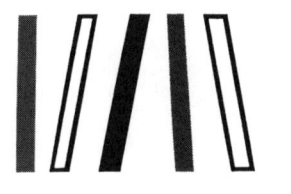

WRITERS AND THEIR CRAFT

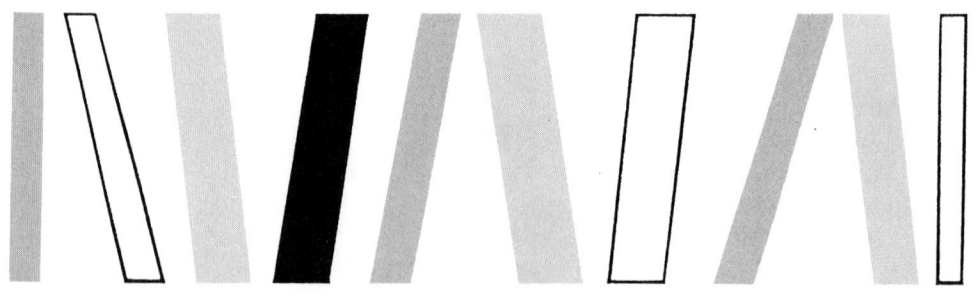
 WAYNE STATE UNIVERSITY PRESS   DETROIT

WRITERS AND THEIR CRAFT: SHORT STORIES & ESSAYS ON THE NARRATIVE

Edited by Nicholas Delbanco and Laurence Goldstein

COPYRIGHT © 1991 By Wayne State University Press, Detroit, Michigan 48202. All rights are reserved. No part of this book may be reproduced without formal permission.

Manufactured in the United States of America.

95 94 93 92 91   5 4 3 2 1

"History by Narration" by Kyna Taylor copyright © 1991 by Kyna Taylor. All rights reserved. No part of this work may be reproduced without formal permission.

"Keeping Order" by Gloria Whelan copyright © by Gloria Whelan.

"Long Work, Short Life" by Bernard Malamud copyright © by Bernard Malamud.

LIBRARY OF CONGRESS CATALOGING IN PUBLICATION DATA

Writers and their craft : short stories and essays on the narrative / edited by Nicholas Delbanco and Laurence Goldstein.
   p.   cm.
  ISBN 0-8143-2193-3 (pbk. : alk. paper)
  1. American fiction—20th century—History and criticism—Congresses. 2. Fiction—Authorship—Congresses. 3. Fiction—Technique—Congresses. 4. Short stories, American. I. Delbanco, Nicholas. II. Goldstein, Laurence, 1943–
PS379.W75   1991
813'.5409—dc20
                                             90-49018
                                                  CIP

DESIGNER Selma Tenenbaum

The editors are grateful to Sarah Townsend for her assistance in preparing the manuscript for publication.

CONTENTS

INTRODUCTION ix

PERSONAL EXPERIENCE AND THE ORIGINS OF FICTION

Long Work, Short Life | Bernard Malamud   2
Beginnings | Joyce Carol Oates   13
An Interview with Max Apple | Allan Vorda   28
A Conversation with Maxine Hong Kingston |
                                              Paula Rabinowitz   36

A SYMPOSIUM ON CONTEMPORARY AMERICAN FICTION

Linsey Abrams 49	Rudolfo A. Anaya 56
James Atlas 62	Asa Baber 63
Russell Banks 64	Raymond Barrio 65
Jonathan Baumbach 69	Charles Baxter 70
Stephen Becker 74	Madison Smartt Bell 77
Joe David Bellamy 80	Anne Bernays 82
George Blecher 83	Corinne Demas Bliss 86
David Bosworth 87	Kay Boyle 93
T. Coraghessan Boyle 95	Rosellen Brown 96
Frederick Busch 98	Nash Candelaria 101
Raymond Carver 103	Fred Chappell 105
Kelly Cherry 107	Alan Cheuse 108
Annie Dillard 111	Thomas M. Disch 112

Stephen Dobyns 113   Susan Dodd 116
Robert Dunn 118   Stuart Dybek 121
Margaret Edwards 124   Irvin Faust 125
Elaine Ford 127   Richard Ford 128
Paula Fox 130   Marilyn French 131
Bruce Jay Friedman 133   Laura Furman 134
Herbert Gold 136   Doris Grumbach 137
Ron Hansen 139   Curtis Harnack 140
Mark Harris 142   Jim Harrison 144
William Herrick 145   Edward Hoagland 146
William Holinger 147   John Clellon Holmes 149
James D. Houston 152   Robert Houston 154
David Huddle 155   Charles Johnson 156
Steve Katz 160   Janet Kauffman 162
Richard Kostelanetz 165   James McConkey 167
Colleen J. McElroy 170   Jay McInerney 172
Clarence Major 173   Frederick Manfred 175
Bobbie Ann Mason 176   Hilary Masters 177
Paul Metcalf 180   Sue Miller 183
Edith Milton 185   Stephen Minot 188
A. G. Mojtabai 191   Mary Morris 194
Marge Piercy 195   Joe Ashby Porter 197
John Rechy 200   Carolyn See 202
Lore Segal 203   Joan Silber 204
Elizabeth Spencer 205   Scott Spencer 206
Wallace Stegner 208   Daniel Stern 209
Richard Stern 212   Gladys Swan 214
Barry Targan 216   John Updike 220
Arturo Vivante 221   Jon Manchip White 222
Allen Wier 225   Dara Wier 228
Nancy Willard 232   Hilma Wolitzer 233
Jose Yglesias 235

▍THE ART OF THE STORY

The Infidel | Lynne Sharon Schwartz 238
Chowder | Stephen Dunning 272

Keeping Order | Gloria Whelan	279
Takes | Stephen Dixon	290
The Anvil of the Times | Richard Elman	299
Turnabout | Richard Elman	303
History by Narration | Kyna Taylor	305
The First Time Ava Saw Angelo Naked | Eugene Mirabelli	310
Mel's Back | Wanda Haynes Fries	319
Here at the Starlight Motel | Andrea Barrett	324

THE PROFESSION OF LETTERS: THREE UNFLATTERING APPRAISALS

The Literary Life: A Portfolio | M. G. Lord	332
The Star System: A Jeremiad | George Garrett	342
Short Stories Are Not Real Life | David R. Slavitt	352

FORMS AND THEMES OF CONTEMPORARY FICTION

Spirit of Quest in Contemporary American Letters | Ihab Hassan	364
Contemporary Fiction and Popular Culture | Constance Pierce	384
Speaking a Word for Nature | Scott Russell Sanders	394
The Agrarian Impulse in Contemporary American Fiction | Gregory L. Morris	408
The Lost Tribe of American Fiction | Paul West	430

CONTRIBUTORS 441

INTRODUCTION

This book first appeared as a two-volume issue of *Michigan Quarterly Review (MQR)*. Nicholas Delbanco, guest editor for that project, worked in close collaboration with *MQR* editor, Laurence Goldstein—we have now joined forces again.

What follows surely must be called a celebration of contemporary American fiction. This does not mean that every author applauds the current literary scene; indeed, the reverse is more nearly the case. Fiction writers cannot claim with a straight face that the novel is dead, but they can, and do, discourse on the decline—the near-extinction—of a discerning audience. Our prophets are at odds with the profit system. Yet most of the authors herein seem engaged by the historical moment, much as Twain, Howells, James, Crane, Wharton, Kate Chopin, and others recognized that the end of the nineteenth century offered a kind of pivotal point for art. How much we would have welcomed such a book circa 1890!

A journal like *MQR* must, of course, take its brief bow and move on. The original issues deserved a second incarnation; here they have it. This is a single-volume version of those two special issues amplified by additional contributions to the Symposium and an interview with Maxine Hong Kingston. The end result, in our opinion, is a kind of road map through the 1990s, a work whose polyphonic structure represents its subject with high fidelity. It may help in the discussion of that subject to discuss our method of approach.

First, it was a process of exclusion. We decided not to represent fiction in translation—although that eliminated what may be among the best of contemporary prose. So, too, we excluded the work of writers beyond our national boundaries, even if they write in English; to have incorporated the work of African, Australian, British, Canadian, Indian, Irish, and West Indian authors — among others — would have been to publish an encyclopedia. The fiction included here is self-contained; we printed no novel extracts, no chapters from work-in-progress. The essays deal only with what James, from his incremental distance, called "The American Scene."

The fiction is, or should be, self-explanatory. We have appended no reader's guide, although each story will benefit from close scrutiny — whether in the living room or classroom. Not surprisingly, our selection argues range; there is work from all sections of the country and from established authors as well as from those at their career's start. Wanda Haynes Fries is publishing her first short story herein, whereas Stephen Dixon has published at least two hundred. Joyce Carol Oates's essay "Beginnings" amply documents what we take to be the case: the house of fiction has many voices, many rooms, and we are the poorer if we visit only one wing.

Taken as a whole, the contents of the Symposium argue enlargement. The virtual consensus of hostile views on the subject of minimalist fiction surprised the editors, but this seems less a rejection of a few fashionable authors than a warning about the engineering of taste that has catapulted those authors into prominence. The underlying protest seems to be directed at a media culture that relegates to the background the larger possibilities of the medium. Writers are omnivorous and scrupulous readers; they are the first to discern when a fashion is stale, a style exhausted. Yet one cannot read either the Symposium or the rest of the book without gaining confidence that the authors represented, and those they recommend, are equal to the task of making sense of American lives in, and for, the twenty-first century. In this sense, too, the book is a celebration.

The intention of the editors is to create a volume both descriptive and polemical. It is descriptive in the sense of allowing fiction writers themselves to define the contours of the literary landscape as they see it. When more than a hundred voices are permitted their say on a matter of such pressing urgency in their lives, the results will have authority. The lay of the land is best defined by those who must traverse it. The book is polemical in the sense that each such description is either overtly or covertly prescriptive. The question posed to the Symposium members invited them to champion a kind of writing — one of their choosing. The question also had a further purpose: to set an agenda of sorts for the 1990s by guiding us as readers to exemplary authors and texts.

Much of the book is advice. Whether framed as memoir (Max Apple and Bernard Malamud), as jeremiad (George Garrett and Paul West), or as reasoned critical discourse (Ihab Hassan, Gregory L. Morris, Constance Pierce, and Scott Russell Sanders), the prose aims at persuasion as well as entertainment. So, these pages clearly show how writers view their immediate culture, their colleagues, and their reading public. But we did not undertake this task in the belief that we would, or could, *define* contemporary fiction or even shape its contours. The work of M. G. Lord should adequately puncture any such pretension; her acid-dipped pen takes the measure of those whose game is knowingness, who consider themselves crucial to the literary life.

It will go on without us. It will survive caricature as well as classification. Our ultimate objective has been to give a hearing to more voices, more models of creative and critical insight. Here is a very large window into the literary imagination of our times. And welcome to the prospect.

PERSONAL EXPERIENCE AND

THE ORIGINS OF FICTION

LONG WORK, SHORT LIFE

BERNARD MALAMUD

I intend to say something about my life as a writer. Since I shan't go into a formal replay of the life, this will read more like a selective short memoir.

Bernard Malamud
photo by
Jerry Bauer

This memoir was originally delivered at Bennington College, in the Ben Belitt Lectureship Series, on October 13, 1984, and thereafter published in a limited edition as one of The Bennington Chapbooks in Literature, 1985.

The beginning was slow, and perhaps not quite a beginning. Some beginnings promise a start that may take years to induce a commencement. Before the first word strikes the page, or the first decent idea occurs, there is the complicated matter of breaking the silence. Some throw up before they can breathe. Not all can run to the door at the knock of announcement — granted one hears it. Not all know what it means. Simply, not always is the gift of talent given free and clear. Some who are marvelously passionate to write may have to spend half their lives learning what their proper subject matter may be.

Not even geniuses know themselves in their youth. For years Emily Dickinson was diverted from her poetry by men she felt she loved, until one day she drew the shutters in her sunlit room and sat in loneliness at her table. She had at last unearthed a way of beginning. Those who loved her appeared in her home from time to time, perhaps less to love than to cause her to write her wondrous poems of intricate feeling and intricate love.

I began to write at an early age, yet it took me years actually to begin writing. Much diverted me. As a child I told stories for praise. I went for inspiration to the movies. I remember my mother delivering me, against her will, on a wet Sunday, to a movie house to see Charlie Chaplin, whose comedy haunted my soul. After being at the pictures I recounted their plots to school friends who would listen at dreadfully long length as I retold them. The pleasure, in the beginning, was in retelling the impossible tale.

When I overcontrived or otherwise spoiled a plot, I would substitute another of my own. I could on occasion be a good little liar who sometimes found it a burden to tell the truth. Once my father called me a "bluffer," enraging me because I had meant to tell him a simple story, not one that had elaborated itself into a lie.

In grammar school, where I lived in a state of self-enhancing discovery, I turned school assignments into stories. Once I married off Roger Williams in Rhode Island to an Indian maiden, mainly because I had worked up an early feeling for the romantic. When I was ten, I wrote a story about a ship lost in the Sargasso Sea. The vessel appeared in dreams, about to undertake a long voyage in stagnant seas. This sort of thing, to begin with, was the nature of my "gift" as a child, that I had awakened to one day, and it remained with me many years before I began to use it well. Throughout my life I struggled to define it, and to write with originality. However, once it had pointed at me and signaled the way, it kept me going even when I wasn't writing. For years it was a blessing that could bleed as a wound.

Thus began an era of long waiting.

I had hoped to start writing short stories after graduation from City College during the depression, but they were long in coming. I had ideas and felt I was on the verge of sustained work. But at that time I had no regular means of earning a living; and as the son of a poor man, a poor grocer, I could not stand the thought of living off him, a generous and self-denying person. However, I thought the writing would take care of itself once I found steady work. I needed decent clothes; I would dream of new suits. Any work I found would make life different, I thought, and I could begin writing day or night. Yet I adamantly would not consider applying, in excess of pride, to the WPA. Years later, I judged that to have been a foolish act, or non-act.

I considered various things I might do to have time for writing, like getting up at 5:00 A.M. to work for an hour or two each morning before hitting the dreadful Sixth Avenue agencies in Manhattan to scrounge around for jobs. More often than not there were none, especially for someone with no work experience. And where there was no work there were no words.

The Second World War had begun in 1939. I was born at the beginning of the First World War, in 1914. The Second was being called "The Phony War." The French and German armies sat solemnly eyeing each other over the Maginot Line, yet almost not moving except for night forays. No one seemed about to launch a major attack. Neville Chamberlain, after Munich, was on his way out. He had rolled up his umbrella and was hastening away from the frightful future; Churchill came to power and was eloquently growling that Britain would never be conquered. Possibly diplomacy was in progress. Perhaps there would be no renewed conflict. Many Americans seemed to think the threat of war might expire. Many of us hoped so, though hoping was hard work; nor did it make too much sense, given the aberrations of Adolf Hitler. We worried about the inevitable world war but tried not to think of it.

Often young writers do not truly know what is happening in their lives and world. They know and they don't know. They are not sure what, in essence, is going on and are years in learning. Recently I was reading Ernst Pawel's book of the life of Kafka, and the author speaks of Kafka's "all-encompassing goal in which the writer searches for his own truth." Truth or no truth, I felt the years go by without accomplishment. Occasionally I wrote a short story that no one bought. I called myself a writer though I had no true subject matter. Yet from time to time I sat at a table and wrote, although it took years for my work to impress me.

By now I had registered at Columbia University for an M.A. in English, on a government loan. The work was not demanding. I told myself what I was doing was worthwhile; for no one who spends his nights and days devoted to great works of literature will be wasting his time as a writer, if he is passionate to write.

But when did I expect to begin writing?

My answer was unchanged: when I found a job that would support my habit: the self's enduring needs. I registered for a teachers' examination and afterwards worked a year at $4.50 a day as a teacher-in-training in a high school in Brooklyn. I was also applying for, and took, several civil service examinations, including those leading to jobs of postal clerk and letter carrier. This is mad, I thought, or I am. Yet I told myself the kind of work I might get didn't matter so long as I was working for time to write. Throughout these unsatisfying years, writing was still my gift and persuasion.

It was now four years after my graduation from college, but the four felt like fifty when I was counting. However, in the spring of 1940 I was offered work in Washington, D.C., as a clerk in the Census Bureau. I accepted at once, though I soon realized the "work" was a laugh. All morning I conscientiously checked estimates of drainage ditch statistics as they appeared in various counties of the United States. Although the job hardly thrilled me, I worked diligently and was promoted, at the end of three months, to receive a salary of $1,800 per annum. That, in those times, was "good money." What was better was that I had begun to write seriously on company time. No one seemed to care what I was doing so long as the record showed I had finished a full day's work; therefore, after lunchtime I kept my head bent low while I was writing short stories at my desk.

At about this time I wrote a piece for the *Washington Post*, mourning the fall of France after the German Army had broken through the Maginot Line and was obscenely jubilant in conquered Paris. I felt unhappy, as though mourning the death of a civilization I loved; yet somehow I managed to celebrate ongoing life and related acts.

Although my writing seemed less than inspiring to me, I stayed with it and tried to breathe into it fresh life and beauty, hoping that the gift was still in my possession, if by some magic act I could see life whole. And though I was often lonely, I stayed in the rooming house night after night trying to invent stories I needn't be ashamed of.

One night, after laboring in vain for hours attempting to bring a short story to life, I sat up in bed at an open window looking at the stars after a rainfall. Then I experienced a wave of feeling, of heartfelt emotion bespeaking commitment to life and art, so deeply it brought tears to my eyes. For the hundredth time I promised myself that I would someday be a very good writer. This renewal, and others like it, kept me alive in art years from fulfillment. I must have been about twenty-five then, and was still waiting, in my fashion, for the true writing life to begin. I'm reminded of Kafka's remark in his midtwenties: "God doesn't want me to write, but I must write."

There were other matters to consider. What about marriage — should I, shouldn't I? I sometimes felt that the young writers I knew were too much concerned with staying out of marriage, whereas they might have used it, among other things, to order their lives and get on with their work. I wondered whether I could make it a necessary adjunct of my writing. But marriage was not easy: wouldn't it hurt my career if I urged on myself a way of life I could hardly be sure of? One has his gift — the donnée — therefore he'd better protect it from those who seem to be without a compelling purpose in life. Many young women I met had no clear idea what they wanted to do with their lives. If such a woman became a writer's wife, would she, for instance, know what was going on in his thoughts as he worked in his sleep? Would she do her part in keeping the family going? I was often asking myself these and related questions — though not necessarily of someone who might answer them. And I was spending too much time being in love, as an uneasy way of feeling good when I wasn't writing. I needed someone to love and live with, but I wasn't going out of my way to find her.

Meanwhile, I had nailed down an evening-school job in September of 1940; I then completed an M.A. thesis and began to think of writing a novel. By now I had finished about a dozen stories, a few of which began to appear in university quarterlies. One of these, "The Place Is Different Now," was the forerunner of *The Assistant*. And a novel I had started while I was teaching in Erasmus Hall Evening High School in Brooklyn was called *The Light Sleeper*. It was completed but not sold. Later, I burned it one night in Oregon because I felt I could do better. My son, who was about four at that time, watched me burning the book. As we looked at the sparks fly upward I was telling him about death; but he denied the concept.

Several years before that, not long after Pearl Harbor, while I was teaching at night and writing this novel, I met a warm, pretty young woman at a party. I was told she was of Italian descent and lived in a hotel with her mother and stepfather, who was a musician. I observed my future wife for a while before we talked.

Soon we began to meet. Some nights she would come to Flatbush to watch me teach. We ate at Sears, or Oetgen's, and sometimes walked across the Parade Grounds to my room. We wrote each other during the week. Her letters were intense and witty, revealing an informed interest in politics and literature; in love and marriage. After the death of my own mother, I had had a stepmother and a thin family life; my wife, the child of a woman divorced young, had experienced a richer cultural life than I. And since we both wanted children we wondered how we would fare in a mixed marriage. She had been Catholic. I defined myself as Jewish.

Life in New York City was not easy or pleasant during the Second World War. Our friends Rose and James Lechay, the painter, had rented a small walk-up flat on King Street, in the Village, which we took over when they went off to live in Iowa, Jim to take Grant Wood's place as professor of painting at the university. After we were married, we both continued working until my wife was pregnant. I taught day and evening classes, with practically no time to write. A few years later I left the evening high school and spent a year teaching in Harlem, incidentally picking up ideas for short stories like "Black Is My Favorite Color," before we decided to go west. I had now received an offer to teach at Oregon State College though I had no Ph.D. degree. In 1949, when my son was two, we moved to Corvallis, Oregon, where I taught three days a week and wrote four. In my own eyes I had become seriously a writer earning his living, though certainly not from his writing.

I think I discovered the Far West and some subject matter of my earlier fiction at almost the same time, an interesting conjunction, in imagination, of Oregon and the streets of New York. One's fantasy goes for a walk and returns with a bride.

During my first year at Oregon State I wrote *The Natural*, begun before leaving New York City. Baseball had interested me, especially its comic aspects, but I wasn't able to write about the game until I transformed game into myth via Jessie Weston's Percival legend with an assist by T. S. Eliot's "The Waste Land" plus the lives of several ballplayers I had read, in particular Babe Ruth's and Bobby Feller's. The myth enriched the baseball lore as feats of magic transformed the game.

Soon we were making plans to go abroad. We had wanted to go earlier but could not afford it until we experienced the fortunate coincidence of a sabbatical leave from Oregon State with a *Partisan Review*-Rockefeller Foundation grant.

We left in late August 1956 for Italy. On board the SS *Constitution* I spent hours studying the horizon, enjoying the sight of ocean as the beginning of more profound adventure, amid thoughts of new writing. One night we passed our sister ship, the SS *America*, steaming along in the mid-Atlantic, all decks alight. I felt I was on the verge of a long celebration.

Previously, my wife had been abroad twice, once at age eight, for a year in Italy, and at another time for her college junior year, in France.

I was ready for a broader kind of living with as much range in writing as I could manage. Before leaving Oregon to go abroad, I had completed *The Assistant*, and had begun to develop several of the stories that became *The Magic Barrel*, some of which I wrote in Rome.

Italy unrolled like a foreign film; what was going on before my eyes seemed close to unreality. An ancient city seemed to be alive in present time. It was larger than life, yet defined itself as our new life. I felt the need to live in a world that was more than my world to live in. I walked all over the city. I walked in the ghetto. I met Italian Jews who had been tortured by the Nazis; one man held up his hand to show his finger-shorn fist. I felt I was too much an innocent American. I wandered along Roman streets and studied Roman faces, hoping to see what they saw when they looked; I wanted to know more of what they seemed to know. On All Souls', I walked in the Campo Verano cemetery. I visited the Ardeatine Caves where the Nazis had slaughtered Italians and Jews. Rome had its own sad way of sharing Jewish experience.

Mornings I walked my eight-year-old son to Piazza Bologna where he took his bus to the American school. At noon, after finishing my morning's work, I picked up my four-year-old daughter at her kindergarten. She would hand me her drawings as we walked home. Home was 88 Via Michelo Di Lando, not far from where Mussolini had lived with Clara Petacci, his mistress. We had made friends of our landlords. Mr. Gianolla was an old Socialist who had been forced to swallow castor oil by Mussolini's fascist thugs. His wife, thin and energetic, talkative, courteous, was one of the rare women university graduates of her time.

I returned to Oregon to an improved situation after our year abroad. From a teacher of freshman grammar and technical report writing, I was transformed into a teacher of English literature, as though a new talent had been discovered in a surprised self. What had happened was that the two gentlemen who administered the English department had heard I was acquiring a small reputation as a serious writer of fiction, and therefore I was no longer required to teach composition only, but might be allowed, even without a doctoral degree, to teach unsuspecting sophomores a little poetry, with even a touch of Shakespeare in the night. For this relief I gave happy thanks.

Let me, at this point, say a short word about the yeas and nays of a writer teaching what is called Creative Writing. I have done it because I teach decently well, but I wouldn't recommend that anyone devote his life to teaching writing if he takes little pleasure in informing others. Elsewhere I've said about teaching creative writing that one ought to keep in mind he is not so much teaching the art of imaginative writing as he is encouraging people with talent how to work as writers. Writing courses are of limited value, although in certain cases they may encourage young writers to read good fiction with the care it deserves. However, I think about a year of these courses should be enough for any serious student. Thereafter writing must become a way of life.

When my Western-born daughter appeared, my father sent us $350 for a washing machine. Once when I was twenty, he trudged up the hall stairs from his grocery store one morning. I had a summer cold and was stretched out in bed. I had been looking for a job without success. My father reached for my foot and grasped it with his hand.

"I wish it was me with that cold instead of you."

What does a writer need most? When I ask the question, I think of my father.

I had already begun to receive literary awards. It seemed to me that I did nothing to get them other than stay at the writing table, and the prizes would mysteriously appear. One day I had a phone call from New York. My publisher, Roger Straus, asked me whether I was sitting down. I said I was. He told me I had just won the National Book Award for *The Magic Barrel.*

I must know how to write, I told myself, almost surprised.

I was in a happy mood when I began to work on *A New Life,* my fourth book. Once, at Yaddo, while I was writing it, a visitor knocked at my door. I had just written something that moved me. He saw my wet eyes. I told him I was enjoying writing my book. Later the legend grew that I had wept my way through it.

During my early years at Oregon State I had gone nowhere, with the exception of our trip abroad, and a ten-day visit to Montana, when Leslie Fiedler was there in the 1950s. He had sent me a copy of an article he had published in *Folio,* in Indiana. His was the first appreciation of *The Natural* that I had read by someone who knew how to read. Fiedler was always *sui generis,* but on the whole generous in his judgment of my work. I shan't forget that he appreciated the quality of my imaginative writing before anyone else wrote about it. That was long before Robert Redford, in his sad hat of failure, appeared on the scene, socking away at a ball that went up in the lights.

Not long after our return to Corvallis from Italy, I had a telephone call from Howard Nemerov at Bennington College, where I was invited to teach a year. I was glad to go. After our year abroad, stimulated by the life and art I had seen, I wasn't very patient with my experience in a small town, though my wife, after a difficult start, now enjoyed her Western life. I seized the opportunity to return to the East. She would have liked living in San Francisco, but there were no job offers. So we traveled to Vermont by way of Harvard Summer School, where I substituted for Albert Guérard. When the class filled quickly, someone at Harvard asked John Hawkes, the novelist at Brown University, to teach a second section of the course. Before long we were walking together in Cambridge streets, talking about fiction. Hawkes is a gallant man and imaginative writer. His work should be better known than it is.

In September 1961, my wife and I arrived with our kids in Bennington, Vermont. The college, an unusual place to work and learn, soon became a continuing source of eduction for me. My teachers were my new colleagues: Howard Nemerov, poet and faithful friend; Stanley Edgar Hyman, a unique scholar and fine critic; and Ben Belitt, a daring, original poet and excellent teacher — from all of whom I learned. My other teachers were my students, whom I taught to teach me.

Stanley Hyman reminded me of Leslie Fiedler in more ways than one. They both knew a great deal about literature, and neither found it difficult to say what. Hyman was an excellent theoretician of myth and literature. His humor kept him young and so did his appetite. Once my wife and I invited him and his wife, the writer Shirley Jackson, to a restaurant, to help us celebrate our wedding anniversary. Stanley ordered the champagne. He and Shirley lived hard, and — I think they thought — well; and almost did not regret dying young. Flannery O'Connor once described them as two large people in a small car, when they came to call on her in Milledgeville, Georgia. She showed them her peacocks.

When I think of Hyman as a critic of literature, what stands out was his honesty of self and standards. One of his favorite words was *stan-*

dards, and you weren't in his league if you didn't know what he meant. He defined and explicated. He was proud of what he knew, though I remember his saying, speaking of himself, "knowledge is not wisdom." He enjoyed the fun of wit, merriment, poker, horseplay, continuous laughter. He died young.

Before I come to the end of this casual memoir, perhaps I ought to say that I served as president of American PEN (Poets, Editors, and Novelists) from 1979 to 1981. PEN had come to life in 1921 as an international organization founded in London by John Galsworthy, the British novelist and dramatist. Basically, PEN brings together writers from all over the world to meet as a fraternity, to foster literature, and to defend the written word wherever threatened.

When I was president, I began to deal more frequently with publishers after the difficult period that followed a time of consolidation in the book industry. The consolidation I refer to was not always helpful to those who wrote, and much remains to be done to improve the situation of writers, dealing in whatever way with their own publishers.

Though my publisher is a good one, I fear that too many of them are much more concerned with making money than with publishing good books that will seriously influence generations of writers in the future. Stanley Hyman had preached standards, but one tendency in publishing today is that standards are forgotten. I can't tell you how badly some books are edited these days; one excuse given is "We can't afford too much time on one book. We've got to make our profit." I'm all for profit from the work of writers, but the simple fact is that we have begun to pay more in a loss of quality in publishing than our culture can afford. Happily, many people of good will, dissatisfied with present-day publishing, are trying to find new ways to improve the industry. And some of the new presses that have begun to publish are quite good, a few even daring.

If I may, I would at this point urge young writers not to be too much concerned with the vagaries of the marketplace. Not everyone can make a first-rate living as a writer, but a writer who is serious and responsible about his work, and life, will probably find a way to earn a decent living, if he or she writes well. And there's great pleasure in writing, if one writes well. A good writer will be strengthened by his good writing at a time, let us say, of the resurgence of ignorance in our culture. I think I have been saying that the writer must never compromise with what is best in him in a world defined as free.

I have written almost all my life. My writing has drawn, out of a reluctant soul, a measure of astonishment at the nature of life. And the more I wrote well, the better I felt I had to write.

In writing I had to say what had happened to me, yet present it as though it had been magically revealed. I began to write seriously when I had taught myself the discipline necessary to achieve what I wanted. When I touched that time, my words announced themselves to me. I have given my life to writing without regret, except when I consider what in my work I might have done better. I wanted my writing to be as good as it must be, and on the whole I think it is. I would write a book or a short story at least three times — once to understand it, the second time to improve the prose, and a third to compel it to say what it still must say.

Somewhere I put it this way: first drafts are for learning what one's fiction wants him to say. Revision works with that knowledge to enlarge and enhance an idea, to re-form it. Revision is one of the exquisite pleasures of writing: "The men and things of today are wont to lie fairer and truer in tomorrow's meadow," Henry Thoreau said.

I don't regret the years I put into my work. Perhaps I regret the fact that I was not two men, one who could live a full life apart from writing; and one who lived in art, exploring all he had to experience and know how to make his work right; yet not regretting that he had put his life into the art of perfecting the work.

BEGINNINGS

JOYCE CAROL OATES

> *I will maintain that the artist*
> *needs only this: a special world*
> *of which he alone has the key.*
> André Gide

I begin with the proposition that the impulse to create, like the impulse to destroy, is utterly mysterious. That it is, in fact, one of the primary mysteries of human existence. We can't hope to explain it but we can't, evidently, resist speculating about it.

Two general theories about the genesis of "art":

—It originates in play: in experiment, improvisation, fantasy; it remains forever, in its deepest impulse, playful and spontaneous, a celebration of the (child's?) imagination.

Joyce Carol Oates
photo by
John Munson

— It originates out of the artist's conviction that he is born damned; and must struggle through his or her life to achieve redemption. By way of art.

If these theories appear to contradict themselves, to the point, very nearly, of comedy — so, as Walt Whitman would say, they contradict themselves. Sometimes one is obviously true; sometimes, the other.

In his classic work *The Structure of Scientific Revolutions* (1962), the science historian Thomas Kuhn makes the point that "discovery," in terms of single, discrete, and readily identified dates, let alone "discoverers," is highly misleading. Scientific discoveries are, in a historically real (if poetic) sense, there to be discovered. Not only are scientific theories developed, frequently, by more than one individual, not inevitably in communication with other individuals, but there is often a good deal of ambiguity about when "discovery" itself takes place. Despite our predilection for believing in isolated and inspired genius, genius *sui generis*, it is not often the case that scientific revolution has to do with the individual. There may be heroism, and heroes, but the drama — the evolution of scientific discovery — would have taken place in any case.

In the world, or worlds, of art, very different phenomena may be observed. Not only is the work of art uniquely identified with a single individual, but, if we look closely, it is frequently the case that, from that individual's perspective, the work of art is in itself unique, and perplexing in terms of its origins. Just as our historical beginnings are utterly mysterious — why are we born? why when and as we are? — so too are the beginnings of works of art and of "artists." Conception (in contrast to the fully public fact of birth) suggests not only the unknowable but the forbidden: our birth dates are matters of public record but our dates of "conception" are permanently shrouded in mystery. Consciousness dominates our thinking about works of art as well as artists, even as we know that the genesis of any creation (in contrast to its execution) must derive from unconscious sources.

Ornamental qualities in prose fiction are invariably the consequence of authorial deliberation and strategy while more powerful qualities — the primitive force fields that generate "theme" (or obsession) — are clearly given. The storyteller experiences the ravishing phenomenon of stories being told through him and by way of him; his single voice generating any number of singular "voices." Is it magic? Is it psychopathology? Is it supremely normal? In Plato's *Ion*, Socrates says:

> God takes the mind out of the poets, and uses them as his servants, and so also those who chant oracles, and divine seers; because he wishes us to know that not those we hear, who have no mind in them, are those who say such precious things, but God himself is the speaker, and through them he shows his meaning to us. . . . These beautiful poems are not human, not made by man, but divine and made by God; and the poets are nothing but the gods' interpreters, possessed each by whatever god it may be.

But this is a logic hostile to the individual; a logic in denial of the wide play of personality that characterizes creative work. For if there is any single quality which we associate with art it is the individual, the personal, the unique, the inimitable. One might add: the inevitable. In many writers it comes to seem over a lifetime that a complex and essentially unknowable drama is working itself out by way of the individual; yet, so far as the individual is concerned, each experience is immediate and singular. And the act of writing itself is likely to be felt as purely and radiantly subjective: "the exalted sense of being above time and death which comes from being again in a writing mood" (Virginia Woolf, *Diary*, September 8, 1934).

After the completion of an ambitious project the writer may try to pass judgment on it, "objectively"; he may try to analyze it as a reader; or probe his own motives for writing. "The port from which I set out was, I think, that of the *essential loneliness of my life* — and it seems to be the port also, in sooth, to which my course again finally directs itself! This loneliness — what is it still but the deepest thing about one? Deeper, about *me*, at any rate, than anything else; deeper than my 'genius,' deeper than my 'discipline,' deeper than my pride, deeper, above all, than the deep counterminings of art" (Henry James in a letter of 1900). Though such analyses are often astute and startling — recall James Joyce explaining that the labyrinthine *Ulysses* was written "to preserve the speech of my father and his friends" — it surely cannot explain the depth, or the subtlety, or the stark originality, or genius, of a work. Virginia Woolf noted that the writing of *To the Lighthouse* seemed to have laid the ghosts of her father and mother, of whom she used to think constantly, "I believe this to be true — that I was obsessed with them both, unhealthily; and writing of them was a necessary act" (*Diary*, November 28, 1928). It remains a surprising (and disturbing) fact to many literary observers that writers should, upon occasion, write so directly from life; that they should "cannibalize" and even "vampirize" their own experiences. But this species of creation is surely inevitable? entirely natural?

The artist is driven by passion; and passion more powerfully derives from our own experiences and memories. Writers as diverse as William Butler Yeats, Marcel Proust, August Strindberg, D. H. Lawrence, Ernest Hemingway, even, to a less obsessive degree, Thomas Mann, Willa Cather, Katherine Anne Porter—all were writers of genius whose imaginations were not constrained but positively energized (in Strindberg's case one might say "demonized") by specific events in their lives.

Strindberg, for instance, used not analogous but exact details from his family life, and in particular from his three marriages, for his fiction and plays; his biographer Olof Lagercrantz has noted that he went so far as to create domestic traumas in order to "rectify" his literary material, and, with the passage of time, developed an intuitive symbolist method of creation, in which individuals no longer seemed to exist save as emanations of meaning—*his* meaning. Equally dependent upon his own life—upon what he called "passional" experience—D. H. Lawrence directly fictionalized his own experiences as "son" and as "lover" in virtually all his novels and poetry, from *The White Peacock* to *Lady Chatterley's Lover* and *Pansies*. Thomas Mann was so "excessively precise" in recording his origins and family life in *Buddenbrooks* and *Tonio Kröger* that he directed a French translator to consult these works of fiction for a biographical portrait. And there falls across much of Albert Camus's work, however obliquely, and allegorically transformed, the presence of the "silent, uncomplaining figure of [my] deaf mother" who instilled in her son fiercely contending emotions of sympathy and helplessness.

Yet how many people, writers or otherwise, have been haunted by families to no productive end. . . ! Clearly the powerful unconscious motives for a work of art are but the generating and organizing forces that stimulate consciousness to feats of deliberation, strategy, craft, cunning.

To be *inspired*: we know what it means, even how it sometimes feels, but what is it? Filled suddenly and often helplessly with renewed life and energy, a sense of excitement that can barely be contained; but why some things—a word, a glance, a scene glimpsed from a window, a random memory, a conversational anecdote, the shard of a dream—have the power to stimulate us to intense creativity while others do not we are unable to say. The early surrealists believed in the empirical world as a "forest of signs"—a rich, largely unexplored region of message-forms that lay behind the apparent irrationality of the surface: just as meaning lay behind the apparent irrationality of the dream. Images yield themselves to those who *see* — like Man Ray wandering through Parisian streets with his camera, forcing nothing, anticipating nothing, but leaving himself open to document *disponibilité*, or availability; or chance. Surrealism's most striking images were, at the outset, purely ordinary images, decontextualized and made strange — as Lautréamont said, "Beautiful as the chance encounter of a sewing machine and an umbrella on a dissection table."

No less open to *disponibilité* was Henry James, who listened avidly to dinner table conversation in London social circles — for years the popular novelist dined out as many as two hundred times in a single season. He heard, and overheard, any number of gossipy tales; yet chose to write *The Sacred Fount, The Turn of the Screw, The Aspern Papers, The Spoils of Poynton*. (Having heard approximately half of the riveting anecdote that would provide the comical plot of *Spoils* James asked not to be told the rest: he didn't want his imagination contaminated by mere factual truth.) In revisiting Washington Square after years of absence from the United States James claimed to have "seen" the ghost of his unlived American self — and wrote that remarkable ghost story, "The Jolly Corner," in which the unlived self, the other James, is both realized and exorcised. After the violent Dublin insurrection of Easter 1916, William Butler Yeats was indignant with the Irish rebels for sacrificing their lives, needlessly, he thought; yet for days he was haunted by a single mysterious line of poetry — a line repeating itself again and again — until finally his great poem "Easter 1916" organized itself around that line: "A terrible beauty is born."

> I write it out in a verse —
> MacDonagh and MacBride
> And Connolly and Pearse
> Now and in time to be,
> Wherever green is worn,
> Are changed, changed utterly:
> A terrible beauty is born.

Karen Blixen, writing under the carefully chosen pseudonym Isak Dinesen ("Isak": one who laughs), transmogrified personal experience, a good deal of it bitter, into apparently distant, if not mythical images; yet the biographical element in her work is consistent if one knows how to decipher the clues. For instance, in a late parable, "The Cardinal's Third Tale," of *Last Tales*, a proud virgin contracts syphilis by kissing the foot of Saint Peter's statue in the Vatican after a young Roman worker has kissed it before her—a detail that aroused a good deal of negative criticism for its apparent "frivolity" since, at the time of the book's publication, the secret of Dinesen's own syphilis, also "innocently" contracted, was not generally known. Young Jean-Paul Sartre was so profoundly struck by the hallucinogen-induced vision of a tree's roots that *La Nausée*, his first novel, virtually shaped itself around the hieratic image; an image that has consequently come to represent, however misleadingly, the Existentialist preoccupation with things in their mysterious and usually malevolent *thingness*.

In 1963, the poet Randall Jarrell received a box of letters from his mother, including letters he himself had written at the age of twelve in the 1920s; he immediately embarked upon what was to be his last period of creativity—virtually plucking poems, his wife has said, from the air. The title of the book says it all: *The Lost World*. Before this, Jarrell had been inactive; after this, he sank into depression. He died in 1965. The poet Theodore Weiss, having written a twenty-line poem, was inspired to work on it in subsequent days—and months—and, finally, years: twenty years altogether. Each line of the poem mysteriously "opened out into a scenario" shaping itself finally into Weiss's first book-length poem *Gunsight*. Eudora Welty was moved to write her early story "Petrified Man" by hearing, week after week, the most amazing things said in her local beauty parlor in Jackson, Mississippi—in this story the writer effaces herself completely and allows the voices to speak. While driving in the Adirondacks E. L. Doctorow happened to see the sign Loon Lake— in which everything he felt about the mountains ("a palpably mysterious wilderness, a place full of dark secrets, history rotting in the forests") came to a point. And there suddenly was the genesis, the organizing force, for his novel *Loon Lake*: "a feeling for a place, an image or two."

For John Updike inspiration arrives, in a sense, as a "packet of material to be delivered." In 1957, revisiting the ruins of the old Shillington, Pennsylvania, poorhouse, a year or two after his grandfather's death, Updike found himself deeply moved by the sight, "Out of the hole where [the poorhouse] had been there came to me the desire to write a futuristic novel"—a memorial effort cast in the form of a parable of the future. So Updike's first novel *The Poorhouse Fair* was conceived—the very antithesis of the typical "autobiographical" first novel. Norman Mailer's first novel, *The Naked and the Dead*, was, by contrast, a wholly deliberate effort, "a sure result of all I had learned up to the age of twenty-five." Mailer's characters were conceived and put in file boxes long before they were ever on the page; he had accumulated hundreds of such cards before he began to write, by which time "the novel itself seemed merely the end of a long active assembly line." But Mailer's second novel, *Barbary Shore*, seemed to come out of nowhere: each morning he would write with no notion of how to continue, where he was going. Where *The Naked and the Dead* had been put together with all the solid agreeable effort of a young carpenter constructing a house, *Barbary Shore* "might as well have been dictated to me by a ghost in the middle of a forest." Similarly, *Why Are We In Vietnam?*, Mailer's *Huck Finn*, was written in a white heat of three ecstatic months, dictated in a sense by the protagonist's voice—"a highly improbable sixteen-year-old genius—I did not even know if he was black or white." Joseph Heller's novels typically begin with a first sentence that comes out of nowhere—independent of theme, setting, character, story. The opening line of *Catch-22*—"It was love at first sight. The first time he saw the chaplain, ———— fell madly in love with him"—simply came to Heller for no reason, could not be explained, yet, within an hour and a half, Heller had worked out the novel in his mind: its unique tone, its tricky form, many of the characters. The genesis for *Something Happened* was the inexplicable sentence, "In the office in which I work, there are four people of whom I am afraid. Each of these four people is afraid of five people." And though, a minute before, Heller knew nothing of the work that would absorb him for many years, he knew within an hour the beginning, middle, and ending of the work, and its dominant tone of anxiety.

Such visitations are experienced as mysterious at first—indeed, often anxiety-provoking—but, in retrospect, as fate. Francine Gray's moments of inspiration have been similarly sudden and unexpected: seeing a photograph of the Jesuit priest Philip Berrigan pouring a vial of blood over draft documents in the 1960s led to the writing of her passionate book of nonfiction, *Divine Disobedience*; the observation of a solitary fellow tourist on a Russian trip was the germinating stimulus for *World Without End*; a visit to an ailing relative in a hospital, and the observation of another close relative as he regarded himself in a mirror, constituted the emotional nexus of *October Blood*. Joan Didion began *Play It As It Lays* with no notion of "character" or "plot" or even "incident." She had only two pictures in her mind: one of empty white space; the other of a minor Hollywood actress being paged in the casino at the Riviera in Las Vegas. The vision of empty space suggested no story but the vision of the actress did:

> A young woman with long hair and a short white halter dress walks through the casino at the Riviera at one in the morning. She crosses the casino alone and picks up a house telephone. I watch her because I have heard her paged, and recognize her name: she

is a minor actress I see around Los Angeles but have never met. I know nothing about her. Who is paging her? Why is she here to be paged? How exactly did she come to this? It was precisely this moment in Las Vegas that made *Play It As It Lays* begin to tell itself to me.

In his *Paris Review* interview of 1976, John Cheever speaks of the way totally disparate facts came together for him, unbidden, "It isn't a question of saving up. It's a question of some sort of galvanic energy." The writing itself then becomes the difficult effort to get the "heft" right — getting the words to correspond to the vision. Surely one of the strangest of all literary conceptions is that of John Hawkes's *The Passion Artist*. In a preface to an excerpt from that novel in Hawkes's anthology *Humors of Blood & Skin*, Hawkes relates how, when he and his wife were spending a year in southern France, he found himself inexplicably unable to write, in the midst of a profound and paralyzing depression — "whenever I entered our house I thought I saw my father's coffin. . . . I had this vision even though both my parents were buried in Maine. Each morning I sat benumbed and mindless at a small table. Each morning Sophie left a fresh rose on my table, but even those talismans of love and encouragement did no good. All was hopeless, writing was out of the question." Then came an invitation for lunch. Hawkes was told a lively bit of gossip about a middle-aged man who went one day to pick up his young daughter at a school in Nice, only to discover accidentally from one of the child's classmates that the daughter was an active prostitute, already gone that day from the playground to a sexual assignation. Hawkes listened to the anecdote; saw himself walking toward a lone girl and some empty playground swings. . . . One or two further associations, seemingly disjointed, and he had the plot of what would be *The Passion Artist*. The paralysis had lifted.

The most admirable thing about the fantastic, André Breton says, is that the fantastic does not exist: everything is real.

In *A Portrait of the Artist as a Young Man*, Stephen Dedalus explains the Joycean concept of the epiphany: "A sudden spiritual manifestation, whether in the vulgarity of speech or of gesture or in a memorable phase of the mind itself. He believed it was for the artist to record these epiphanies with extreme care, seeing that they themselves are the most delicate and evanescent of moments." That Joyce's concept of one of the most potent motives for art has become, by now, a critical commonplace, should not discourage us from examining it. In his own practice the young Joyce, in his late teens and a student at University College, Dublin, began to collect a notebook of "epiphanies" fueled by the ambition not only to write but to write works of genius. He collected approximately seventy epiphanies — sudden and unanticipated moments of "spiritual manifestation" — of which forty survive. Many were to be used with little or no change in *Stephen Hero* (Joyce's early uncompleted novel) and in *Portrait*; the stories of *Dubliners* are organized around such revelations, rather like prose poems fitted to a narrative structure. It might be said that *Ulysses* is a protracted celebration of epiphany fitted to a somewhat overdetermined intellectual (Jesuitical?) grid: a short story tirelessly inflated to encompass the cosmos. (In fact, *Ulysses* had its formal genesis in a story for *Dubliners* tilted "Ulysses," or "Mr. Hunter's Day" — a story that, according to Joyce, never got beyond its title.) The epiphany has significance, of course, only in its evocation of an already existing (but undefined) interior state. It would be naive to imagine that grace really falls upon us from without — one must be in spiritual readiness for any visitation.

Yet is the writer in truth the triumphant possessor of a secret world to which (in Gide's words) he alone has the key? — or is he perhaps possessed by that world? The unique power of the unconscious is that it leads us where it will and not where we might will to go. As dreams cannot be controlled, so the flowering of any work of art cannot be controlled except in its most minute aspects. When one finds the "voice" of a novel, the "voice" becomes hypnotic, ravishing, utterly inexplicable. From where does it come? Where does it go? As in any fairy tale or legend, the magic key unlocks a door to a mysterious room — but does one dare enter? Suppose the door swings shut? Suppose one is locked in until the spell has lifted? But if the "spell" is a lifetime? But if the "spell" *is* the life?

So, the familiar notion of a "demonic" art; the reverse in a sense of Plato's claim for its divine origin — yet in another sense identical. Something *not us* inhabits us; something insists upon speaking through us. To be in the grip of a literary obsession is not so very different from being in the grip of any obsession — erotic love, for instance, in its most primary and powerful state. Here the object of emotion is fully human, but the emotion has the force of something inhuman — primitive, almost impersonal, at times almost frightening. The very concept of the "brainstorm": a metaphor nearly literal in its suggestion of raging winds, rains, elemental forces. The extravagance of William Blake's visions, for example; the ecstasy of Kafka in writing his early stories — writing all night! tireless! enthralled! — no matter that he is in poor health and physically exhausted. "Odd how the creative power at once brings the whole universe to order," Virginia Woolf observes, (*Diary*, July 27, 1934), but she might have gone on to observe that the "universe" is after all one's own very private and unexplored self: "demonic," "divine."

The genesis of Mary Shelley's *Frankenstein* is nearly as primitive as the appeal of that extraordinary work itself: after days of having failed to compose a ghost story (in response to Lord Byron's casual suggestion), the eighteen-year-old Mary Wollstonecraft Godwin Shelley had a hypnogogic fantasy in her bed—"I saw the pale student of unhallowed arts kneeling beside the thing he had put together. I saw the hideous phantasm of a man stretched out and then, on the working of some powerful engine, show signs of life. . . . His success would terrify the artist; he would rush away [hoping] this thing . . . would subside into dead matter. He sleeps; but he is awakened; he opens his eyes; behold the horrid thing stands at his bedside, opening his curtains." One of the central images of *Frankenstein* is that of a stroke of lightning that seems to issue magically in a dazzling "stream of fire" from a beautiful old oak, blasting it and destroying it: a potent image perhaps for the violence of the incursion from the unconscious that galvanized the author's imagination after a period of strain and frustration. (It cannot have been an accident that *Frankenstein*, telling of a monstrous birth, was written by a very young and yet-unmarried pregnant woman who had had two babies with her lover already, only one of whom had survived.) Following this waking dream of June 1816, Mary Shelley had her subject—spoke in fact of being "possessed" by it. So too the brilliantly realized vision of the monster comes to us with such uncanny force it is difficult to believe that it owes its genesis to so very personal an experience—and did not evolve from a collective myth. *Frankenstein; or, The Modern Prometheus* was published in 1818 to immediate acclaim; yet with the passage of years the novel itself has receded as an art-work while Frankenstein's monster—known simply and inaccurately as Frankenstein—has achieved dominance. The nightmare vision ends as it began, with a curious sort of impersonality.

The writer commonly writes to articulate a mystery he seems in a way to understand: the most paradoxical of situations. His vision is experienced as a totality but can be narrated only by slow painstaking degrees, as if one were trying to assemble a vase broken into thousands of pieces. In the afterword to *Memoirs of Hadrian* the author Marguerite Yourcenar speaks of her moment of inspiration when, in 1927, as a young woman, she happened to come upon a sentence in a published volume of Flaubert's correspondence—"Just when the gods had ceased to be, and the

Christ had not yet come, there was a unique moment in history, between Cicero and Marcus Aurelius, when man stood alone." Yourcenar then adds, "A great part of my life was going to be spent in trying to define, and then trying to portray, that man existing alone and yet closely bound with all being." Partly due to interruptions in the author's life and partly because she felt inadequate to the task—"There are books which one should not attempt before having passed the age of forty"—*Memoirs of Hadrian* required twenty-seven years to write: it was finally published in 1951.

Why the need, in some rising very nearly to the level of compulsion, to verify experience by way of language?—to scrupulously record and preserve the very passing of Time? "All poetry is positional," Nabokov notes in his autobiography *Speak, Memory*, "—to try to express one's position in regard to the universe embraced by consciousness is an immemorial urge. The arms of consciousness reach out and grope, and the longer they are the better. Tentacles, not wings, are Apollo's natural members." For Nabokov as for many writers—one might say Boswell, Proust, Virginia Woolf, Flaubert—surely James Joyce—experience itself is not authentic until it has been transcribed by way of language: the writer puts his imprimatur upon his (historic) self by way of writing. He creates himself, imagines himself, sometimes—recall Walter Whitman changing his name to Walt Whitman, David Henry Thoreau changing his name to Henry David Thoreau—renames himself as one might name a fictitious character in a work of art. And the impulse can rise to the level of a sacred obligation, at least in a young author's ambition: "There is a certain resemblance between the mystery of the Mass," says James Joyce to his brother Stanislaus in a letter, "and what I am trying to do . . . to give people a kind of intellectual or spiritual pleasure by converting the bread of everyday life into something that has a permanent artistic life of its own . . . for their mental, moral, and spiritual uplift." (One is tempted to note here in passing that it was for their "mental, moral, and spiritual" preservation the citizens of Dublin suppressed Joyce's *Dubliners* and in effect drove him into his life's exile in Europe.)

No one has analyzed the complexities of a writer's life so painstakingly as Virginia Woolf in her many volumes of diaries and to a lesser extent in her correspondence. The slow evolution of an idea into consciousness; the difficult transcription of all that is inchoate, riddlesome; the sense of writing as a triumphant act; the necessity of surrendering to the unconscious (the "subconscious" as Woolf calls it, imagining it as "her"); the pleasure in language as sounds, beats, rhythms—Woolf writes so meticulously about these matters because she is trying to understand them. In a letter to Vita Sackville-West of September 8, 1928, she says:

> I believe that the main thing in beginning a novel is to feel, not that you can write it, but that it exists on the far side of a gulf, which words can't cross: that it's to be pulled through only in a breathless anguish. Now when I sit down to write an article, I have a net of words which will come down on the idea certainly in an hour or so. But a novel . . . to be good should seem, before one writes it, something unwriteable; but only visible; so that for nine months one lives in despair, and only when one has forgotten what one meant, does the book seem tolerable.

And of style:

> Style is a very simple matter, it is all rhythm. Once you get that, you can't use the wrong words. . . . This is very profound, what rhythm is, and goes far deeper than words. A sight, an emotion, creates this wave in the mind, long before it makes words to fit it; and in writing . . . one has to recapture this, and set this working (which has nothing apparently to do with words) and then, as it breaks and tumbles in the mind, it makes words to fit in.

One thinks of the young Ernest Hemingway writing each morning in a Parisian cafe, groping his way into what would be his first book, *in our time*: writing at first with extreme slowness and difficulty until he set down his "one true sentence"—usually a brief declarative sentence—and could throw the earlier work away, and begin his story. One thinks of Theodore Dreiser composing, as he claimed, much of *Sister Carrie* in a trance—that masterpiece of "American naturalism"; and of William Faulkner's composition of his greatest novel, which began with a troubling and inexplicable image (the vision of a little girl with muddy underpants climbing a tree outside a window) and slowly expanded into a long story that required another story to amplify it, which in turn required another, which in turn required another, until Faulkner had four sections of a novel he had not, in the most literal sense, thought to write. *The Sound and the Fury* was published in 1929; but it was not until two decades later when Malcolm Cowley edited *The Portable Faulkner* that Faulkner added the Appendix—that remarkable document that is, of course, always published as an integral part of the novel.

"I am doing a novel which I have never grasped. . . . There I am at p. 145, and I've no notion what it's about. I hate it. Frieda says it's very good. But it's like a novel in a foreign language I don't know very well—I can only just make out what it is about." So D. H. Lawrence writes in a letter of 1913 in reference to his work-in-progress, *The Sisters*. So vague and unformed was the young author's sense of his novel in its early "crude fermenting" he had intended it to be a potboiler of a kind: the novel that would eventually become *Women in Love*. He made several false starts in its composition before realizing that he must give his heroine some background: this background rapidly evolves into the germ of a new, separate novel about three generations of Brangwens—a social history of the English Midlands from before the industrial revolution to approximately 1913. In short, the "background" for the heroine of *The Sisters* became *The Rainbow*, published in 1915. (*Women in Love* was published in 1920: the two novels are radically different in structure, style, narrative voice, and tone.)

Is it as a consequence of Lawrence's method of composition, or in defiance of it, that he published within a few years two of the greatest novels of the twentieth century, *The Rainbow* and *Women in Love*? Lawrence was the most intuitive of writers, yet he was willing to write numerous drafts of a work and even to throw away as many as one thousand pages, as he claims to have done with *The Rainbow*. His deep faith in himself allowed him the energy to experiment in following his voice and his characters where they would lead; temperamentally he was the antithesis of James Joyce, who imposed upon his work a purely intellectual scheme meant to raise it to the level of the symbolic and the archetypal. "Don't look for the development of [my] novel to follow the lines of certain characters," Lawrence says in a letter of 1919, "—the characters fall into the form of some other rhythmic form, as when one draws a fiddle-bow across a fine tray delicately sanded, the sand takes lines unknown."

The sand takes lines unknown. What more beautiful and precise image to suggest the very imprecision of the creative enterprise?—the conjunction between inner and outer forces we try in vain to understand and must hope in the end only to embody?

Postscript

On the genesis of my novel *Marya: A Life*.

In 1977, I wrote a short story, very short, deliberately spare and uninflected, I decided to call "November Morning." It was about a boy of eight whose father has been killed, though the boy himself doesn't quite understand what has happened. He is taken to see his father's corpse, in a county morgue; but his father has been so badly beaten or mutilated (it isn't clear which, to the reader), that the boy doesn't seem to recognize him. The story is told not by the child but by way of his limited consciousness and his reluctance to understand what has happened in his family. The setting of the story was rural: naturalistic but dreamlike. The time was several decades ago.

I finished "November Morning" in a few days, and sent it to my agent. Though I went on to other projects I found that I was still thinking about the story, haunted by it, as if I hadn't really finished it. My practice as a writer might be defined as an active pursuit of "hauntedness": I can't write unless I am preoccupied with something, sometimes to the point of distraction, or obsession. But rarely am I haunted by a piece of writing, after I have finished it. . . . Though the story was accepted by a magazine, I decided I didn't want it published in that form; but when I tried to withdraw it from publication I learned that I had waited too long. So the story, incomplete, teasingly "wrong," was published.

The test of a work's integrity is its appearance in print: you know then, if you didn't know beforehand, if it is honest or not.

(Cocteau said that writing is a force of memory which is not understood. Certainly there are times when the prospect of writing leaves me virtually faint with longing; a yearning, a desire so palpable it's almost physical, bound up in some complex, undefinable way with memory. This yearning can't be satisfied except by the head-on plunge into work, in which, somehow, God knows how, raw instinct and critical acuity come into some sort of equilibrium. People who don't write might think it is easy. Or, considering me, as a writer labeled "prolific," that it is easy for *me*: but nothing is farther from the truth. Writing is not easy for most writers nor is it easy for me.)

So I rewrote the story another time. At some point it struck me that the protagonist should have been a girl, and not, as I'd thought, a boy. And that would make all the difference.

Except for the bare outline of the plot everything was recast entirely: tone, texture, rhythm, the silences and spaces between words. Immediately I had my "real" character; I knew her thoroughly; Marya, Marya Knauer, eight years old as the story opens but already in my imagination an adult woman — the thirty-six-year-old woman she would be when the novel ends. (I seemed to know too that Marya's story could not be eight pages long but would be novel-length. Many pages, many years, many experiences would be necessary to bring her into focus and to the culminating point of her life.) I had the ending, now; the final image; I had a number of scenes, "dramatic interludes," in the middle; I saw, or seemed to see, the ghostly outlines of characters whom Marya would encounter, who would act upon her in crucial ways, if not radically alter her life. Most of all I "saw" Marya — a girl, and then a woman, with a face not unlike my own yet not my own: kin of some kind, perhaps sisterly, but unknown to me.

It wasn't until I had finished a first draft of the novel that I learned, by chance, that the story I believed I had invented recapitulated an incident in my mother's early life. Not my father, of course, but her father had been murdered; not I, but my mother, had been "given away" after her father's death, to be brought up by relatives. Marya is eight years old at the time of the event that changes her family's life; my mother was an infant of six months. Somehow, without knowing what I did, without knowing, in fact, that I was doing anything extraordinary at all, I had written my mother's story by way of a work of prose fiction I had "invented."

AN INTERVIEW WITH MAX APPLE

ALLAN VORDA

AV: What are your feelings about contemporary fiction? Do you feel comfortable with labels like metafiction or experimental fiction, which are sometimes applied to your work?

MA: The truth is, I don't like to categorize. I'm as likely to enjoy fiction that is old-fashioned as something avant-garde. My current colleague

Max Apple
photo by
Jerry Bauer

Lynne Sharon Schwartz's novel *Disturbances in the Field* is perfectly realistic, conventional narrative and could have been written, stylistically speaking, in the nineteenth century. It's wonderful. It is a great novel in the way that George Eliot's and Joseph Conrad's novels are great—intricate plot, richly realized characters, acute social commentary. So I can appreciate that. I can also appreciate Frederick Barthelme or Raymond Carver and other writers who shade away from the mainstream. I consider what I do as sometimes experimental, sometimes very conventional.

AV: Or postmodernist?

MA: I was invited to write "Post-Modernism" [reprinted in *Free Agents*] for a panel discussion at a museum. First, I went to a library to find out what postmodernism was. I ended up reading a book of literary criticism that used my work as an example. So I thought, if I'm part of it I ought to be able to describe it. But, of course, it's critics who make the categories. That's what I was playing with in the "Post-Modernism" piece: writers don't say, "Today I'm a realist" or "Now I'm going to write a minimalist story." We write what we can, including the bad writers. I think Louis L'Amour might have his existentialist days and Judith Krantz now and then feels minimalist. You hope that the critics won't stick you with a label—Georgian poet, Decadent novelist—that will diminish you. You hope that like Dickens or Joyce your work will defy any one label and accommodate all of them.

The real question is, when will I have time to read all the contemporary fiction I want? I think there are an enormous number of good writers in the country today. I think this is a golden age in fiction writing. Some people are upset that there is no Faulkner they can pick out. Of course, in Faulkner's lifetime, until almost the end, no one picked him out either.

AV: Would you be willing to name writers you admire? Or those who influenced you?

MA: There are so many that I would just as soon not answer. I read my contemporaries with admiration and respect. I know a lot of them now, too. That's why I'd feel badly if I started giving a list and left some out.

I can tell you that when I was young, and by that I mean eighteen or so, it was a great discovery for me to find the Jewish writers. Not only Bellow and Malamud, but Herbert Gold. A whole group of writers who seemed so different from me, though their idioms and characters were intimately familiar.

I knew as a teenager that I was going to be a writer, whatever that meant. I was living close to stories. My grandmother was a great storyteller. And I knew that being a writer meant being a reader too. Reading was the most important thing in the world to me. When I was sixteen or seventeen I read everything I could get my hands on. I didn't know when I read Dostoevsky that I was reading a translation. I just read any book I could find, and given my later practice, I was strangely attracted to immense realistic novels like *Les Misérables*. I made the jump, literally, from juvenile fiction to that book; I couldn't stop reading it. It turned out that I was reading great fiction, though I didn't know it at the time.

I thought that real writers were not people like me. Essentially, I thought they were Englishmen or Frenchmen or Russians. I thought you had to be full of high seriousness like T. S. Eliot. Then when I got to college and took a closer look at all that high seriousness and great tradition, I knew I didn't belong to any of that. When you realize that you're not going to be writing about the Russian artistocracy or the French bourgeoisie, you look around for models closer to home, and this is where Malamud and Gold, especially, were so helpful.

I feel enormously close to E. L. Doctorow's writing, too, both to the life he recounts, the autobiographical stuff, and to his style as a fiction writer. I also love Grace Paley's stories. Some of these stories just sing to me. Once I was teaching a short summer session at Berkeley with Grace Paley and Ed Doctorow. Students could go from one class to another. One student work called forth an allusion from me to a certain Chekhov story. Another student stood up and said, "This has got to be a fix. I was in Doctorow's class and Grace Paley's class and they were both talking about the same Chekhov story!" Of course, we had not mentioned it between us, but it shows our affinity as readers and writers.

AV: *The Oranging of America* was one of the most distinctive collections of short stories in recent decades. I think it stands up there with Borges's *Labyrinths* and Barth's *Lost in the Funhouse*. How did these stories develop?

MA: I had a long apprenticeship, a quiet one. I tried to hide from being a writer. All the time I was working on my Ph.D. at Michigan I didn't send any stories to magazines. Finally, I knew when I was ready. I sent "The Oranging of America" to Ted Solotaroff at *American Review*, and after he published it, other stories came rapidly. When I started to be published I realized I had some readers.

I wasn't alone, as I had been all those years in graduate school, writing my secret stuff in the back of my Shakespeare and Milton notebooks, almost as if it were Hebrew starting from the other side of the page. None of these stories was published — they were typical juvenilia set down in my mid-twenties without hope.

I felt I was going to be a writer someday, and I thought I was going to be a teacher, but I knew I was never going to be a literary critic. Writing a dissertation was a pose for me, but I wrote it on a text that was intriguing: *The Anatomy of Melancholy*, a seventeenth-century book that addresses subjects I take up in *The Propheteers*. The career I have now is the one I still want. I still teach. I spend some hours almost every day being a writer, but I spend more hours being a reader. If you ask me what I am, I'm a reader.

AV: Regarding your narrative style, you have said in an interview with the *Mississippi Review* [Fall 1984] that "Gas Stations" was a crucial story for you "because it was the first time I consciously trusted my fantastic impulses completely." Can you elaborate on this statement? Does this following of fantastic impulses apply only to the short story?

MA: I hope so. I don't want to follow too many fantastic impulses in the world, though I have them. About "Gas Stations," Nora Ephron called me from *Esquire* and said she liked my work and wanted to know if I'd write something for their bicentennial issue. She started running through a list of possible topics, which always strikes dread in my heart. I had never had anything published in any large circulation magazines. So I said I would write on gas stations, my suggestion. And yet I began to follow her advice in writing the essay; it was more than advice, it was directions. There was a lot of money at stake and I nervously produced a rather dull essay on gas stations, which I threw away. Then I wrote what I wanted. I remember this so distinctly because I sent it to her with trepidation — with real fear that I'd blown my big chance for money and fame.

I was on vacation when Nora tracked me down and told me how much she loved the piece. I said, "But it's not an essay." She said, "Who cares! When it's that good, who cares!" That gave me a lot of confidence just at the time I needed to trust my own instincts and personal style. Maybe that dull essay would have been published anyway, but I wouldn't have *emerged* as a writer, following my own directions.

AV: Speaking of editorial matters, I understand that your new novel *The Propheteers* was originally titled *The Disneyad*.

MA: A lawyer for Harper & Row insisted on the change and I'm sure he was correct. The content of a book is protected by the First Amendment, you can use the name *Walt Disney* in the text, but the book jacket and title are considered advertising. So using the name *Disney* might be construed as an infringement on what the Disney people own.

I couldn't think of any other title since I was so wedded to *The Disneyad*. I was in Buenos Aires when I got the call that I needed a new title. My children and I walked the streets, but we couldn't think of one. Ted Solotaroff, my editor, came up with the new title. I'm very satisfied with it, but all those years I had the book in mind it was *The Disneyad* to me and always will be.

I was trying to write a mock epic. Behind *The Disneyad* was the *Iliad* and the *Aeneid*, and another mock epic, *The Dunciad*, which is why the title was so important to me. Just as every reader or listener of Homer knew that there was a Troy that had fallen, and knew all of Priam's sons, so I'm counting on my readers to be familiar with Walt Disney and Disney World in Orlando. Of course, there's a big difference between Troy and Disney World — that's part of what the novel is about, part of its Kafkaesque and modernist comedy.

AV: The use of popular culture in contemporary fiction is a fascinating subject. Your novel contains some household words as characters: Howard Johnson, Walt Disney, Clarence Birdseye, C. W. Post, and Margery Post Merriweather. Why did you select these historical figures and did you research their lives for accuracy?

MA: No I didn't research them. I didn't even know Margery Post had met Birdseye. I like the names. I always liked the name Birdseye and that little trademark has been in my mind since I was a kid. The disclaimer at the beginning of the novel, where I said that I was mostly acquainted with these people from my breakfast table, is the truth. I grew up in Grand Rapids, which is down the road from Battle Creek, and one of the earliest trips I took was to a cereal factory. People like the Posts and Kelloggs have been in my mind since childhood. Obviously they are easily recognizable symbols of American success, and for that reason I can use them, as names or ciphers, not as realistic historical figures. I wanted to suggest that what motivates people who become household words is something more complicated than money. If I called those characters John Smith or Allan Vorda or Max Apple, I would have to treat them more realistically, perhaps write about them as people who *do* want to earn money. I don't believe anybody does anything for money.

I know that sounds perfectly crazy. I mean everyday people, men and women who go to work in the morning to a store or factory, work for money. But someone who has ninety motels: Why do they want ninety-one or ninety-two or ninety-three? Or if someone has Disneyland, why do they want Disney World? I'm just trying to imagine what it would be like because I think all of us everyday people know why we work. We work for a paycheck every week or every two weeks, but if I had one hundred million dollars or five hundred million dollars, I'd still work. You'd still work. Why does a writer with three books want another one? It's the same thing. Why does someone who's drawn a series of cartoons want to draw another one? What's the blank page or the open celluloid? Those are life and death questions. I can't just state them baldly, theologically, or religiously. There's no way to do it.

The novel becomes a vision of what life is. Now maybe I've romanticized it, sentimentalized it. Maybe these moguls are awful people. No doubt some of them are. I read the paper too; and, unfortunately, I've met some of them.

I was looking for a vision that is generous. I honestly believed from the few things I know about Post or Kellogg that they still held an idea of making money for the sake of stewardship. C. W. Post believed very seriously that the world would be better if animals weren't killed. For me this makes Post a much more interesting character. So he's not a case study in how to get rich or what money is. That is what most popular fiction, what little I've read, is about — rich people and how they got rich. You know, the page-turning bestsellers by people like Judith Krantz.

I wanted to write another version of this fundamental American story. I was interested in the concept of money, but in a different way. I was interested in why C. W. Post didn't want his money. Why money doesn't mean anything to him or to Howard Johnson or, finally, Walt Disney. When I was creating Walt Disney, I was trying to make a portrait of the artist. I think Disney was a great artist. You know Whitman's remark that "money is a form of poetry"? What if getting rich is not the sordid thing it's depicted to be in so many American novels? Or say that wealth might serve a writer now as Priam's wealth served Homer, as an opportunity to investigate the whole national character, its sweetness, its pathos, and its existential terrors. Maybe that's what more formula writers ought to be doing in their novels? I'm just asking.

AV: That's an unusual perspective on modern America.

MA: Perhaps it's because, although I was born in the United States, I've lived so close to an immigrant generation. My first language is Yiddish. I'm still fascinated by America in the way an immigrant is. I didn't eat in a restaurant until I went to college. America is still new and interesting to me. I don't see it the way a lot of other people do. Even in middle age I'm not quite jaded yet by the everyday world. I've internalized my grandmother's attitude about America, which is looking at it with wonder, stupor, and some satire.

AV: The ending of *The Propheteers* is somewhat demonic. Walt is mildly electrocuting the Disney children who wait to return for more electrical-shock treatment. "As awful as it looked," you write, "as awful as it was, he was giving them what they wanted." Can you elaborate on this unconventional ending?

MA: I think the quote says all I can say. I wanted the end to be both a surprise and inevitable. That is, here we have the world as it is. I've showed in the novel that Walt Disney, who's depressed and brooding on death, is an artist who can't help but wonder what happens when he erases a line, thereby raising existential and metaphysical issues. He is not a happy man. So we wonder: What is the magic of Walt Disney? Like any artist, he works in loneliness. He works in that dreamy, dark undercurrent that produces both great joy and inexplicable despair. Margery Post, by contrast, works in a straightforward way. Money can do this; power can do this. I'll hire the lawyers. She understands the world, she thinks. So when there is a confrontation, I wanted it to be a confrontation between the artist and the world.

AV: Disney makes the analogy on pp. 166–67 that the artist is like God drawing lines (life) and then erasing them (death). And in Chapter nineteen, Nurse Bloom is unable to get any blood from Disney. Essentially, he is like an animated character, isn't he?

MA: Exactly. I wanted him to be as lifeless, as full of death, as I possibly could. It's the blank-page idea again. The novel in part is about how the imagination creates words, people, out of nothing, as God did the world. So for all that I've made an anatomy of melancholy in Disney's character, I've also made the kind of affirmative statement, I hope, that I described earlier. It's a comic novel. Like the Disney children we're all attracted to humor and humorous people because we sense the sorrow and pain behind the humor, and that's real life.

AV: You're fond of fanciful ways of saying something abstract.

MA: Fanciful isn't the word. Maybe the word is epiphany, but I don't see it as quite that either. I read an interview with Gabriel García

Márquez a few years ago and someone asked him a similar question. I'm not comparing myself to García Márquez, but he said that he needed to render reality through surreal images in order to be faithful to its eerie strangeness. In one particular episode every time the woman touches a glass the glass turns blue. That was the way he found for saying "falling in love," for defamiliarizing it, as the critics say.

In my short story "Vegetable Love," the man and the waitress put on their running shoes and go off to Mexico. It means that his quest is for nothing less extravagant than the meaning of life. But if I put it like that, who'd want to read it? Who'd want to write it?

So I find a dramatic or metaphorical way of talking about, I hope, things that matter most to people. Poets get away with these tropes all the time. Really, twentieth-century fictions owe a lot to the narrative stock-in-trade of poets, and makers of fairy tales and folklore.

AV: Finally, what direction do you see your fiction going?

MA: In an article I published this year in the *New York Times Book Review* I talked about finding my place on the dying body of fiction. This goes back to Henry James's phrase, about the novel being the body of American fiction. I said, "Finally, I found a place. It was under the left middle fingernail, an aging subdivision called 'Jewish, Jewish-American, not so Jewish and not so American either.' It was one of the noisiest sectors on the body, but I slipped in and found a place that had been vacated when the inhabitant moved to Hollywood. As crowded and argumentative as the subdivision was, I was relieved to have finally found my own place."

In the act of writing a novel or story, I'm dreaming. I'm daydreaming. It's the most real, the most profound *me* there can be; which doesn't mean it's very real or very profound. I was learning, even before I went to the University of Michigan, how to tell a story and also what to leave out. I don't consider myself a master of this. I give myself assignments. They come from my unconscious and, when the raw materials are there, I work with it as well as I can. I'm still learning. I hope to learn to do this better and better. That's the work of my life. My writings are my motels. My hope is to have a chain.

19 February 1987

A CONVERSATION WITH MAXINE HONG KINGSTON

PAULA RABINOWITZ

PR: My questions to you range from broad philosophical matters to more narrow concerns focused on your work, but all address the significance and politics of memory for women writers in the United States today.

Maxine Hong
Kingston
photo by
Franco Salmoiraghi

In your 1983 lecture at the University of Michigan Hopwood awards ("Imagined," 565], you said that you had not wanted to go to China before you had finished working on your two books. In an earlier interview you said you had not wanted to ask people to repeat their stories to you while you were working on the books, either [Pfaff]. I saw some connection between the use of memory and the function of imagination — the image of China, in particular for you as a writer, and in general for Chinese Americans.

MHK: The artist's memory winnows out; it edits for what is important and significant. Memory, my own memory, shows me what is unforgettable, and helps me get to an essence that will not die, and that haunts me until I can put it into a form, which is the writing. I don't want to get confused by making new memories on top of the old ones which were already such a large vision — the mythic China. Going to China would have meant the creation of, and the beginning of, another memory.

PR: So, when you subtitle *The Woman Warrior, A Memoir of a Girlhood among Ghosts*, "memoir" and "ghost" represent the same thing. And they both needed to be exorcised.

MHK: Yes, but not *exorcised*. I have learned that writing does not make ghosts go away. I wanted to record, to find the words for, the ghosts, which are only visions. They are not concrete; they are beautiful, and powerful. But they don't have a solidity that we can pass around from one to another. I wanted to give them a substance that goes beyond me.

PR: Then memory is essentially a visual quality?

MHK: Visual, and emotional. Sometimes, there are words, too, like when someone says something that's violent and it echoes through time.

PR: Like the father's insults in *China Men*?

MHK: Yes.

PR: Well, in that context, memories have meaning for you in a sense very different from the Freudian notion that what we remember is what is insignificant, since what's significant is repressed and we never entirely get it back.

MHK: Yes, that makes sense, in a way, in that memory is really nothing. It's not substantial, and it's not present. It has to do with past times, and in that sense, it's insignificant, except when it haunts you and when it is a foundation for the rest of the personality. Somehow, though, words are a medium to get to the seemingly subconscious.

I think that these visions don't just come full-blown and with details such as chairs and clothes, and where everything is placed—

the relationships between bodies in a room. All that becomes more and more accessible as I approach them with words. Words clarify the vision and memory.

When you think about it, words are also insignificant, insubstantial, not things. So we can use them to arrive at insignificant, insubstantial memories. As I paint part of a vision, the next part of it becomes clear. It's as if I am building the underpinnings of a bridge, and then I can cross it, and see more and more clearly.

PR: So, memory is the starting point for your work, but once the writing begins, it's actually language that takes over the next level of memory, and words become traces themselves.

MHK: Because then you find the next memory, all of the time keeping an eye on what's happening in real life, right now. I think that my stories have a constant breaking in and out of the present and past. So the reader might be walking along very well in the present, but the past breaks through and changes and enlightens the present, and vice versa. The reason that we remember a past moment at all is that our present-day life is still a working out of a similar situation.

PR: Because the present reenacts the past. Memory becomes a structuring device to mediate past and present.

MHK: Understanding the past changes the present. And the ever-evolving present changes the significance of the past.

PR: I was wondering about your decision to divide off your narratives in terms of a male and a female ancestry — dividing them off by gender. Did you feel that one narrative could not fully contain both kinds of memories?

MHK: At one time, *The Woman Warrior* and *China Men* were supposed to be one book. I had conceived of one huge book. However, part of the reason for two books is history. The women had their own time and place and their lives were coherent; there was a woman's way of thinking. My men's stories seemed to interfere. They were weakening the feminist point of view. So I took all the men's stories out, and then I had *The Woman Warrior*.

Historically, of course, the men went to a different country without their families, and so they had their adventures by themselves. It was as if they went to a men's country and they had men's stories. This is hindsight now; but it does seem as if the women's stories have a convolution and the men's stories have more of a linear passage through time. The men's myths and memories are not as integrated into their present-day lives, and that influences the structure of both those books. In *The Woman Warrior*, when the girls and women draw on mythology for their strengths, the myth becomes part of the women's lives and the structure of the stories. In the men's stories, I tell a myth and then I tell a present-day story, a myth, and then another present-day adventure story; they are separate narratives. The reason I think that happened was that those men went to a place where they didn't know whether their mythology was giving them any strength or not. They were getting very broken off from their background. They might not have even been drawing any strength, or they may have gone against the teachings of the myth. They were so caught up in the adventure of the new land that they thought, "What good are memories and the past?" Memory just hurts them, because they can't go home. So, the myth story and the present story become separated.

PR: What you are saying, in a way, is that there is geographical difference in terms of genders. One might roughly say that China is a landscape inhabited, at least in the narratives, by the women and their myths, and the Gold Mountain, America, is really where the men are and that's where history is.

MHK: Yes, those men were making history. They were making a new myth, too. They were not so caught up in the old myths as the women were.

PR: Yet, even in the narratives of the men, the sense is that these are narratives that have been retold through women. Perhaps, then, the women's voices and women's memories become a cultural connection between those China myths and that American history?

MHK: Yes. In fact, I wrote the characters so that the women have memories and the men don't have memories. They don't remember anything. The character of my father, for example, has no memory. He has no stories of the past. He is an American and even his memories are provided by the mother. She says that he went dancing, or whatever; he is so busy making up the present, which he has to build, that he has no time for continuity from the past. It did seem as if the men were people of action.

But I am trying to think whether we can make any generalizations about men and women. I have thought about the animus and the anima, Jung's terms, as I work. I have had dreams about two women, and they both have a left toe on all four feet. Somehow, if I could get to the point where one is a man and one is a woman, I'd be a more balanced person. Somewhere, in the writing of the two books, things did sort out: there was a man and a woman.

PR: Since I just reread them, I was struck by the way you played with intertextuality in the two books, where an insignificant reference in one of the books will be elaborated to a great extent in the other one. Some little statement that Brave Orchid makes in *China Men* had been a whole section in *The Woman Warrior* or vice versa.

It struck me that the way the two books work is the way that memory works, where some large memory often just comes out of the most ephemeral beginnings and then gets blown up from there. So that you don't ever really remember the whole picture. What you remember is a smell or a "sharp white triangle" [Kingston, "Imagined," 569].

MHK: Yes. Yes, and then, that triangle turned out to be the trouser leg glimpsed on a ship while my father was stowing away. I think life works like that. There are various themes and people, and obsessions, that come and go and sometimes they take a major role in life. And then, on another day, you have to devote your whole day to going to the grocery store . . .

PR: Yes. I wanted to ask, now that you have been to China, what happened?

MHK: I was very afraid to go because it's really there. What if China invalidated everything that I was thinking and writing? So, one of the great thrills was to see how well I had imagined it. Many of the colors, and the smells, the people, the faces, the incidents, were much as I imagined. Many people said to me, "Welcome home." I did feel that I was going back to a place that I had never been.

Actually, it was a new adventure, too, but there were just small things that I wish hadn't happened, in a way. There were some things that I wish I had seen before I had written my books. The tight quarters of the rooms and of the villages. If I had been in those rooms earlier, I would have understood even bettter the sense of a village and how each person's drama reverberates throughout the village. I would have seen that people did not have to walk as far as I said to go from one place to another. At my father's village, the well where the aunt drowned herself was right next to the Hong family temple. My mother said that the guys used to hang around on the steps of the temple and make remarks at the girls to try to get them to drop and break their water jars. That is so real to everyone, of all cultures. You know, guys whistling at girls, and, also, it's so sexy. I wish I had had it in the book. I saw small things like that that I wished I had had earlier, but nothing large that invalidated the whole work.

The trip made me see another use of memory or imagination or "talk story." Toward the end of *The Woman Warrior*, I wrote about the savage barbarians shooting off arrows with whistles on them. I wrote that, and then, not very much later, I saw one of those whistling arrows in a museum. I felt that I created it. I wrote it; and therefore, it appeared.

I think that I found that China over there because I wrote it. It was accessible to me before I saw it, because I wrote it. The power of imagination leads us to what's real. We don't imagine fairylands. I've begun lately to realize that if I were to know you, as my friend, the best way is for me to imagine you at life so well that I sympathize with you. Well, that means that imagination is reaching toward a real person. Now, if I imagine something about you that is totally off the wall, that's not you, then my imagination is off. To have a right imagination is very powerful, because it's a bridge toward reality.

PR: Your books also seem very American, even though they are about "China Men" or "Warrior Women" in China. I was wondering if you were also imagining America?

MHK: Oh yes. Actually, I think that my books are much more American than they are Chinese. I felt that I was building, creating, myself and these people as American people, to make everyone realize that these are American people. Even though they have strange Chinese memories, they are American people. Also, I am creating part of American literature, and I was very aware of doing that, of adding to American literature. The critics haven't recognized my work enough as another tradition of American literature.

PR: What tradition?

MHK: I directly continue William Carlos Williams's *In the American Grain*. He stopped in 1860 and I pick it up in 1860 and carry it forward. When I was writing "No Name Woman," I was thinking about Nathaniel Hawthorne and *The Scarlet Letter* as a discussion of the Puritan part of America, and of China, and a woman's place. I use the title, "The Making of More Americans," from Gertrude Stein, because when I read *The Making of Americans*, I thought, "Yes, she is creating a language that is the American language; and she is doing it sentence by sentence. I am trying to write an American language that has Chinese accents; I will write the American language as I speak it." So, in a way, I was creating something new, but at the same time, it's still the American language, pushed further.

PR: In that sense, then, there is a kind of political agenda to your writing.

MHK: Yes, there is. There has been exclusion socially and politically, and also we have been left out of literature.

PR: I was thinking about the way, in your two books, the characters become Americans by appropriating bits of American popular culture.

MHK: Fred Astaire—yeah.

PR: Or the comic books that the little girl reads, and I was wondering whether that appropriation is an example of a kind of subversion of the erasure of Third World cultures. In other words, instead of seeing it as, "Everyone comes to America and—

MHK: And we disappear"—

PR: —rather it's a way of turning America into yet another aspect of one's own culture?

MHK: Yes, and I think that the highest form of that appropriation is art. In a sense, when I wrote these books, I was claiming the English language and the literature to tell our story as Americans. That is why the forms of the two books are not exactly like other books, and the language and the rhythms are not like other writers, and yet, it's American English. I guess my thought is, "If I can use this language and literature in a really beautiful, strong way, then I have claimed all of it for us."

PR: I don't know if you saw Mel Watkins's article in the *New York Times Book Review* berating Afro-American women writers for not presenting positive images of black men.

MHK: Yes, the men are doing that now.

PR: Well, I recently read in Elaine Kim's book [198] that you had gotten some of the same kind of criticisms.

MHK: All the minority women get exactly the same thing from the minority men.

PR: What do you think is going on?

MHK: Oh, I think what's going on is that the men have had a very bad time, and the men writers are equating the novel with their manhood. They are not publishing as many novels as the women are, but their anger is toward the wrong people—us. I mean, they are angry at what they think is the white publishing establishment. But they also think that the women are in conspiracy with the white male publishing establishment to get our work published. We are getting to be anchors on television news programs—and the men, where are they? But their anger is misplaced. They aren't reading us right. Instead of being angry with us—I mean, it takes a lot of words to write articles against us—they ought to be home working on those novels. The other possibility is that they feel that they have been castrated by American society. Maybe what they say is exactly what's going on: the novel is castrated out of them and all that's left is tremendous anger at women.[1]

PR: Well, I was thinking about this in another context, which is the white, male, postmodernist establishment of writers, who have outlined the boundaries of what is considered contemporary writing. Certainly the critics who write about them would never consider putting your work in that category. Your work seems as insistently reflexive about questions of narrative, form, representation, and language as theirs, and yet, because your work is about culture, and comes out of a history that has been kept silent but now has a voice, it lacks that whole sense of *ennui*. So, it seems that you and other minority writers have been put in a peculiar spot, and "eccentric" position.[2] You are being deleted from the mainstream of contemporary American literature while being denied a position as writers within a Chinese-American or Afro-American tradition.

I was wondering if you feel, therefore, an affinity with other minority women writers? Do you see a connection between your work, and say, that of Toni Morrison or Leslie Silko?

MHK: Yes. Yes. It's funny you mention the two of them, because we went to China together. I do feel an affinity not only because I love them as people but because we seem to write alike. There is so much human emotion and richness and story and imagery and colors and things to eat. Nobody is alienated from life; everybody is warm. I feel that we write like that because we are warm, and even though we all—I hate to say master—we are all very good with words, words aren't the only thing that's important. We care about stories about people, and also that magical real place that we are all visiting. When I compare our work to some of the mainstream work, it seems as if many of them are *only* playing with words. The "language" people's world seems grey and black and white. Toni's and Leslie's and my aliveness must come from our senses of a connection with people who have a community and a tribe. We are living life in a more dangerous place. We do not live in new subdivisions without ceremony and memory; and if those other writers have to draw from that non-magical imagination, then of course, their writing will be grey and black and white.

PR: So then the idea that you are speaking out of a cultural community is crucial?

MHK: I don't see how I would live without a community, family, friends.

But I am always very interested in how one can be an individual and be part of a collective people and a collective memory. Of course, that's very American too, because Americans strive to stand alone. I am always figuring out how the lone person forms a community.

PR: Well, it seems that memory does that for you in a way. It becomes the translation between an individual narrator and the family, whose stories have been narrated, and the history in which that family has lived its stories.

MHK: Yes, and then that brings us to the tribal memory, the family memory, the cultural memory. Well, I guess I contain them all in my own individual memory, but some of the stories that I write began with memories that we all have. Those collective memories are the myths. For example, immigration stories about how you got through Angel Island — having four or five versions of your immigration — that's not just the way my head works, that's the way narration and memory and stories work in our culture. So, that's a gift given to me by our culture, and not something that I imagined on my own. I invented new literary structures to contain multiversions and to tell the true lives of nonfiction people who are storytellers.

PR: Your books are categorized as autobiography or cultural history and as fiction and I am wondering what you see as the relationship between fact and fiction?

MHK: It doesn't bother me very much; it bothers other people more than me. It has caused problems. When the British reviewed my work, they could not get past the question, "Is this fiction or nonfiction?" There have been articles that just addressed that, and never got to what I am talking about.

The question of fiction or nonfiction has become a very political debate. Some minority critics have really elevated the novel as the highest form. They say that autobiography is a lesser form because you are not using imagination, and you present yourself as an oddity, an anthropological specimen, not as a literary creator. Since both *The Woman Warrior* and *China Men* were called nonfiction, I have had attacks from that point of view. When people pointed that out to me, I said, "Sure, I could have classified them as fiction." Our usual idea of biography is of time-lines, of dates and chronological events; I am certainly more imaginative than that; I play with words and form.

After going back and forth on my classification for a couple of years, I've decided that I am writing biography and autobiography of imaginative people. I am writing about real people, all of whom have minds that love to invent fictions. I am writing the biography of their imaginations.

PR: What are you working on now?

MHK: I am working on a novel that I should finish soon. It is definitely fiction. I mean, I made up everything; I invented the characters and the situations. I can tell the difference between fiction and nonfiction. Almost everything I've written was conceived in a process that would seem to produce essays. I imagined an event, an image, a person; and I thought of explication. I suppose that if the explication took up most room, I'd have an essay. Since I write about subjects that many people are ignorant about, it would seem that social forces would dictate the essay as my form. The begining chapters of *The Woman Warrior* are very essaylike. The later chapters and *China Men* are a letting go of the explicable. I present the events, images, and people and allow the reader to find the logic, which I've already suggested. In my forthcoming novel, *Tripmaster Monkey: His Fake Book*, I make up cause and effect, and I make up history. Now that I've almost finished such a long book — 750 [manuscript] pages, 8 years — I have a strong desire to write poetry, a form which seems to be close to the essay. Maybe I'll write essays instead of poetry if I can't resist putting in all the bridges. In a sense, fiction is so much easier, because if the narration needs an exciting moment, I can invent the exciting moment. Whereas, in the other two books, structurally it may be time for an exciting moment, but if the characters decide to go do their laundry or something, then somehow I have to make that a compelling part of the whole narrative.

PR: So you are saying that you felt constrained by the real people who were inhabiting those memories.

MHK: Yes, but they were an inspiration and a guide, too. They were always helping me shape the books; whereas in this fiction that I am writing, there is another kind of shaping, where I, as the writer, have a lot more power. In writing the other two books — finding the form, finding the language — I didn't always feel that it was me who was the most powerful. Some of the characters helped shape it, the way they spoke —

PR: Certainly Brave Orchid looms —

MHK: Yes, she dictated it, dictated it.

PR: So for the writer, fiction gives more power than writing autobiography. That's interesting, because one would think that if you are constructing the story of your life, you have a power; but you are suggesting the opposite.

MHK: Different kinds of power. Now that I have written fiction and two nonfictions, I just don't see why everybody doesn't do both. Each kind of writing draws on other kinds of strengths needed to find new ways to create a literary reality, to get at life. Just playing with another form, I feel that I am in another world.

PR: Do you think that fiction comes out of the same locus of memory and imagination that generated the other two books?

MHK: There seems to be a fantasy at work that's different from memory and imagination. For fiction, we fantasize about what we would like to happen: I am making what I would like to happen happen. And so, this writing always feels new and going forward. If there is such a thing as reverse memory, maybe that's what I am getting into; because it seems to me, I'm writing the memory of the future rather than a memory of the past.

September 1986

NOTES

1. For an elaboration see Kingston, "Cultural."
2. The narrator of *China Men* speaks directly to "The Father from China": "I wanted to be able to rely on you, who inked each piece of our own laundry with the word *Center*, to find out how we landed in a country where we are eccentric people" (15–16).

WORKS CITED

Kim, Elaine H. *Asian American Literature: An Introduction to the Writings and Their Social Context*. Philadelphia: Temple University Press, 1982.

Kingston, Maxine Hong. "Cultural Mis-reading by American Reviewers." *Asian & Western Writers in Dialogue*. Ed. Guy Amirthanayagam. London: Macmillan, 1982. 55–65.

———. "Imagined Life." *Michigan Quarterly Review* 22 (Fall 1983): 561–70.

Pfaff, Timothy. "Talk with Mrs. Kingston." *New York Times Book Review*, June 15, 1980: 1, 24–25.

Watkins, Mel. "Sexism, Racism and Black Women Writers." *New York Times Book Review*, June 15, 1986: 1, 35–37.

A SYMPOSIUM ON CONTEMPORARY AMERICAN FICTION

The editors posed the following question to a number of distinguished American fiction writers:

I Granted that contemporary American fiction is a variety of things, what kind of recent writing interests you especially, and, in your opinion, is most deserving of more attention and more readers? I

What follows are responses to this question.

Linsey Abrams

LINSEY ABRAMS

Is it any wonder, in this age of Star Wars, budget deficits, ayatollah diplomacy, the homeless, and a declining middle class, that mainstream American fiction has charted a more conservative course? The 1980s has seen a retreat from the proliferation of subject matters witnessed since World War II: a body of work of first Jewish then black and other minority men, which dominated the 1950s and 1960s, was followed by a landslide of books written by mostly middle-class white women in the early 1970s, then by women of color, until the late 1970s seemed to bear extraordinary promise for literature's future. The writing of that decade both reminded and informed us of our multiplicity. Work by Chicano/a, Chinese-American, Hispanic, Native American, and gay and lesbian writers helped reflect a truer America, as lives largely unseen became subject matter for a more public readership. (One thinks, for example, of Toni Morrison's Pecola, a twelve-year-old black girl whose wish for blue eyes exemplified the anguish with which she understood her own unrecognized life and how different it might have been had she been white.) Interior and exterior realities of a wide variety of characters enlarged our sense of the experience of others, of ourselves, of the confluence of diverse cultures in our own country.

The 1980s, in contrast, has seen a paring down of fictional territory. The minimalist stories and novels that have dominated this decade's postmodern literature document a retrenchment from our earlier pluralism. While scrutinizing the lives of sometimes working-class but mostly middle-class white people in individual and often meaningless predicaments, these slices of life tend to be without the surround, both historical and societal, that we have come to expect of fiction. Perhaps this is because this work skimps on interior lives, too, the surest mirror to a larger world.

But literature is a tree of many branches, and while one may outstrip the other for a time, the rest keep growing toward the light. A more complicated notion of ourselves — we could call this an eye to community or the moral placement of the self in society — continues to inform the novels of many of our most interesting writers of the 1980s. And if these books have met with individual rather than group fanfare, it may be because at first they seem less easily categorizable owing to the variety of their subject matters and forms. Nevertheless, if the solutions in these novels are different, their task is, it seems to me, the same: they have evolved in the spirit of our earlier pluralism, and in each of them a writer takes on as his or her opportunity (and burden) our *multicultural society.*

What separates the contemporary work I'd like to talk about from most of its antecedents is that these writers are attempting to *synthesize* a multiracial and multicultural experience. Where before (with notable exceptions) we had books by black writers about black experience, woman writers about women's experience, Native American writers about their experience — too often placed outside of "literature" shelves in their own categories in bookstores — today we are seeing an increasing number of books peopled according to a reality that is racially and culturally diverse, as these writers try to paint an accurate and inclusive American canvas. Not only are we offered characters more usually peripheral to the preoccupations of much contemporary fiction — walk-ons in which gay characters provide the humor, nonwhite characters the service or the urban surround — but also a kind of cross-referencing of experiences starts to occur, so that the lives of these characters resonate in the context of others. In this way, each comments on society, too.

Naturally, this alternative vision to minimalism tends to be more operatic in form. While minimalism, particularly among its youngest practitioners, borrows heavily from TV in its scenic movement, "synthesis" novels structure according to a more flexible and literary conception of time. Often, a variety of voices, points of view, create a refractory image of the world. This literary impulse is opposite to the spirit of deconstruction.

Her First American (1985), by Lore Segal, takes on two themes fundamental to this multicultural literature: the place of black people in a white-dominated United States and also the inclusion of immigrants into American society. Ilka Weissnix, a twenty-one-year-old Jew who arrives in the United States from post-Hiltler Europe, as without references as some alien dropped to earth, enters into an unlikely love affair with Carter Bayoux, a middle-aged intellectual and writer who is black. With his help, she begins to construct an understanding of her new country and a vocabulary of American English. The great achievement of the novel is the way the progress of their exchange, of both love and culture, is mirrored in Ilka's changing *language*. As a friend pointed out, Carter's alcoholism functions as the other, more internecine language of the book: what I take to be the psyche's language, in which there is always a more charged expression than that of words, in this case the insupportable weight of racism. Carter refers to the Talmud in explaining what, ultimately, he and Ilka have in common, "Property can be restored by the action of the court, but to cause another to blanch with shame is like drawing off his life's blood and is tantamount to murder. When a people — a whole race — is systematically humiliated, it is tantamount to genocide." The devastating irony of the book is that Ilka finds entry into American society from someone who finds himself, and his people, marginal to it. Not only are we made privy to the intimate and cultural center of these two characters but also to the larger reality against which both measure their lives. Though the city is New York, the locale is *America* (in the way that Gertrude Stein's hometown was forever Paris).

Rosellen Brown's *Civil Wars* (1984) also handles overtly the subject of racism, but in the contemporary context of the South and with reference to the history of the Civil Rights movement. Though the characters whose points of view we share are white, their interior and exterior lives are conducted in the context of a black and white community. When a couple who were Civil Rights activists in the 1960s adopt a niece and nephew whose white supremacist parents have died in a car accident, what results is the characters' inability to become a family. Though this inability is based, first of all, on differing beliefs, it is the experiential truth of living in an integrated world that becomes the rope in the tug-of-war between the two children and their guardians. The niece's clenched facial expression one morning at the table gives some sense of the fanaticism on both sides and is indicative, of course, of a larger societal struggle: "It was what one expected of a political prisoner, not a thirteen-year-old orphan girl at breakfast." The reader is left with the unsettling feeling that both children's resistance is to psychological rather than social change, and for that reason intractable.

Maybe it is this sense of psychological context that prompts contemporary novelists who take on black-and-white America (black culture evolved from African, slavery roots, that is, not the variety of cultures of recent immigrations) to explore the *past* the two races share. If it's true that as a country we face too squarely into the future, still the part of our short history that is most viscerally alive today is the memory of slavery. The slave narrative, in particular, has drawn the attention of a variety of contemporory writers, mostly black, though one of the earliest and most stormily received examples of the genre was Williams Styron's *The Confessions of Nat Turner* (1967). This invention by a white man as to *why* a black slave led a bloody insurrection against white society — without remorse and according to what Styron sets up as a pathology created by the institution of slavery itself — exemplifies the enormous risk of the kind of literature that is before us. The imagined interior life of Nat is where Styron's critics found their argument, not in the labyrinthine narrative at whose center the flashback of the bloody insurrection waits. Nat's obsession with a white woman as the maniacal force to his revolution, his defining of himself only in opposition to white society — these are what skew and ulitmately render inauthentic the characterization of Nat Turner. Imagination, then, is what both fuels and restricts the writer's reach; gaining subject matter means making it believable.

Charles Johnson's *Oxherding Tale* (1982), a slave narrative that must be read, in part, as an answer to Styron, is a celebration of imagination. (In the face of postmodernism, the novel is shamelessly modernist.) Johnson enriches the psyche of a mulatto slave living in 1858 with the language and sensibility of a modern man, in particular the tradition of Western philosophic thought. Andrew's interior life serves as a metaphor for a kind of spaciousness of thought that is lacking in Styron's Nat at the same time that it brings up very real questions about black and white identity. While he is running away from a slavecatcher, a predicament that is due to the man's being considered black, his mental life partakes of white culture, which eventually he joins: living as white, hence free. In the hands of a lesser writer, this scenario might simply be funny (which it is), but as usual in Johnson's fiction, the past makes commentary equally on the present. By the end of the novel, after all,

Andrew has lived both as a black man and as a white man. The either/or nature of his identity and position is not lost on the reader. Nor is the dilemma of intellectual and literary dominance, in a racially diverse society, by white culture.

Certainly, our most grievous loss to the primacy of a single culture has been that of the country's Native American heritage. Following on the work of such writers as James Welch and Paula Gunn Allen, Louise Erdrich's *Love Medicine* (1984) documented both the devastation to, and the endurance of, modern Indian life. There is an awful isolation to these characters' lives that is both figurative and literal, a psychological displacement from the larger culture alongside the displacement of reservation life. Erdrich's subsequent novel *The Beet Queen* (1986) extends her fictional scope to include a variety of immigrant and native North Dakotans, local to the small town of Argus. These characters work side-by-side, the dailyness of their difficult lives bringing them together over the course of forty years (from the Great Depression to the 1970s), until they are united, even in their differences. In this world, tragedies, miracles, and the exigencies of human nature are understood to dominate any one person's hopes or expectations. Being well-to-do or white offers no exemption from *living*.

As we have witnessed the small but significant introduction of Native American characters into a broader literature, we have witnessed also the revision of contemporary paradigms of human placement in nature. Indian history is also the history of the land. It is no accident that in Toby Olson's *Seaview* (1982) it is the presence of a Native American character, Bob White, that vitalizes both the other characters' (a white couple) and the reader's participation in a cross-country journey from the Southwest to Cape Cod. This journey takes as its ground a luminous, sacred landscape that we internalize as a description of the soul, the missing density in so much of contemporary literature. Olson speaks to us according to the logic of dreams (interior reality) and of causal reality as he tells this quintessentially American tale. The fantastical ending of *Seaview* crosses these two vocabularies as the individual stories of his characters flower into the larger story of the Native American struggle to regain their land.

Olson's more recent novel, *The Woman Who Escaped from Shame* (1986), shows a continued widening of American subject matter. This time he places Mexican characters and culture in a weave with our own; the effect, as before, is to break through the sealed culture of a society whose shared information seems to be exclusively of life's *surface:* brand name products, money, the TV news — to deeper paradigms for consciousness and living. A pair of white horses the size of dogs are the quasi-magical beings of Olson's story. Considered by some to be the invention of legend, they turn out to be real animals, who in the action of the book are, for humans, carriers of deep hope, of self-knowledge, of triumph against impossible odds.

Similarly, Russell Banks gives voice to myth and the imaginal in his novel, *Continental Drift* (1985), where he, too, creates a more inclusive America. Here an omniscient voice sets up the inescapable boundaries of the characters' lives, before they themselves see them, as we anticipate the coming together in Florida of a Haitian woman en route to the United States illegally by sea and a blue-collar New Englander who, with his family, is seeking a second chance in the South. We witness their approach, and rightly, with the horror reserved for radioactive halves nearing critical mass. Dickensian in its plotting, the novel becomes psychologically acute through the point of view of Bob Dubois, whose flashes of self-respect and desire for meaning qualify an otherwise bleak victimization. Depriving Vanise Dorsinville—Bob's opposite pole in the mechanism of the novel—of a similar interior life (particularly when she is repeatedly raped in the hold of a boat) seems a flaw in an otherwise impressively imagined narrative of two cultures. She becomes less a fully human character alongside Bob than a figure to which like an idol he bows at the novel's violent end. Banks's vision is both more explosive and bleaker than Olson's, in that the spiritual underpinnings of his tale have no power of redemption.

This mythic overlay to the real is one of the most remarkable changes in recent literature and is, I think, the direct result of the inclusion in it of a variety of nonwhite cultures. One thinks of Toni Morrison's *Song of Solomon* (1977) as an early example of how profoundly the description of the landscape we think of as American—the place we summon up in imagination when thinking about where we live—has been altered. In *Tar Baby* (1981), the first of her novels in which she wrote about black and white characters together, we witness, in an American household on a Caribbean island, the psychological minutiae of power, both societal (meaning racial and economic) and personal, focusing on the relationship of servants and employers. Morrison's evenhanded treatment and revelation of all her characters gives this novel the kind of breadth, and layering, that makes of a handful of lives a story equally about society. We are all living in that household. Similarly, her inclusion of a variety of cultures in both the action and ambience of the novel catapults us into a global reality, as Banks does. We are all living in that world.

The life of the servant has attracted the attention of writers of other recent books in this category, too, including Joseph Olshan's *Clara's Heart* (1985) and Paula Fox's *A Servant's Tale* (1984). Olshan's Clara is a Jamaican who forces the coming-of-age of the boy she raised in his parents' house by banishing him from her transplanted home in Brooklyn when he most needs her love. As in *Tar Baby*, we are met with the fact that personal relationships infiltrate and change societal roles, that the human is larger than any boundaries set to contain it. It is through the sharing of language, interestingly, that this transaction occurs between David and Clara, the same way it did between the characters in *Her First American*. But while Carter taught English to Ilka, this time it is the other way around. The boy learns Clara's Jamaican patois to get closer to her and, by implication, to her culture. The trueness of this voice is Olshan's own imaginative leap and what, ultimately, authenticates Clara.

A Servant's Tale is the first-person narrative, told by Luisa de la Cueva, of her childhood on a Caribbean island and her subsequent emigration to New York, where she works for the rest of her life as a servant to the well-to-do. In fact, this is a tale only a servant could tell: wanting nothing beyond working in other people's homes, Luisa stands in opposition to the *ambition* of the modern, industrialized world she has joined. But the larger story carried by this autobiography is the story of the two worlds its narrator claims. When finally Luisa recognizes that her only desire is to return to the island of her childhood, she does, to find the way of life she remembered, and everything of value, gone. The "ambition" of the United States is the "progress" of her home, and both translate into a change beyond human scale. Not only have the cultures of the world all clustered to America. But America, in turn, is now everywhere.

Many readers will have noticed that the minority of these books I've mentioned are by white writers. Let me say, first, that this is by no means an exhaustive list, that these novels simply have come to my attention and stuck. However, I think there are other reasons why fewer writers of other races have embraced this more culturally diverse subject matter. One is that minority writers and others with subject matters and perspectives outside of what has become a narrower mainstream of culture are having a hard time getting published now. A fact, and one we need to do something about. The other is that writers whose cultures and truths have in the past been denied inclusion into published literature are rightly interested in setting the record straight on *themselves* first. In a *New York Times Book Review* article of last year, Reynolds Price — in pondering why male writers over centuries have invented a number of major female characters, whereas the opposite has not been true — overlooked these same two facts. Tradition is the springboard from which individual writers leap. Building a literary vision takes publications and time and belief.

The vision of these multicultural novels is not postmodern. It's pre-global. Practitioners of this larger literature understand that American society with its various races and experiences is like the planet itself, whose population taken together describes difference as the norm, not the exception. What these books have in common is an attempt at synthesis of multiplicities, of finding in them a dialogue, if not a common value. People whose cultures, whose religions, whose skin colors, whose social institutions and mores, whose ideas . . . are different . . . must take on one another's subject matter, if imperfectly, to *learn* it.

These novels remind us of the role of imagination in literature: the awesome task of imagining not only one's self but others. It is the first leap the young writer takes: moving from self to other in the *imagination*. We are faced with similar leaps all our writing lives: across gender, across age, across work, across region, across race. Taking each one, responsibly, is to cultivate a larger moral ground. This garden of possibilities forms each writer's unique world, though what we ask of that world is that it both describe and recast the world we inhabit together.

RUDOLFO A. ANAYA

When one speaks of publishing in this country today, one must sadly note that the mainstream publishing industry has still not acknowledged the writers who come from our multicultural communities. Given the nature of our society and the politics of publishing, many of our most important multicultural writers are not visible in the bookstores or in the columns of the reviewers who help create taste in contemporary fiction. Those of us who belong to multicultural communities, therefore, take every opportunity to remind the public that a richness of literature exists around the periphery of mainstream publishing. It's a message we have to keep repeating. It's a message that bears repeating!

I want to discuss those writers in this country who write from a multi-

Rudolfo A. Anaya

cultural perspective in English, and at the same time to touch upon the content (or worldview) of the multicultural perspective. That presentation by the writer reflects and helps shape the communal ethos of the writer. These two elements, language and content, seem to me to be at the core of the richness and importance of the multicultural writer's work. It is my conviction that the multicultural writers of this country are expanding and enriching the literary heritage, but only in isolated cases is the challenge and richness of their works acknowledged.

It's precisely the two areas of language and content which seem to keep the publisher, the critic, the book reviewer, and eventually the reader at arm's length from the works of some multicultural writers. Those of us who were suckled in Spanish-speaking communities in the Southwest, the Hispano/Chicano writers, quite naturally have wrenched English from its unilateral, one-dimensional movement of expression and fitted our own Spanish cadence, rhythms, and the sensibility of our oral tradition to the story at hand. The English language belongs to all of us: each writer is free to experiment with all the aspects of language, to enrich the story and broaden the very language itself. That seems a natural course, a course which enriches the language, makes it cyclical, and makes it more serviceable to more people.

It's that usage which brings the first criticism from those who subscribe to a universalist approach to the language. Very often the reviewer of a multicultural work will complain that because the language reflects the writer's original language or culture, the meaning is not clear. That was, and is, a criticism of my first novel, *Bless Me Ultima.* Even recently I was told by an eastern publisher that my work is better served if it's published west of the Mississippi (they really meant west of the Rio Grande) because that's where it's better understood. Those people in control of publishing and of reviewing contemporary fiction upon whose promotion of universal literature we have relied have employed harmful and narrow definitions of literature. On the other hand, the multicultural writer has served contemporary fiction by promoting and embracing the literature of all the communities in this country.

The second point that bears discussion is the idea of content, that is, the worldview of the multicultural writer which permeates the story. Each writer from each multicultural community envelops within his work a particular ethos of the community. This is true of the Native-American, Black, Asian-American, and Chicano writer. This, too, has generated criticism. Most often, the safer story (safer because it did not create problems of meaning and it did not challenge the reader by presenting a new ethos) coming out of mainstream America remained the accepted story to publish, critique, and include in the American canon. Only the most adventurous readers (and at the beginning largely others of our multicultural communities already mentioned) were interested in the perspective presented in, say, my first novel. We have lived in this country for over four hundred years, our worldview is older than Plymouth; our Hispanic and indigenous perspective is tied to the earth and history of the Americas. It also is as new as the crucial social issues in civil and ecnomic rights denied to Hispanos, Native Americans, and other multicultural groups. It is as explosive as the Chicano movement of the sixties and early seventies, and it is as vital as the Mexican workers crossing the Rio Grande in search of work.

The black writers have constantly challenged the American status quo, both in literature and politics. They have learned to use the English language to serve their need for story: in the sixties some of the other multicultural communities followed their lead. Each community of multicultural writers created contemporary fiction out of its needs, out of its sense of history, and each has used its particular language code to enrich the stories written in English.

Yes, the literary canon in this country is being revised, but every small step seems a hard-won battle. The fact that the *Michigan Quarterly Review* asked me to share my thoughts in this essay may not seem momentous, but it is important to those of us expanding the literary voice of the great Southwest. I am a writer from the Mexican-American, Hispano community, I am a Chicano writer; I do not come seeking acceptance, I come to tell you that what I find exciting in contemporary fiction is its multicultural nature.

Reed Way Dasenbrock, in a recent article on intelligibity and meaningfulness in multicultural literature written in English (*PMLA*, January 1987), states that "multicultural literature dominates literature in English today." He uses the term *multicultural literature* "to include both works that are explicitly about multicultural societies and those that are implicitly multicultural in the sense of inscribing readers from other cultures inside their own textual dynamics."

He further suggests that "some of the greatest writing being done in English today is coming from outside the traditional Anglo-American mainstream." This is my text for the day. We, and the literary power brokers, have to acknowledge our own narrow views on literature and discover the work of the multicultural writers of our country. The impetus of the seventies should not be lost as we complete the eighties. The earlier infiltration of mainstream literature by the multicultural writers is a reality, but power structures are defined by the nature of their resistance. We must continue to expand the process of awareness of our role in the literary heritage.

The politics of publishing in this country have become stagnant and boring. Perhaps even the freshness of creating the literature of the country has become mired in packaging and sales projections. (Many of the new writers in creative writing programs and those who regularly attend the summer writing workshops become too quickly involved in the sales pitch, in who they know and how soon they can be blessed by an eastern publisher.) What a waste of talent when the writer looks to the publisher for guidance instead of to his soul.

I suggest we take a lesson from the multicultural writers in this country, those who have so long been denied, those who are still publishing their stories through the small presses. It is precisely here where language is being used in new, exciting ways and at the same time presenting a new, local (regional) picture of the world. I'd like to suggest a few books coming from the multicultural perspective. The problem with the list is that it would quickly grow to include books from India, Africa, New Zealand, and many other places. I think I serve the purposes of this special issue best if I stick closer to home, alert you to the writers from my Chicano community. The multicultural perspective is right here in our backyard, it's the new perspective trying to work its way into American fiction.

Chicano writers are involved in a renaissance of literary works. The production began in the mid-sixties with the Chicano movement, and it has continued to grow and expand, despite the fact that it has not yet acquired mainstream publishing currency. The Chicano writers of this country write in English, Spanish, bilingually and with various combinations of languages. It is exactly their usage of English that makes their work exciting. The presentation of their world (which had not been portrayed en masse by the writers from within the community before the sixties) through the filter of a different language creates one of the most interesting phenomena in contemporary fiction.

Some of you are familiar with the recent fiction of Gary Soto and Alberto Alvaro Rios, both writers who have won prestigious literary awards. All of you should be familiar with the classic, *"y no se lo trago la tierra"* by Tomas Rivera. Written in Spanish and then translated into English, the novel captures the essence of the Mexican workers of the Rio Grande Valley of Texas and their migrations in search of work. The novel forces the Anglo-American reader to look for the first time at a community of people living within the confines of the Anglo-American culture and to see the oppression the workers suffer. It is probably one of the most existential novels within the Chicano canon.

The Road to Tamazunchale by Ron Arias has been called an example of magical realism written by a Mexican-American writer. It is that, but it's more. It recreates the world of the village within a Los Angeles barrio with all the attendant characters. What we learn about death, the main theme of the novel, touches precisely on the character of our culture.

The novels of Oscar Zeta Acosta touch not only on the theme of identity, they touch on the relationship of the Chicano writer to his contemporaries. We do not live in a vacuum, we know, read and respect other writers, and these influences create interesting hybrids.

Antonio Villareal should be read. His novel *Pocho* stands out as a precursor of the Chicano novel. He has continued to write, exploring the consequences of the Mexican Revolution on the Mexicans who came north into the United States, those who would later call themselves Chicanos in the sixties. His novel tackles the theme of the American Dream: the acquisition of job, home, money, power, and what you give up to acquire them.

Arturo Islas's recent novel, *The Rain God,* has much to tell our community of our new role in Anglo-American society as we acquire an education and move away from the confines of the group. The communal pull is strong in Chicano prose and poetry, family and culture are motivating forces, sometimes characters in the novel. What happens when we leave the nexus of the group? Can we as a community recreate our heritage and history in a comtemporary world? Or do we have to give up our history to live within the confines of Anglo-American society? An important theme and one which I wrestled with in my novel, *Heart of Aztlan*, a theme so important that it is at the core of the current discourse within out intellectual community.

Also there are important works of younger writers, the second wave of the Chicano movement whose works are just now being published. The tragedy here is lack of attention by publishers to these young writers. I know many gifted writers who have a long wait ahead of them because the publishers with power just aren't interested in that group west of the Rio Grande. It is a tragic waste in our community, because we need their stories for a clearer reflection of our soul, as does the broader society.

Within this group the women writers are adding to the expression and rich texture of the literature. Denise Chavez just published a novel, *The Last of the Menu Girls*. It is a coming-of-age novel, but it also provides sensitive insight into the world of women, the mother who copes with family and struggles with her dream for girls in a small, New Mexican town.

The House on Mango Street, by Sandra Cisneros, is wonderfully crafted. Again the view is of women, the central metaphors have to do with those elements in culture which trap women. The novel forces a new dialogue on us, as good fiction should. One of the most exciting recent novels is Ana Castillo's *The Mixquihuala Letters*. (Notice how she challenges you immediately with her title?) It is the story of two women traveling through Mexico, daring the old prejudices against women. It is well written, with great strength in style.

I could go on mentioning names and works and introducing you to writers from my community, but the list is long. What I intend to create in this short space is awareness. Those of us who continue to draw materials and inspiration from the content and language of our groups may well represent the yet-unrecognized vitality of an untapped root of American literature. It's the well-crafted presentation of that local (regional) universe which creates the excitement in contemporary American fiction. I hope I've been able to point to a new direction for readers of contemporary fiction.

James Atlas
photo by
Thomas Victor

JAMES ATLAS

There is such a profusion of contemporary American fiction worth noticing these days that one is tempted to speak in grandiose terms of a renaissance. Scarcely a week goes by without some new novel or collection of stories landing on my doorstep, adorned with endorsements from well-known writers and fervent claims by the publisher. What's amazing is how often these pronouncements turn out to be valid. This year [1987] has brought us Mona Simpson's astonishing debut, *Anywhere But Here;* Max Apple's *Propheteers;* Bret Lott's *The Man Who Owned Vermont;* a new novel by Padgett Powell; a thick, much-touted novel by David Wallace entitled *The Broom of the System . . .* and these are just the titles that come instantly to mind. Bantam has started a New Fiction line with two estimable first novels, Glenn Savan's *White Palace* and Ann Hood's *Somewhere Off the Coast of Maine.* Penguin's Contemporary American Fiction series has a hundred or so books on its list; the ones I've read are very good.

How to characterize or quantify this outpouring? I hesitate even to try, so diverse and original are the voices I've mentioned. One tentative generality: New York is no longer the center of things. The geographical distribution of talent is random. There are writers out at the University of Iowa, writers in Mississippi, writers in Texas. . . . The impulse, not only to write, but to write as a vocation, a career, is very strong; and I wonder if the success — after much patient labor — of Raymond Carver, Richard Ford, and a handful of their contemporaries hasn't made the dream of becoming a writer more attractive. Their lives and work testify to the fact that it can be done.

Is there *more* good writing now than there was, say, a decade ago? Again, I'm not sure. There have always been good writers. But it does seem to me that the willingness of publishers to support new fiction, the flowering of anthologies, the enthusiasm of magazines — the latest among them Gordon Lish's quarterly — have combined to produce a climate highly favorable to what used to be a very tenuous enterprise. This much is clear: an audience for literature exists. Books are being published; they're being sold and read. What more could a writer ask?

ASA BABER

Asa Baber

If fiction writers in the USA are going to be able to maintain any sense of individuality while they struggle to make a living and get published, they are going to have to come face to face with The Bear: publishing is now nothing more than a branch of the entertainment business. "It's showtime, folks!" might be publishing's trademark. This includes the increasing concentration of power in publishing conglomerates, the need for fiction editors to find a trend and ride it (they are being judged by the bottom line and little else), the tyranny of a marketplace that is frightened of any true diversity of ideas, the influence of marketing and demographic experts on fiction lists. McDonald's Fiction, you might call it. Fiction that sells, not fiction that illuminates. I'm not sure that "contemporary American fiction is a variety of things." Nope, to me it seems mostly bland, similar, unexciting, academic. North American fiction, that is. Travel south of our border and you find in Latin America the best fiction being written today. McDonald's hasn't conquered Central or South America. Yet.

I
RUSSELL BANKS
I

Russell Banks
photo by
Thomas Victor

We're talking Serious Fiction here, of course, and as Thomas Pynchon noted, serious fiction is determined by its attitude toward death. That is to say, it has one. Which is perhaps the reason most serious fiction writers spend their writing lives obsessively returning to the terms of the trauma that occured when, cast into a larger world than the world provided by their tiny immortal self, they discovered mortality and other people. In war, in the family, in the streets, in a trailer park, in the back seat of a '62 Chevy — wherever the serpent happened to appear first. Accordingly, most fiction writers reserve their deepest affection for work that teaches them how to make that obsessive return with efficiency, honesty, elegance, and pith. Every generation of writers needs to learn how to re-tell the Fall. Thus I'm especially interested in the work of novelists and story-writers of my own generation (born betwenn, say 1935 and 1945) whose historical locus was created by entry into a large social world that happened at the time to be preoccupied with sex, race, and violence, and the politics of same. Unpopular themes, maybe, or at least not very chic these days, but it's where we found death and other people, and as a result, for many of us who emerged from the cocoon of adolescence in the raging sixties, the terms are an unavoidable vocabulary of self and mortality. Robert Stone, Don DeLillo, John Wideman, Rosellen Brown, Alice Walker *and* Ishmael Reed, Ray Carver, John Irving, Clarence Major, and a dozen more, who don't necessarily need more attention: they need a different kind of attention. For they are clearly a generation of grown-up writers who are usefully different from the generation of writers that preceded them (whose Fall seems to have occurred in universities, suburban bedrooms and divorce court) and the one coming along behind (whose Fall so far seems to have occurred somewhere between the men's room at the Palladium and a health food store in Vermont).

I
RAYMOND BARRIO
I

Once upon a time . . . no. I'm a year older than Kurt Vonnegut, who was born in 1922. In WWII we were both young soldiers, sent overseas against the hated Nazis. He was captured. I was lucky. The Nazi Super Panzers bypassed my division and stunned the rest of the line with the Battle of the Bulge. Then our Allied armies smashed back into the German heartland, triumphant.

Raymond Barrio

In 1969 Kurt Vonnegut published his wry, dark, daft *Slaughterhouse Five*, a novel dealing with the Allies' dreadful firebombing of beautiful Dresden. That same year I self-published my novel *The Plum Plum Pickers*, which deals with the exploitation of Mexican field-workers in California agriculture. *Plum* went through several printings and was excerpted in more than twenty-five literary anthologies nationally. A nice reward, a nice feeling for a serious writer. Very little money.

Despite his ferocious facetiousness Kurt Vonnegut is a very serious writer. I like his work. I like his visions.

What I don't like—and it certainly isn't Vonnegut's fault—is the way I've been seriously mistreated as a serious writer. My gripe has to do with the way cheap, shoddy, meretricious businessmen have mishandled America's publishing establishment. Way back, even during my dewy-eyed high school daze I quickly learned I mean fast that there are two kinds of fiction in America: serious and commercial. And this in a ratio of about five percent to ninety-five percent.

Don't look for the differences between the two in either money or fame. Both fields, both serious and commercial fiction can make their authors famous and rich, and both, at the same time, can lead to failure, frustration, and fooey.

The main difference between these two worlds lies in motivation, in what you are willing to give up, or to invest in, in order to get into print.

Every writer must confront a crucial decision, usually at a young age, which is either to write what other people (editors, publishers, friends, relatives) think he should write—or else what the writer feels, deep in his heart, come heels or high wasser, he should, indeed *must* write. Not:

what he thinks sells, but what he feels most deeply about. Whether to be a fiercely independent thinker, or whether to sell out for some comfortable promised pittance: that is the real question.

(Incidentally, I should point out here that I am speaking principally of poets, dramatists, and writers of serious fiction. Nonfiction writers face a far different set of circumstances. Nonfiction writers had better know what the hell they're talking about for if they don't they won't get past the editor. If by alcoholic oversight they should, thousands of alert readers will give them the heave-ho, along with the editor and the publication unlucky enough to let it slip by.)

Fiction is a Jezebel. She is wild, loose, and heart-thumping. She uses every tricky lure in the book to snare you. Both good fiction and bad. (Remember Mae West? "When I'm bad I'm very very good.") So it's OK for bad fiction to outsell serious fiction. But those sales figures must be ignored by the serious writer. What I'm talking about here is principle, and not selling out.

It takes a lot of guts to go after success, recognition, achievement in serious fiction. It can be done. The very act of trying is in itself a high act. In fact, my whole thumping thesis here is to convince you young waverers out there to go all out for serious writing. You might not achieve recognition, sure, or money. But you can't really fail if you write seriously. Hey, you get to keep your integrity. And integrity is what it's all about, not pimping. In writing seriously, you are advancing not only your own miserable elf but the whole waffle, society.

The days of gentlemen publishers are long gone. Many old-line publishing houses were started by refined gentlemen. As a hobby. They could afford to finance risky books. Their educated taste led them to choose manuscripts they liked. Making a profit wasn't their top priority. What they liked were the prestige and honor they received reflected from publishing authors who became famous under their aegis. The small press movement and little literary magazines now take their place.

For that ole debbil started rooting and snuffing around. Now we have the Rupert Murdochs peddling fake romance, filth, and trivia for that famous bottom line. And the public swills it. And pays hot bucks for it.

But we're still holding the line. Serious writers don't give up. They just go underground. Where the poets have been all along. Move over, poets. Serious writers simply have to practice Emersonian self-reliance.

All art must go public. Singers give recitals. Dancers dance. Painters exhibit. Musicians play. Writing must be printed. A serious writer, once he feels ready, must break into print. Somehow. Sure you can be rejected. A thousand times.

While you're making all those submissions, however, you should also seriously investigate self-publishing. The vanity vultures discovered this lucrative field long ago and have bilked thousands of hopeful tyros ever since. Instead, you go do your own typesetting and you go to a printer yourself, direct. The difference is a ratio of about five to one in cost. And you get to keep your pride intact. Think of how old Henry Ford made his first tin Lizzie by hand.

Now I have another gripe. No, not the commercial robber barons. They simply and cleverly snuffed out a fat golden cow and boy are they milking it. This has nothing to do with serious writing. It is merely a naturally evolved market. Just because it's writing, a serious writer has to turn his back on it.

No, my other gripe has to do with serious writers who have achieved high fame and fortune. While I wouldn't expect commercial moneybags to suddenly grow charitable and subsidize serious writers — what a laff! — I would, however, like to see some signs of sympathy from successful writers (heck no I won't name no names) toward overcoming the frustrating blocks faced by serious tyro writers. Grants, commissions, whatever.

Specialty workshops could be set up to help writers and thereby help advance America's serious culture. My favorite would be a printing shop, with typesetters, graphic arts, layout people, offset press, copy machines, and so on. Over the years I've taught myself all of these skills. Or access to computerized desktop publishing. A writer could then submit his plan, his manuscript, and get it into print just for the cost of materials. What? Who says it can't be done?

Also, a distribution center for little magazines and small-press books, on a bigger scale than CCLM or Dustbooks. Subsidize the distribution of little mags to libraries. Well, you get the idea. . . .

I've devoted my entire mature life to serious writing, at great personal and financial sacrifice. As inspiration; that has been my chief reward. I earned my living by part-time teaching and supported my family, badly, over the years. I hate to guess what my devoted wife and our five wonderful grown children think of the tremendous sacrifices I've subjected them to. I can personally take penury. But it is very difficult for one's children to understand the rationale thereof. I've not simply paid my dues. I have forced my innocent family to help in making those heavy payments.

I think some of those rich and famous authors out there should pitch in and help a little. (As James Michener has done.) If anybody wants any specifics, shop ideas, programs, plans, etc., it's easy to get in touch with me. I've been listed in *Who's Who* and *Contemporary Authors,* and other reference works for years.

I
JONATHAN BAUMBACH
I

The kind of contemporary fiction that interests me the most, the kind of fiction I recommend to friends and others, has some or all of the following concerns.

1. Words. Sentences.
2. The hostility of certain readers who believe the novel must abide by certain rules — rules that have been inductively arrived at by myopic observation of the nineteenth-century English novel.
3. A romantic refusal to believe that everything has already been done.
4. A sometime compulsion to devise a work of fiction that determinedly breaks the rules or, as Robert Bresson in his "Notes on Cinematography" puts it, "To bring together things that have never yet been brought together and did not seem predisposed to be so."
5. A certain rebelliousness against received notions. A turning of received notions against themselves. Orneriness.
6. A refusal to take literally such dichotomies as intellect and feeling, form and content.

Jonathan Baumbach

7. An attempt to revise the notion of what is possible.
8. An investigation into ways of telling a story and ways of not telling a story.
9. A withholding of empathy—an engendering of distance. A refusal to allow the reader to be passive.
10. Fiction as self-contained object separate from the reader's life.
11. A refusal to create the illusion (or the convention of the illusion) of reality.
12. Surprise.

I also read and admire and recommend books that have few or none of these concerns.

I
CHARLES BAXTER
I

Charles Baxter   photo by Robert Turney

If there has been a growth of interest in the American short story in the 1980s, this interest has been spurred not only by the stories themselves but also by attacks on them from various organs of official culture such as *Newsweek* and *Commentary*. The claims against the new short story have to do with what it represents and how that is represented. What we are getting, the argument runs, are affectless characters with no histories or commitments who don't do much except talk in stupefying ways (or whine) before acting out their preprogramed impulses. This, or some variation of it, is represented in flattened prose with moments of sensual narcissistic flash, in scenes set up without transition, in the present tense, no background provided, plot eliminated as is social background. The new things are short, sketchy, and cold.

Although this looks like a squabble over aesthetic strategies, it is in fact a contest between competing versions of American life, in which class interests are deeply implicated. The refusal to provide more epic versions of American life—a project by now taken over by mass-market middlebrow writers—has made the writers of the new short story seem *almost* subversive, radical (in some sense), and therefore oppositional in late-modernist style. This being America, the debate about this fiction goes on in a curious ahistorical way. The fact is that we are experiencing a revival of modernism, call it neo-modernism or modernist revival, in which the style of Stein in "Melanctha" and Hemingway in *In Our Time* have become, without anyone remarking on it, all the rage. But it's still rage, which signals that the moment does have something to do with modernism: the new stories appear to be an assault on psychologism and traditional ideas of character. The assault works formally by eliminating depth, shadow, and the explanatory past, and thematically by giving us characters who could, most of the time, care less. It's American nihilism: cool, even cheerful. It is opposed to any late-blooming epiphanic moments. Hemingway's "A Very Short Story" or "Hills like White Elephants" might serve as the models here, with their spare and somewhat indifferent characterizations and no-bullshit-please brusqueness.

These are ahistorical times, at least in America, but the history of America has habitually included a good deal of ahistoricism. Americans, as Tocqueville never tired of pointing out, don't believe in the explanatory power of history, and they don't really believe in the power of the past to shape *them*. As a result, they don't much believe in tragedy (exception being made for the South, where history and tragedy have been communal obsessions). New beginnings—*the* New Beginning—are at the heart of American business-secular and religious-revival thinking, and the short story of all the available literary forms is the one that tends most aggressively to bracket history, both personal and cultural. Short stories that try to include history often turn into summaries and explanations; they turn discursive. It's no wonder that the American short story form has recently been struck by the craze for present-tense narrative, a form that suggests that the only thing that has happened is in fact happening now. The present is the only past there is. One may freely complain about the present tense and about characters who can't think about anything anterior to the day-before-yesterday, but the problem is not so much literary as cultural. In the age of Reaganism, why blame Ann Beattie for writing about young urban types who can't remember, and don't care about, what they were doing a few years ago?

Whatever happens in short stories happens, in one way or another, somewhere else. The reason that short stories are newsworthy is that the inability of the form to incorporate much history is pleasing to readers in a radically ahistorical time and culture. Stories seem to have caught the pastlessness of things faster than novels have. American culture these days emphasizes moments rather than sequences—the current drug of choice is cocaine, not acid—and to that degree stories act as formal representatives of the way some people live now.

It seems to me, however, that American fiction of the 1980s has been largely constructed out of anger, and its formal and aesthetic difficulties have originated in the problem of what to do with anger in a commercial medium. I am assuming here that anger is *prior* to apathy and depression, that it is, in effect, the source of both of them. This cooled-out anger—and this is the tricky part—has two components, politics and taste. Mainline American culture is the target of that anger; no one engaged in the fiction I am talking about seems to doubt that this culture is guilty of social, ecological, and political crimes. Anger against these crimes is conflated, however, with a distaste for middle-class American culture as vulgar, unreal, or silly. Not some of it: all of it. This distaste comes from writers who are inescapably part of that class. The result of this mixture of politics and taste is that snobbery, elitism, and *personal* isolationism become confused with political anger, with several distinct results: a ban on tenderness and lyricism stylistically as collaborationist, and a new pastoralism concerning lower-middle-class and working-class characters, as if they were immune from the guilty culture-as-a-whole. There are several notable exceptions to the trends I am trying to pinpoint, but I think it could be proved that in current American fiction, politics and aesthetics have become badly confused.

This is most apparent in quarrels over style. Visible language, we are given to understand, is radical. It functions in a Brechtian way, to strip us of our illusions. In a postdeconstructive, postmodern era, the high visible style calls attention to the depredations of language (Brecht, Hemingway, Derrida). The problem here is that all the old truisms of modernism, circa 1925—*The Dehumanization of Art,* for example—are being recycled as conventions, with the style of the avant-garde moving straight into mainline academic and commercial culture. We are witnessing the repackaging of modernism into pseudo-oppositional fiction published by big commercial houses, the return of the repressed as glossy merchandise. What was once avant-garde in the 1920s returns, in the 1980s, as avant-garde kitsch. Avant-garde kitsch, perhaps the one true invention of the American short story of the 1980s, is kitsch in large part because of its air of nostalgic nihilism, or, its twin, glossy hip radicalism. Its dirty secret is that it is nostalgic for an adversarial margin it no longer can lay claim to. It comes from the mainstream and goes into the mainstream but pretends that it does not. It proclaims crisis, collapse, burial, and sells these proclamations for $17.95. This is the merchandizing of the apocalypse, an apocalypse that nonetheless seems all too plausible.

My objection here is not to any style as such but only to self-righteousness about any particular style and to anyone who claims to speak for history with reference to style or subject. History does not dictate that characters must be deprived of an inner life or that political radicalism precludes tenderness in human affairs. Virtually all other world cultures of the present time have discovered techniques for combining passion, politics, and postmodernist techniques. Only we in America (and, perhaps, those in perpetually Futurist France) have the idea that character is unreal, that language is our enemy, and that what happens on the surface is all there is. Because history dictates nothing, editors, writers, and readers attempt to dictate in its name. *Necessity,* by contrast, is silent, and makes us do what we do often without our knowing it.

I don't wish to name names. The bookshelves behind me are filled with books by current and past American writers whose work I admire. The finest of these writers strike me as generous, willing to give away everything they have, for the cause, whatever that cause may be. They have used their minds and their hearts; everything is at stake; everything is on the line. That kind of generosity may be the truest radicalism.

"Art must claw at the neck of the bourgeois as the lion does at the horse," says the German artist Dieter Hacker, quoted by Donald Barthelme, in a catalogue for a showing of the work of Sherrie Levine, at the Mary Boone Gallery. Well, all right. Maybe so. But the lion, clawing at the horse, kills the horse. Then, traditionally, the lion *eats* the horse before taking a long nap. There is no evidence that art has, in any sense at all, killed off any sector of bourgeois society or consumed it. Rather, the opposite. The customer lines up, happily enraged, checkbook at the ready, at the Mary Boone Gallery. Barthelme knows the ironies of this situation all too well and, an expert spinner of these cultural webs, is amused. Writers less conscious of cultural ironies than Barthelme who pretend to be the lion have to be careful; thinking themselves the lion, they have often played (by accident) the less romantic role of the horse.

STEPHEN BECKER

Stephen Becker

No recent writing interests me. "La chair est triste et j'ai lu tous les livres." I concentrate on old friends and old favorites. Twice a year, urged, I explore; once would do.

Nowadays our arts conform to ludicrous and ephemeral theories; a poetry student once told me that "we use free verse now because the old forms aren't flexible enough for our complicated emotions."

Well! How many of the scores of old forms she was acquainted with is one conjecture; how complicated her emotions were, another. Our burgeoning world of amateurs scoffs at effort, at purity of tone or language; the memorable line has vanished. A poet who knows too much about poetry is considered a freak, an academician, possibly a Platonic fascist; a writer or politician who uses words right, and works in complete sentences, is considered a snob, a pedant, a show-off, surely an elitist and possibly an Anglophile.

Consider current cinema's addiction to violence; current journalism's sleazy appeal to "new age" and "soft science" mentalities (setting us up for demagogues).

Consider Andrew Wylie's comment (he is a literary agent), "Every week on the *New York Times* best-seller list there are thirty books, two of which are written in English."

Consider television, impossible to praise and impossible to malign.

Consider paintings, happenings, temporary or self-destructive art; or the ingenious and boring squeaks and shrieks that have replaced Mozart and Stravinsky (about whose work similar complaints were lodged).

The new short story, resurgent and triumphant, blurs into one vast shallow slice of life; the vocabulary and range of emotion are so limited that one author reads much like another, squeezing the tube of basic English for a swatch of banality. "Anybody can write a Barthelme story. Only Cheever can write a Cheever story."

Yet Cheever admired Barthelme. And I am in principle happy about the explosion of letters.

What the hell is going on?

Well, democracy is going on. The richly wrought novel is to public letters what the mansion is to public housing. In politics I march with tenants, not landlords; why should I reject my comrades' (let us reclaim the word) rocklike simplicities?

Art has become self-expression. Some selves are grubby and self-indulgent; that is an unavoidable risk. (Remember Yoko Ono's famous remark, almost twenty years ago," To be an artist today, you don't have to have talent." Still, when my students say, "I have to find myself," I answer, "There may be nothing to find. You must *make* yourself.")

Or: the arts have become a way of life, like banking or plumbing or farming. Or change the figure, for the more serious writer: where the novelist used to be a great hooded vulture, consuming whole societies and excreting gorgeous heaps of particolored compost, he is now — with perhaps a dozen exceptions — a maggot, barely able to digest the least granule of history's horror, and consequently excreting mainly his own innards, which are of little interest or importance and less beauty.

Even our trashy novels are read by perhaps one American in fifty. Taken as a whole, American writing is shallow and banal; weak verbs prevail (as in "you don't have to have"); meanings vanish like endangered species; efforts at significance are solemn, indignant, derivative, pretentious, and infinitely tedious. One is tempted to sympathize with the aficionados of cockfighting and pit bulls.

The two poles are Plato's rigidly ordered republic in which reside no poets at all, and the United States of 1999, when every citizen who can print his mark will call himself a poet. In half a century, we have emerged from elitism to enter an age of universal semiliteracy. Frost's "tennis without a net" is pertinent: with every sag, droop, and frayed cord, more poets and novelists joined the rally, and now we cannot see the ball for the players.

Much current poetry is read by poets, subsidized by academe and of no interest whatever to the general public; it is unmusical, subjective, and trite; it is solemn mooing. "There are nine and sixty ways of constructing tribal lays, and every single one of them is right"; there was only one way to write Kipling's poetry, and everybody says it was wrong, but quote me three consecutive lines of any current poet. Quote me a line that you live by, love by, dance to.

Perhaps the computer culture has arrived to dispatch the literary culture decently, and spare it a lingering demise, incontinent upon its own deathbed. But probably not: the flood of writing since 1960 will be refined to a literature by time, but also by attitudes that do not now prevail or perhaps even exist. Think of the sexual revolution — *Lady Chatterley's Lover*, published today, would be a middling melodrama with quaint overtones of class struggle, and plenty of clichés in the prose.

Yes, I was educated when Latin was required. First moved by the ancients, I live with my mortality and need arts to the scale of human pain. Your hangnail, sir or madam, does not move me; I have loved and lost whole countries, whole decades, a whole lifetime, I need greatness as consolation; I need art not to improve each shining hour, but to hold back the night.

Loss, despair, annihilation itself emerge from great works without ignoble tears or bourgeois sullens. Audiences used to understand that, and were not afraid to bring some effort to the experience of art — they did not believe, as we seem to, that an artist ought to work long and hard to produce something immediately accessible to the untrained observer, just because the untrained observer was in the majority. Past audiences seem to have expected that the artist would use all the culture at his command; that he would dominate them and not pander to them; that the experience of his work would deepen, broaden, and enrich them. Not now; today's mass audiences need popcorn, and the cordon bleu is reserved for dog shows.

So — as subjective as any of them — I retreat to my Authorized Version and my Greeks and my Shakespeare. Yet I teach "creative writing" and script-writing with a clear conscience (and with *Dubliners* as occasional text). Any paradox or polarity is a tool and not a barrier. The gods and heroes are dead, so we tailor fate to our own small measure. Myriads of poets capture the emotion of the moment, recommended in tranquility. James or Kilmer: you pays your money and you takes your Joyce.

Art for all. Well, it beats heroic wars, in which those we love are maimed or incinerated; and how many of us these days would fight before Troy for ten years and wander home for ten more?

I
MADISON SMARTT BELL
I

Madison Smartt Bell
photo by
Andrew French

As an omnivorous reader since I first learned how, I like almost everything I read, by definition. There'll be occasional exceptions; there's always a little bandwagon fiction around, jouncing and clanging after whatever trend, but one learns to hear it coming and so avoid it. "Fashionable" fiction, one presumes, is reassuring to its readers in its very sameness, but what I'd always rather have is surprise, variety—the swerves, sidesteps, and prestidigitation that maybe can add up to magic. I'm interested in writers more than "schools" of writing, where every individual gleam vanishes into the shiny mass of fish. Schools stultify; that's what they're for. But if a writer can keep you guessing, light on your feet from book to book, then so much the better.

Effective hype is a relative thing, and literary publishing operated on that principle as much as any other form of show business. Only so much talent can crowd into any spotlight; some limit, usually arbitrary, must always be invoked. So, having no time to talk about all I admire, let me only mention a few of the writers I'd like to *steal* from.

Of these, the first must be George Garrett (from whom I've begged and borrowed all I can). Garrett is the most protean writer on the American scene today that I know anything about. The easiest sample of his extraordinary range is found in *An Evening Performance*, a recent gathering of some thirty years' worth of his short stories. That book should prove to a great many people who could use the lesson (myself included) that the short story can and sometimes ought to be an arena for trying things out. Garrett is willing to try almost anything and can usually make it work. In this collection he runs the whole spectrum from pure horse-laugh comedy to whip-stroke satire to the altogether serious dissection of the practical morals of human behavior on earth.

On his serious side, Garrett has written two historical novels which absolutely change the definition of "historical novel," *Death of the Fox* and *The Succession*. His Elizabethans are not mere moderns in fancy dress, as is most usual for this genre, but genuinely people of their time, not ours, with a very different language, an entirely different set of fundamental assumptions, and so a world to live in which is almost completely other than our own. These books offer a privileged glimpse into what is really a parallel universe, interrupting the stream of time so completely that the reader learns to think of his own period as the future. There's enough of an achievement here for anyone else's whole career. Then, just as a pigeonhole labeled "profoundly contemplative historical &c." has been prepared for him, Garrett comes back with *Poison Pen*, a satiric maze of tripwires and mirrors in which Swift, Twain, and Nabokov would all have to struggle to keep their bearings.

The scope of Garrett's abilities is always something to aspire to, but there is another quality as important to his work, which helps to bind the whole of it together: voice. His writing is much more of a sound than a pattern on the page; it's a voice that talks right to you, buttonholes you, clasps your attention and draws it deeper in. It seems to me that he knows more than any other writer now in business about writing for the ear, and it's that ability that I would most want to appropriate, if I could.

Two other writers who'd tempt me to larceny are Robert Stone, in his first three novels, and Denis Johnson in *Angels*. They write about what I consider my kind of people: moral outsiders propelled by energies they can't control or completely identify, internal or external, angelic or demonic, they don't know for sure. Stone and Johnson write books which go a long way to prove that if the old abstractions of God and the Devil are not autonomous actors in our affairs, then they might just as well be. So whenever I'm reading one of their books, my first wish is that I'd written it myself. That kind of envy adds its dose of salt and lemon to the dish, a sharper edge to what is probably still the greatest pleasure a reading writer can enjoy.

I'm more a reader than a writer of short stories, and a list of recent story writers whose work I like could run the page. Say for a start, Ellen Gilchrist, Andre Dubus, Ron Carlson, Charles Baxter, Ellen Wilbur, Leigh Allison Wilson, Mary Hood . . . and all the others that won't fit. Speaking strictly as a thief, what interests me most are a few writers who've found ingenious ways of organizing stories into books of forceful unity, like Louise Erdrich's *Love Medicine*, Harriet Doerr's *Stones for Ibarra*, Carolyn Chute's *The Beans of Egypt, Maine*, and most interestingly and unusually, Michael Martone's *Alive and Dead in Indiana*. They've found their very different ways of making many stories somehow one, and in the process have invented, if not wholly new forms, at least important variations on the old ones. Innovative form is a great good they have in store, and maybe you don't have to steal it either, just use it as example and encouragement to devise your own.

With maybe just enough exceptions to prove the rule, *all* writers, somewhere along their way, steal style. A talented thief of style has all the skills of a pickpocket: the goods are not missed and once they're displayed you wouldn't imagine they'd ever belonged to anyone else. Of all the strong stylists now at work, my personal favorite is Cormac McCarthy, in any of his five novels but most especially *Child of God* (far and away the best American novel ever to be written about necrophilia), *Suttree*, and *Blood Meridian*. I will bet money that McCarthy can write a more dazzling and perplexing sentence, paragraph, and page than almost anyone else now trying it. And, notably, he is one of the very few writers to pass under the long shadow of Faulkner's wildest stylistic extremes and survive the experience, even come away all the stronger for it. Who knows but that he may have opened up that whole treasure trove for a whole new generation of enterprising bandits? But like any powerfully original stylist, he's painfully hard to steal from himself.

These aren't all the writers I'd sometimes like to plunder (and maybe already have at times), just all I'll admit to, at the moment. Still, I'll claim that in this craft a conscientious thief is no better or worse than a dutiful apprentice. I am talking not about imitation, but outright pillage, where the truest admiration is expressed. It is often easier to admire writers who operate in far-off territories you have no interest in annexing. But in the end you love best the work *you* should have done, in the lively hope that one day yet, you'll do it.

I
JOE DAVID BELLAMY
I

In the last twenty-five years, it seems to me, we have witnessed an astonishing turnaround in the kinds of fiction that our leading writers are writing. This is partly because we have several new leading writers, but also because the spirit of the times is so utterly transformed. Not surprisingly, we have also seen radical changes in the favorite aesthetic theories that writers subscribe to — when they wish to deal, self-consciously, in theories at all. Recent developments tend to reveal a wholesale escape from theorizing, since it was theory, some feel, that was the bane of the now exhausted superfictionists.

To portray the evolution of American fiction from, say, 1960 to 1987, one might describe it as a movement from middlebrow realism or modernist realism to superfiction — a radical departure that captured center stage for a few brief years — followed by a return to a different sort of realism, minimalist realism or dirty realism or designer realism or lifestyle fiction. Lifestyle fiction is not merely a return to the modernist realism of the early sixties or a sort of attenuated or watered down version of modernist realism, as some seem to feel. The best of the newest fiction we have now, it seems to me — the work of writers such as Frederick Barthelme, Tobias Wolff, Jayne Anne Phillips, Richard Bausch, Dianne Benedict, Raymond Carver — consolidates some of the bizarre moods and diverse discoveries and errant experiments of the superfictionists and makes them more accessible and plugs them in to the realistic tradition in ways we couldn't have imagined.

But, to my taste, some of the newest work that has gotten a lot of attention — not any of the writers mentioned above — is a little thin. Some of the so-called minimalists have sacrificed stylistic richness or sophistication in search of other values. Of course, pure styles can be conceived and delivered in six-word sentences and in fiction that more or less eliminates exposition, as Hemingway sometimes tried to do. But it isn't easy. It isn't the sort of feat everyone should be trying for at once. So, whatever else the newest American fiction might try to do in the years ahead, my hope is that, stylistically and imagistically, it will strive for more robust, more muscular, more ambitious performances — a swing of the pendulum back in the direction of Faulkner and Flannery O'Connor. That would be the sort of writing I would like to read (and write) and that I imagine might even be therapeutic (consciousness-expanding) for readers with six-word attention spans too.

Joe David Bellamy					photo by Melon Grover

*Anne Bernays
photo by
Justin Kaplan*

ANNE BERNAYS

I think that Ann Beattie's work—brilliant as it is—has had the unexpected effect of making young writers think that if they write in the present tense and take a documentary stance toward their material that the story will be "realer," "truer," and more immediate than if they wrote it in a more traditional mode. They're wrong: it's much more difficult to write a good "minimalist" story than the other kind and you have to be spectacularly good to bring it off.

As to what kind of recent writing interests me, I can't answer because I respond to writers rather than genres. I like the short stories of Deborah Eisenberg, Pamela Painter, Marian Thurm, Sharon Sheehe Stark, Lynne Sharon Schwartz, but I'm afraid I don't read as much short work as I should.

I like the novels of Lore Segal, Isabel Colgate, Anne Tyler, and Muriel Spark (her early work).

I see that I haven't mentioned a single man — there must be somebody. Charles Portis and Mark Harris — but only their early novels; John Updike for his prose but not his stories.

I prefer a strong plot to a weak or rambling one and humor to the deadly serious (which I can never take quite seriously).

GEORGE BLECHER

Kathy Acker's *Literal Madness* has been on my mind (and desk) for months. Sometimes she strikes me as our last hope, the only one who's found a way to write about how the enormous range of language (or languages) once available to us has been trivialized by mass media to the point where we've lost the means to describe — or even perceive — how complex our experience really is.

Apart from Acker and one or two others, I haven't run across much exciting work in recent American fiction. The established voices seem to me tired and self-indulgent, the new ones terribly old-fashioned. Most

George Blecher

American fiction is stuck in a small-scale realism that was outdated in Europe a century ago, and our attempts at modernism (let alone postmodernism) lack passion and subversiveness. Maybe the most disturbing thing of all is that nobody moans, complains, struggles against the mindlessness of the marketplace and the narrowness of our fiction; at least publicly, we seem content with our work, we learn little from others or the past, and when we actually discuss literature with each other, it's a hallowed event.

The interesting thing, though, is how many talented people are around. One can feel the talent, energy, and brightness bursting out of them; sentence by sentence, many write like angels. But underneath their public self-assurance, one also feels their frustration and doubt. Aside from the never-ending obsession with making (and keeping) it, they—we— face deeper quandaries: What should I write now? How should I write? Do I dare to take risks and write something that hasn't been written yet, either by me or anyone else? If I do, will anyone publish or review it?

I don't think that the problems of contemporary fiction are ours alone. Even though the atmosphere in many countries (in terms of their respect for literature) is more congenial than in ours, I don't find the work they produce much more stimulating. I read Handke and Kundera, but not with the deep excitement I once felt. I admire Lessing, but she's broken no new literary ground. I translate Scandinavian writers who I think have something to say, but their work is never totally realized. It may simply be that we're in a trough; it's happened before. Or it may be that modern society, at least in large countries, is too fragmented to furnish its writers with a cohesive enough overview of human behavior to write anything other than Pynchonesque satire. (Soviet writers seem to be faced with this dilemma, too.) Exhausted by stressful, unfulfilling jobs, even our small intellectual elite may not be able to tolerate the demands that "serious" writing makes on them; and if society expresses no *need* for complex thinking, the wish to create ambitious work may also shrivel up. Or perhaps—and Kathy Acker's work suggests this—by facing how impotent we really feel, we may be at the beginning of a new literature of mutual anger and indignation.

It's clear that most of these issues are imponderables, out of our control. But I think as American writers there is one important thing we ought to consider: that our passion might better be put into our work than where much of it goes now—into envying other writers' successes, both real and imagined. I think that this envy, and the competitiveness that goes with it (both of which serve to isolate us from each other), are largely responsible for the whine of anxiety I hear inside and around me: Is he/she doing better than I am? What does "better" really mean?

There's an obvious reason we envy and compete with each other: we have such a tiny portion of the pie. Bellow was right when he said recently that the Founding Fathers forgot to make any provision for culture — so, like any deprived minority, we fight bitterly over the few scraps of money, prestige, and notoriety available to us. Yet I'm sure that this fighting (mostly in our heads) is bad for our work: it constricts our imaginations, uses up too much mental energy, and makes our work brilliant in surface polish but disturbingly thin in ideas. I assume that this is why virtually every important American writer of the last hundred years — James, Eliot, Pound, Stein, Fitzgerald, Hemingway, Miller, Burroughs, and so on — went to Europe: to clear the air and recover a sense of adventure by connecting not with the past but with their contemporaries, with a group of living people who wrote poetry and prose, were accepted for it, and therefore weren't quite as eager as we to do each other in.

Two Postscripts

I'm a little surprised at how few fiction writers pay attention to the recent literary theory and art criticism that's been coming out of France, Germany, England, and the United States. However convoluted the prose (and sometimes unconvincing the merging of philosphy and philology), underneath this work, it seems to me, is an effort to rescue language from TV and advertising and restore some of its complexity and strength — an admirable goal. Unfortunately, at this point critics and academics seem to take literature more seriously than do publishing houses — and most writers.

To answer your original question, maybe there actually is a neglected genre of American fiction: the headlines in the *Star*, the *Weekly World News*, and the other supermarket rags. "85 Year Old Man Gives Birth to Twins," "Martians Use Tooth Decay to Destroy Earth," "Congresswoman Crushed by Giant Frog" — these ministories have many of the qualities good fiction ought to have: imagination, pithiness, surprise, immediacy, humor. Next to them, all the books in the bookstores with their dazzling covers but grim lines of text seem so lifeless!

Corinne Demas Bliss
photo by
Matthew Grahame
Roehrig

CORINNE DEMAS BLISS

I've long been an advocate for the short story, not just because of its intrinsic merits or because as a writer I find it's a genre that gives me considerable pleasure along with my toil, but because it's still something of a poor relative to its more corpulent cousin the novel. When the collected short stories of John Cheever hit the best-seller list, in the late seventies, I optimistically thought that the short story might be ascending once again to the kind of popularity it enjoyed in Fitzgerald's heyday. The climate for the short story has improved in the last decade, but although the genre itself is flourishing, the readership is simply not there. The home of the literary short story is still primarily the literary magazine. With the exception of the fortunate stories that are plucked up for the few annual antholgies that use that peculiarly antiliterary label "best," most short stories never make it to the hands, let alone the eyes, of more than the select audience (like you who are reading these very words) for literary magazines.

For the past few years I've been a fiction editor for the *Massachusetts*

Review. The quantity of submissions is awesome, and I'm saddened by how many good stories we end up having to turn down (a problem I know we share with a few dozen other literary magazines). I sometimes fear there are more Americans writing short stories today than reading them, and if that is true, the fault is not with the genre—which is versatile, and vivacious—nor with its potential readers, but with the publishing industry that hasn't yet figured out how to best bring the two of them together.

I
DAVID BOSWORTH
I

A Prescription for Contemporary Fiction
Including:
a Sermonette on Aesthetics
a Psalm to the Senses
and an Ethical Sucker Punch
(to arrive disguised as the
mandatory Ronald Reagan joke)

David
Bosworth
photo by
Joe Freeman

Wanted: A fiction whose fundamental design and whose worldview, therefore, is not a mindless (or even mindful) projection of nineteenth-century mechanistic science: characters with no more spirit or will than the naive materialist's conception of the atom, the ruling forces of the fictional world always external and random, the whole characterized by thoughtlessly episodic, pinball action. Enough of the entropic soap opera, of the hero as neutron. In their place a fiction whose organization is ecological or biological in nature; which gathers and conserves energy, which regulates and moderates and multiplies possibilities of meaningful interaction through symbiosis, allowing in a small space a complexity of life forms and a depth of perception. There are *rules* in this sort of fiction — not abstract but concrete and adaptive, and at least slightly unique for each new fictional environment — and just as one can't pollute at will or introduce a new species to a pond without threatening the whole, so one can't violate the separate orders of these fictional worlds without serious consequences. In this fiction, in other words, decisions, both by the author and by his characters, *matter*. In this fiction, unlike so much that is published today, not just anything can happen.

A fiction, therefore, which doesn't condescend to its own characters, which allows them the possibility of a complex inner life, a chance at perspective, an opportunity to be held accountable for their own confusion, fear, and pain; in particular, if about blue-collar Americans (a topic so in vogue these days), a fiction that doesn't sentimentalize their state with the sort of secret snobbery that presumes a fifty-word vocabulary and a hundred-proof liver. Who says that Thoreau is the only one allowed to retreat to the pond? that Lincoln is the only man or woman who has, in some way, made a courageous stand against slavery in any of its many baneful forms?

A fiction whose rhetoric isn't pellet-sized; whose tab button isn't stuck "on," paragraphing automatically every second declarative sentence; whose model of engagement isn't commerical TV, presuming a readership with the attention span of a gerbil on speed; whose vocabulary is diverse, intelligent, lively, allowing itself moments of clarity yea-even-unto eloquence; whose style, when reticent, has the reticence of stoicism (Kawabata, the best of Hemingway), of passion contained by discipline, rather than the dumbly inarticulate or wan ennui.

A fiction, therefore, which is not tone deaf, which understands that music is not merely decoration but an essential quality of our shared environment. This, too, is a philosophical question. I pose it this way: given that one's attitude toward the human condition embodies a certain necessary sadness, whose range can stretch from the high tragedy of Shakespeare to the feculent farce of Beckett's cave, how does one respond to the nonhuman setting in which we live? The world *I* experience is, however ugly or desparing its human element, astonishingly beautiful. And I don't just mean mountains or shorelines but also the play of light on ice in a glass, the hitch and skip of a boy entering a room, the profusion of colors from books on a shelf. Pay attention, please! Everywhere the extraordinary beckons from within the ordinary; everywhere small harmonies, *rhymes* if you will, sensory if not thematic epiphanies. (The wonder of John Updike is his rare ability to rescue for us just those smaller harmonies.) Whether one finds, simply, a momentary consolation in all this splendor or—as I do—senses in it the hint of something more profound, to denude one's fictional world of its presence seems to me a violation akin to strip mining: the unconscionable devastation of a living landscape.

Wanted, too: a shift in contemporary literature away from parody, pastiche, and urbane irony toward forms more serious, passionate, and profound. One could assert, and I would, that parody is essentially parasitical and, therefore, a lower art form, but the more telling argument is strategic in nature. In the culture that produced the Timothy Leary and G. Gordon Liddy Traveling Debate and Talk Show, in the culture that actually conceived and built a *drive in* funeral parlor (a grief-burger and a large fries to go?), a culture whose current leader, a walking if insensate parody, actually trained for the job playing second banana to a chimp in a film (yes, George Bush, there's hope for you still); in *that* culture, our culture, can a literary parody have any bite at all? Can a cartoon be cartooned? I say no. Better a sermon than another sight gag. Better a jeremiad than another in-joke. Better an allegory, a parable, a fairy tale, a morality play than another burlesque on the excesses of middle-class greed.

Wanted, finally: a fiction which matters; whose existence poses a serious challenge, which reorients, clarifies, vivifies, chastens. A fiction which is useful, a fiction pragmatic. My life is different, I am a better man because of certain stories I have been privileged to read. I understand the ritual of passion far better for having read Marguerite Duras's *Moderato Cantabile*, the pathos of adolescence for having read and re-read John Barth's "Lost in the Funhouse." The abstract aphorism "Character is fate" was brought to life for me with incredible potency by Yukio Mishima's very short story "Swaddling Clothes." Want to feel the possibility of art as communion sacrament?—read John Updike's beautiful "The Music School." Want to experience in riveting if repulsive detail the psychology of evil?—spend a week with Pär Lagerkvist's *The Dwarf*. Every man and woman should read that novel, as they should Faulkner's lynching story "Dry September": the world might be a safer place if they did. Wendell Berry's essays in *Standing By Words*. John Gardner's story "John Napper Sailing Through the Universe." Graham Greene's *The Heart of the Matter*. All of Conrad and Flannery O'Connor.

I *use* these works—not just to write or teach but to live, to navigate my way through our difficult world, day to day. Watchwords, examples, vivid symbols. *Remember Major Scobie!* I admonish myself when my compassion begins to turn egocentrically imperial. *Remember Marlow, steer the boat toward the spears!* I remind myself when, to avoid a momentary trial, I let my life drift toward a much more consequential disaster. I actually met the Dwarf once. I didn't recognize him soon enough, but I'm convinced that the disguise would have been prolonged, the wreckage he caused far worse, if I hadn't been instructed first by a terrifyingly accurate fictional world.

I won't pretend that all, or even any, of the authors I have mentioned would subscribe to my emphatic aesthetic beliefs. There are many paths but only one Way. Behind the diversity of style, content, and philosophy, there lies, I believe, a quality shared, a harmony of accomplishment we long to hear. And what would that quality be? The rarest thing of all, I think, the only commodity whose value never changes, whose standard, indifferent to the vagaries of fashion, is fixed only to the everlasting. What these great works share is wisdom. And we need it as much as the air that we breathe.

What should contemporary fiction be like? Who, as a writer of contemporary fiction, do I want to become? I want to become Don DeLillo wed to Wendell Berry, to marry DeLillo's relentlessly contemporary wit with Berry's sanity, clarity, sense of history. I want to merge the passion of Duras with the intelligence of Barth, the inventive zest of Paul West with the laconic sagacity of Lagerkvist. And more, of course. I could go on and on; there's no end to one's appetite when shopping in the market of literary delights. The hard truth is, though, that art isn't made by mere addition, that too many ingredients, like too many cooks, can spoil the brew of any ficion. A single name, then—one writer to serve as the arch exemplar of what fiction can be.

I am thirty-nine years old as I write these words, the exact number of years Flannery O'Connor lived. Teaching her stories to my writing students has been among the most humbling experiences of my professional life. I found, for example, that in order to do justice to "The Artificial Nigger," I had to bring to class, by way of introduction to the content of the work, a copy of the Bible and a volume of Aeschylus. A weighty armload, that one. In twenty-five pages the revivified essence of three thousand years of civilization. Now *that* is the real prescription for a "contemporary" or any other sort of fiction. I want to read, to write a fiction like that; I want to enter new worlds which, whatever their accent, have that potency, that clarity, that honesty — that *depth*.

. . . which brings me, believe it or not, (*Here it comes — duck!*) to my favorite Ronald Reagan anecdote, one gleaned from a newspaper article more than ten years ago now when citizen Reagan, trying to win the nomination, was speaking to caucuses across the nation. After one such talk, a Southern Republican, when asked to assess the candidate's performance, conceded that Mr. Reagan was exceedingly smooth, but then he added (one can almost hear the honeyed drawl, see the wry wrinkling of eyes and lips) that behind the practiced gestures and smiling face, the man was, in his considered opinion: "About as deep as piss on slate." A good one, no? Oh the power of a pungent simile. Serious people all, we readers and writers of literature, our political sympathies carefully attuned, our powers of observation safely removed from the vulgarity and superficiality of our age, we smile as one, cynically amused, in our dens across America.

Wait a minute, though. Isn't it time we took an accounting, too, asked our own constituency to provide a review? Would it be any more odoriferous, any less contemptuous? And I'm not speaking of the usual contempt the public is wont to show us when we venture beyond the ambit of our specialty to comment on matters of public policy (the Jane Fonda syndrome), but their response on matters closer to home, their assessment of our stewardship of the very household we call our own. We, after all, are looked to for leadership, too. However remote, we canvass for support and are, in our own odd way, soliciting votes. So look to your desks, then, pretenders to the throne of Dickinson and Melville, Hawthorne and Thoreau. Is the fiction which appears in that glossy magazine you've subscribed to for years, which thickens those quarterlies you collect, those reviews you edit, which is studied in your classes and praised in your blurbs, which is bought and borrowed and lent to your friends, is the fiction right now scrolling down your screens or filling up my pads in our smoke-filled dens — made to last? Is, it only seems fair to ask, *our* performance any deeper than that of Bonzo's friend?

Another prediction of decline unto Doom, then? Not exactly. Yes, we do live in a vulgar and superficial age and, yes, much of what passes for serious fiction is utterly insubstantial, the literary equivalent of bleached white bread. But has it ever been different? Dickinson wasn't published at all, Mellville harrassed out of fiction writing at the peak of his powers by hostile reviews. Only Hawthorne of the four luminaries mentioned above was an indisputable success in his own lifetime, and that percentage, one out of four, might well be predictive for ours or any subsequent literary generation.

Whatever the exact numbers prove to be, we can assume this: much of the best in contemporary letters will not be recognized as such until our time has passed, the authors themselves aged or dead. Nevertheless, sustained by other rewards, the good work goes on, in unexpected places — discretely, ignored. And now, when more people are writing than ever before, the possibilities for quality fiction would seem to abound. Surely even as I write these words down, someone "contemporaneously" is inventing a new fictional world whose habitat will house those old truths we need to hear. Decades may dissolve before its value is noted, its cause promoted, but the fiction that is made to last *will* last, the merely fashionable will eventually pass.

So let a hundred thousand fictions bloom. Time, relentless as ever, will ruthlessly prune.

A Coda
In Which the Author Is Upended, the Ending Amended

The ending seemed smooth, don't you think? An aphoristic couplet, assonantally rhymed, suggesting completion, an organic design. That's what I thought, anyway — I had been aiming to arrive there since the second page. Now, though, that my destination has been reached, the design complete, I find it offensive (slate-deep?) in a number of ways. The political reference, the revised Maoism, given the authentic oppression of the Chinese artist, seems to me now inexcusably flip. And the sucker punch I had so carefully planned seems instead to have been a roundhouse hook which, circling back, has sent me flying on my own derriere. For doesn't the couplet, in an unplanned irony, seem to suggest those very points of view — Reagan's politics and mechanistic science — which are the constant targets of this piece? Isn't relying on "Time," that stuffy abstraction, to provide for our children a literature which matters something akin to "trickle-down" economics where, eventually, the theory goes, the needy will be fed by the drippings left by the crapulence of the "Marketplace"? And doesn't the passivity of the statement suggest as well a process driven by forces, "external and random," beyond ourselves? providing results indifferent to our will? *Someone,* I'm reminded belatedly, discovered Dickinson at last; *someone,* and not Time, resurrected Melville from critical contempt. And what would have happened if in the year Lagerkvist was awarded the Nobel Prize, another Pearl Buck had been named in his place? Would *The Dwarf* have ever ended up in my hands?

Sobering questions. They beckon action. They remind me once again that we musn't be passive, that we should embrace opportunities such as these to hound the poseur and herald the substantial. The prescription, then, is this: promote the books you love, defend their achievement. If the authors are living, send them money, food, bouquets of praise in honest letters of appreciation. Don't let the apparent but transient triumph of bad taste, the cant of age, depress you into acquiescence, for silence, too, is a kind of ratification — more applause for the fake.

Take faith instead in the discipline we love, the wisdom of its craft. For we have an advantage over the economist, the scientist. We know that *once upon a time* is a better beginning, a more fruitful way of thinking, than *studies have been done* or $x = y$; we know that the history we are living is best understood neither as a "marketplace" nor as a "mechanism" but as a story — a complex, important, ongoing novel. And in this chapter, to be entitled "The Living Word," you and I — lovers of literature, the guardians of fiction — *we* are the characters whose choices matter, who are shaping even now the plot's direction. A second ending, then. A reformation of a sort — the first born again.

Yes, Time will prune. But we are her agents: be responsible when you choose.

KAY BOYLE

I am concerned with the difficulties and obligations that the writer and the teacher inevitably share. And both as writer and teacher I refer those with whom I work to Albert Camus. In his life of action, as in his writing, he sought to define with modesty and clarity, with patience as well as impatience, man's predicament. "Pas par nature," he explained with characteristic honesty, "mais par volonté et réflexion, j'ai essayé de ne pas me séparer de mon temps." That is what he asked of all of us, from the days of our youth until the finality of old age, not to separate ourselves from our time.

Camus believed that he had not the right, either as man or writer, to sever himself from the plight of other men. He believed that the miner

Kay Boyle
photo by
Bob Bryant

who is exploited, the slave of the concentration camp, the silenced population of the totalitarian state — in other words, the persecuted legions of mankind throughout the world — were in such desperate need that those who could speak (and by this he meant the writers above all) should not in fear, or evasion, or in sanctimonious judgment hold themselves apart from other men.

After the activity and dedication of his years as a resistance fighter, Camus found it impossible to accept the atmosphere of Paris literary circles, and he often spoke of the "uncomfortable career" in which he found himself involved: the career of the writer. "The trial by vanity" he called it, and from the beginning of that career he was resolved to be "a man with an ethic," and this, he said, was of all the struggles in his life the one that caused him the most pain.

Yes, contemporary fiction is indeed a widely varied thing, and I am excited by fiction that has a profound belief as source. It is of no importance whatsoever if the belief is not recognized, not identified, not given a name. William Carlos Williams, one of our greatest for all time, had a belief as pure and as fervent as that of Camus, and this is true of Nelson Algren as well. Their fictive characters do not mention their authors' beliefs, but speak with humor or irony, with joy or tragedy, of other things entirely, yet we know the belief is there.

The contemporary literary scene exists for me in the work of Grace Paley, of Louise Erdrich, of Russell Banks. Their characters talk of the mundane and at rare times of the mysterious and spiritual, but never reveal the sacred source. But whether that source is compassion, or an unquestioning commitment to the lives of others, or the total negation of the self and its tiresome ego, that gives to the people they write of an enduring life, I cannot say. I know only that the power of the source is given substance in their work.

I
T. CORAGHESSAN BOYLE
I

Actually, contemporary North American fiction is too much of one thing — the safe, minimalist/realist story purveyed by a group I like to call the Catatonic Realists. (You know the story, you've read it a thousand times: three characters are sitting around the kitchen of a trailer saying folksy things to one another. Finally one of them gets up to go the bathroom and the author steps in to end it with a line like, "It was all feathers.")

In contradistinction to this school, we have the colorful, exuberant and imaginative novels of Denis Johnson (*Fiskadoro*), Don DeLillo (*White Noise*), Louise Erdrich (*Love Medicine*), and Robert Coover's new collec-

T. Coraghessan Boyle
photo by
Alan Arkawy

tion, as well as his marvelous Aesop story that appeared last year in the *Iowa Review*. This is the fiction that excites me. A fiction that is unfolding, opening up, rediscovering the joys of language, story, imagination, and chance-taking. I hope to see a whole lot more of it.

ROSELLEN BROWN

What interests me most and is least read these days is fiction that acknowledges a world outside our own psyches, our own bodies. Are there forces that — objectively — put pressure on individuals, make their lives conform to patterns they might not have chosen, or cannot even see? Not everyone has the leisure to be aimless; not everyone can loaf and invite his soul — and yet there is very little *work* in today's fiction, there is little history, and there is certainly next to no anger or impatience for change. Women gave forth that sense of agitating grievance for a while, and blacks, of whom there are still too few repre-

Rosellen Brown
photo by
Marv Hoffman

sented by mainstream publishing. Now gay writers are beginning to ripple the waters, but their negotiations still tend to be with self-and-other, family and lovers, not with their pressure points with the body politic. And there are the Vietnam novels finally emerging, though, with some exceptions, they too tend to spend their energy (understandably) on settling old grievances, not on finding their characters' place in the continuum of events.

Since I've published a novel that attempts to see individuals and families in a larger context, I receive a dismaying number of manuscripts — requests for help in marketing them — from others with similar interests who are bewildered by the respectful "no's" they've received from editors who praise the quality of their work but send it back nonetheless. The "no's" achnowledge that the fate of my *Civil Wars* is a common one for books preoccupied with "social issues": no one reads them but those who've been similarly preoccupied themselves — and that leaves out almost everyone, certainly the young and affluent. (Of course there are thousands of *individuals* who are pleased to have such work to read, but they don't add up to the kind of numbers publishers pay attention to.)

A few years ago, my friend Elinor Langer wrote a good piece on fiction by women for the *New York Times Book Review*. In it she asked the inevitable question: What has become of seriously inquiring, challenging, or socially-concerned fiction by women? Why has so much of it returned to subjectivity? My answer was, and is, that we have no certainty that women aren't writing those books; all we have is the visible phenomenon, which is in the hands of the publishers whose eyes are on the market, that such books are not being published. Or if they're being published, they're not getting much attention. Everone knows, or ought to know and pay attention to, the dismal facts of shelf life, advertising budgets, print runs, and so on — dreary, crass-sounding, but the expression of the publishers' death wish for a majority of their books: the self-fulfilling prophecy that dooms the not-quite-fashionable to the pulp machine before it even comes off the press. Of course such "realities" have a chilling effect on the writers who would like to fly in the face of fashion but give up. They also suggest to a new , young reading public that given the current bias of the readership, if *War and Peace* were to come across somebody's desk now in the era of Beattie-McInerney-Janowitz, the *Peace* sections might be smiled upon. But all that war, Leo — why don't you go home, have a drink and think about it a little and maybe give it another rewrite? Then we'll get together and do lunch and see if we can make it the really good read it wants to be.

*Frederick Busch
photo by
Judy Busch*

FREDERICK BUSCH

I write for a living. I write, that is to say, for my life — for my life's sake. Which is to say: when I write, I consider my life to be at stake; the values that help me to measure it, and the moments, memories, and emotions of it that I cherish — the people, therefore, whose presence in it makes me want to keep experiencing my life — all are at risk when I work. It feels that way to me. I believe the feeling to be true, and I write from that belief. And my characters — aspects of, reflections of, extensions of, meditations upon, the people I hold dear — are therefore also at risk. So when I write I feel that I deal with danger, and that the danger confronts what I cherish.

My physical response to danger, like yours, is a metabolic surge. And when I write, I write like a laboring man: I move a lot, I feel a worker's fatigue, and my temperature increases, and I sweat. The sort of fiction I think I write, and the sort of dangerous stories of danger to which I'm attracted, have to do, then, with body heat. I am thinking, now, of human warmth, of people in the world reacting as creatures of passion.

I am interested in reading fiction by writers who believe as I do, who feel as I do, and whose language, characters, and belief in *story*, that fever and thermometer, have to do with 98.6 Fahrenheit, or higher.

John Updike, who can write the coldest, most precise and omniscient undercutting of romantic love, can also, by taking the temperature of flesh, create remarkable feeling. In his "Killing," a woman sits by her dying father:

> His face, parched and unfed, grew rigid. His mouth made an O like a baby's at the breast. His breathing poured forth a stench like a stream of inexpressible scorn. His hand lived in hers. He could not die, she could not stay; as with the participants of a great and wicked love, there was none to forgive them save each other.

Dying and sex: they are startlingly, rightly, together: the temperature here is high, though not feverish, and we feel with, and for, those sad others. Updike tempers the precise instrument of his prose, not cutting so deeply as to kill the moment in order to show his extraordinary wit. The moment belongs to his characters, and their stake in the moment, and Updike's generosity encourages us not only to feel for the daughter and the dying man, but to feel in terms of our own sexuality, our own disgust with the stench of death, and to think of how to reconcile our life and death.

I would like, in answer to the question, then, to say that I declare on the side of stories and novels, novellas, meditations, that deal with, generate, body heat. I am on the side of fiction that deals with *stuff*, things of specific gravity that fall to earth and hurt us when we try to toss them up or lift them into, or out of, our lives. I am on the side of fiction that yields characters loved or feared or even needed by their authors (and then readers). Must I make a list? I think of this volume's editor, Nicholas Delbanco, of Reynolds Price and Paula Fox, Richard Russo, Lee K. Abbott, Richard Bausch, Francine Prose, Rosellen Brown, Leslie Epstein, Pam Durban, Jayne Anne Phillips, Paul Theroux; I honor with my passion and attention those whose names did not spill instantly, but who work in my mind with their care and their craft.

And so, I suppose, I must declare my opposition to—and, often, anger toward and about—the work I call Chilly Fiction. It is a fiction of attitude, not feeling; it is therefore, as any middle-aged parent of teenagers can tell you, a youthful form of fiction. It perverts the dignity and reticence of the best of Hemingway and says: I want to complain, and I'm going to pretend to act as though I'm not complaining. I'm going to snort so much coke, it says, drink so much tequila, have sex with so many people and machines I haven't met before (much less like) that you're going, at last, to feel that you must get behind my pages and ask, "What's wrong?"

And then, the adolescent-writer persona continues, I'm going to show you: Nothing can really be wrong because there is, in such works, no person and no lived life, no conflict of values because nothing's at stake. What's there for the reader is the writer's basic sense that life is tough and he's unhappy. I will not name names. But we do know the books. We're reading them now, and we want to know why it feels so much like hole and so little like doughnut. We sense a kind of attractiveness to it, the way we have felt attracted to a woman with a go-to-hell expression or a boy with orange hair and crazy eyes; but we also wonder what we might discover to *talk* about when the lights and underthings are low.

Chilly Fiction is made of books — they're mostly little books of rather short stories — about sadness in the city, deliberate submergence in a psychic underground, but with enough money for a car, a meal, a snort, a pop; Chilly Fiction's about Yuppie deprivation, after all, about being on the bum with a master's degree: Lite Dostoyevsky. This Chilly Fiction is about the self — how the self feels sad, or bad, or mad; it's why we can't get it *together*, and it's often by kids who make statements about generations, just as Hemingway did. The Chilly Writers seem to speak about no generation honed, or blunted, on war, but about a generation that feels deprived of having been, in any romatic way, deprived. While Hemingway spoke of a Lost Generation, Chilly Writers give interviews about a generation giving interviews.

There is nothing to feel in Chilly Fiction. It's accomplished, crafted, cunning, correct in many technical modes. It is about having the stance of a Hemingway character — man or woman who is victim and hero at once — without possessing the felt history of such a character. This emptiness about emptiness speaks directly *to* lack of character.

So I am declaring on the side of Grace Paley, who in "A Conversation with My Father" can write:

> My father is eighty-six years old and in bed. His heart, that bloody motor, is equally old and will not do certain jobs any more. It still floods his head with brainy light. But it won't let his legs carry the weight of his body around the house.

I am declaring on the side of hearts, bodies, weight, and pulse, on the side of bloody motors and brainy light, the side of Ernest J. Gaines and Beverly Lowry and Lee Smith, Kay Boyle, Alice Adams, Walker Percy, James Welch, Alice Munro — all those who work in spite of the icy, wily self, and offer love, in fleshed metaphors, to a cooling world.

Nash Candelaria

I
NASH CANDELARIA
I

In his book *The Literary Situation*, published in 1954, Malcolm Cowley explored the geographical origins of U.S. writers. The fewest native-born writers were among Spanish-Americans and Native Americans in mountain states like New Mexico and Colorado.

The world, literary and otherwise, has turned upside down since that time. The Civil Rights movement has energized U.S. minorities. Political movement in the rest of the world has seen the rise of less powerful nations and required coining of a new term: *Third World*.

Current population estimates show that the non-Hispanic, non-Indian United States is a minority country in the Western Hemisphere. For every 100 English-speaking people in the United States and Canada of "Anglo" culture, there are 158 Spanish-, Indian-, and Portuguese-speaking people in Latin America. By the year 2020, this ratio will widen to 217 Latin Americans to every 100 New World Anglos.

In spite of this, U.S. politicians have failed to lead the way toward a peaceful, cooperative hemisphere. Our colonial myopia and history of frequent intervention run contrary to our highest ideals. We do not seem to realize the kind of future that we are sowing. One day we may no longer be the most powerful nation in the New World and may have to reap what we have sown.

How do such matters impact American fiction? Why should more North Americans be acquainted with U.S. Hispanic writing? If we do not understand our own internal Third World, that is North Americans whose ancestors came from Third World countries, how can we come to terms with people outside the United States?

The key is better understanding, and this is where fiction has an important role to play. Novels, short stories—it doesn't matter. Minimalist, maximalist, schmaximalist—it doesn't matter. What matters is the ancient role of stories to teach and to help us understand. To put us into other people's hearts and minds.

There is a growing richness of U.S. Hispanic writings today. Hopefully there will be growing recognition of these works. Never mind that major publishers ignore such writings. They ignore other fine writings, too. What we need is greater recognition among discerning readers who will try unpublicized books by small, unknown presses. Publishers like Arte Público Press, Bilingual Press, Floricanto, and now-defunct Tonatiuh International, Inc. They represent many fine Hispanic writers, men and women, novelists, short story writers, poets. Many of these works make us more aware of the varied, rich, and different lives other North Americans have lived and endured. Lives, attitudes, history, and experiences that can give us insight into that other Third World outside our own borders.

The academic community has a particularly important role to play in the recognition of U.S. Hispanic writings. Not only are universities and colleges the repositories of today's culture—the monasteries, as it were, of today's materialistic Dark Ages—but they are the spawning ground for the enlightenment of our youth. It is an important responsibility to see that students no longer accept the erroneous belief that the United States is white, male, and Anglo-European. To be taught so and believe so is to be relegated to a golden ghetto that is out of touch with real life.

Students need to know more about other cultures and attitudes that make up this complex country of ours. Probably the greatest immigration in our history is occurring right now. It brings to us people whose predecessors have been in the minority, while soon it will be Anglo-Americans who are the minority in the United States. The price of ignoring this changing culture is too high. Students need to know more about Hispanic, Native, Asian, and black Americans. This is where literature teachers can further the proper education of our youth. American literature is more than what we once thought it was. It is a growing body of work that has to change in order to reflect and explain the changing world.

U.S. Hispanic writings exploded in our post-Civil Rights era as part of emerging ethnic studies programs in colleges and universities. Much, though by no means all of this writing, was in Spanish. Much of it fit into literature courses within these programs. The merits and demerits of ethnic studies have been debated endlessly. Declining enrollments and resistant attitudes caused retrenching of curricula. In many cases, U.S. Hispanic literature became part of Spanish departments. As if the writings were a foreign language from a foreign country. And this not only for works in Spanish, which properly belong in such departments, but also for writings in English. Strangers in our own land again. It's the all-too-familiar relegation to "outsider" status that is the result of generations of basic Anglo ignorance if not outright prejudice about other cultures—even other U.S. cultures. For in truth, all literature is ethnic literature if we but recognize it. Unfortunately, for too many people "ethnic" is the other guy, not me.

Let's see more U.S. Hispanic works in their rightful place. If in English, incorporate them into American literature courses. If in Spanish, let's see more translation into English much the way North Americans read Latin-American writers.

Nobel laureate Gabriel García-Márquez has acknowledged that his greatest reading audience is in the United States. At the risk of being a North-American-Hispanic chauvinist, I urge you to try U.S. Hispanic writings too. Widely read works from New Mexico writers—Malcolm Cowley's stepchildren—like Rudolfo Anaya's *Bless Me, Ultima*, Orlando Romero's *Nambe—Year One*, Sabine Ulibarri's *My Grandma Smoked Cigars*, or my own *Memories of the Alhambra*. Or works by other Mexican Americans or by Puerto Rican-, Cuban-, and Native Americans. You may be pleasantly surprised. They're better than you imagine.

RAYMOND CARVER

I'm interested in the diverse brands of work being done these days in the short story form by a large and increasingly significant number of writers. Many of these writers, some of whom are quite

Raymond Carver

talented and have already produced work of real distinction, have publicly declared they may never write any novels — that is to say, they have little or no interest in writing novels. Should they? they seem to want to add. Who says? Short stories will do nicely, thank you. If money enters into it (and when, at some bottom-line level, does it ever not?), it ought to be said that advances presently paid for collections of short stories are as large, though some would say as modest, as those paid for novels by writers of comparable stature. An author who publishes a collection of stories can expect to sell, generally speaking, roughly the same number of copies as his or her novelist counterpart. And, besides, as anyone can tell you, it's mainly the short story writers who are being talked about these days. Some people would even say it's where the so-called cutting edge is to be found.

Has there ever been a time like the present for short story writers? I don't think so. Not to my knowledge, at any rate. It wasn't long ago, as recently as ten years back, say, that a short story writer had a distressingly hard time trying to place a first book. (I'm not saying it's an easy matter now, I'm only saying it was even harder ten years ago.) The commercial publishers, expert in ascertaining what the public wanted, knew there wasn't an audience out there, felt sure there wasn't a readership for short fiction, so they dragged their corporate heels when it came to publishing stories. That unrewarding enterprise was, they figured, better left — like poetry — to a few small independent presses, and an even fewer number of university presses.

A vastly different situation exists today, as everyone knows. Not only are the small presses and university presses continuing to publish collections, the truth in fact is that first collections (or second or third) are now regularly issued in significant numbers by large mainstream publishers — and just as regularly, and prominently, reviewed in the media. Short stories are flourishing.

To my mind, perhaps the best — certainly the most variously interesting and satisfying work — even, just possibly, the work that has the greatest chance of enduring, is being done in the short story. Minimalism vs. maximalism. Who cares finally what they want to call the stories we write? (And who isn't tired to death by now of that stale debate?) Short stories will continue to attract more attention, and more readers, insofar as the writers of them continue to produce work of genuine interest and durability, work that merits the attention, and approval, of increasingly large numbers of perceptive readers.

The current profusion in the writing and publishing of short stories is, so far as I can see, the most eventful literary phenomenon of our time. It has provided the tired blood of mainstream American letters with something new to think about and even — any day now, I suspect — something to take off from. (Where it's going, of course, is anybody's guess.) But whether or not such a claim can be permitted, the fact is the resurgence of interest in the short story has done nothing less than revitalize the national literature.

I
FRED CHAPPELL
I

I have been particularly impressed in the last few years by the quality and quantity of fiction lately published by southern women. They have always had sure hands in fiction, but it is as if the prestige of the preceding generation that included Katherine Anne Por-

Fred Chappell

ter, Eudora Welty, Flannery O'Connor, Caroline Gordon, and others, had opened the way for them.

Already some of the newer names are beginning to become household words. Most knowledgeable fiction readers would recognize Anne Tyler, Bobbie Ann Mason, and Lee Smith at least. But there are others whose works, though fewer and less well known, are equally impressive.

Joan Williams has a solid body of work, and her early *The Morning and the Evening* I think of as a minor classic. A major comic classic, *Augusta Played*, was written by Kelly Cherry; it is one of the funniest books ever written. The short stories of Eve Shelnutt—brief, bright, and adventurous—will soon come to be known as they ought, I hope. Candace Flynt's first two novels were impressive, and her forthcoming *Mother Love* a real achievement. There are brilliant first novels by Angela Davis-Gardner, Elizabeth Cox, Marianne Gingher, Louise Shivers, and Jill McCorkle. Anything that Sylvia Wilkinson writes is fascinating, and I hope that the recent reissue of *Cale* establishes the proper reputation for that fine book. Lee Zacharias's *Lessons* is only the beginning of a stellar career.

I shall have omitted others out of sheer forgetfulness—a great many others.

I can't account for this wild and lovely proliferation of bloom. Perhaps the fact that more southern women now attend college has something to do with it, or maybe the women just got fed up with books by Good Old Boys. Whatever the reason, the appearance of these books and others has made me happy.

And envious. Of course.

I
KELLY CHERRY
I

I would be glad to read any contemporary novel published by a major house, say, Knopf, in which the heroine did not lay her book on the table when she ought to have laid it. It is difficult to say whether the problem here is one of shyness or illiteracy.

As for larger matters, well, is there a larger matter anymore? Where is vision? Where is music? Where is truth, that unseemly tear in the fabric of literary convention that allows a glimpse of the naked human soul? Unpublished, mostly.

Kelly Cherry

Alan Cheuse

ALAN CHEUSE

If this were a story instead of an off-the-cuff piece I would have it begin in a German restaurant in the basement of a little shopping mall in San Jose, California. We're eating pretty good Wiener schnitzel when all of a sudden lights go up on a little bandstand and a quartet of young men starts to play. The saxophonist, a kid about twenty-one, sounds like Charlie Parker! If the lights didn't reveal him to be a student from a local music institute, you would think that someone had put a Parker recording on the sound system. But in music schools these days young white kids can learn how to play exactly like Parker and Coltrane, if they want to. The technique they acquire has produced a generation of instrumentalists unparalleled in American jazz. Technicians of the first order roam the land, so many of them that even funky German rathskellers can hire pick-up jazz bands who sound great.

MFA programs have done the same for American fiction. Dozens and dozens, perhaps hundreds of writers between the ages of thirty and forty now write every day in the United States, and scores of books have come out of their workrooms, some of them with a technical proficiency that would make some of the masters of the West give pause and wonder. We live in a Silver Age of American fiction. Never before have so many well-made and interesting books, novels, and stories been written and published. There are writers of every stripe and tendency, creators of short fiction and long, and they can write sentences and paragraphs and stories with skill that would make Sherwood Anderson tear his hair and Dreiser weep and James Jones scowl.

The paradox is that hardly any of them has written anything worth reading twice. Most of the writers at work today have either closed themselves off from the world outside their workrooms, most of which seem to be located on or near university campuses—a point that E. L. Doctorow has recently made in the *Michigan Quarterly Review*—or they have not given themselves over to the true stories of their own lives and stay, rather, within the fashionable boundaries of the styles in which they have been tutored.

The former difficulty seems self-explanatory, or at least Doctorow has illuminated it with real power, so that I don't have to add to it. As for the latter, consider this: two really gifted writers; say that one is a former drunk and a family man whose California cottages fell on him like houses of Usher; he has developed a lean, spare style as a stance toward life that helps him explain his past to himself; and say that another is a former addict and a drunk and a petty criminal and has crafted a wild, witty highly enameled story-style in order to stave off the onrush of the horrifying past. Say that I don't know these writers, or don't know at least one of them, but I am making a kind of surmise about the relation of their crafting powers to their lives, to the realities of their pasts and presents. Studying under them you might notice only the power of the style, not the force of the past that created it. Take away the life force that injures people into art, leave only the technique, and you have mannerism, not great writing.

The underside of our Silver Age is mannerism. The alternative would be a cadre of clunky writers with great stories to tell. I'm not suggesting that I want that, a generation of Dreisers, rushing to the table with our big main meal of the day and in their haste and lack of grace slopping food over the tray and onto their trousers and shoe-tops. You can't train to become a Dreiser anyway. Ignorance and pain and accident does that for you. But you can imitate a Nabokov or a Barth or Barthelme. You can apprise technique — catastrophe that hurts you into story-making comes free of charge and at odd intervals in your life. You have to have the former in order to be ready for the latter. Most writers of our Silver Age seem to be indoors playing board games while the storms rage when they should be outside under the spreading oak, waiting for the lightning.

I guess that I'm suggesting that a true distinction may exist between the achievements of writers who have given over their craft to their obsessions and those who have made an obsession of their craft. The difference for me is that the former can produce work of rough beauty that has the possibility of remaining around for subsequent generations to take up. The latter makes for natty little raves in the Sunday book reviews, jobs at the assistant professor level, and mildew of the imagination.

But in America in these days we all lie down with the beast, wherever the place, whatever the position. That's what we do in order to bring the stories back alive. And it is fair to say that some of our finest writers have moved in and out of the faculties of colleges and universities. Some have simply failed to reemerge intact, while others have used the institutions as patrons for their art. For many it's a living, as the church was in nineteenth-century England. For those for whom it's faith, there trouble might arise. In any case, their presence there has produced subsequent generations of these extremely competent technicians.

But after technique, what?

Some answers lie, I think, in the work of a number of writers whose productions I admire deeply: in the novels and stories of Wright Morris and Eudora Welty, in the broad palettes of George Garrett and Norman Mailer, in the work of Herbert Gold and Doctorow and Didion, in the novels of Cormac McCarthy and Richard Ford and Josephine Humphreys, in the prose of Annie Dillard, Richard Elman, Barry Lopez, Edward Hoagland, Frank Conroy, James Houston, Al Young, in the stories of Grace Paley, Ursula Le Guin, Raymond Carver, Max Apple, Mary Robison, James Robison, Charles Baxter, Jayne Anne Phillips, William Kittredge, Richard Bausch, Ron Carlson, in the fiction of Mary Lee Settle, Robert Stone, William Kennedy, John Wideman, Madison Bell.

You may want to add to this list. I think that you'll subtract at your peril. These are the writers, among others, whose new books I wait for with deep anticipation and the highest expectations. They stand as exemplary artists who use what comforts come their way to create fiction that wounds us into recognitions of our time and place. That's the kind of book I've come to demand of all of us these days, the gold strand in a time of silver, beginning with myself. When I fail, throw me from the life raft and leave me for the sharks.

Annie Dillard
photo by
Shana Sureck

ANNIE DILLARD

Lots of the best of the new fiction is coming out of the South, as usual, and, as usual, no one believes it unless hit over the head: Larry McMurtry, Anne Tyler, Cormac McCarthy, Reynolds Price, Lee Smith, George Garrett, Bobbie Ann Mason, Kate Lehrer, Mary Lee Settle, Peter Taylor, Jill McCorkle, Harry Crews, Madison Smartt Bell, Jayne Anne Phillips, Fred Chappell, Blanche McCrary Boyd.

I find Mark Helprin, Marilynne Robinson, and Scott Spencer to be very talented young novelists, outside the South. Mark Helprin's *Winter's Tale* should be much better known.

Among established writers, John Updike continues to delight me.

Thomas M. Disch   photo by Spracher

THOMAS M. DISCH

Forgive me for not being a trend-spotter. There isn't any "kind" of fiction that looms large enough to be a category that isn't probably already (like most new suburbs) having sanitation problems. I.e., if there's enough of it to constitute a "kind," the larger part will be mediocre. The recent *individual* works of fiction that I can most heartily recommend have generally all been successful within their literary econiches. *Lonesome Dove* was a great read and deserved its Pulitzer and its place on the best-seller list. Everyone who reads short fiction knows that Alice Munro is top-notch. Elizabeth Jolley is a phenomenon, a black comedienne on a par with the late Joe Orton, but at this point her work probably doesn't lack for readers. Within the field of science fiction Greg Bear's *Blood Music* has been widely and deservedly applauded, but it is *echt* science fiction.

Friends are a special category, and whenever I see catalogues of the insufficiently appreciated I am suspicious as to why X should be stumping for Z. On the other hand, this is the area where one is likeliest to know of buried treasure. So, in the friendship category, I suggest the following. . . . Happily, in the case of Norman Rush's *Whites* the world has already got the message. Fred Pfeil's *Goodman 2020* is a dystopian satire published by a university press (Indiana), and undoubtedly many readers who would enjoy it have yet to discover it. Probably, the single most (critically) neglected vein of fiction is the historical novel. John Calvin Batchelor's Civil War epic *American Falls* did not get a fair shake (and neither, I've often fretted, did my own collaboration with Charles Naylor, *Neighboring Lives*). Probably because its proper appreciation requires aesthetic receptors that purely "literary" training doesn't provide, the historical novel tends to be snubbed by those academics in charge of the distribution of laurels (and the defense of their own boundaries).

On the whole I think any large and persistent talent will reap something like its just reward—but that *may* mean being treated as caviar: honored in theory but not widely consumed. Some very good works of fiction are meant to be hermetic and exclusionary of all but a special "initiated" class of readers. E.g., Harry Mathews's trilogy that concluded with *The Sinking of the Odradek Stadium* or Jaimy Gordon's *Shamp of the City-Solo*. Readers have a natural reluctance to submit to the demands on their time and attention of yet another modernist maze/language lesson/semiotic seminar. Such books demand serial monogamy at the very least, if not (as with the votaries of Joyce and Pound) a wedding unto death. Writers are always entitled to ask for such total devotion, but they ought not to be surprised when it is not forthcoming.

I
STEPHEN DOBYNS
I

Because of the great number of graduate writing programs, there are probably more fiction writers at this time than ever before. Because of television, movies, and various aesthetic theories that see fiction as "untruth," there is probably less fiction being read than ever before. There are, of course, many magazines tied to universities, and this is where most short fiction gets published. But these magazines have small circulations and they are read mostly by other writers, while the editors tend to be writers themselves who are only a few years out of graduate school.

A lot of serious fiction today reads as if it wanted to be a screenplay. The language is competent but undistinguished. The plots are linear.

Stephen Dobyns

The subject matter is strong on sincerity and earnestness. It deals with first marriages and first divorces, the complications of well-meaning middle-class men and women under the age of thirty-five. It is written as if modernism had never happened. Its strategies are basically pre-modern, even Victorian. Sometimes it seems as if such work only existed to be optioned to TV or the movies. The postmodernist fiction that one reads seems equally vapid. It is more experimental than meaningful; it takes its "risks" in its form and tries to link with the reader intellectually rather than emotionally. One is often impressed by its methods without caring for its content.

Film and TV have offered a serious challenge to fiction by taking over the traditional methods of storytelling: the linear unraveling of an emotionally engaging narrative. Even if a movie isn't better than a book, it is often more entertaining. Instead of fighting back and writing differently most young writers go on as before, and if their books or stories are bought by the TV or the film industry they are only too happy to see it, even though it may mean the destruction of their work as a piece of language.

It seems that fiction writers should be offering alternatives to TV and film. Of course some are. For instance it would be hard to imagine a film being made from a Stuart Dybek story. It is not that film is wrong or TV is wrong or that it is wrong to make movies from books. It is just that fiction cannot use the same narrative methods and strategies as film. It can't compete with film and TV. It can't be made up of language that tries not to call attention to itself, where the language works as a kind of invisible window. A piece of fiction can't release its information in the same way that a film does because a film can do it better. But much fiction continues to attempt this which is why so many stories and novels read like treatments for film scripts.

What fiction has that cannot be duplicated or improved upon in film is language and a greater variety of strategies, voices, and tones. A story or novel, no matter what it is about, is first of all a piece of language. That language should not be merely serviceable; it should be unique. All the energy and beauty and emotion and idea of the work should swim within that language like fish in a river. The language should be unduplicable. This is not to say it should necessarily be ornate. Raymond Carver's language is unduplicable and simple at the same time. He may be parodied and copied, but no one can do what he did.

And then structure, the way the fiction is built and arranged: this too must be unique. Ditto tone and strategy. Think of how striking many people found Jay McInerney's use of the second person in *Bright Lights, Big City*, an otherwise unremarkable novel. The point is that the fiction writer should make use of the whole gamut of strategies and tones, perhaps even avoid linear structure, avoid doing what a film can do better. The fiction that resembles a failed screenplay can't hope to be successful.

Fiction also has to be more aggressive; it needs to snatch up the readers' attention right from the start. The writer can't expect that the reader will give him a couple of hours of his time like giving a vagrant spare change. Earnestness and sincerity aren't enough. Intelligence isn't enough. The writer must make the reader want to read and he must make the reader believe that within these pages there is something that will be meaningful to him, that will grip his heart. Again Carver had a wonderful way of beginning a story with a first paragraph that was so compelling that it was almost impossible not to read the second. A work is compelling through its language, emotion, originality, structure and idea, as well as through its compassion and energy. It must convince the reader from the beginning that he will find elements within it which will touch his life. Kafka said something to the effect that literature should be an axe to smash the frozen sea of the heart. A piece of fiction needs to break through the reader's complacency and astonish him, and it must do it through language.

I think it is wrong to say that writing is in a healthy state. It is dying.

Writing cannot compete with film and it cannot pander. It needs to be its own unique area of creative endeavor. First of all it is language, secondly that language must make the reader want to read it, thirdly that language must be original and unique. Fiction and poetry teach us to think and feel in a way that films can never do. Fiction and poetry also invite the reader to participate in the creative process by engaging his imagination with the language, by using words to allow the reader to create events in the mind. A film only asks its viewer to remain relatively silent, to mimic the dead. In reading the reader is still an actor; in film he is acted upon. But it can be uncomfortable to participate. More and more it seems that people would prefer to be passive, to do nothing. We have already reached the point where the reading of poetry is not a natural activity but a cultivated taste. To my mind that is a tragedy. I fear the same thing will happen to fiction.

I
SUSAN DODD
I

At twenty, I indulged in a celebration of what I knew; it seemed, at the time, like quite a lot. By thirty, I had succumbed to

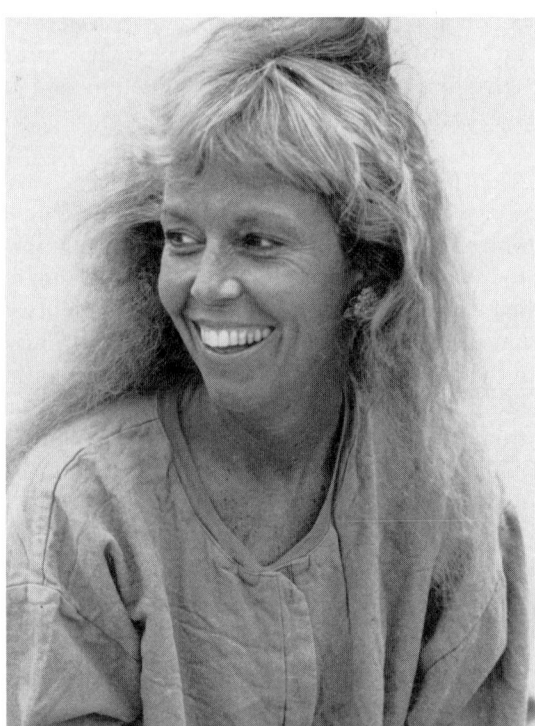

Susan Dodd
photo by
Art Seeman

an almost holy terror of all I had to learn. Only now, at forty, do I begin to understand that I am embarked on a more complex mission: the discovery of what I love.

It is slow going, but I am learning. Writers (Chekhov, Cather, Cheever) help. *Writing* helps. Indeed, I suspect I write primarily to discover what I love.

Andre Dubus, a writer who in my opinion — lest you think I am never going to get around to your question — *deserves more attention*, writes, "We like to believe in this quarter of the century, we know and are untouched by everything; yet it takes only a very small jolt, at the right time, to knock us off balance for the rest of our lives." That jolt, that moment, that subtle, heartbreaking, permanent imbalance — those are what I love in literature. I prize above all others those writers who seize the moment, force me to experience the jolt, recognize the *sanctity* in humankind's perpetual tilt.

Chekhov: "The end was still very far away, and the hardest and most difficult part was only beginning."

Frank O'Connor: "And anything that ever happened [to] me after I never felt the same about again."

Welty: "I did not know, any longer, the meaning of my happiness; it held me unexplained."

The words are simple, their knowing profound. But the *unknowing* is what staggers. To confront such unknowing humanizes, wises us up. And no one — character, writer, reader — is left untouched.

To know it all, to be untouched by it all, is brash perhaps, but not brave. Bravery is what I love, the kind of bravery Tolstoy summoned to face down his obsessive fears of physical suffering and mortality by writing *The Death of Ivan Ilyich*. Every student who falls into my clutches is shamelessly cajoled to read *Ilyich*. I am shocked and disheartened by how many reject the book, charging Tolstoy with sentimentality. Knowing, untouched, too many writers seem mortified by rage, terror, grief. Passion embarrasses them.

Passion is what I love. *Le feu sacre.* And even — yes — excess.

As writers, we confront a perpetual choice of failures, I think. Aiming for a perfection we know is out of reach, we choose our shortcomings the way duelists choose weapons. The choice may not always be conscious, but we make it nonetheless, and it is vital: shall I err by not going far enough . . . or by going too far?

The writing I love, the books I believe should be read, celebrated, *attended to* are those which risk the latter course. Caution, no matter how elegant, adept, knowing, is a far cheaper commodity, in literature or in life, than passion.

I miss John Gardner, though I never knew him. I miss the delicious can of worms he opened with *On Moral Fiction*, the shooting war of letters he provoked with his wondrously loose tongue and his prodigious irritability, "True art clarifies life, establishes models of human action, casts nets toward the future, carefully judges our right and wrong directions, celebrates and mourns. It does not rant. It does not sneer or giggle in the face of death, it invents prayers and weapons. It designs visions worth trying to make fact. It does not whimper or cower or throw up its hands and bat its lashes. . . . It strikes like lightning, or *is* lightning." Gardner, bless him, was always going too far. . . .

It is tempting to say there ain't much lightning around these days. I believe it's still there, though, always has been and always will be. Maybe we just haven't been paying enough attention?

Blessed are the lightning-makers.

ROBERT DUNN

When I read a work of fiction these days, I often can't shake a nagging, perhaps unfair question that pops up in the back of my head: Why was this short story or novel written? I've become obsessed with motive: not so much what the author thinks he's trying to say, but why he decided to say it; what, in terms of the real world, he is trying to attain. This is, perhaps, an unfortunate curiosity about perceived rewards, but with the labors of fiction so intense, and what can come out of publication so little, I keep wondering what an author thinks he's up to.

There, of course, is the great hope of overnight success, even though experience tells us that truly worthy books never blaze popular glory, at least not at first (cheerful aside: *A Portrait of the Artist as a Young Man* is Penguin's largest-selling book ever; millions of copies). A *New Yorker*-managed literary success is still possible, and yet books by David Leavitt and Deborah Eisenberg, for instance, though well reviewed and well sold, seem rather thin, minor efforts, hardly inspiring as works of literature. There's Jay McInerney running around with the Hollywood Brat Pack. And then there's what most of us settle for, the warm smile

Robert Dunn   photo by Patricia Woodbridge

of one's husband or wife, the good notice in the *San Diego Union*, the huzzas from one's creative writing class when a story "works."

I like to see my fascination with quick literary success as a particularly contemporary fallacy, culturally stimulated and driven. These days our culture seems less than ever interested in significant, long-term accomplishment. Instead it rewards the attainment of access to our attention (usually through the media) and celebrates strategies employed to gain access. The greatest attention, of course, comes to those on television, which remains, even with the plethora of talk shows, resistant — perhaps deeply antipathetical — to the serious use of words, as in good writing, good writers, anything truly literary. I guess in glib terms, my concern with what an author thinks he's up to is a simple desire to shake his collar and say, Hey, can't you see what's going on? What matters out there — what people are interested in — is TV, video, computers, visual art, and you keep writing books! But of course we all do, for love, for the desire for something well-made and true, and, most of all, as I more and more believe, to prove to ourselves that today, sitting in front of the typewriter, we can still do it — still bang out a well-turned sentence, cobble together an interesting character, catch an epiphany. The struggle with questions of potency, essence, self-discipline and rigor, and the answers only serious literary labor can provide, may suffice.

Still, there is that world out there, all set to traduce good writing and celebrate the facile and glib — yet we all hope we'll be the one to beat it, write well *and* successfully. As it should be. I'm also fascinated with what the literary world has come up with to keep going in the face of indifference. (The latest: designer paperbacks such as Vintage Contemporaries which publish worthy books, but do so by commodotizing literature and, just as we were warned when corporations started buying up publishing houses, selling it prepackaged, like the proverbial soap.) In truth these days the writer's lot seems newly improved in many ways, from creative writing sinecures to a panoply of available, finally well-paying grants to more and more programs of author readings to the new paperback editions which, thank goodness, do sell books. And, perhaps not ironically at all, as these small but significant rewards become available, their pursuit becomes all the more avid, and writing runs the risk of overconforming to the needs of book packagers, grants managers, a developing bureaucracy of literature.

My problem is that I don't want to read stories or books and find I'm wondering what kind of success the author's after. Who asks what was Shakespeare's motive, Emily Dickinson's, or William Blake's (or, if we ask, who can do more than begin to answer)? Or if an author announces his motive, I want it so clear and grand it takes your breath away.

> . . . What in me is dark
> Illumine, what is low raise and support;
> That to the heighth of this great Argument
> I may assert Eternal Providence,
> And justify the ways of God to men.

A motive worthy of awe.

In these times of gross attention to quick success — succumb, or risk feeling foolish or irrelevant — it's valuable to remember some of the still-worthy motives of literature. Here are a few: To turn ourselves inside out, light up unexplored corners of the self. To cover the breadth of society, explain connections hidden to the mundane eye, explore the way things actually work, how lives are truly lived, on levels of spirit as well as accountable action. To sum up in gnomic, boundless perceptions the new mysteries of postindustrial society and technologically determined man. To create or recreate a new myth of our existence, do for our half of the twentieth century what Joyce, Eliot, and Freud did for theirs. Or maybe simply to tell a good story, expertly, with resonance.

Tall orders, these — standards anyone would despair of meeting — but ambitions, the whole of which, only literature can hope to attain; and if not met by literature, then by what? What I really look for in these times of confusion and duplicity are books that pierce the sad and dismaying unreality of our political lives, books that work to expand the shrunken, battered self, books that try to shake the invisible walls of the empire.

Here are the novels I've read in the last few years which come closest to fulfilling some of these hopes:

> *White Noise*, Don DeLillo
> *The Sportswriter*, Richard Ford
> *In Country*, Bobbie Ann Mason
> *Continental Drift*, Russell Banks
> *Angels*, Denis Johnson
> *Money*, Martin Amis (though English, through flash and guile just as American as any of the others)
> *More Die of Heartbreak*, Saul Bellow (a model for us all).

STUART DYBEK

I wonder how many other writers have, as I do, tucked away somewhere in files or boxes or trunks unopened for years, unpublished stories and poems written by friends. Or, for that matter, stories and poems that *were* published, perhaps in some obscure, poorly circulated, little magazine that has long since folded and been forgotten. I'm thinking especially of work by people who for any multitude of reasons no longer write, or who have turned to other kinds of writing, yet whose early work we privately save, not merely out of friendship or nostalgia, but because something in the work itself seemed promising. I'd guess many writers have such collections. It might even make an interesting feature in a magazine to ask a number of writers to dig out and submit a piece or two that they've saved—but then again, maybe the trunks are best kept locked.

In any case, such a friend, a DJ among other things who ran a jazz show out of East Lansing, showed me many years ago some very brief stories he'd written. As I remember, the *longest* was three pages, double spaced. This took place in an era when literary ambition was measured at least in part by the magnitude of book spines, when writers were supposed to be concerned with the quest for The Great American Novel, and so I suppose my friend's short pieces seemed even more compressed

Stuart Dybek
photo by
Robert Wulkowitz

than they might now. I know I hadn't read many pieces that short before. They reminded me in their brevity more of the vignettes that Hemingway calls Chapters in *In Our Time*, than they did of the prose poems of Rimbaud. I thought they were exciting—extremely fresh—both the jazz DJ's and those Hemingway had written nearly half a century before.

Of course, a tradition of short prose pieces existed. Continental writers, especially, had been working with the form at least since Baudelaire who, in the preface of *Paris Spleen*, wrote that in his ambitious moments he had dreamed of the miracle of a poetic prose, musical, and supple and rugged enough to adapt itself to the lyrical impulses of the soul. But neither the DJ nor I were in touch with that yet. The news hadn't reached Connally's, an Irish bar on Chicago's North Side, its decor suggesting that one had entered a shrine of the Kennedys, where we sat on a Sunday afternoon in spring, reading one another's work as we always did when my friend would drive in from Michigan. He'd bring the manuscripts he was working on and a stack of records, and maybe it was merely that juxtaposition, but those little stories he showed me seemed jazzy—tight, rhythmic, incisive like bebop, timed for a world to bloom within the limits of a song on a jukebox.

The immediate interest I felt upon first reading those short pieces is something I've sustained. I've kept an antenna tuned for writers working with the short prose form — including its various offshoots and permutations such as Italo Calvino's brilliant "novel," *Invisible Cities.*

And, if The Great American Prose Poem phenomenon of the 1970s is any indication, there must have been a fair number of other writers, holed up in their various versions of Connally's, who were attracted by some aspect of the short prose form — the scale, the novelty, the freshness, the compression, the possibility of a prose as supple as poetry.

As this is simply an appreciation, I don't feel any obligation to stop and try to sort out the distinctions between the prose poem and the short-short form of fiction. Clearly, they overlap. The easiest way out is to say that generally poets write prose poems and fiction writers write short-shorts. Whatever one calls the short prose form — and it hardly lacks for names — I was pleased when poetry editors opened avenues for pieces that often read like very short stories.

Within the past year [1987] two anthologies of short-shorts, *Sudden Fiction* and *4-Minute Fictions* have appeared. Apparently writers continue to be intrigued by the form.

What continues to interst me most about the short-short form is that it so often serves as a vehicle for the exploration of the lyrical possibilities of prose. In this, I think of it as a writer's form, though certainly believe that it can be made to appeal to the mythical "general reader," as well.

In *The Art of Fiction,* John Gardner, disccusing the poetic beauty of sentence rhythms, talks about "rhythm so subtle only prose can achieve it." I think of the short-short as a laboratory in which one hears writers timing out such rhythms, often developing those qualities that become the sound of distinctive styles.

I think that often within its small boundaries one stands on the border between the narrative and lyric, that shifting, invisible line where story crosses to image and image into story.

One of my favorite writers, and a master of the short-short story, is Kawabata. He wrote over a hundred of the short pieces he called palm-of-the-hand stories, and it would make a wonderful book, I'm sure, if they could all be gathered together and translated into English. What he said about them goes to the heart of what fascinates me: "Most literary men write poetry when they are young, but I wrote these vignettes instead."

Margaret Edwards
photo by
Joel Gardner

MARGARET EDWARDS

In museums it depresses me to stand in front of art that asks the question *What is art?* I'm willing to accept the conventions of paint and canvas and frame, and of casting and carving. I'd rather rest my attention on the subject being portrayed. And likewise, in reading short fiction, I'm drawn into stories more by topic and character and tone, less by an experiment in form. Not that I'm insensitive to the brilliance of a new style that can put a spin on often-tossed subjects, nor that I'm unaware of how much my own writing owes to experimentalists. Yet as a reader, I am pedestrian, conservative, and desirous of being caught up in a narrative. I want a story to hustle me, handle me, sweep me along, leaving aside even my admiration of how well it might be written. The deepest pleasure of reading is — in my opinion — that experience of having the author's voice and vision wholly invade the mind.

As for current fiction, specifically short fiction, I pick it up always curious to see how much of life as we know it has managed to make its way onto the printed page. I don't mean to measure the time lag between say, the new watch on the wrist and a literary reference to the digital time-face. In fact, name brands and all mundane artifacts that are part of modern *texture* seem to spring from life into art relatively quickly. I'm speaking more of the impact of various social events that are blinding in actual advent, but complete only as their thunder rolls through our fiction's pages. Vietnam, for instance, seems only beginning to emerge as an experience. Distance has been crucial, too, on the sexual revolution of our era, a revolution that has set so many fond assumptions in motion (i.e., reeling).

Did anyone else feel, along with me, a certain suspense about how AIDS would find its way into the *New Yorker*? Of course, there would be a caught, held breath — and an unmentioned Unmentionable quality — in such a treatment. I was therefore unprepared for the power of Susan Sontag's "The Way We Live Now," which skirted the chasm of Taste the taboo-makers had dug for her, yet managed to suggest the hideous facts enough to reveal a situation so stunning and unbearable.

I'm interested in the stories that come stitched together to make novelistic quilts, like David Huddle's brilliant *Only the Little Bone* (David Godine Press, 1986). One must judge the marketing device of stories-as-novel by the integrity of each separate piece. His book works. Yet it remains to be seen if the push for unified story collections won't promote some dashed-off and flimsy stories that function only as glue and can't stand alone.

I
IRVIN FAUST
I

I am concerned about, and worry over, writers who *dare*. Writers who refuse to be typecast, another definition for playing it safe. This means that they will, and have, *truly* dug into other personas, other miseries and ecstasies, other pasts. One such who comes quickly to mind is George Garrett, a writer who has accomplished especially splendid things with an item called history. People like Garrett sometimes get clobbered for adventuring (a recent review of his latest was hilariously dumb), but they don't retreat. Like a literary Foch, surrounded on the left, on the right, they *attack*.

Coover does the same thing to some extent, although *The Public Burning* left me cold. The point is that he gives this thing known as literature a variety of shots, and has had the nerve to develop a career along a

*Irvin Faust
photo by
Jean Faust*

number of truly felt divergent lines. Even when I don't like the results, I admire them.

Here are two things I wish:

1. I wish we had protean writers like Tom Keneally, the Australian. Anyone who can pull off literary marvels with Joan of Arc, the American Civil War and the armistice negotiators of the First World War deserves our rapt attention. Perhaps we can be inspired by him; on the other hand, perhaps we're not good enough. Incidentally, or not so incidentally, it should be clear by now that I am particularly taken with explorations of history, and with pushing those explorations beyond the traditional "historical novel" (I've tried this twice, myself; success or failure aside, it crashed me excitingly through the typecasting wall).
2. I wish James B. Hall was writing more short stories, or at least stories I can find. The man from Oregon was careening all over the internal and external map when I chanced on him in the 1960s. The young of today who have *discovered* the short story, should try one of the masters. If he can't be found, have them dig into *Us He Devours* and *15 by 3*. I should note that Verlin Cassill and Herbert Gold were the other two-thirds of that group and at the top of their estimable form. Hall dared in his stories; I have an idea that if he is still with us, he is thrashing beautifully and precisely around.

Finally, I would add, that in addition to history, I've become fascinated with mystery (both very much connected). Again, not in the genre sense, but in ways that can redefine it. The PI has become a bore, so have transvestite or idiot-savant cops (there are two throwaways for characters looking for really *different* problem solvers). I'm not at all sure that I know what *I'm* looking for, but it's not Hammett or Chandler, great as they were, and they *were*. One magazine trying to break through the old parameters is *A Matter of Crime,* edited by Bruccoli and Layman, supported by HBJ. It may be hung up on Hammett (after all, he *is* box-office), and it frequently strikes out, but at least it goes down swinging. And when it connects, it's worth much more than the price of admission.

ELAINE FORD

Last weekend I read twenty-one short stories, the maiden efforts of my students in English 205, Introduction to Creative Writing. The stories were about: a retarded woman whose boyfriend dies in a fire; an eleven-year-old who steals candy and has to deal with

Elaine Ford

the guilt; an exhausted and financially pressed medical student contemplating the advantages of suicide; a janitor who befriends a mentally ill teenager; male friends in a tiny Maine town engaged in a pointless competition that leads to disaster; a college boxer whose most formidable opponent is himself . . . and so on.

Each kid got inside a situation that was real to him and explored the ramifications. To be corny about it, each, in his own way, wrote about life. Or *life*.

I hope these young writers and others like them never learn what "sells" or what styles or subjects are in fashion at the moment. I hope editors will nurture those who have talent and who persevere and that publishers will publish them. And if they are really lucky, they may even make a buck or two.

I
RICHARD FORD
I

I don't like much of anything implied by this question; that writing — recent or old — gains by being divided artificially

Richard Ford
photo by
Allan Titmuss

into "kinds"; or — more perniciously — that one spurious kind might deserve more attention or readers than some other; or that I should accept such a classifying in order to turn a reader toward one writer and, inevitably, away from some other. And, just to make a clean sweep of it, I don't like the idea that "recent writing" is judged or even spoken of as separate from older writing — the classics. Such a division concedes what I don't: that writers are any less likely today than a hundred or four hundred years ago to write superbly.

Categorizing art — naming it, likening it to other art, explaining and describing it generally, simplifying it for the purposes of focus and convenience — is critics' business, and as far as I can tell is posterior and quite often opposed to what, say, a writer does when he writes a short story — an activity inclusive if not always generous in spirit, commencing from nothing, in which form is always created new, and for which no reliable category preexists. Moreover, affection for writing-by-category encourages a profusion of invidious "schools" or "camps," and such name-mongering irrelevancies as "minimalism" and "postmodernism," as well as the deeply banal "women's fiction," "Southern literature," "gay writing," and worse yet, scrambling along after all that, a whole set of tedious minds armed to ambush and guard only these very terms. This winter, a friend of mine — a teaching writer — wrote me from one of the "good colleges" in Minnesota, saying: "Where do students learn to pick quarrels with literary modes so early on? Is it all affectation?" And my answer is, *not at all*. They learn it from their teachers, people with not enough of literature on their minds. It seems to me that fuller attention to the best being written now could and would lead a student elsewhere — toward where great writing usually leads readers — toward complexity, toward the new, toward, as Schwartz wrote, redeeming the species. But not, for Christ's sake, to *isms*. Not to tag-names or to categories.

To the second part of this question — what writing I believe is most deserving of more attention and readership — I have only this little to say: Why would I want to make a tyrany of my reading preferences? I like some books; most books I don't and never finish. I don't like them for a vareity of reasons — mostly they don't seem smart enough, not even as smart as I am. Sometimes they aren't skillful enough. And sometimes I *will* like a book, but then only because it concedes a world I myself accept as true, or imagines it in a way I find kindred — books, I admit, that remind me too admiringly of my own work.

My preferences, in other words, are aimless, unreliable (except to me), possibly self-serving. Sure, I like a *good* book. Who doesn't? But couldn't it be possible to like and dislike books merely singly and absolutely, without excluding whole bunches of them in contemptuously general and categorical terms? Relative choosings of this latter sort is critics' business again and has nothing to do with what I care about — reading stories and writing them. It's bad enough that demonstrably excellent writing goes, by large lots, into and out of vogue among readers. But it's especially unappealing that writers champion their own preferences just to give faddishness the appearance of judgment. I think now is a fine time to be writing in this country; good diverse work's being done all over, and people should read whatever they want to — books I like, books I hate. It's their business not mine. My own work, what I write, is enough public evidence of what I care about. If I can't be persuasive there, I ought to quit trying.

PAULA FOX

I wonder if good writing *ever* gets the attention and readers it deserves? Emerson wrote, "People do not deserve to have good writing, they are so pleased with bad."

Flaubert distinguished between readers (those who *read*) and an au-

Paula Fox
photo by
Thomas Victor

dience that wants stimulation — ("Outrageous stimulation," Wordsworth said) as two opposed things.

It is a continual complaint that good works are often shoved aside by books which serve the sentimentality of the age, which hold up before the book-buying middle class a stylish picture of itself, which present its gossip as serious concerns, falsify its fears and exaltations, and are profound only in the self-satisfaction, the amour-propre they express. When hasn't it been so since printing gave books a market value?

"What is so wonderful about great literature is that it transforms the man who reads it toward the condition of the man who wrote," said E. M. Forster. To be transformed, to have one's imagination awakened, to feel always on the edge of mystery and discovery — these are things that *readers* seek.

I am now reading stories by Andre Dubus. They have the surface of life: season, hour, costume and custom, the furnishings of a world with its duplicities and uncertainties; and they have, below the surface, hard, patient meditation on what it means to be human.

When I see a new book by Mr. Dubus, I feel stirred and a touch alarmed — because good writing wrings one. I feel similarly about the work of James Purdy, Alice Munro, Gina Berriault, Frederick Busch, and Marilynne Robinson.

I
MARILYN FRENCH
I

Any *kind* of writing attracts me — especially stories, novels, and poetry — if it is well done, that is, if it is alive, honest, unpretentious, not purposely obfuscational or hermetic. No, I have to qualify that. There are two kinds of writing I do not like even when they are well done. I very much enjoy mysteries/police procedurals/spy stories — except when they involve carefully detailed physical violence toward women. I expect I would dislike detailed depiction of physical violence toward men just as much, if I were to encounter it. I have not; but certain writers seem to love lingering depictions of torture/injury/maiming of female bodies. I loathe such writers in direct proportion to their attention to such details — in any genre, not just mysteries.

The second kind of prose and poetry I dislike even when it is written with stylistic skill is work I privately call self-indulgent. It is work in

Marilyn French   *photo by Annelise Jackbo*

which the protagonist is clearly the writer idealized, and the plot or texture functions to aggrandize or justify the protagonist. There is a great deal of such work these days, by both male and female authors; it is offensive not primarily because it is self-serving (many good authors have used literature in a self-serving way, for revenge—Joyce, for instance), but because it is false to experience while claiming "seriousness"—truth to experience.

The contemporary works I like most are fictions or poems that deal with the texture of life, the day-to-day feel and throb of experience, works that suggest we are formed by small daily choices rather than isolated dramatic events, although we may not realize this until afterwards—when it is too late to change anything—and that "tragedy," (if we can still use the word to describe our literature) lies in that fact. I like such work even more if it suggests an awareness of the larger political ramifications of our everyday experience. I like literature that emerges from a sense of human beings as morally neutral and desirous of the good insofar as we know it, that sees human cruelty and evil as arising from imaginative and emotional limitation, from unthinking acceptance of the morality of a given society rather than from transcendence (whether super- or subhuman). I do not believe in transcendence and cannot read seriously serious works (fictions or poetry that present themselves as offering truths about experience) that invoke these realms. This means I cannot read seriously works that posit a villain or a near-perfect protagonist; although I can tolerate villains or heroines/heroes in "nonserious" writing (mysteries, spy stories, works which do not claim to offer truth to experience—although some in fact do).

Above all I love novels that border on poetry—Christa Wolf's *Cassandra*, for instance, or Marie-claire Blais's Quebec novels, David Plante's *Francoeur Trilogy*, the work of Luisa Valenzuela. My own first novels (unpublished) were of this kind. It is "poetic" prose—along with poetry itself—that American publishers tend to slight or dismiss, to refuse to publish. I feel this lack to be a profound loss to our culture, but I place only secondary responsibility for it on publishers, who prefer to publish books that they believe will sell in great numbers. I believe the primary responsibility for this failure lies with grade- and high-school (and perhaps college-level) English teachers, who do not know how to read poetry (and therefore do not really know how to read) and so cannot teach their students how to read poetry *or* serious prose. Perhaps even they do not deserve such blame: perhaps the real responsibility lies on all of us, who refuse to pay teachers decent wages, and who tolerate impersonal, centralized, bureaucratic educational systems.

In any case, a few students are lucky enough to have gifted teachers or learn on their own to read poetry and prose that does not spell everything out; but the majority, which does not, loses a most intense and brilliant experience, perhaps the most ecstatic reading experience. Two authors whose work I know who are underpublished because they write "poetic" prose are Barbara Greenberg and George Chambers. I am sure there are many others. But even well-published writers are devalued if they write "poetic" novels: Norman Mailer's brilliant *Why Are We In Vietnam?* was, last time I checked, out of print.

|
BRUCE JAY FRIEDMAN
|

My reading doesn't have much method to it. A friend came by, looked at a shelf and said: "Who *lives* here?" Some books that stick with me—ones I've read in the past year, include: Bellow's *Him with His Foot In His Mouth*; the first three Philip Roth *Zuckerman* books; the twelve volumes of Powell's *A Dance to the Music of Time* and a number of books in the excellent Virago series—novels by Anita Brookner, Marguerite Kennedy, Nancy Mitford—all of the novels and short stories of Elizabeth Taylor. One that lingers particularly is *Mrs. Palfrey*

Bruce Jay Friedman

at the Claremont, not necessarily the best but the one that lingers. Most of my reading is nonfiction — recently *Nicholas and Alexandra*, *Napoleon and Josephine*, Barbara Tuchman's *The March of Folly*, Michael Howard's *Franco-Prussian War*, the finest work of history I've ever read. One book kicks me into another. The preference is for areas I know nothing about. My education wasn't much, so I suppose it's an effort to fill in the gaps. Gaps — that's all there seem to be.

LAURA FURMAN

Your question about American fiction strikes me as a critic's question, best answered with the name of a school or kind of writing, and this seems far away from what I do (for I don't feel particularly close to any school), but maybe that's the way all writers feel. In any case, a short route to an answer is to say that I would like to read and be able to celebrate more fiction that has engaged the writer's heart, writing that is fully imagined and has evolved into mature fiction. I read contemporary writers who seem to be more interested in form (sometimes just in voice) than in the life they are creating on the page. What is created is writing without much interest as anyting but an exercise. And the reader is left, I suppose, to admire the writing. In the writers I like best—Anthony Powell, Ivy Compton-Burnett, Natalia Ginzburg, Yasunari Kawabata—there is joy in form, but far more for the reader than trained skill.

In her essay "The Novel Démeublée," Willa Cather spoke out against the overly furnished novel, one stuffed with a catalogue of journalistic details or unnecessary physical sensations, and she called for an imaginative art that works through "the inexplicable presence of the thing not named, of the overtone divined by the ear but not heard by it." When Cather wrote her essay fifty years ago, perhaps much of the prose she read was too fleshy, or at least fat with details she didn't admire. Now I would say that there is much fiction that is too slim or unfurnished and that its bareness masquerades as meaning.

Though I won't name writers I don't like, I'll cite the stories of Mavis Gallant as models of full prose, and *The Madness of a Seduced Woman* by Susan Fromberg Schaeffer, which was a transforming book for me, one that made me feel like writing. Like most good books, it is so idiosyncratic that I don't think it qualifies as a kind of writing, but it does embody the spirit that I seek as a reader, and as a writer, in whatever voice it speaks.

Laura Furman *photo by David Crossley*

Herbert Gold
photo by
Lonnie Wilson

HERBERT GOLD

I need both stories and language. I like the spaces between the words, so long as the words are there, too. The kind of "experimental" writing which gains its esteem from, oh, not being printed square on the page, not putting down enough of the words, doing all vasty space and no language, angst & anomie & muddled griefiness and no novel. . . . I guess I sort of mean that post-pre-modern antestructuralist Sixth or Seventh or Fourteenth Arrondissement starwars prose . . . doesn't stick in my Derrida. It just whizzes right past.

Recent American writing gets too much attention and not enough readers. I would prefer that people pay no attention, just leap right in and let it happen. May conscience and soul be our guide.

DORIS GRUMBACH

What kind of recent writing interests me, you ask. I am tempted to answer with a clever contradiction: all of it and yet none of it. I have read so steadily (and thus so much, too much) in the past thirty years that I have grown weary, after a while, of most of the "kinds." There are the long, hyperthyroid, overgrown fictions, stuffed like Victorian sofas with unnecessary material, books ponderously self-indulgent and suffering from severe cases of logorrhea. And there are the anorexic, Giacometti-like minimalist productions. When I am feeling charitable I see some value in both sizes of fiction, but usually both have the same effect upon me: they hold me to the ground, like Gulliver, making it impossible for my spirit to soar, my imagination to be freed, my mind to burst into fire, my ears and eyes to burn with pleasure. The real world, what we perceive as reality, binds, imprisons, depresses, and enervates. Fiction was devised, I have always believed, to undo the restraints of the world as it is. Reading my way through new fiction now I feel indentured to it; I yearn to *escape.*

So what am I left with to praise? A few stray, wayward (in the sense of uncataloguable) books that have sustained and delighted me in the past twenty years. I have made a list, out of my head, of eleven such

Doris Grumbach
photo by
Jerry Bauer

books I would not part with, or lend, or sell, at any price. I examine them and see they fit into no category whatsoever. They tend to be short, I discover, although a few are normally sized, and one is rather fat, to my dismay. But none is elephantine and none is starved in concept or embodiment, and every one is distinguished by its style, its unique manner of telling its unique story. All belong to that vague category of fiction distinguished by fidelity to language, by the use of the exact, graphic, inevitable word in the appropriate place, settled perforce into the well-shaped sentence, or incorporated into the right image. One or two experiments with language, plays games with it. I find that irresistible.

For what it is worth, here is the list, printed out from the retentive personal computer I carry around in my head, in no special order:

John Updike's first novel, almost a novella, *The Poorhouse Fair*, a finely crafted story of a mutiny in a poorhouse by old men against a young, good prefect, Connor. Updike went on, after 1958, to write a great deal more, but nothing better than this, and much that is far longer.

Walker Percy's first novel, *The Moviegoer*, published in 1961, won the first National Book Award for Fiction. Binx Bolling the moviegoer and his beautiful cousin, Kate Cutrer, are, for me, unforgettable Southern characters (not too many of the thousands of others I have since encountered are) and the writing is impeccable.

Giovanni's Room, by James Baldwin (1956). Not a first, but a second novel, and the best, I think, Baldwin ever wrote. It is about the discovery of love, the kind is immaterial, a model of concision and verbal beauty.

Grendel, by John Gardner (1971), a masterpiece of imaginative recreation, a brutal and loving story of the monster Grendel, told by him, who sees men (including Beowulf) as monsters and tries to love them. This small book supersedes in elegance all the more heavy-handed later fiction by Gardner and acts as a model for his instructions to the young writer in *The Art of Fiction* and *Becoming a Novelist*.

Bridgeport Bus, Maureen Howard's early novel (1965), has as its main character a wonderful, fat, Irish-Catholic narrator, Mary Agnes Keely, who makes an amazing trip to New York. Neither Keely's New York nor Howard's extraordinary economy of language have I ever been able to forget.

It appeared six years ago [1980], and yet I have not been able to put it out of my mind: Russell Hoban's *Riddley Walker*, a futuristic novel (usually I abhor them) which is an adventure in creating and using a language suitable to a remarkable story. I loved every "broken-up and worn-down vernacular" word of it. The quotation is from Hoban.

Philip Roth's *Zuckerman Bound* seems to me to be overextended, being rather more of Zuckerman than I wanted, but one volume within the trilogy, *The Ghost Writer*, is a masterpiece containing a small masterpiece within *it*, the resurrection or survival, or imaginative re-creation, of the character of Anne Frank. It is the kind of leap Roth rarely makes, and it is plain wonderful.

I first read William Kennedy's *Ironweed* in manuscript and thought what I think now, that it is an achievement in the power of language and a superb piece of magic realism. By now I know some of it by heart, and it has become one of those books that will live with me and with my own feeling for what constitutes exceptional writing.

Now, you ask, how can it be? *Ragtime*? E. L. Doctorow's *Ragtime*? Yes, because it influenced me, by the strong imaginative amalgamation of the created and the real characters, and by the writing, to try to do something of the sort myself. I have read it again and again, always with pleasure. I believe it will survive its great instant popularity, the scorn that inevitably followed the acclaim, and the present silence it has fallen into, and will assume a place in the canon of seminal books of the century.

Two books that have the unusual form of novels-as-memoirs, or perhaps memoirs in the form of novels: Clancy Sigal's *Going Away* and Frank Conroy's *Stop-Time*. Sigal's story of a boy growing up and Conroy's similar odyssey into manhood are models of stylish narrative. I compare them with every similar account and find nothing written since has equaled them. Both volumes, I understand, have become cult books: entirely understandable to me.

RON HANSEN

There is an unhappy but possibly convenient tendency in our criticism and reviewing to pigeonhole writers or place them in camps and clubs, each with his own raccoon cap and complicated handshake. It happened in the 1930s with the Proletarian Writers and the Algonquin Club; in the 1960s with the Jewish Writers, the Black Humorists, and the Fabulators; and it is happening now with our petty arguments over the Southern Hicks, the Minimalists and Maximalists, the Old Fogies in Great Britain. I agree that there are differences in approach and subject matter, but that seems no more interesting than where the Elks hold their weekly meetings. What *is* interesting in all these con-

Ron Hansen
photo by
Linda Fry Poverman

temporary writerly movements is their common pursuit of hyperbole and misrepresentation. Everything is made either bigger or smaller or eerier than it really is in life; and that is what storytelling has always been about. Probably ever since the advent of daily newspapers, and certainly since television, it has become increasingly necessary for fiction writers to report on the unreported, the underside, the hidden and horrible and otherly, even the clearly impossible. In many ways, contemporary American fiction is spookier than it has ever been, and, given the complacent and arrogant disposition of this country, I think that's both appropriate and important.

I
CURTIS HARNACK
I

I read almost anything, all the time (though not necessarily to the end), and I only wish there were more like me out there. The trouble is not that certain fiction isn't noticed, but that general readers don't know what's available or how to get hold of it and often don't care sufficiently to make an effort. We're in a rich, various, quite splendid period of fiction-writing, the most fecund in the English-speaking world, but without a voracious audience to back it up, I can't see it running anywhere except into sand before long. Compared to many other countries — most of Eastern Europe, Japan, China, parts of South America — literature isn't all that important in American life, and this has been true for some time. One can't hope to change ingrained cultural habits, but no writer can avoid sizing up the situation and trying to figure out some strategy for dealing with it.

Today there's a great emphasis on fictional technique, almost for its own sake, and many new writers burst forth with dazzling performances. Professionally, one can take a good deal of pleasure in the pyrotechnics, though writing workshops in the universities often do their jobs only too well and the question, What new is being said? isn't supposed to be asked.

I'm still interested in fiction being meaningful to those readers who aren't writers, just general people. I have my clients of that sort who take my advice, follow my reading lists at the library, at paperback stalls, wherever they can find what I tell them they'd enjoy. The pleasure of a "hit" is wonderful — when a book really knocks them over and they keep thinking about it, are somewhat changed by it. For me this remains the central purpose of writing, and I'd like those readers to feel that way about my books. Some of these, like *Love Medicine, During the Reign*

Curtis Harnack

of the Queen of Persia, or *The Counterlife*, are well known but need to be word-of-mouthed anyhow. Others, like Alma Stone's *The Banishment*, Douglas Unger's *Leaving the Land*, Linda Collins's *Going to See the Leaves*, and T. Glen Coughlin's *The King of New York* are less so; the mission becomes all that much more urgent. Reissued forgotten gems like Alfred Chester's *The Exquisite Corpse* have to be noticed.

Of course, I'd rather just be writing and let this huckstering be done by critics or somebody else — or would I? The cause is everybody's who is in this business and I fall upon each new crop of glistening-jacketed books with excitement and an anticipation that never tires. The good ones must be ferreted out and talked about. There're never enough of them.

MARK HARRIS

Part One. I don't mean to be rude but the question has holes. What's the good of "more," as in "more attention . . . more readers?" I won't speak to the ratings. Admire me for my virtue.

Mark Harris
photo by
Layle Silbert

Part Two. Think of the novelist as biological. Most of my students are young, and I read what they write, but they do not tell me anything I do not know, and if you send me the young people's writings bound in cardboard stitched together by an eminent publisher it's still the writings of young people and it still doesn't tell me anything I don't know. Nor does it reveal a style I haven't read or even tried myself, among many I tried until I found my own.

Not every *old* novelist is going to interest me, either, but if anything is going to come to me with the thrill of enlightenment it's going to have to come from a writer of my own age and generation. It may even come from one of the hundred thousand young people writing prose fiction everywhere in the world (Melville was in his early thirties when *Moby Dick* appeared) but I know no way of searching out the one in a hundred thousand amidst the clamor of competing claims.

Writers evolve. They are like everybody. Most of their lives they are trapped in themselves. Their struggling realities get in their way. They are working something out of their own psyches, or they are imitating someone else's style. They are raising families and struggling with careers and racing against their peers: still swept up in that old fruitless ratings game.

Difficult for me, overwhelmed by memories of process, to be able to read almost anybody's fiction without noticing his/her intervening or crippling anxieties. I have heard it said that when fine baseball players retire they can't watch baseball games.

"Don't leave your scaffolding up." That's a good rule. Most new novels come to me scaffolding still up — the author's thinking out loud. Stuck into the book is the painful letter of the publisher's editor young but already exhausted, telling me this book will be "exciting," and so forth.

Think of my awful problem as teacher. Nobody told me when I was young how very dim my prospects were, so I don't tell my students. I am the soul of optimistic enthusiastic encouragement. I say, "Go, go, go, you can do it, don't quit now just when you're . . . " I deceive them to stimulate them.

But I'm expecting you'll forgive me if I can't come out in a public statement like this and name the names of authors of "recent writing" more deserving than others. I say "Do it, go for it," cherishing the wisdom of Voltaire's everyday practical experience when Boswell, age twenty-four, in 1764, went to him at Ferney on the day before Christmas, and came away and wrote in his own journal, "I told him that Mr. Johnson and I intended to make a tour through the Hebrides, the Northern Isles of

Scotland. He smiled, and cried, 'Very well; but I shall remain here. You will allow me to stay here?' 'Certainly.' 'Well then, go. I have no objections at all.'"

Am I being clear? Sort of, you say? But come back tomorrow and the day after and again and again and again and it will come clear.

JIM HARRISON

What disturbs me about the situation of the contemporary novel is that it seems mostly a bourgeois preoccupation. Perhaps this is only a reflection of the tertiary period of postmodernism — we have minimalism as a new fixture in the house when it is only naturalism rendered and written very small: it is literature as ornament à la Ronald Firbank, Michael Arlen, Speed Lambkin, et al.

Perhaps in reaction to this sort of writing that seems to emerge from the academy with such resolute insistence, I read a lot of Canadian, South- and Central-American novelists. Also, my tonic for suffocation

Jim Harrison

by the lint which is our contemporary obsession with the media, I read quasi-natural history writers like Peter Matthiessen, Barry Lopez, Gretel Ehrlich, Edward Hoagland, Edward Abbey, and Douglas Peacock. I also do a great deal of reading in poetry, also the history of Native Americans.

I
WILLIAM HERRICK
I

Novels that delve into the politics of our time, that is, the last seventy years. Undogmatic, unpolemic, undidactic political novels that are fueled by the energy of their characters — characters drawn to their political actions by motives *other* than political, as well as characters formed by history. There is enough material there for any writer to equal the output of Anthony Trollope or Honoré de Balzac — the "de" of course a political fiction. If a writer wishes to live and work outside politics, that, too, is a political decision of sorts, and I for one will fight to the death to allow him or her that prerogative.

William Herrick
photo by
Dick Duhan

*Edward Hoagland
photo by
Thomas Victor*

EDWARD HOAGLAND

I don't have much to say about contemporary American fiction. We've got lots of good, serious writers around but no great ones, no geniuses — we're in a trough right now, as far as geniuses go; Singer seems to me the last one alive. We can't help that; genius is an accident of birth. But I am tired of minimalist fiction, or "dirty realism," or whatever term the repetition of Anderson-Farrell-Dreiser-Garland-Crane travels under nowadays.

What would be new from many of our contemporaries would be some demonstration of faith and joy. I don't mind pessimism. God may be dying, but I do suspect that there *was* a God, and most current fiction doesn't think so. One can even believe that the world is about to blow up and yet still be transported with joy at being alive sometimes.

Also, we remain incredibly provincial. Three-fourths of the human race lives on continents never visited by most of our writers, including the more prosperous, peripatetic ones. They buzz back and forth between Michigan and London, instead; visit nowhere that Henry James and F. Scott Fitzgerald didn't go. My point is not that everybody should start writing travel books, but that the Hemingway-Fitzgerald generation got a new view of life, and of America, by traveling places uncommon sixty years ago. And we might too.

It is customary in round-robin commentaries like this to name one's good friends as the best hope for literature, without confessing that they are your good friends. I'd rather just say that Howard Frank Mosher is perhaps my best writing friend, and also an admirable novelist; as are a number of old pals and benefactors of mine — the prodigious Updike, the poignant Roth, the inventive Barthelme — and some former students I've had, like Susan Minot and Charlie Smith; and still other writers whom I've never met, such as Anne Tyler and Louise Erdrich. Blessings on them.

I
WILLIAM HOLINGER
I

The question immediately brings an answer to mind: fiction by Vietnam veterans. I've just read Larry Heinemann's *Paco's Story*, and it made a deep impression on me. It's one of a number of novels "about" the Vietnam War, written by veterans, that deserves a wide

William Holinger
photo by
John Shultz

audience. I'd especially like to see a lot of young people read it. What if it were mandatory reading for all Americans aged 14 to 17? Maybe people would stop joining up. That would force the government to reinstate the draft. That, in turn, would make the government more accountable for the way it uses troops. It might also make young people more politically aware and active.

I am alarmed to see that recruitment in the armed forces is way up (thanks especially, I understand, to the film *Top Gun*).

I am alarmed that current fashion idolizes and idealizes the "military look."

I am alarmed that so many toys sold at Christmastime are replicas of weapons.

If fiction can be political, perhaps one of the political things it can do is this: put readers in touch with the reality of war, with the evils of combat and the horrors of its (combat's) aftermath. Strange irony, isn't it? — that we might rely on fiction to inform us about "reality." It seems as if one sort of fiction must be called on to counteract the illusions created by another sort. So Larry Heinemann's *Paco's Story* must be read as an antidote to *Top Gun*.

(A digression about the film *Platoon*: although you can see Americans feeding blanks into their M-60 machineguns, and although it was difficult to believe Elias outrunning NVA regulars after taking three M-16 rounds in the chest, *Platoon* is still and otherwise a realistic and mostly unromantic depiction of the war in Vietnam. It treats its black characters as complex and valuable individuals; it doesn't sacrifice credibility for narrative excitement, much; and it leaves room for moral ambiguity, and complexity of theme and character. Besides, any film that depicts GIs using diesel fuel to burn off 50-gallon drums full of shit can't be all bad.)

But enough about movies. The question before us is contemporary American fiction.

Paco's Story is about the sole surviving member of a rifle company that has been wiped out by artillery. Paco, still recovering from many wounds and in pain all the time, returns to the United States and settles where his money runs out. As Paco goes about trying to live this strange new life he's been given, the narrative occasionally flashes back to Vietnam. The novel is narrated — at times in the first person plural — by the ghosts of his company's dead, and this spooky narrative voice addresses the reader — sometimes angrily — as "James." It can be disconcerting; it probably takes a touch of masochism to read this book. Given its subject and intent, this is appropriate. We are meant to suffer, along with Paco. It is a redeeming experience.

Two other compelling, nonromanticized novels with the Vietnam War in them are Kenn Miller's *Tiger the Lurp Dog* and Tim O'Brien's *Going After Cacciato*. I can recommend them highly; these works of fiction deserve a wider audience.

Of course, in our discussion of American fiction, let us not overlook fiction by non-Americans: stories and novels written by Vietnamese, Koreans, Nicaraguans, Africans, Filipinos, Mexicans. . . . Americans are often insensitive and ignorant where other cultures are concerned; in fiction, not only do we get information about others (again: "facts" or "reality"), but we also get their *point of view*. Fiction, more than film, far more than journalism, has the power to put us, so to speak, in someone else's shoes. To read someone else's story — if that story is true and honest and well told — is to *become* that person (character). I'm in favor of that. It's more difficult, morally and emotionally, to blow people up if you know and understand them, if you've fully imagined their lives — if you've "been" them. I wish our leaders read good fiction. And I hope our young people will.

JOHN CLELLON HOLMES

My thoughts on recent American fiction are somewhat jaundiced by the circumstances that led me, a year ago, to resign from the staff of the Writing Program at the University of Arkansas after a decade there. It had been a good ten years, but I wasn't sorry to leave. Every nine months or so, I worked on a dozen or so student stories, nursing them from conception to term, mother-henning them, good or bad, as if they were my own, and by the spring of 1986 I was as viscerally sick of the act of fictioning as a gynecologist is of human plumbing. Simply, I had come to detest the nuts and bolts of making stories.

Now after a year of preparing two collections of nonfiction for the publisher, I feel like a fiction writer again — wayward, impatient, nervy, curious, and eager for that first magic seizure in the imagination that might eventually become a story. Nevertheless, my opinions about what's been happening in the genre during the last years are neither generous nor balanced, I'm afraid.

John Clellon Holmes

I still wait, mostly in vain, for the big novels that so pulse with human riches, fair and foul, that one's life is enhanced for having read them. I still look, again mostly in vain, for the great *styles* that make a collection of characters and events mysteriously cohere into a world, that peculiarly mesmerizing way with language that is the ultimate vehicle for a writer's vision. I find no Faulkners, no Fitzgeralds, in American writing now; no Gabriel García Márquez or Yukio Mishima. No one seems seized by the big emotions any more, neither the writers nor the people they create. We shy away from the oversize passions as if they were uncool. We work within our successes, no longer going for the risks that result in the important failures. Well-crafted, cautious, safe, instantly gratifying, the fiction of today seems to do little but reassure us in a sulky and unexamined pessimism about the human condition. Cleverness, bitterness, and irony seem to at once vitiate and express the extent of our energies.

Perhaps the very nature of late-century American experience is such that any single, encompassing perspective is impossible to maintain beyond midnight, and vivid moments surfacing out of the general confusion are all that we can manage. As always at such times, the short story flourishes. Raymond Carver, Andre Dubus, Cynthia Ozick, Tobias Wolff, Anne Tyler, Jim Harrison, Lewis Nordan, Lee K. Abbott, and others still pull me up short sometimes, and give me that marvelous and creepy feeling of having looked through a lighted window on a winter's night, and seen into the mystery of existences utterly separate from my own.

These writers occasionally suggest the sort of moment that Dostoyevsky caught in *A Raw Youth* when Dolgoruky's peasant-mother, confused and shamed by her son's insufferably exacerbated ego, actually *bows* to him when they part, just as if he was the well-born Versilov who had fathered him and refused to marry her. When Alfred Kazin wrote of that bow that Dostoyevsky had somehow been able to "lift the whole curtain of history and its appearances, and that what is before us is nothing less than the innermost pang of life and the eternal appeal, beyond all the power of speech and action, that one human being can make to another," he was describing the kind of truth that only great fiction can reveal, the sort of perception that is beyond the reach of philosophy or psychology, that rarefied sphere of intuitive recognitions that is the special realm of art. I see little of this sort of thing being sought for today. Are we to conclude that we don't experience life at this intensity any longer? Have we become so guarded one from the other that our characters are no longer willing to bet their lives on love and rage, hope and despair? When do accurate, needle-nose accounts of the impossibility of human contact cease to be laments and become celebrations of the condition?

The stuff I tend to like shares something with the so-called Magic Realists. Not fantasy, sci-fi or otherwise; not fable or parable. But realism (always the lifeblood of fiction) touched with the wilder swings of the freed imagination engaged in *redeeming* existence, the urgent response of a highly individualized sensibility to the drama of human character in confluence with time.

Fortunately for all dire prognostications, there's never been a lot of exceptional fiction around at any given time. The Chekhovs, Lawrences, and Hemingways were rare birds in eras more conducive to fiction than ours. Still, I never lose hope. What sometimes haunts me, however, is the suspicion that the audience may be changing. The attention span relentlessly shortens. Diversion seems to be as imperious a need in the modern reader as sensation in the orgiast. But great fiction demands that we think and feel as whole, and wholly conscious, human beings, and it is dependent on a moral vision that is as innate in the reader as it is in the writer. Whether such conditions exist today seems to me to be up for grabs. But I prefer *not* to believe that new and narrower and more gelid sensibilities have been machine-tooled by our computerized culture to survive the bleakly technological winters that lie ahead.

In my own case, it's once again become a matter of putting up or shutting up, and I look forward to the perilous plunge into the dark and heedless river of fiction again, hoping that it may get me to the moment (which must have been triumphant for Faulkner) when the returned-convict in *The Old Man* could finally say, "All right. Yonder's your boat, and here's the woman. But I never did find that bastard on the cottonhouse."

That bastard on the cottonhouse — the most elusive prize of all, the one that's worth the perils of the river-flood. It seems to me that at the very least we should go on looking for him.

JAMES D. HOUSTON

They say this world we all inhabit gets a little smaller every day, thanks to satellites and direct dialing and jumbo jets. Yet in the realm of human-to-human knowledge, huge gulfs remain. Maybe they will always remain. But in recent years I have learned a lot from writers who possess a grasp of two cultures at the same time. It is a rare gift, always accompanied by a special wisdom. They open windows from one world to another, from one culture to another. I always listen

James D. Houston
photo by
Barbara Hall

carefully and watch closely when I come across someone who has seen beyond a cultural border.

I think first of such writers as Leslie Silko, James Welch, Louise Erdrich, N. Scott Momaday, Gerald Vizenor, who bring to their works an implicit understanding of two opposing ways of life that have been in struggle on this continent for centuries: the Native American and the transplanted Anglo/European.

I think of Maxine Hong Kingston, whose books, *Woman Warrior* (1976), *China Men* (1980), *Tripmaster Monkey: His Fake Book* (1989), explore two worlds simultaneously. Her stories depend upon a knowledge of both China and the United States, Chinese dreams and American dreams. Early in *Woman Warrior*, she writes:

> After I grew up I heard of Fa Mu Lan, the girl who took her father's place in battle. Instantly I remembered that as a child I had followed my mother about the house, the two of us singing about how Fa Mu Lan fought gloriously and returned alive from war to settle in the village. I had forgotten this chant that was once mine, given me by my mother, who may not have known its power to remind.

An old chant crosses the wide water, from a village near Canton, where the mother first heard it, to nourish the daughter/writer growing up in Stockton, California.

The Woman Warrior also plays along the border between fiction and nonfiction, drawing upon Kingston's Asian ancestry, via an amazing mix of personal memory, family history, myth and magic and humor, to give us a fresh and original trans-Pacific vision.

In a darker and more violent way Robert Stone accomplishes something similar in *A Flag for Sunrise*, his 1981 novel set in the imagined Central American republic of Tecan, during a time of political turmoil. His characters come from both sides of the U.S. border, north and south, and the writing reveals a detailed understanding of these two joined but vastly differing regions and populations. In this novel, three groups of Americans, unknown to one another, are being drawn toward the ferment of impending revolution. Stone does a great deal more than chart their adventures in an exotic landscape. American attitudes and values are being profoundly tested. It is a novel wherein one social and cultural environment tests and illuminates some fundamental assumptions of another.

In that sense, Stone's novel has a kinship with D. H. Lawrence's *The Plumed Serpent* and E. M. Forster's *A Passage to India*, two classic works of this type. Through Lawrence's double lens we see into Mexico. Through

Forster's we see into India; at the same time, against that landscape and history and climate, something essentially English and Western is being measured and held up to a relentless light.

The point is not that some new level of cross-cultural harmony should emerge from such writing (though one always hopes it is a possibility). Rather, one culture can hold a mirror to another — just as the female can define the male, and vice versa — helping us to see *the other, the stranger,* with clearer eyes, and more importantly, helping us to see and know ourselves.

I
ROBERT HOUSTON
I

The kind of writing that interests me most is work in which something matters because the people matter, and the world of those people matters. Hollywood doesn't matter much, nor do the people to whom Hollywood matters. Somebody whose greatest perceived conflict is whether or not to ride the subway doesn't matter much, at least to serious fiction. A character who is in despair because she or he has to pay $2,000 a month for a cubbyhole apartment in a city that's

Robert Houston
photo by
Boyd Nicholl

uninhabitable anyway doesn't matter much except to the relatively few other people who despair over the same thing. People in books who maunder about the nuances of their "relationships"—fashionably neurotic ones at that—in redone farmhouses are only microcosms of the microcosmic. Writers who write stories full of one-liner jokes and call that humor don't matter much more than postmodernists—not much more, but some.

John Berger, the art critic, says that Picasso was a "vertical invader," someone who suddenly sprang onto the stage of European art from a trapdoor that none of the other actors even realized was there. Those trapdoors are springing open in the Midwest, the West, the South, New England, now. Writers like Garrison Keillor and Raymond Carver and Edward Abbey and Ron Powers and Rolando Hinojosa have sprung them, writers who are finding the sources of their fiction and nonfiction in the people who have been ignored (as subjects *and* as readers) in favor of the superficial and manufactured and marketed. A return to anything—dull regionalism or shopworn realism—isn't what's going on, or if it is it won't be much more interesting than it was the first time around. What's truly of interest is the discovery that America is still here, after all, and that its potential for writers who will look at its heart is still vast. Call the movement Anti-Slick, and be glad for it: it may just give us back our readership.

I
DAVID HUDDLE
I

What I keep hoping for is somebody who will really put to use that manic prose we've been seeing in flashes for the past twenty years or so, in Leonard Michaels's "City Boy," Tom McGuane's *Ninety-Two in the Shade*, Toni Cade Bambara's "Gorilla, My Love" and "The Johnson Girls," Barry Hannah's *Airships*, Jayne Anne Phillips's "Lechery," and elsewhere. I'd love to see an emotionally substantial, thematically rigorous novel or long story sustained in that quirky, souped-up, highly textured prose so filled with energy that it almost flies off the page. Long stories, such as Peter Taylor's "The Old Forest" or Andre Dubus's "The Pretty Girl," seem to me to be the least appreciated fine work of the day. But I think it's a lively time for fiction; various good novels and stories are being written, published, and read. I can think

*David Huddle
photo by
Donna Kaplan*

of thirty or forty American writers whose first or next books I'm eager to read.

CHARLES JOHNSON

In his December 1986 essay in the *Washington Post*, entitled "Americans Don't Value Good Writing," Jonathan Yardley places the blame for our present crisis in education and the tragedy of widespread illiteracy where it properly belongs. "The skill of writing — not to mention the art — has never been held in especially high repute among Americans, but its standing in the age of television and technology is especially low, with the entirely predictable consequence that it is not being taught competently in the schools." And why is this? Yardley adds, "Americans are too busy getting ahead . . . to care whether their writing does anything more than get the job done; and since just about everybody writes poorly, or indifferently, it doesn't take much to do that."

Unlike the British, and one might add the French and Germans, we do not have a tradition of writing excellence, according to Yardley. "Writing," in America, he says, "as something to be mastered—as a skill valuable in its own right—is, and always has been, given short shrift." And he observes that "skillful writing—forceful, witty, persuasive—is almost as common in British culture as it is rare in America." Sadly, he sees little reason for hope, concluding that since "Americans are not regular readers, and most of what they do read is not well written," we have virtually institutionalized "minimal competence" in our schools, our books, even in our thought about education.

I've bullied all my students and friends into studying this grouchy essay because what is at stake in the idea of writing as a centuries-old *discipline* is our very capacity to reason, which democracy itself, at least in its classical definition, requires, i.e., a voting public smart enough to recognize rot, rhetoric, and demagoguery when they see it. Each word in Webster's is, when you think about it, like an old coin handled by millions; each, with its various meanings, is a tissue of experiences and interpretations of our predecesors crystallized into word. Each sentence, whether it takes the form of asyndeton or antimetabole, is a basic unit of logic or reasoning insofar as the structure we impose on experience subtly transforms the expression and experience itself. Technique *is* vision. Style *is* sense. "Every sentence is a risk," Sartre once wrote, because what is at risk whenever we speak is what things *mean*. And once you move to larger units of expression—the novel or story—you see beyond all doubt that fiction is not simply about "entertainment," though it pro-

Charles Johnson
photo by
Wayne Sourbeer

duces this pleasure too, but is at its core one of the most important means at our disposal for the ongoing chore of making sense of the world of consciousness and culture. Fiction's materials, being as close as they are to those of other interpretative disciplines (such as philosophy and history), demand that we see the act of writing well as identical to the act of thinking well.

For these reasons, and a few more, I'm only interested in ambitious, carefully wrought, innovative, intelligent fiction by writers who exhibit what Northrop Frye once called, "an educated imagination." Minimalist stories and supermarket fiction that sidestep the adventurous possibilities of metaphor, skim the surface of life, and hold back the explosion of many forms of diction on the page produce, in my opinion, stories that are thin and *detotalized* and lacking in the rich, interpretative possibilities of language and literary form. They deny us breadth of vision, depth of seeing, the thrill of exploring new territory, and scale down the cross-cultural treasure of words and ways of speech that are our inheritance as creators. And as human beings. Similarly, I prefer writers who are conscious of the possibilities of literary form — the innumerable forms and styles of narrative art, each of which can be seen as a distinct method of reasoning, with its own strengths and limitations: forms that are for a smart writer the very foundation of contemporary literary practice. And to this, finally, I must add that I prefer writers who have something original to *say*. Excuse me, but I think that's important. I read for three reasons: to laugh, to cry, and to learn something. You can call these "philosophical writers," if you wish. But a better way of putting this is to say these are the American writers, most of them still young or at least under fifty, who are guided by aesthetic goals greater than the best-seller list or the latest literary fashions; they are creators who find in the processes of fiction a way to carefully dramatize right down to the last detail a complex, convincing vision of the world. And, by doing this, they bring a measure of clarity to our own lives. These are writers who can probe lives other than their own. They can plot. And yes, they are prose-stylists as well, artists who in their work teach us anew how to use the common, expressive instrument called English.

Such writers are rare among us, these novelists and storytellers who first of all understand the theory and technique of great fiction; who, secondly, find in their predecessors models — artistic and metaphysical — for the future; and, thirdly, who *advance* the form of the novel or story with each new work they attempt. But, though rare, these are the writers I believe deserve readership in a steadily declining culture where, as

Yardley observes, true language skills and thinking skills have nearly been lost.

Among these American writers I would list Barry Holstun Lopez, whose books *Winter Count* and *Arctic Dreams* I'd be proud to give as presents to anyone, even to the grumpiest philosopher. Even to a positivist. No, especially to a positivist. Other gifts worth giving are the brutally honest short fiction of James Alan McPherson, novels of Linsey Abrams and Russell Banks, Clarence Major's fabulous *My Amputations*, virtually anything of Scott Sanders, Nicholas Delbanco, and Fred Pfeil, all of John Gardner, Larry Woiwode's gentle but little-read *Poppa John*, the plays of Jay Wright, poetry of James Bertolino and Liz Rosenberg, and whatever you can lay your hands on by Robley Wilson, Jr. and Mary Elsie Robertson. Obviously, this list could go on and on, naming dozens of fine writers I fear may not be familiar to you, for one consequence of daring to write seriously—for trying to *think* seriously, and with both eyes fixed on the high-wire of artistic and intellectual achievement set by our elders—is that in an age dominated by television and throwaway fiction you may, for all your sweat and sacrifice, remain unknown.

Underground is often where you find our most exciting writers of fiction, their painstakingly sculpted works appearing in literary magazines with goofy names and through small press and university publications. Clearly, these magazines, always short on money and space, deserve more readers, especially now when "industrial fiction" (as Pfeil calls it) from the commercial houses reads as if it were written for instant translation into a Hollywood film. A librarian friend of mine recently called my attention yet again to the lack of formal and linguistic complexity in American mass-market writing, to the absence of challenging characters, and dramatic scenes multilayered in their meaning (as in, say, certain scenes in William Gaddis's *The Recognitions*), as if anything that could not easily be rewritten as a film-script had been eliminated. Many editors, I know, are *trying* to release first-rate fiction, and hunger for it, and celebrate with parties for the whole staff when they score the acceptance of a risky novel with the sales department. But they can't do enough, which means that the proving ground for our literary pioneers must be, as it was for many authors in the 1920s and '30s, in the small presses.

Go there.

Steve Katz

I
STEVE KATZ
I

What do we read? I read whatever is in front of my eyes when I have time to read. Some of it is the wrong stuff, like the latest manufactured trend, so-called new minimalist fiction where banality gets another flutter of attention, as in the last two issues of the *Mississippi Review*. This clutters the desk and bookshelf with a lot of bland, timid stuff. Most of the writers collected by their guest editor, David Leavitt, seem like clones off one of John Updike's warts, producing tedious sentimental reiterations of American middle-class values. That seems to be the trend promoted by an increasingly conformist, cowardly corporate publishing establishment. It was refreshing to get a new publication out of Buffalo, N.Y., called *Blatant Artifice*, with an intense, passionate, righteous response by its editor, Edmund Cardoni, to the *Mississippi Review* blancmange. He also selects an exciting range of mostly young writers for his publication that give me some reassurance that a few new writers are trying to respond to the need for a storytelling appropriate to the nauseating double-talk of our recent history with something more passionate, more formally explosive, more impulsive, more educated in its investigation of the heart of America. Some other journals are trying to survive the deadening trends, like *Black Ice* out of Oregon, and of course *Fiction International* in San Diego, trudging along with Larry McCaffery and Harold Jaffe at the helm.

Of course I think some writers who captured and held my interest in the last ten years or so are being neglected, so "deserving of more attention and readers." Some of them are formally or linguistically complicated, like Paul Metcalf, whose carefully choreographed montages, like *U. S. Department of Interior* and *The Middle Passage*, cut an interesting track through several histories, and Carol Emshwiller's wonderful lost book *Joy in Our Cause* that makes you feel the whole cerebral dance of her womanhood. Paul Zelevansky's unique books, obtuse, personal, inspired storytelling through visual signifiers and reinvented language, deserve some celebration somewhere. And why doesn't someone bring out again and celebrate Madeline Gins's *Word Rain*, a playful, serene book that puts self-reflexivity to rest forever, would save a lot of young writers a lot of trouble. One of the most energizing books the Fiction Collective has published is Yuriy Tarnowsky's *Meningitis*, a sequence of fictions that reconstruct the Updike milieu in formal patterns that expose the addictive, destructive obsessions of middle-American life. Two books by young writers under the same imprint that should get more attention are Mark Leyner's *I Smell Esther Williams* and Judy Lopatin's *Modern Romance*. Bernadette Mayer's recent prose works should be available to more than its New York audience, as should Dallas Wiebe's adventurous fictions find an audience beyond Cincinatti. What happened to Michael Stephens' *A Season at Coole*, and to Ted Mooney's *Easy Travel to Other Planets*? Rudolph Wurlitzer's low-keyed, luminous novels, a unique threesome in American fiction, *Nog*, *Flats*, and *Quake*, are nowhere available, and his recent Hollywood novel, *Slow Fade*, faded before its virtuosity and intelligence found its witness. Being published by the major houses is like being erased these days. They seem to print the books in order to see how fast they can get them to the remainder house, or better yet, the shredder. All the books mentioned above need time to build their audiences, time on the bookstore shelves, and that kind of bookstore, with real shelf life, hardly exists any more. Even mainstream books I admire, like Norman Rush's *Whites*, or Russell Banks's *Continental Drift* are disappeared from consciousness before the dialogue and debate they can potentially stimulate begins. In the struggle to sell more product, the publishing industry seems to be eating its own tail. Two other potentially mainstream books I admire, Chuck Wachtel's *Joe the Engineer*, and Vicki Lindner's *Outlaw Games* got lost in the flood of product. Happily Sun & Moon Press has just reissued in paperback one of my favorite novels, Michael Brownstein's hilarious, poignant, innovative, crazy, *Country Cousins*. If you haven't read it, treat yourself. Marianne Hauser is a national treasure kept in the attic. Her peculiar point of view of the world and her impeccable, witty, acerbic prose are displayed brilliantly in her two last books, *The Talking Room* and *The Memoirs of the Late Mr. Ashley*. But she herself can't find copies of *Ishmael*, and her other, early, highly praised works. Our culture is amnesiac. What has happened to Hubert Selby, Jr.? An evening alone with *Last Exit to Brooklyn* will minimalize the "new minimalists." I could go on, but I'll stop here in Brooklyn. A lot of wonderful writing has passed my quirky taste test in recent years. We live in one of the most exciting "periods" of American writing. There's great variety, and an intensity of deep formal, spiritual, and social exploration. It's a time as rich as the post-World War II period in American painting, and the seventies in American music, but only the most conservative trends are touted. The "reality" is obvious, and inevitable in our time, the business of publishing is only business.

I

JANET KAUFFMAN

I

In American culture, the supply and demand economy of *things* — real things, or at least things that look real — has driven a tremendous technology. We want strawhats; we get strawhats. We find them — handmade or manufactured. Imported, maybe. We find them. We order what we want. American know-how and "technique" encourages (whether in fiction or in the Taiwan factory) the fabrication of strawhats in quantity, in intricate detail, very often plastic of course, but realistic, strawlike hats, good for a couple of parties. In the trademark no-nonsense, good-humor spirit of American realism, we point out, yes, what they do with presses and plastics, it's really something. Ambivalent, but accustomed to the ambivalence, we admire, it's cheap, but that's a wonder. Look at the detailing. What a world. What a hat.

The myth of the cheap party hat in American economic life has a mirror-myth in American fiction. In his introduction to *The Best American Short Stories, 1986*, Raymond Carver praises and grants special value to stories with "realistic, 'life-like' characters . . . in realistically

Janet Kauffman

detailed situations." He is drawn to these, he says, rather than to "stories where method or technique is all — stories, in short, where nothing much happens." But think about it: what Carver describes is a completely *technical* realism, as conventionally American as a Burger King Whopper, and not a fiction necessarily truer or better or more worthy of praise — though such stories may be praiseworthy and remarkable for plenty of *other* reasons.

In notable foreign fiction, and in less-noted American fiction, realism of the technical, "life-like" variety is not a crucial element and certainly not a goal. There are all the names we know, from elsewhere: García Márquez, Nathalie Sarraute, Beckett, Kundera, Calvino, Coetzee, and on and on. These fictions acknowledge various realities and allow the world, in its various conceptions, to assume a shape in words. The language is not made transparent, to offer a see-through, realistic story. Instead, we find these fictions variously, idiosyncratically, confronting the real-worldiness of language; or the invisible life of the mind and imagination; or the mix and mess of life in nature, not necessarily human.

American fictions in the 1980s often remain as automatically "realistic" as the President figures walking and talking at Disney World. Yes, what we do with presses and plastics, it *is* something. But for American fiction, and no doubt for American culture, it is crucial to acknowledge the conventions, the devices, the paradox of its realism. One of the conventions of realistic characterization, for example, is this: objects are clues to personality; and the personal, psychological "self" is some kind of core. This fiction centers on interpersonal drama and event, so that if Mr. Montauk, in a strawhat, goes to the party, that is a realistic action (but if the trees along the way lie down, or stand there, cumbersome, extraneous — that is something else). A customized, realistic American story is a written story, of course, made up of words, although the words are typically *disappeared*, as *trompe l'oeil* hats, husbands and wives, Camaros, unencumbered trees. I am a great fan of trees in literature (in fact a fan of all weather and unhoused nature in fiction). But I love most of all when those trees, that weather, are undeniably, blatantly wordmade.

Some of the most interesting contemporary American fictions diverge from technical realism and make themselves evident as written-out fictions: consider Donald Barthelme, just about any day; Barry Hannah, in extremis; Lydia Davis; numerous poets-in-fiction — Grace Paley, all that talk; Ron Silliman, in *Paradise*; and think of Carver, too, whose work is surely less praiseworthy for its "realism" than for its severe and scrupulously cut sentence-work, in *What We Talk About When We Talk About Love*, for instance, where the writing sets one stark sentence after another. What is real in reading those stories is the fearsome order and blunt, cumulative power, for sudden, sheer dead-endedness, of the sentences. It is not the "life-like" detail or realistic situations that make these stories important reading, but the visible language itself, the human evidence of it.

American fiction needs, as the culture needs, all kinds of *dis-illusioning* (not illusioned; not disillusioned) work. We need to attend to fictions that are variously worded — with vagaries of talk, speculation; with unfamiliar patterns and meshes of ideas and attentions to a world-at-large; with human event skewed sometimes away from the center of things; with nothing guaranteed, for a change; with a visible language circuitry, wherein the mind can move.

When I open a book, I want to read. And it matters to me, not so much whether there are characters or events I can believe, as whether the words comprise crucial human evidence. I want to have the writing. In my ears, in my head. Some readers may not recognize fiction except as a see-through story; some writers may not either. But fictions are *always* worded, written. At least as long as the paper lasts, that's where the human record lies.

Richard Kostelanetz   photo by J. Nebraska Gifford

I
RICHARD KOSTELANETZ
I

My taste in fiction matured during the editing of two anthologies, *Future's Fictions* (1981) and *Breakthrough Fictioneers* (1973), which I'm told remain indisputably the most "way-out" ever done. There has been no need for me to progress beyond those touchstones, because hardly anyone else has caught up. In fiction, as in everything else in art, I am most impressed by alternatives that are radically unlike anything already known; and so in fiction, I am especially interested in work that moves well beyond not only the masterpieces of modernism but the avant-garde that became accepted as I came of critical age (in fiction, Barth, Pynchon, Burroughs). Examining my current taste, I find that the new works I like best innovate either within the materials of literature itself, especially language, or by mixing literary concerns with the materials of such other arts as design and music. Out of the former motive of purification come the distinguished sentences of, say, Kenneth

Gangemi's *Olt* (1970) and Richard Grayson's best stories, the abstract semantics of Madeline Gins's *Word Rain* (1969) and many books by Stanley Berne and Arlene Zekowski, the fictionalizing of nonfiction conventions in both Richard Horn's *Encyclopedia* (1969) and Donald Porter's *As If a Footnote* (1974), in addition to Raymond Federman's *Take It or Leave It* (1976) with its explorations of a bilingual sensibility and Bradley Lastname's *The Secret Presidential Diary of William Henry Harrison* (1986) with its ironic facsimiles of various expository styles. I know enough French to recognize the stylistic originality of Jean-François Bory's *An Auteur sous Influence* (1986), but wait for an English translation before I risk characterizing it. Need I add that even in 1987 I still read with continuing wonderment James Joyce's *Finnegans Wake* and the more experimental prose of Gertrude Stein.

When literature is mixed with calligraphy and picture the result is visual fiction, where a lot of major work has been done: Duane Michaels's photographic *Sequences* (1970); Raymond Federman's *Double or Nothing* (1971), whose recent German translation gives a clearer notion of how the American edition should have been looked at; M. Vaughn-James's books which appeared in Canada more than a decade ago, while his shorter pieces appear nowadays in Paris; Tom Phillips's *A Humument* (1980), which finally appeared between hard covers, even though it was finished more than a dozen years before and pages had appeared in magazines around the world; Paul Zelevansky's multipath visual-verbal fiction for Apple II computer disc, in addition to his several spectacularly designed volumes with both image and text. To me these books, among others similar in kind, represent a continuing avant-garde in fiction.

More recently, I've been attuned to discovering, and perhaps making, acoustic fictions, which is to say narratives that must be heard to be understood, because they exist primarily on audiotape. Consider Mark Ensign Cory's description of a crucial episode in Naoya Uchimura's radio play *Marathon* (1958):

> The plot is carried by two micro-durational or rhythmic figures: the anapest of [the runner's] breathing and the iambus of his footsteps. Each can be extremely effective, as in the moment when the steady rhythm of [the runner's] controlled breathing begins to falter, or when the clean beat of his footsteps becomes uncertain and then is momentarily obscured by a passing competitor.

I have found inklings of such fictional possibilities in the audiotapes of Walter Bachauer in Germany (especially the *Das Ohrenlicht*, 1984, produced with Ronald Steckel); Frits Weiland in Holland (*Orient Express*);

and Lars Gunnar Bodin in Sweden. Because such fiction speaks mostly in the international language of expressive sound, it need not be translated to be understood. Having become myself heavily involved in radio composition, especially for German stations, I've been planning to work in this area myself; but without a position in American radio, or sufficient sympathy for such experiment in our literary agencies, it is hard to get appropriate support here to use machines and materials that are, alas, more expensive than typewriters and paper.

I could go on, talking about principles and enthusiasms I've advocated for over a decade now — principles and enthusiasms that have so little presence in classrooms today, at a time when everything prominent has been heavily merchandized, if not by merchants then by publicists, that I am prepared to give a B.A. (bull's ass) to anyone who has read five of the authors mentioned above, an M.A. (mother's amulet) for anyone knowing eight and, finally, to anyone knowing them all, a D. Fict. (fictitious doctorate) *cum very louda*. While this work hasn't penetrated self-styled literary consciousnesses here, it does have impact upon practitioners, and enthusiasts, in the other arts; and that fact, always true for genuinely avant-garde work in this backward and innocent country, leads me to believe that it will survive, as art can only survive, not in the classroom or in the publishing houses but in the aesthetic memories of cultured people.

I
JAMES McCONKEY
I

Though President Reagan would be surprised to hear it, and most practitioners of fiction would indignantly deny it, I believe that our chief executive has primary responsibility for the current renaissance of fiction in America. As the expression of the individual voice, one separate from the social realm, poetry gains ascendancy in periods of national crisis and doubt, as during the Vietnam War; fiction, connected as it is to the societal framework, composed of characters who are responding to the "real" world, requires at least a minimal acceptance of, and faith in, society.

The revelations about our clandestine selling of arms to Iran, with a portion of the proceeds from the sale illegally supporting the Contras in their struggle to overthrow the leftist government in Nicaragua, pres-

James McConkey   photo by Jim C. McConkey

ently have diminished Reagan's popularity, based as it is on his personal appeal as a practical-minded and honest man, as well as on his faith and confidence in free enterprise, national purpose, and the morality of the United States. Still, his optimism has bolstered traditional values and the institutional status quo; and, in so doing, has provided fiction writers with a social environment respectable enough so that their characters can be defined within it.

I say this with considerable irony, but without facetiousness. For quite a few years, the most influential fiction writer in the country has been Ronald Reagan, who has been refashioning the happy myths we most would like to hear, the stories that dispel social malaise and support pride in personal and national achievement. Certainly the genre of fiction has been abetted by the wide-flowing praise of things-as-they-are that has its central fount in the Oval Office.

It should be added, however, that self-respecting writers of fiction respond not only to general attitudes of the populace but to their own, often unformulated, musings about human potential, particularly about the possible inability of our race to survive its greeds, fears, and aggressions. Generalizations always simplify; but, to my mind, the above explains the antithesis that I find in the contemporary storytelling renaissance. On one hand much of our fiction acquiesces in the status quo, in an acceptance of institutions that reflects our president's good cheer and mighty sword; on the other, it tends toward a minimalism that suggests spiritual paralysis. The latter quality emanates from the writers' own insights, and prevents them from permitting hope or even enlightenment to the characters they have dreamed up to live in the strengthened society. The antithesis itself has produced a tension congenial to creative prose, though undeniably it prevents the writers from obtaining the popular success of the master artificer of the age.

A vital and durable fiction probably requires a more justified belief in human structures and in the spiritual integrity of the people who live within them than we now possess, and so the renaissance may be a temporary affair. Nevertheless, the young and still unpublished writers currently studying at Cornell, undergraduate and graduate students alike, are writing some of the strongest fiction I have read since the days of Thomas Pynchon and Richard Farina, and their work shows a happy disregard of all institutions, including the one that pays for my upkeep. If Ronald Reagan has had an unacknowledged hand in their achievements, I can say only that the seeds of conservatism, like all other seeds, contain a few capable of destroying the intended crop.

Recently I have read some novels that, because they elude any possible generalization about the current state of fiction, may not get the attention they deserve. I admire Roberta Silman's second novel, *The Dream Dredger*, because it first establishes a seemingly coherent social environment and then convincingly demonstrates a woman driven into madness within it; I admire Edward Hower's *Wolf Tickets*, also a second novel, because it uses as social metaphor a reformatory for young women, and makes the troubled and rebellious inmates matter to me, while showing the degree to which the institution abets their feelings of alienation and hopelessness. I think Joanna Scott's first novel, *Fading, My Parmacheene Belle*, a remarkable achievement by a young writer, for it contains the most moving scenes involving an elderly and lonely and hallucinating man I've come across since my first exposure to Lear on the heath.

I suppose one reason I am attracted to these works is that in none of them does a central character passively accept the contemporary world, as he or she finds it. Maybe only in rebellion do we truly exist, as characters or citizens. And maybe Ronald Reagan's ultimate contribution to fiction has been to give us, at last, something tangible enough so that we can rebel.

Colleen J. McElroy
photo by
Carl Vandermevlen

COLLEEN J. McELROY

What saddens me most about trends in contemporary American fiction is the general notion that good writing depends on a best-seller list (however that is compiled), as if good can only be equated to what ($)sells and what sells is dependent on what is reviewed as good. While best-seller lists could, and sometimes do, reflect the craft and energy a writer has brought to the work, too often readers fail to use their own judgment in selecting books, and instead, depend exclusively on these lists to steer them to what is "good." Everyone (who is anyone) reads the same handful of books. This type of dependency promotes a general illiteracy among readers. Some lose their sense of adventure, their need to explore new realms of literature. The country becomes, then, a democratic state with socialistic reading habits, habits that would have us all swimming in the same waters, hooked on the common notion that only a best seller is worth reading.

Viewed objectively, not as a writer or teacher of writing but as a curious bystander, I might say the trend is partly caused by a so-called consumer appetite that ravenously eats and discards, with equal speed, everything new, everything that cannot be cut into a series of episodes or put on instant replay available in supermarkets everywhere. I see readers who spend more time perusing the best-seller lists and the quick-fix review columns than the lists of books-in-print. Unless a book is prominently displayed in recent magazine or newspaper review sections, it goes by unnoticed. But this notion only makes the victims, in this case, the reading public, solely responsible for the crime against them.

Perhaps, then, the real culprit is the conglomerate business concern that has supplanted the legendary publishing house of the past. Books have become a product of business, and as with any other business, the product is ranked (by laboratory tests? by independent researchers? by reviewers?) according to lists of popularity. Could the fault lie with a voracious business that supplies all those supermarket book racks and bookstore shelves cluttered with the pop pablum stock-in-trade, a business that says, "If it sells it's good and whoever sells is a good writer? But if there is supply, there must be demand. Somebody is writing That Stuff.

What is That Stuff? Too often, those books hit the list as a result of media hype over some instant biography by some instant "personality," or worse yet, writing that seems to have the same popularity as the newest fad in jeans, the newest wave in cocktails, the hottest war, or the latest angst of political failure — this decade's celebrity literature. Many of the writers have found their niche by relying on superficial images, or stereotypes, or in worst case scenarios, misinformation, and the books are as facile and brittle as any midday soap opera. After all, how far can you go with an eight-year-old's autobiography, a twenty-year-old's tiresome account of boredom in the big city, or a former politician's confession of corrption?

A sad state. By my best recollection, my love of literature — and certainly, my romance with language — came as a result of a favorite aunt telling me to "read everything." I did. I became a subversive reader, discovering writers I would not have encountered otherwise. In my search for lessons on how to survive childhood, I read stories of adventuresome young girls. For want of dark-skinned female characters, I read stories with dark-haired women as heroes (or villains — I hadn't made up my mind as to which side I would join, and perhaps I haven't yet). Feeling distanced from the culture of mainstream middle America (that mythical place that supposedly embodies all of our desires), I read stories of distant cultures. I discovered a world — not an elliptical, singularly Western-minded English-language world, but one of such diversity, its possibilities seemed endless.

These were not books read only because they appeared on a best-seller list or the required "great books" assigned by the English teacher. These were no looky-loo writers of pop culture full of risk-free stories of easy reading that would not disturb the melting pot myth. These were stories by writers who wrote from experience, who used life as stock-in-trade, and knew the heart of their own cultures. Thse books were not written for readers with limited attention spans—built on a history of television viewing—the authors of these stories used the language of authority and authenticity to cause readers to think. And thankfully, they are still out there. Younger, perhaps; wiser, no doubt; and just as often beyond the confines of the latest best-seller list.

Take an afternoon and look for them. With luck, you might discover, as I have, Cecile Pindar's fine novel, *Face*, Sherely Anne Williams's *Dessa Rose*, Al Young's wonderful blues trilogy of nonfiction essays, *Stones for Ibarra* by Harriet Doerr, Gloria Naylor's *Mama Day*, the reprint of Jane Bowles's *My Sister's Hand in Mine*, or Octavia Butler's *Kindred*. You'll need to search those small bookstores that thrive, somehow, without national syndication. More than ever, these stores need your support. You'll need to frequent university bookstores, those ubiquitous suppliers of literary anthologies and textbook supplies. Quite often you'll need to make demands on a local book-seller. Take heart. The search is well worth the effort.

JAY McINERNEY

The kind of fiction I am most interested in is that which is in some sense not a kind at all. Ezra Pound said "make it new," and I humbly concur. The fiction that I want to read shocks me into looking at the language and narrative anew, makes me privy to an act of primary perception. A great deal of what we read borrows established tools and conventions, and whether the regnant orthodoxy is metafictional or minimalist realism, most of what we read leaves us in the realm of the secondhand.

I look for what might be called character, novels or stories that are unmistakably individuated. I don't say, "Not meatloaf again, honey," when I pick up a book that begins, "When I am run down and flocked around by the world, I go down to Farte Cove off the Yazoo River and

*Jay McInerney
photo by
Jesper Haynes*

take my beer to the end of the peer where the old liars are still snapping and wheezing at one another. . . . " (Barry Hannah's *Airships*.) And by character I don't necessarily mean the thinly disguised voice of the author; Richard Ford has created three very different, arresting personae in three successive novels. The sense of character, or voice, does not begin to encompass the ways in which fiction reinvents itself again and again. Don DeLillo has a unique voice, and is capable of knocking my socks off with a sentence, but what I find most original in his work is his breadth of vision and his appropriation of large areas of American culture and experience — areas previously unexplored by American fiction writers. Fortunately, I could name others.

I

CLARENCE MAJOR

I

I like fictions that "look back" at you with a life of their own. This idea of looking back (Paul Klee's concept) is easier to understand when it is applied to painting or drawing. The painting that achieves a life of its own, that breaks its link with models in the "real"

Clarence Major

world, despite representational elements, is the true, disturbing, breathtaking, joyous entity that, as Rilke observed, stands for all glory. The fictional text (and subject matter is unimportant) that elevates its properties to this level is the kind of thing I respect and enjoy. Its ability to "look back" means that, from the closure of its own life, it is a small universe unto itself, held together by the skill and magic the writer has laid on it. This is why no great, truly great, work of fiction can be merely representational. Some of the writers I have read recently who occasionally achieve this are Charles Johnson, William Melvin Kelley, Charles Wright, John Edgar Wideman, Thomas Pynchon, Russell Banks, James Welch, Jim Harrison, Toni Morrison, James Crumley, Rudolph Wurlitzer, Leonard Michaels, Gloria Naylor, T. Coraghessan Boyle, Don DeLillo, Paul Auster, Marianne Hauser, Jerry Bumpus, Harry Mathews, Rachel Salazar, Judy Lopatin, Robert Coover, and Stephen Dixon. The list would have been different had I been approachd with the question at a different time. But I think the point is clear.

I
FREDERICK MANFRED
I

In a way your question is a devilish one for me to answer. I haven't got time to read widely in the modern American age; I'm still busy exploring Old Masters of the world. Some of the old ones I've read many times. I'm going through *Don Quixote* for the fifth time. I've read all of Chaucer a half-dozen times. I've read Charles Montagu Doughty through three times. I can't seem to get enough of them. And in the last ten years I've become very interested in Emily Dickinson, especially since I bought Franklin's *The Manuscript Books of Emily Dickinson* as well as Sewall's *The Life of Emily Dickinson* and Longsworth's *Austin and Mabel* and Shurr's *The Marriage of Emily Dickinson*. She's probably our best American writer.

But of the modern Americans I've read there aren't many that I admire. I don't care much for Updike's muddy sweetness, nor Barth's antiblood osmotics, nor Bellow's rasp filings, nor Mailer's outhouse discoveries, nor any of Alain Robbe-Grillet's American followers who find themselves holed up in a cul-de-sac. I do admire the early William Gass—he's a good writer and he has a deep mind. I thought Flannery O'Connor wonderful—now there's my kind of gal as well as writer. And

Frederick Manfred
photo by
Larry Risser

our best of all, Robert Penn Warren, who is getting better as he goes along—the mark of the true genius—is inexhaustible.

Of the modern poets, I admire Bly, Wright, Stafford, Hall, and McGrath.

Of the western American writers I've read and admired, Fisher, Waters, Morris, Stegner, Cather, Fergusson, and Clark; all of them not only have a wider lense, they come up with wonderful life detail. All of them deserve more attention and many many more readers. The heavy minds of the Eastern Literary Establishment still haven't learned how to read them. If they could learn how to read them, as they've learned, finally, how to read the great Faulkner, the Western American writers would finally come to be known for what they really are—our glory.

But each man and each woman to his or her own last as best they can.

BOBBIE ANN MASON

Although I admire many individual writers of various styles and subjects (and I'm usually partial to stylists), I'm especially interested right now in the new American fiction about the lives of so-

Bobbie Ann Mason
photo by
Thomas Victor

called ordinary people, people whose lives weren't written about much before, but whose dreams and difficulties are nevertheless complicated and rich. I hear these new voices coming in from all over — small towns, farms, prairies, factories, reservations, night shifts, car radios, backyards, prisons, shopping malls, condos, big city apartments and offices, riverboats. It cuts across class lines. It's "people like us" instead of romantic heroes.

American fiction since *Huckleberry Finn* has been about the alienated hero (usually male) who rejects society because of its corruption and goes off to follow his own rules. But nowadays there are so many of us, and so many feel left out and are in no position to reject society and light out for the territories, that the focus has shifted away from the romantic hero to the ordinary person's struggle to get by in a mass society. Now the emphasis is on characters who make up the mass culture and away from the privileged few who can remove themselves from it. The new arena for fiction is the mainstream. Instead of the hero going outside society, we have people carrying on their daily lives within it, in spite of it, and we have marginal folks trying to get in, to get some basic advantages they've been denied. In the past we weren't willing to take salesclerks, for instance, seriously in fiction — especially black female salesclerks. But now we are. And that's important, I think.

I
HILARY MASTERS
I

During a recent radio interview, one of the moment's more celebrated novelists offered as proof of his dialogue's realism the claim that he could "hear it on television." He also opined that Huckleberry Finn's dialogue was "inarticulate."

His allegiance to the tube as an interpreter of reality, along with his perplexity over a classic item of American literature, makes me wonder if this isn't the voice of a new generation of writers (and the editors who publish them) who were weaned on "I Love Lucy" and came to maturity while watching "Miami Vice."

Some years back, Lincoln Kirstein suggested that the candid camera technique, which came with the Leica 35mm format introduced in the 1920s, had influenced the documentary or proletariat fiction of his period. These novels, he thought, might have adapted the photographic use

*Hilary Masters
photo by
Thomas Victor*

of a sensational image that passes for "real testimony . . . an accidental shock (which) obliterates the essential nature of the events it pretends to discover."

Today, it's difficult to tell where the shock becomes schlock, perhaps it's all one, but much of the contemporary fiction I have looked at—to differentiate from reading—seems to utilize a sitcom technique: an accumulation of fast scenes and sensational incidents and with no serious attempt to evaluate the subject of the narrative.

Do I digress when making this distinction between looking and reading? Up until now, there's been a tacit understanding between novelist and reader that they are engaged in a form of argument. This discussion has been at the writer's initiative but the reader responds with intellect and emotion. Reading has always been an active sport and pastime.

To look, to be an audience, can also be active, and theater audiences have given many examples of this particular dialogue—from the Ancients down to the incensed Dublin audiences of O'Casey's plays to the rude cowhands of our own West who would sometimes rise from their seats to challenge the stage villain of a touring melodrama. But these were naive audiences, long gone; even more important, not conditioned by the screens that have made us into passive receptors, looking only for the "good," the sensational passages. So, a passive reader is an oxymoron but, alas, the same can no longer be said of a passive audience.

Television cannot be made totally responsible for the shock-schlock being manufactured as fiction for the patented *frissons* of a stupefied gallery. The motion picture screen, much larger and far more attractive, came before television and now, the even smaller but perhaps more potent screen of the computer has presented itself for our attention.

In this product, the genius of our computer scientists has created the ultimate passive mind which materialists since John Locke have been asking for. The Macintosh is the *tabula rasa* to end all *tabulae*, but is this wonderful imitation of human memory so passive? Has it not turned around and made us imitate it as we sit before the display, a captive and passive audience even as we punch the key marked ENTER?

For myself, I am as conditioned by the silver and the green screens as anyone else may be, and, as a writer who has just used a computer to create a long work of fiction, I wonder if this extraordinary mechanism has not affected the quality of my novel's prose. Yes, let's hear the parallels that are to be made with previous changeovers in technologies. Gutenberg's movable type. The pen for the typewriter. But all these techniques of composition, whether setting the letters of a word by hand, or scratching it with a goose quill onto parchment or pecked out on an Underwood — all of these techniques provoked the critic in a writer as every word and every sentence was laid down. "A writer's best friend is his wastebasket," Ernest Hemingway advised.

But the transition to the computer has introduced the act of looking and given the writer a new, possibly dominant, persona, that of an audience, and he is a unique audience in that he arrives simultaneously with his own creation: the thing to be looked at. Is there a temptation, gratified by years before the screen, to sit back and enjoy the show?

To read and to write for readers is to engage in an argument that involves the entire human being, not just the memory. To be an audience as one writes for an audience is to give only a show that passes for the "real testimony," to quote Kirstein once more.

Here is an old question in new software; this argument between Plato and the Sophists. The debate has been an unhappy feature of this century in which the human spirit has been under almost continuous attack — from the early 1900s to the hot ovens of Auschwitz and down to the cold aim of deconstruction. The machinery becomes more and more efficient and the reduction rumbles on. Appearances *are* everything. The show-offs have won the amusement of the whole theater, whether in the pit of politics or the loge of literature or the elevated balconies of academia.

The object seems to entertain the outside dimensions while eclipsing the argument within: that stubborn search the human spirit has always made for truth.

If we become content to put up on the screen only those scenes, those sensational incidents that tickle the tops of our intellects and to do so for an audience that has been conditioned to turn away from the narrative during the serious messages (i.e., the commercials), then may this not be one more measure of the tyranny in store for us — a tyranny of one-liners?

Enter Lucy. (Audience laughter up — and out.)

▮

PAUL METCALF

▮

Let's assume that the fiction writer — like all good writers — is trying to convey some truth, or something that he conceives as truth, about the human condition. Such an assumption probably eliminates, right at the start, the great bulk of what is published today

Paul Metcalf

as fiction, but so much the better: we are winnowing down to the serious writers.

The "truth" may loom large and incontrovertible in the writer's mind — and it is probably best that it does so. The poet Theodore Enslin has a line somewhere (which I will misquote from memory, but I have the sense of it): "You say you fear the man obsessed, and I say, I fear the man who is not." There is a corollary truism: "The subject matter of a work of art matters only insofar as it be something about which the artist cares passionately." That quality of caring, that obsession, may be the writer's only hope when he enters those dangerous waters of *actually writing* — committing his "truth" to paper, to literary form.

It is a curious fact, a fact to which, blessedly, good writers seldom become adjusted, that the act of writing, of transferring the thing from inside the writer's skin to outside it, is more than just a transference, it is a transformation. The material itself is radically altered, in the process. This is often to the author's horror, when he realizes it — or *if* he realizes it: he tends, rather, to cling to the notion that he has managed to sneak it through the gates, unaltered. And it is to the reader's delight, for the "thing" is no longer that amorphous lump that so brightened the writer's eyes when he talked about it, before writing; it is now an object, something finished, a work of art.

It is this process of transformation, I guess, that makes writing so intensely subjective. It is what makes writers so childishly vulnerable to both criticism and praise: we have no real way of knowing. And it is why I never, ever, accept a writer's self-evaluation. Whenever a writer tells me how good his poems or stories are, I slam my ears shut. If those judgments had any value, he would be no writer at all, but a first-class garage mechanic — where the action is all "outside," and the parts truly measurable. It is because of the helplessness of the writer, mired in his processes, that we quite legitimately have literary critics.

Often a reader and writer, talking about a recent work by the writer, find themselves talking about two different things. This is why a reader's comments, either pro or con, so often surprise the writer.

All of which is preamble to — or circumlocution around — the question at hand: "Granted that contemporary American fiction is a variety of things, what kind of recent writing interests you especially?"

American fiction is indeed a variety of things. And I'm not sure I want to pick and choose, as to preference.

In 1966, Truman Capote published a book called *In Cold Blood* — and therewith was born a new genre called the nonfiction novel. In the same year, Jonathan Williams published my book, *Genoa* — a blend of fact, history, and fiction. A friend of mine, Don Byrd, suggested that Capote must have read *Genoa* before he wrote *In Cold Blood*. Given that both were published in the same year, this is patently unlikely. More likely, there was a notion floating in the air — like the spores of the morel mushroom — to which Capote and I were vulnerable: the notion that the old-fashioned novel — pure fiction — had played itself out, that it must be refreshed, revivified, by the incontrovertible force of *facts*.

For me, today's realities, and that heavy freight train of antecedents that we call history, became a method.

But there is another aspect to this, which is almost contravening. If history, if reality, if facts are placed on the page, in some literary form, are they, in the process of writing, transformed? In being forged into a novel, does the quality we most trusted in them — their factuality — become suspect?

Suppose we look still further. Given the writer's highly desirable passion, his obsession — is his view of history, of reality — *before* he sits down to write — is this view to be altogether trusted?

I have recently been reading *A Voyage to Pagany*, by William Carlos Williams. This is a novelized account of a trip that Williams himself took to Europe in 1924. The author has made one major change, though: Williams made the trip with his wife Flossie; and his counterpart in the novel is a bachelor, who has affairs along the way. The good doctor is clearly fantasizing. Is it for his delight? For our delight? Or is it at his expense? At our expense? (And I wonder what Flossie thought?)

All writing, be it factual or fantastic, is to some extent autobiographical. All that we have experienced, seen, heard, read, is available to us as resource, and, in the heat of writing, any of it may be thrown into battle, in ways of which the most cynical and "objective" writer may not be aware.

And writing, like all the arts, is kin to magic. There is an element in us that wants to con the reader. To the extent that we get away with this, like actors and politicians we subtly create for ourselves a reality that is not quite real. We come to believe in ourselves, to believe our own cons.

As to the question, which sort of fiction I prefer: I don't think I really have a choice. Although my own method, my own obsession, has been largely historical, I can take great delight in stories that give the appearance, at least, of being totally made up. I love to teach fiction workshops, and in every class it is my hope that the tales come out in all shapes and forms.

I guess what it comes down to, in truly preferential reading, is to find a story or novel that delights me on the surface; that presents depths that

I don't at once understand; that urges me to find out more about whatever it is the author is writing about; and—perhaps most importantly—that urges me to find out more about the author. No, this is not a taste for gossip—at least, not at first. It is germane to the argument I have been making here: What is this process we call writing, what materials is the author using, and how did he come by them, and finally, how are they altered in the forging? What is this particular writer's method of magic?

Perhaps it's because I'm a writer myself, and I tend to think shop; but these are the questions that fascinate me.

I
SUE MILLER
I

Recently I lugged with me across the country a posthumously published novel of Christina Stead's called *I'm Dying Laughing*. I recommend this book to no one. To call it a loose baggy monster is outrageous flattery. In a way it's perhaps most accurately seen as the lavish outpouring the author might have done—of endless dialogue, monologue, almost random scenes—before getting down to the disciplined

Sue Miller
photo by
Thomas Victor

business of shaping a novel. (Of course, we wouldn't even know Stead's work if this kind of logorrhea was all she was capable of. But she also produced a long list of fine and shapely novels and stories.)

In a world where fictional characters sometimes seem marginally alive, seem to exist only for the sake of a story's elegant shape, are animated by what seems a few arbitrarily chosen tics or quirks, it's bracing — and challenging — to read a writer like Stead, who clearly knew her characters so thoroughly that she could fill page after page with their obsessional ravings, their idle chatter, their solitary anguish, the details of what they ate, what they wore! for God's sake. That she *wanted* to fill page after page with this stuff.

It is this lavishness itself that interested me in *I'm Dying Laughing*, that made me want to have it with me for a month's working stay in California. And in general it's fiction that seems to carry the weight and authority of this lavish kind of imagination — either on the contemporary scene or from the past — that is most compelling to me.

It seems immediately more difficult to call up the names of American writers working this way than it does Europeans or South Americans — or Australians, like Stead. But of course, there are many. It's just that for the moment the American work that seems to receive most attention is quite different from this. It shares a tone, a flat, affectless damaged tone that traces its ancestry, I suspect, to the wounded narrators of Hemingway's fiction. Sometimes, as in many of the fine short stories by Raymond Carver, this tone seems natural to the work, seems earned. But often it doesn't, it carries no moral weight, no charge for the reader.

But we do have writers creating fiction in which the flesh that meaning must wear — the *embodiment* of the meaning — is as convincing and rich and compelling as the meaning itself, writers who are as generous as Stead with their imagination. Toni Morrison or Larry Woiwode, for example, have both written numerous novels as lavish and complex as Stead's finished work. But there are other forms of this lavishness. I think for example of the vastly disparate and intricate turns of Tom McMahon's and Robert Stone's imaginations. And sometimes more compressed, more "minimal" writers too seem to be working with such a deep knowledge of their characters, their characters' lives, that their much shorter works seem equally full, by implication equally complex: *Monkeys* by Susan Minot. *That Night* by Alice McDermott.

All certainly worthy too of lugging across the country.

Edith Milton
photo by
Fleur Weymouth

EDITH MILTON

I seem unable to isolate a particular kind of writing I most wish well, or, in fact, to divide American fiction into categories at all.

The possibility that I may have a blind spot in that area first suggested itself to me some years ago when an article in *Harper's* identified me as a member of a sect of writers who, the author argued, were united in pernicious devotion to various trends of fashionably nihilistic thinking. It sounded rather unhealthy — the article certainly suggested that it was very unhealthy. But some of the members of the sect were quite famous and several were writers I admired: I failed to recognize any of the factions and subfactions the article evoked, but I accepted my membership, *ex post facto* and with pride. Probably I had joined the sect inadvertently.

A year or so later, at a conference for women writers in New York, my instincts of allegiance failed again when they were put to the test. A woman in the audience asked me how I accommodated my stance and outlook as a writer to the fact that I was female. She meant it politically; and I took it idiotically: as if I had no feminist sympathies whatever. At Town Meeting I come out sounding like Medea; but in that setting of militant Womanhood I turned into Phyllis Schlafly. I suppose identity is always defined by opposition, and it became clear to me that literary loyalties and the colorations and distinctions to which they applied were beyond me, since to my eye they are constantly shifting.

In fact, American fiction, like American cooking, seems to me governed by a pretty easygoing federalism. Writers here are not strongly divided by regional traditions of style or flavor or emphasis, and our literature easily incorporates a complex variety of differences, of ethnic histories, political biases, and local preoccupations without discovering real antagonisms among them. We are good at living with diversity and at unifying it. Such antagonisms as there are, like those two I ran into myself, tend to be artificial and arbitrary. And we borrow so heavily and randomly from each other, we move so rapidly across geographical and cultural borders that terms like *Southern* or *feminist* or *West Coast* or even *minimalist* tend to limit and deprecate more than to describe the writer to whom they are applied.

So I have settled for not seeing current American fiction in terms of category and style at all, or even direction. My enthusiasms run to specific writers rather than to kinds of writing; and my choice in writers ranges from big guns like William Styron and Philip Roth to the totally obscure, some still — and some perhaps doomed to remain forever — in manuscript. Nothing holds these preferences together. I would say that I have a taste for undernourished prose and for understatement; but my deep admiration for Styron and also for Rosellen Brown, bears witness against that.

In writing, as in cooking, American federalism, with its search for common denominators and mutual agreements, has its dangers. It allowed us, gastronomically, to invent McDonald's, and it also created a sort of literary Big Mac, which the phrase "American fiction," itself, brings to my mind — and probably to the minds of many American and most non-American readers, as well. Something large, schematic, and flossy; something more apt to describe violent action than the daily inner or outer lives of women or men or children. The antithesis of Henry James, it borrows its ingredients from a tradition of Romantic Calvinism that stretches from Melville to Mailer and Poe to John Barth, but it uses them without the strength, the economy, and the honor which that tradition demands.

I should confess that my reaction to the juicy, beefy image the term *American fiction* brings before me is blazingly neurotic. The response of one of those awful mothers with a full-grown son still living at home, trying to nag him away from the shallow company to whom he seems perversely addicted. Since I cannot comprehend what attracts him so, I go over and over the situation in my mind, looking for answers.

Foremost in the litany of literary failings, which I repeat to myself when I lament this unfortunate attachment, is evasiveness. God knows our fiction can claim as many horrors to tame into print as anyone's can, but I have doubts about its willingness to do so. Even on such a massive subject as human rights it has been generally feeble: look at South Africa, look at the grandeur of fury that emanates from there! While in our fictional studies of social justice a memorial, historical tone prevails as though all the problems were fifty years gone by or a continent away; we seem reluctant to embrace the tedious sickness of racism as still belonging to us. We are dainty about outrage.

We are also delicate on other subjects: for instance, the question of whether we will lead the world to the farthest stars or whether we will offer convincing proof the human race is a cosmic error in evolution. If American fiction touches that issue at all it only tickles it gently, an alternative approach to the Holocaust as entertainment. I am morose about our overriding frivolity.

But possibly what dismays me most about our literature is its social life. Its lack of it, I should say. I read Barbara Pym and wonder why Ann Beattie's people have so few friends. I ask myself why Robertson Davies's academic colleagues in Toronto have so much more fun at parties than Alison Lurie's in Upstate New York. Perhaps the habits of thought which invented Hester Prynne and Captain Ahab have hardened; and there are certainly too many novels about being single, about tenuous relationships, about breaking up. The most frequent fantasy of the 1970s was about a woman learning to live alone and liking it; no one wrote much about the more likely case of a woman learning to live alone and not liking it. Do we sentimentalize independence as the Victorians sentimentalized passion, to keep ourselves from laying claim to the real thing?

So much for my neurosis.

The worst, most sinister quality of that bland monster which it leads me to evoke is, of course, that it can be taken quite differently—heroically, and, Heaven help us, profitably. A phantom very similar to the one with which I frighten myself seems to be conjured up by the publishing world with considerable enthusiasm and even romantic longing. The Great

American Novel, all things to all readers, John Irving without the pathology of self-quotation. Like other institutions of American art and culture, publishing has fallen victim to costs and to the blockbuster, best-seller mentality that goes with them. And panicked editors, who have learned to love precedent more than lawyers do, call up the same ghostly image of American fiction that haunts me, but they use that ectoplasmic familiar as a measurement for what is likely to succeed. We have innumerable writers of brilliance and power; probably more than ever before in our history. But I think we are threatened by a monolith.

So I will cast my vote for all fiction whatever so long as it lives in the vast decentralized limbo outside the narrow focus aimed for success. All of it, which takes in a great deal of fiction indeed, including some which may incidentally be very successful. My vote comprehends the well-known and the anonymous, the quietly eccentric, well-written little book and the wildest in experimentation, without reference to level of fame, style, form or Weltanschauung: whatever is not on the main road to stardom. I am, of course, speaking not merely of printing, but of nurturing and cultivating this fiction; of its being distributed and above all reviewed with some modicum of understanding somewhere where the review is even likely to be read. These days that does not happen to many books. In an age of shrinking criticism, of bookstores which keep hardcover novels a bare ninety days, being noticed and being available is not an easy task. Perhaps we should follow the theater, which once seemed ready to sink under the weight of Broadway, by putting greater emphasis on regional publishing and on small-press distribution.

The climate has already become oppressive. If our fiction is to stay healthy, it will need air to breathe, room for surprise, for mistakes, for variety, for the probable failure which may still prove itself a masterpiece; but I have no prescription. And meanwhile the behemoth is growing.

STEPHEN MINOT

Trying to categorize the fiction one admires is like attempting to describe in a single phrase the food one enjoys. Easy enough to identify that which one finds boring, inedible, or potentially poisonous, but what do the favorites have in common?

For me, rewarding fiction usually falls into one of three different

Stephen Minot

categories — the socially committed, the socially aware, and the personally concerned. If this seems to cast too wide a net, I should point out that it excludes a great deal of highly skillful, sophisticated work which appears in a variety of publications from the *New Yorker* to quarterlies that ought to know better.

Socially committed has unfortunate overtones for many. It brings to mind the heavy hands of Dreiser and Dos Passos. But the contemporary practitioners I have in mind are light-years away from those worthies. I am thinking of writers like Peter Matthiessen who displays a deep concern for the damage we do the world about us and expresses himself with language which is highly innovative. Nothing heavy-handed there.

Far Tortuga, for example, is as difficult to read as William Gaddis's *JR*, and both novels were more often displayed on coffee tables than actually read. For those who completed *Far Tortuga*, however, that extraordinary Caribbean misadventure becomes embedded in the memory. It returns whenever one reads about the slow death of any culture, be it Indian, African, or ethnic American. Mathiessen's fiction gives shape and substance to concerns which we may have only perceived in the abstract.

Socially committed writers often display what John Gardner described (in *On Becoming a Novelist*) as a "daemonic compulsiveness." They have pushed themselves to extremes — or are themselves pushed by their convictions. To some degree this is true of Matthiessen. To a greater degree it applies to the fiction of Ishmael Reed whose rage spills over into the absurd like a dream which becomes grotesque in the face of truths too awful to be faced directly. I also see "daemonic compulsiveness" in the work of Fred Pfeil whose recent first novel, *Goodman 2020*, rails at our corporate and military structure through scenes which are often grotesquely comic. He has been described (by Scott Sanders) as having an Orwellian vision, but Orwell was more restrained, almost pedantic, and far less interested in language. Pfeil's is a fresh voice of conscience.

My second category, fiction which is socially aware, includes authors who are less willing to commit themselves to a specific political or social position but who are nonetheless incurably concerned with social issues. Milan Kundera comes to mind first. In *The Unbearable Lightness of Being* he deftly dramatizes the unbearable weight of commitment and the equally intolerable insubstantiality of remaining neutral and detached. These are alternatives which face us whenever our society is in trouble — which is to say daily. Although the novel happens to deal with Czechoslovakians, it applies to Americans who lived through the Vietnam period and who today face (or refuse to face) issues of racism and gross economic injustice. Kundera does not take sides as uncompromisingly as do writers like Matthiessen, Reed, and Pfeil, but he sharpens our sense of social and personal responsibility. In some ways, his political conscience, always couched in irony, resembles Graham Greene's religious conscience. Faith and lack of faith are part of the same problem and are of equal concern. Like Kierkegaard, Kundera sees the threat of damnation on both sides.

Kundera's high sense of irony is his method of psychological survival, and in this he is similar to Joan Didion. We know where she stands when it comes to issues, but none of her characters has fully satisfactory answers, and none can be taken as a model for "right behavior."

The third category is fiction in which the concern is not for society but for an individual. This includes a large group of contemporary writers, but three who come to mind are Bobbie Ann Mason, Alice Adams, and Ursula K. Le Guin. Their approaches differ, but each cares deeply about the characters she develops and, equally important, makes us care too. As readers, we have the sense of having met and come to know an individual who is worth knowing. This is not a cocktail party meeting; it is one of those haunting experiences which sometimes occurs in planes or buses when total strangers manage to share a significant part of themselves — either intentionally or unintentionally.

What kind of writers does this exclude? Were I a critic rather than a writer of fiction, I might take pleasure in listing names. But we are all members of a small fellowship — this odd little tribe which takes fiction seriously—and we spend altogether too much time and energy as it is with attempts at fratricide. Let me describe two frequently acclaimed types of fiction in anonymous terms.

I think of the first as poor-little-me fiction. Such stories often present us with a poker-faced young woman who is beguiling in an offbeat sort of way, charmingly neurotic, and devoid of feeling. We are asked to share one of her more meaningless days, meeting a number of her unfeeling but exotic friends and coming to know, largely through dialogue, a certain social scene which appears to be the East Village or a West Coast imitation. At the end of a sequence of unrelated exploits, she retires, having learned no more about herself than we have. Life, it appears, goes on.

Some of these stories are superbly done. There is a polish there which is as admirable as a freshly waxed car. Occasionally there is just a whiff of erotic—a highly muted version of sophisticated porn which manages to arouse without indulging in so much as a hint of love or compassion. It remains, as John Gardner put it, frigid.

I am also put off by those dreamlike stories and novels in which the characters behave largely without motivation, plot is slow except when spiked with flashes of violence, and theme is ingeniously hidden. I keep having the uneasy feeling that this must have been more fun to write than it is to read. I don't mind listening to the dreams of someone I know well because sometimes they help me to know him or her better; but these are dreams of strangers. They are not Kafkaesque (the author's claims notwithstanding) because they have not caught a universal sense which would allow me to enter them emotionally as well as intellectually. I know what it means to be locked out of the castle, I can feel it; but being locked out of a story is sheer tedium. I keep thinking of more important things to do.

It is concern which concerns me—concern for the society which we depend on, for people with whom we share this most insecure life raft. Good fiction is more than effective use of language. It is also a commitment to the human condition.

A. G. MOJTABAI

The daily newspaper—even the Mesa Petroleum Annual Report—is more absorbing reading to me than most contemporary American fiction.

*A. G. Mojtabai
photo by
Jerry Bauer*

I must admit that I have never been an avid fiction reader (which makes it all the more strange that I should be in the business of writing fiction). As I grow older, I am even less inclined to pick up the latest acclaimed novel. I always wait for the shouting to die down.

During the past five years, my writing has been devoted to nonfiction and focused upon the nuclear question. The books that have meant the most to me in this time have been works of history, historical interpretations and social and religious commentary—not fiction.

Which books?

John Dominic Crossan's *In Parables*; Ronald A. Knox's *Enthusiasm*; Alasdair MacIntyre's *After Virtue: A Study in Moral Theory*; Richard John Neuhaus's *The Naked Public Square*; Richard L. Rubenstein's *The Cunning of History*; Ernest Lee Tuveson's *Redeemer Nation*; Walter Prescott Webb's *The Great Plains*.

These books are not on anyone's best-seller list, yet they are full of imagination and intelligence.

What I find in most contemporary American fiction, my own included, is a debilitating constriction. I am not speaking of *scale*, but of vision, a failure of vision. A failure to dream beyond what we know.

I remember somewhere in one of Ann Beattie's novels—*Falling in Place*, I believe—a man and a woman talking about a famous wishing well he visited in Europe. She asks him what he wished for when he tossed in a coin. "The usual," he says.

To me, this is a terribly poignant and revealing moment. He cannot say what it is he wishes for; he does not know. Most of us, writers and nonwriters alike, do not know what to wish for, and we are unwilling to hazard a vision — or even a guess — as to what lies beyond the here and now.

In an essay comparing "The Blind Man" by D. H. Lawrence with Raymond Carver's story, "Cathedral," Monroe Engel praises contemporary fiction writers for telling us, with unerring accuracy, how bad things are, but laments a prevailing inability or unwillingness to tell us what "better" might be.

I agree and, in so doing, I indict myself as well.

Let me disappear into the collective category "contemporary American writer," so as to indict all of us more freely:

Writing programs abound. We are technically adept. We are industrious to a fault.

We are, in varying degrees, astute reporters of the actual. We are, many of us, vibrant with nostalgia. Or we are innovative tumblers and jugglers. Our fantasies are often bold, yet we are timid and deficient dreamers of the possible.

I am well aware of the dangers that lurk in our attempts to correct these failings. I do not think literature can be written to a program. I know the difference between literature and propaganda. The dangers of correction, and overcorrection, are real.

But we are faced with another real, and *present*, danger. I think of Tim O'Brien's novel *The Nuclear Age*, which speaks powerfully to our present impasse: "But the future is always invented. . . . And if you can't imagine it, I thought, it can't happen."

And I think, too, of W. S. Merwin, in his poem *The River of Bees*:

> We are the echo of the future
>
> On the door it says what to do to survive
> But we were not born to survive
> Only to live.

Mary Morris   photo by Nancy Adler

MARY MORRIS

The kind of contemporay American fiction that interests me the most is a fiction that examines not only the details of our lives, but also is able to take in the bigger picture. I like a fiction that is obsessive, passionate, crazed about power (whether political or erotic), about love, about the world we live in. I've grown weary of the so-called minimalist school, the K-Mart fiction, where the tidbits, the bargains of life are sold, and long for a fiction where the tragic is still possible, as in Sue Miller's excellent (and successful) first novel, *The Good Mother*, which reminded me of Hawthorne; where the dark side may be seen, as in the novels of Robert Stone or Joyce Carol Oates; where the failure of the American dream is revealed, as in Russell Banks's *Continental Drift* or E. L. Doctorow's *The Book of Daniel*, which I think is perhaps the most intelligent novel written in and about America in the last twenty years.

The minimalist school seems to be a kind of sociological phenomenon, the way the "nouveau roman" served a certain sociological function in post-World War II France. I think it is a digression, away from what our real concerns should be, and the literary merits of that digression remain to be seen. The digression is happening because Americans have been diverted from our real concerns — our poverty, our elderly, our alienation, our nuclear arsenals. I am not a postmodernist. I crave content over form. I think the American fiction that deserves more attention and more readers is a kind of fiction that is "about" something, as Tim O'Brien would say, that has a "moral aboutness." I think the fiction that is attempting to do that is the kind that deserves more attention and more readers.

MARGE PIERCY

In my own approach to fiction I am always balancing between my belief that *story* is primary and that the most basic most primitive impulse in narrative (what then? when then? and then what?) is also the most sacred; and an equally passionate absorption in *character* and a belief that fiction is simply the expression of character in action through time. I survive happily as a fiction writer with both of these contradictory theories and impulses always active in me, and find my

Marge Piercy photo by Thomas Victor

best ideas in this tension. I like and read work from both tendencies. I consider both approaches undervalued at present by a preference for certain styles and types of subject matter, rather a narrow range but able to be produced at the yard by any bright writing student with a yen for grants and approval.

The problem I have with minimalism is that I find the passive rather bland and empty characters frequently found in it mental anorexics, who bore me and about whom I find it hard to muster much reaction. I don't think passive characters are more realistic or more "American" than characters who take an active role in their own lives. On the other hand, I recognize that we are being trained from infancy into a people who expect to have images fed into us, with the attention span of a puppy and the intellectual curiosity of a stale doughnut. However, I have experienced the extraordinarily rich and deep capacity of ordinary people many times in my life. It is that ability to open and grow that often exercises my imagination as a writer. I am interested often in characters who seize or are seized by the currents and necessities and opportunities of their particular time and place. I always see characters as *in* history. I find that the lives of ordinary working people generate sufficient struggle, passion, hope, conflict, terror to sustain infinite fictive exploration.

I have written realistically and surrealistically and speculatively, and none of these modes commands my loyalty and none seems to be in truth any more faithful to the reality of living than any other mode. I am loyal to the story, and I find as much meaning in weird tales of dragons and androids as I do in tales of advertising men and dope dealers. To me the self is vast, amorphous, part animal, part collective, overlapping with others underground, tapping hidden rivers that flow through us.

One of the sorts of fiction still lacking sufficient serious attention is finer speculative fiction. Joanna Russ and Samuel Delany are among my favorite writers. Both of them possess a great deal more intelligence and wit and learning than most contemporary fiction writers; both have unusually rich (and completely different) ways of dealing with sex, politics, and violence. Both of them demand that you read their work actively, demonstrate little patience with standard transitions but are uninfected with the dead eye of the overly cinematic.

I also wish more attention would fall on fiction that makes imaginative and totally assimilated use of myth and the religious imagination, as in Esther Broner's *A Weave of Women* and Elizabeth Thomas's *Reindeer Moon*; and work like Manuel Puig's that deals wittily with popular culture and the mass media.

Work by women is constantly undervalued and frequently ignored. Reviewers still tend to review fiction that corresponds in its values to those opinions on politics, sex roles, economics, and religion they share or are used to hearing over dinner; fiction that embodies different opinions of right, wrong, what people ought to do in bed and in the marketplace to whom and how . . . who has got it all in the brains and lovability departments, who ought to win and lose and what winning and losing mean — such fiction is reviewed in terms of its politics, called polemical (meaning said opinions are not viewed as being mainstream) and generally denounced or dismissed. Reviewers only seem to notice opinions that differ from their own; those they agree with are not opinions but just the way things are, part of the quiet background.

Just as North American poetry has never been the same after we finally did begin seriously to attempt to digest Vallejo and Neruda, North American fiction is going to have to digest the South Americans, and I don't mean the bad imitations I've seen. I mean a more organic sense of our history expressed in our fiction and a livelier imagination, less obsession with isolated and alienated narcissists and more sense of the vast social and earthly web we all live in and through. Writers like Toni Morrison, Gloria Naylor, and Leslie Silko are already doing so.

JOE ASHBY PORTER

Already the threshold of the third millennium is exerting its arbitrary irresistible pull all through Western civilization and thence elsewhere, too, and so it seems a good time to crane our necks for a bit of overview. The historical moment naturally enough makes us, me anyway, wonder about what kind of deep future written fiction might have. In addition, my own forty-fifth year seems a proper time for taking some stock in a commitment that can still bemuse me even though it's been irrevocable for a good two decades.

My original statement for this symposium begins:

> What kind of fiction? The kind that makes me stop and pay attention to nothing but it, the kind I don't stop reading even though I really didn't have time for it.
>
> That fiction interests me especially, but I don't know if it deserves more attention and readers. Maybe, but maybe not. It's easy

*Joe Ashby Porter
photo by
J. D. Burns*

to think of any number of writers I've more or less happened on and immediately cottoned to, only to feel my interest ebb as more and more readers have read them.

Estimating just deserts across contemporary fiction before answering the question didn't seem feasible. Furthermore, for me there's no necessary correspondence between, first, what I'd wish for any good fiction and for the world and, second, how and why some good contemporary fiction interests me a great deal and some less. The fiction that interests me most tends to be fiction I as a writer can learn most from, and of course what I can learn is a function not only of the fiction in question but also of what I happen to be needing, which in turn is a function of what I've been writing and reading, and hearing and talking and reading and writing about. What I learn isn't necessarily something I promptly ape, either. Sometimes it is, but sometimes a mere widening of the range of possibilities is what I need.

The first version of my statement continues:

> But the kind of fiction that interests me has its own hidden agendas. It might make me think, "Stay cool till we know what the deal is." It feels reckless and keeps on feeling that way. It might be a story that seems almost too simple to be told, or a story you almost knew by heart. It looks like just a piece of string, or a mailbox — you look harder at it and it looks the same, but more. It might have a breathless rhythm.

The agendas may be hidden by the author or from the author, but they are agendas and achievable, by the fiction and in the world. For example, I believe that some of the fiction that interests me works to smoke out and send up doctrines like "The poor are always with you"—and the fiction in some cases seems to achieve that end beneath the level of the author's full consciousness.

I used to say I had very good antennae for fiction, because I can almost always know right away, after a few sentences or at most a page, whether a piece of fiction interests me. That's the story from my side and, as it implies, I find a high correlation in contemporary fiction between the interest of the whole and the interest of its smallest parts. Maybe in all fiction. I no longer assent as readily as before to received wisdom that this or that writer is mediocre locally while great globally, or vice versa. Anyway, the story from the fiction's side is that it has authenticity, excellence, for the antennae to pick up.

This excellence or authenticity can't be pinned down with any definitions I or anybody I know could crank out, but it certainly is recognizable to me, and I can talk some about it, as in some of the last sentences quoted, and also when the original statement continues about the fiction that interests me:

> It's postminimalist and also postfeminist, I think, and it's post-postmodernist at least. It doesn't sit up and say, "Here, this is what I am."

Postminimalist doesn't mean antiminimalist. Postminimalist fiction doesn't take a stand against minimalism, it goes beyond minimalism, acknowledging minimalism, using what is worth using, keeping what is worth keeping in minimalism, much as the next century and millennium will, I hope, go beyond this. Ditto for postfeminism and postpostmodernism. Other isms and ists can hitch to the same post, and the post can keep them all off the streets I might want to take. I mean, contemporary fiction too serious yet to have a handy label interests me the most.

The original statement continues and ends:

> Fiction like this interests me especially because it heartens me. I'm interested in fiction that stops me: even if it makes your hair stand on end, it heartens you. And we need heartening, I do.

I think I would say the same even if I weren't a writer, so long as I still did read the way I always have read, ready for another double take. Maybe the heartening amounts to pleasure, distinctive absolute pleasure released when undreamed-of vantages open.

*John Rechy
photo by
Tony Korody*

JOHN RECHY

By a subtle process that camouflages as "acceptance," an effective silencing of essential voices is occurring in our time. I am talking about the voices of homosexual writers who emerged since the 1960s, the decade that culminated in gay liberation. The growing ghettoization of such writers depletes all of literature of a sensibility that has produced some of the world's greatest artists, from Michelangelo to Proust. Is it logical to believe that that creativity withers out of the closet?

No. But openly identified, its literature is more easily shoved into another closet. "Acceptingly" dubbed as a new genre known as "gay writing" (and sentenced in bookstores to a corner labeled "alternative lifestyles"), it will be reviewed obscurely if at all (a safe token excepted now and again). Prejudged by narrowing labels, it will not be considered by those whose views determine "importance." It will not be allowed into the flow of *literature*.

The *New York Times Book Review* and the *New York Review of Books,* perhaps the most "important" journals for literary acceptance, have clinging roots in antihomosexuality. In the 1940s the *New York Times* refused even to advertise Gore Vidal's *The City and the Pillar*—and banished the author from its pages for years. Today, homosexual writers who manage to get attention in its powerful pages are often "coupled"—two writers in a single review relegated to the back pages, a review withheld for months. This may occur whether or not the openly identified "gay writer" is exploring overtly gay themes. (Closeted homosexuals are allowed greater attention, either because they are undetected or as a reward for remaining undisturbingly in the closet.)

As late as the 1960s, *New York Review of Books* unabashedly headlined a scurrilous review of a gay novel with the words "Fruit Salad." More recently, it *did* give front-page attention to homosexuals, not for their literature but because of a deadly illness. When everyone else was baffled by AIDS, that literary journal front-paged "The Truth About AIDS." In review of several books, it strongly propouned the now dismissed but highly judgmental theory of "immunity overload" as causing the illness. The same journal refused to print an indictment by Vidal of antigay bigotry in some intellectual quarters.

Occasionally an article about "gay writing" appears in a national mainstream magazine, like a recent one in *Newsweek.* The effect of this gratuity is to further separate. Imagine a similar article about "heterosexual writers." And imagine John Updike and Norman Mailer identified as "self-avowed heterosexual spokesmen." Imagine novels by Saul Bellow and Philip Roth joined in one review because both deal with "the Jewish experience."

Academic criticism that sets out to determine "permanent" importance joins in this "gentleman's agreement" of quiet prejudice. Frederick Karl's *American Fictions* received wide critical attention by purporting to be a "comprehensive history and critical evaluation" of the "most striking movements of the past four decades." He ignored the Stonewall Riot, its impact resonating throughout the entire culture as the beginning of gay liberation.

Had similar separation occurred in earlier times, Proust, Gide, and Genet would have been forced into, at best, a tiny tributary off the main stream—and all of literature would have been powerfully lessened.

The present process of ghettoization is shutting away some of the best writing being produced today, writing which will become even more essential in the time of AIDS, the days of daily dying, when homosexual writers will be providing the clearest, most eloquent voices of survival and courage.

I
CAROLYN SEE
I

Here's what you *don't* have to pay attention to in contemporary fiction: any more novels by women about being married to pig-husbands. Any more novels by men about (A) war, payloads, thrust, death and/or victory, or (B) intelligent husbands (married to pig-wives with fat thighs) who luckily find women half their age who love and understand them. We can go on reading these novels, and even writing them, but we don't have to pay attention to them. They simply restate what we already "know."

We should pay attention to the crossovers. Carol Hill's *The Eleven*

Carolyn See drawing by Don Bachardy

Million Mile High Dancer is what we should read and read again, because here's a woman who writes about a female astronaut who's a perfect roller skater and a mathematical wizard who drives the American military establishment crazy because she combines intuition with facts and then laughs about it. We should read *The Eleven Million Mile High Dancer* for its long and wonderful passages on particle physics, and Carol Hill's insistence that the phrase "Cosmic Dance" is not just a dustbunny of the mind, but words that describe what is *going on*, if we have the wit to see it.

We should pay attention to *This Magic Moment* by Gregg Easterbrook, a man who wears masculine credentials like wreaths, who contributes to the *Atlantic Monthly* and writes fact-filled cover stories for *Newsweek*, blah blah, but who, in his first novel, postulates that a man and a woman can fall in love for centuries and work out their destinies through repeated reincarnation; that falling in love is a moral act that can drastically improve not just our globe but the whole universe; that by falling in love (*and* paying close attention to our computers) we can give God Himself a helping hand.

What I'm saying is: for all our stylistic innovations, we still, repeatedly, leave war and adventure to men, love and suffering to women, and — most disturbing of all — the state of the Larger World to fantasts who create characters named Alf and Delf, and who don't always write very well. American youth eats up this stuff; it recognizes the subject matter as surpassingly important, and it often scorns the education that deplores the fantasy style as being dippy (calling each other "thou," slaying dragons, riding worms — all that).

The novel we should pay attention to? The one that's riddled with masculine knowledge, glowing with female secrets, the one that sets its sights on the Big Picture, our true place in the time continuum and Deep Space. All that with the assumption that this should be not *science* fiction but real fiction, those books that enable their readers to make great leaps of understanding, knowledge, joy.

LORE SEGAL

I take the writer's privilege to answer not the question posed but the question in my head: the book I want to read and

Lore Segal   photo by Marilyn McLaren

to write cannot be written in our time. Our books are of two kinds — the kind I like reading and the kind I admire. In the nineteenth century it would have been the selfsame book. Today I need a William Gass to write me a Jane Austen.

JOAN SILBER

I don't have strong feelings about stylistics — a lean or a dense style is fine with me. When I think about it, it seems that my moments of high literary passion — when I get really angry or thrilled with someone's work — are moral responses, objections, and assents to attitudes.

One pretty obvious characteristic of our times is that we're never very far from high levels of violence and misery; the global village that the media makes for us has, as everyone knows, the tendency to harden us by bombarding us with painful information. It's important to me that fiction not be another part of that hardening process, either by its being flashy and mean or being vapid and blanked-out.

So I am most attracted to fiction that seems, well — wise — and thought through. In the writing that I like — the fiction that I go back to — I can feel the author bearing down on the material to get to the meaning;

Joan Silber   *photo by Thomas Victor*

there's a thoroughness and intentness to the writing. Two authors I think don't get enough attention are Susan Engberg, who writes wonderful, quiet, meditative stories with little kernels of transcendence in them, and Charles Baxter, who writes sharp, toughly intelligent prose about small, unsafe lives.

ELIZABETH SPENCER

American writing at this time seems spread out over the whole country. No one area or ethnic approach seems to dominate. There are pockets of first-class writing on the West Coast, in the South (as usual), suburban to New York (to be expected), and around Houston, Texas, to mention a few areas I know of. The poet Yeats's dire prediction, "the center cannot hold," has come true for us in just the ways he meant it: there is no one controlling myth, tradition, or set of critical values. Yet we have fine talent—readable, serious, informed, entertaining and working hard.

We are all—in terms of supermarkets, shopping centers, schools, "housing," wars, assassinations, and national politics—living a similar life, bound historically to that crazy roller-coaster ride we call our own time.

Elizabeth Spencer

Fewer American writers are trying to bring us news from abroad: more, from a position in the here and now among us, are searching outward (Richard Ford in *The Sportswriter*), looking back (E. L. Doctorow in *World's Fair*), looking forward (Walker Percy in *The Thanatos Syndrome*). Yet the American experience outside the country can still be explored with great imaginative force, as witness Norman Rush's *Whites*, a collection of stories which limns the cultural encounters, often perilous, often comic, of the U.S. civil servant in Africa. As witness also Cecile Pineda's *Face*, creating out of a few facts the courage of an accident victim in Brazil.

Overworked though it may have been in the past, the Southern scene can still be brought to vivid new life, fresh as a flower from an old root: here note Padgett Powell's moving *Edisto*, Nancy Lemann's *Lives of the Saints*.

I

SCOTT SPENCER

I

Nearly every year, there are many more books published here than I find time to read. Perhaps if I were a speed reader, or did not spend the better part of the day writing, or did not have small

Scott Spencer
photo by
Gary Green

children, then I could at least get neck and neck with the thundering herd of new books that every month go racing around the sweetly antique track we call the literary world. But I can't and so my comments about the current state of literary affairs are tempered by the realization that I read five percent of the novels published annually — and in this five percent I am including books begun and then thrown against the wall.

With that in mind, let me venture the opinion that despite the dire state of the publishing industry, the demise of the independent bookseller, the increasingly obnoxious national obsession with celebrity and the big score, there seems to be a steady supply of novels worthy of our attention and a steady supply of writers foolish enough to devote their lives to composing decent, intelligent, often compelling works of fiction.

As to what *kind* of fiction is capturing my imagination these days, I'm afraid my response is a quarrel with the question. I don't like *kinds* of fiction, which is to say I have not staked out a certain subject matter or approach and cooled my ardor for the others. For example, while *Lolita* may be the finest novel written in my lifetime, I'm not sure that *Lolita* is the kind of book I am looking for — in fact, judging from the number of books that come to me with letters from the publisher assuring me that this author or that one has written "another *Lolita*" I can safely say there is nothing in the subject matter or overall literary strategy of that novel that has anything in particular to recommend it. Likewise, a book like Lorrie Moore's *Self-Help* seems to me to be the *kind* of book that could be mistaken for one of those trendy collections of short stories written by someone whose points of reference are wholly contained within the golden ghetto of pop culture. But, in fact, *Self-Help* is a stirring, admirable, often profoundly intelligent book whose success comes from the ineffable individuality of the writer, and the mysterious singularity of her voice.

So the task of the curious, open-minded reader cannot be made any easier by discovering a kind of novel worthy of his or her attention. Books come one at a time and all of the good ones form a category of their own.

I
WALLACE STEGNER
I

When I was presiding over college seminars filled with gifted young writers, I felt that I had a good overview of the fiction of the immediate future. I could see it being written before my eyes, and from it get a notion not only of fashions that were coming in, but also of the state of the American society and the American mind.

Wallace Stegner
photo by
Leo Holub

Sixteen years after retirement from that privileged place, I no longer have such an overview. I also find that, with the obligations of teaching removed, I read less fiction than I used to. I do not have new writers discovered for me by enthusiastic students, and when I read around trying to make my own discoveries I am as often as not disappointed by what I discover. Much of what I pick up seems to me self-conscious in one way or another — self-consciously Alexandrian in its techniques (probably the effect of too much college teaching of writing, or the wrong kind), self-consciously self-absorbed in its subject matter, self-consciously hermetic in its intellectual pretensions, or self-consciously minimalist in its rhetoric, or all four.

Therefore, when I mention Harriet Doerr, Raymond Carver, William Kennedy, Louise Erdrich, I do not claim anything more for them than that they are writers I have recently read and admired. They do not constitute either a Great Tradition or a New Wave. They are simply good writers, not in everything of theirs that I have read, but in one special and powerful book each: Harriet Doerr in *Stones for Ibarra*, Raymond Carver in the stories of *Will You Please Be Quiet, Please?* William Kennedy in *Ironweed*, and Louise Erdrich in *Love Medicine*. If I am going to judge writers, I prefer to judge them by their best.

What these four books have in common is that they are all *about* something, and they are all passionately *felt*. Not one of them is of the kind that can be read as well backward as forward; not one tries to reinvent the art of storytelling or impress readers with its author's nimbleness or profundity. Each is a little world, a scale model of human living; and if three of them — *Will You Please Be Quiet, Please? Love Medicine*, and most especially *Ironweed* — are about undistinguished people in circumstances that range from sad to appalling, I take that to be the fault not of the authors but of the world. What matters is that their people live and bleed and endure. I like the toughness of these four books. It seems to me a salutary antidote to the whining and self-pity that mark too much contemporary writing.

DANIEL STERN

Undoubtedly, the editor's statement that "American fiction is a variety of things" is true. But is it true *enough*? Undoubtedly

Daniel Stern

Robert Stone is quite different from, say, Lorrie Moore or Jay McInerney. But are Lorrie Moore, Gordon Ray, Joy Williams, and Susan Minot different enough from each other?

Let me stop beating around the bush. Here's my problem: I have to reshape your question to make it something I can answer. If you like some "recent fiction" more than other writing, why? — and what's your complaint about the stuff you don't think is so good? Okay — maybe it's a dumb question, but it's mine — and it's a sibling of yours, so here goes.

The so-called minimalist writers — some people have called them the children of Gordon Lish — are thin, self-regarding, narcissistic and, although very talented all, do not make one eager to return to them, for new works or, for the greatest pleasure of all, rereading.

Now, don't go away! All that has been said before! I have a different take on the situation!

Some writers who have been, on occasion, published by the same editors and magazines and publishing houses as the defamed minimalists who I think are quite fine and deserve reading and rereading are Cynthia Ozick, Raymond Carver, Philip Roth, Don DeLillo, Lynne Sharon Schwartz, Alice McDermott, Robert Stone. . . . A peculiar lot, perhaps, since Roth and Ozick have been publishing for decades and Alice McDermott is the author of one extraordinary novel and has just published her second novel . . . and Carver honed his craft quietly for years in the littlest of magazines, until his moment arrived . . . yet all are "recent fiction."

But here's my point: the writers on the second list have something which I believe the others lack, for all of their artistic gifts. I do not refer only to their life-experience—it is also the reading—or its absence—which I sense in their work which is thin, narcissistic, and limited. In short, I would like to raise the issue of the role of a wide world-literature reading or its absence, as a real problem in the writers of "recent fiction." Just as so many of these writers seem born yesterday in their personal/family historical naivete—they also seem born yesterday as artists.

When you see a painting of Mondrian or Jasper Johns—to pick two famous minimalists—there is the unseen, unheard, unspoken but nevertheless present sense of other painters, even of music and literature, in short of aesthetic life. Has any character in a novel by Gordon Ray or a story by Deborah Eisenberg—two very gifted minimalist writers—ever read a novel by Stendhal? There is utterly no doubt that Raymond Carver has read a hell of a lot of Hemingway—and somehow made it his own and become himself in the process.

What I'm suggesting is that recent fiction is a very real notion, but it is not simply a matter of time. For example: Dumas is not recent fiction, but the Balzac of *Lost Illusions* and *Père Goriot* is. What I'm suggesting is that the questions we ask of ourselves and each other need to be radically revised. The question is not what book published in the last year or two or three do we admire and think under-admired. The question is: What are we reading and liking and being nourished by and what is unfairly dying of neglect, in the short and long run?

Two of the best books I've read recently are by two relatively, and unjustly, unknown writers. One is a book of personal and literary essays by Natalia Ginzburg called *The Little Virtues*. The earliest piece in the book was written in 1944, the latest in 1962. Several of them are tiny enough to be called "minimal." They have the timeless and timely resonance of someone who has lived—through war and Italian fascism, in this case—and read—everyone, one would guess, though it's impossible to pinpoint, precisely. Ms. Ginzburg is almost eighty and is a magnificent, humane, unsentimental voice. She deserves to be read—not for her sake but for our sake.

The other book is by a middle-aged American writer, James Salter, called *Light Years*. The book was published by Random House in 1976. It met with small success. Larry McMurtry, who will always be a "now" writer but not a "recent" one, judged *Light Years* to be deficient in characterization in his *New York Times* review. Yet the book was one of the richest experiences I've had in a long time. Unspectacular and almost cool in its long look at a sophisticated literate family, it carves out its own territory in elegant language and a concrete address to experience which could be called Proustian if it weren't so American. (And, to my point, there is a moment in which someone actually dares evoke the reading of Henri Troyat's biography of Tolstoy as an important personal experience.)

The reading of a book as an important experience? Well, *Light Years* (now reprinted by North Point Press) by James Salter was just that, for me. But it is not by recommending books by Natalia Ginzburg and James Salter that some imbalance will be righted. It is by attending the values which those authors care about.

More life, more experience, more personal history, more reading as part of our lives and our literature. And less limiting of the "recent" to the recent.

RICHARD STERN

Richard Stern

As I become more and more whatever small thing I am, I become less and less open to literary alteration. Yet a crucial element of what I am has been literary pleasure. Such pleasure does, willy-nilly, alter one's attention, one's awareness of what constitutes crisis, scene, and personal distinction, and just as important, techniques of sharpening tools and, very occasionally, new tools. In the past ten or twenty years, I've been drawn to a great variety of work. I've enjoyed such masters of the small hint, small comedy, small disaster, and small revelation as the Mary Robison of *Days*, Tobias Wolff, Bette Pesetsky, Ann Beattie, Amy Hempel, and fifteen or twenty other literary lasers. There are also a good many masters of the social middle, brilliant registrars and arrangers of more or less large social chunks, novelists such as Craig Nova and Douglas Unger, storywriters such as Christopher McElroy, Mavis Gallant, and Elizabeth Tallent (to skip around ages and to omit twenty or thirty favorites including the editor of this issue). The grandchildren of Joyce and Kafka still flourish. I prefer most of the Americans to most of the French, whom I know less well. (I might add that I think a great deal is going on in German writing, far from the baroque shores of Grass, closer to the subversive calm of Uwe Johnson.) I stick here to the Americans. To cite only the B's, disciples of Barth and Barthelme, Beckett and Borges: there's the T. Coraghessan Boyle of *The Descent of Man* and that sheathed dagger of a first-person Frederick Barthelme ships around supermarkets, single condos, and other crowded American solitudes. Most after my heart and closer to my own small work are the latest masters of the perennial mimetic center. They are often treated as regionalists in a time when regionalism is little more than a chemical flavor trying to preserve a few old loves and hatreds. The Barry Hannah of *Airships, Ray,* and *Geronimo Rex* can stand for the new lights of the New South. The John Updike of the stories, of such essays as the one on Melville and the one on his own psoriasis, and *The Coup*, the one novel which fetches up what exists under the begemmed hysteria encrusting the other novels, can stand for the two slabs of eastern seaboard which sandwich New York. The last third of Joyce Carol Oates's *them* and fifteen or twenty of her stories can represent the literary Midwest of Dreiser, Anderson, James T. Farrell, and Nelson Algren. Philip Roth's recent *The Counterlife* shows the vitality that forceful, disciplined brilliance can wrest out of long-contemplated material. Some of the most brilliant technical innovations have come from such "traditional" writers as Roth. For me, the greatest of these — almost in a class of one — is Saul Bellow, whose latest book, of which I've read only a draft, testifies to the most extraordinarily productive career in American literature (with the possible exceptions of Henry James and William Faulkner). I've left out ninety-eight percent of those I admire. At this time, I don't have time to be equitable, comprehensive, or just. This is a great age of American fiction, wider in range than Elizabethan literature, although it lacks, of course, a Shakespeare. (Most of us still live off Tolstoy, Proust, and Joyce.) We have a handful of very remarkable writers and perhaps half a thousand marvelous ones.

I
GLADYS SWAN
I

Gladys Swan

Some ages are given more to reality, Wallace Stevens observed; others, to the imagination. Perhaps this distinction offers some perspective of those currently at the center of attention and those at the sidelines: Bobbie Ann Mason and Raymond Carver and Joyce Carol Oates in all the anthologies, but not, for instance, William Goyen, who is a master of the craft and one of our foremost writers.

Reality has a number of dimensions, certainly, and it's hard to categorize those who go after it, by whatever route. Some take their occasions from the familiar surface of the culture, with computer, shopping mall, condominium, and all the familiar brand names. I pick up stories now and then and read about urban blight and cultural sterility and fragmented lives. No doubt the suffering depicted is real: the alienation and entrapment, the passivity and despair, the emotional deadness, the disconnection from social bonds or larger meanings. Allowing for some notable exceptions, writers of this particular bent seem to be getting on better than the rest of us. But I can't stomach most of it. And right now the subject of despair seems to me a dangerous indulgence for both artist and audience. The streets are too full of it as it is, along with a corresponding cynicism, which is perhaps only a wittier form of despair. Our health, if not our survival, may very well depend on the redefinition of our humanity, the recovery of our passion, the exploration of new potentials of the imagination.

I hope that writers engaged in such pursuits, as yet unrecognized and unknown, are out there. I don't have the time to forage around to discover them. Reputation, accident, the recommendation of friends have put me onto the writers I've enjoyed: Saul Bellow, Ralph Ellison, and Toni Morrison; Patrick White, Kawabata, Ruth Prawer Jhabvala, Salman Rushdie, Russell Hoban, Frank Waters, Márquez, and others. So my reading of contemporary American writers is sporadic and limited, and I'm too busy with my own work to keep up with what is going on, much less comment intelligently on it.

Not that one is given a great deal of help. It is difficult to find a book review that gives any real sense of a writer's vision, any real assessment of the depth or complexity of his concerns. Nor is it easy for a reader to gauge what might be the reviewer's underlying prejudices and assumptions about literature. Where so much is published, a writer gets the luck of the draw. And how often then does that mean a sensitive and thoughtful reading of the work, with judgment, whether praise or blame, substantiated by evidence? At times reputation rests on such slender chances.

Oddly enough, since I don't read all that many reviews either, friends of mine put into my hands three long pieces damning the so-called minimalists. That means that someone had to read through all those yards of passionless prose and that three widely circulated magazines gave a great deal of space and attention to the message that their books are hardly worth the effort. Then why not get on with it, and focus attention somewhere else? How much space, except occasionally in the quarterlies, is given to writers from the Midwest and the West, who, it seems to me, still have a tougher go than most, still find themselves subject to prejudice. For instance, an anthology of Southwestern writers, *Writers of the Purple Sage*, managed to get published in Gotham, but Alex Blackburn's *The Interior Country: Stories of the Modern West*, which will reach a far smaller audience, owes its existence to the Ohio University Press. How often are the stories appearing in various of the university press series anthologized in books headed for the classroom? Yet I can think of stories by Mary Gray Hughes, Gordon Weaver, Stephen Minot, Jack Matthews, and others of my generation, that deserve that distinction. (No, I haven't made it either.)

Fortunately, good books, good writers do somehow carve out an audience, be it small or slow in coming: *The Awakening* shines through nineteenth-century prudery and sexism, and Barbara Pym is finally published. The business of attention and neglect is complicated by the fact that certain books are a response to a momentary twitch of the nerve or a passing mood in the culture, or speak to a social problem of immediate consequence — consider, for instance, Jay McInerney — whereas others never hit the trends of their times but speak to another age, another sensibility, and outlive their authors.

As I've said, I'm not much help. I've lived and worked too long in isolation, reading very little of my contemporaries. It would have been, would be still, too much of a distraction to do otherwise, in my own efforts to define the way I must go.

I
BARRY TARGAN
I

I'm not sure that the writing that most interests me needs or is deserving of more attention than it is already getting. It is doing just fine. What characterizes that writing, the literature that has most attracted readers of fiction for the longest stretch of fiction's history, continues to do so: textures — the realistic, sharply sketched images and details of life. The often pungent smell of human-ness. The quotidian and mundane rhythms and heft of life.

I have no great argument with the various spikey projections of contemporary American fiction — minimalist, conceptualist, sur-fiction, post-

Barry Targan

modern fiction, deconstructionist fiction (if that is not an oxymoron), and the like. I am against nothing that is done with intellectual honesty and with great care. I am not against any kind of writing. I am against war, outrageous poverty, substandard living conditions, the creation of a permanent subclass. *That* is bad stuff. *That* is damaging to a society, to the human spirit. Not writing of any kind.

But the fiction that has mattered most through time, like the painting that has mattered most, is the fiction that is "most directly about" the human condition and is written in the terms in which we (in any age, in every age) seem to think we experience that human condition, that predicament. Painting that takes paint as its subject exclusive of the larger and more complex world of event and consequence is unlikely to matter to us over time. And novelty (that "sick disease of modern life" in Matthew Arnold's words) must, perforce, feed upon itself. It can interest and delight us and inform us, but not for long. Much the same can be said of fiction that serves an ideological master, a critical polemic, a fixed aesthetic idea.

Maybe we cannot know — will never know — absolutely the ultimate meaning of things: that which is unalterably true in the universe. But so what? Such philosophical limitations are not limitations to writing. Such certainty as the postmodernist theoreticians demand (but reject) has never been the expectation or goal of fiction. Keats's Negative Capability — Shakespeare's strength — is more like it. Not the certainty but the uncertainty, not the answers but the ambiguous and paradoxical and enigmatic. Sure. But the best fiction (the most honored by being most read fiction) has never taken ambiguity or enigma *itself* as its subject. That best fiction has always positioned itself morally. It takes a stand regarding what we think of as human issues; it comes from somewhere, not everywhere or anywhere. It is not about its means; it is about the glory, jest, and riddle.

Now I'm not saying that these positions are right, that there is, necessarily, a shared "correct" moral view of life. Of course the writer in any age is centered by prevailing moral attitudes and debates which change in time. But we can't ignore the obvious fact that though the specific positions change as societal attitudes and values change, the taking of positions does not. We might not agree with the moral stance of Ben Jonson or Sam Johnson or John Dryden or Alexander Pope, with Jane Austen or Charles Dickens, or Hardy or Conrad or Hemingway or Faulkner, Updike, Roth, Styron. We might even argue that all of these writers serve (unknowingly) a hidden agenda, the economic and political ends of a ruling class or even just the psychology of language and other signs. Maybe. Let's even say that they do. But that doesn't alter at all the clear and dominant impulse of the act of writing fiction itself: to have one's say, and to say that this is how the world is and this is what it feels like.

But to come back to my specific point. What characterizes the fiction "that has mattered" (whether it should have or not is not the point) is texture, the feel and weight of place and substance that brings about the penumbra of authenticity that vitalizes and convinces. Dickens's London or Defoe's island, Tolstoy's wheatfields or salons, Conrad's storms, Hardy's heath, Hemingway's war, Roth's Newark, Updike's beds. How can we possibly fail to notice such power, how can we fail to heed it?

We cannot. We do not. For better or worse we root our Being itself in the "things of this world," and that includes our fictions. Things, not ideas or concepts or theories. Things first. You can have a story—or at least some pleasurable reading experience—that is nothing more than description or the evocation of "thinginess," but you can't have a story that only or mainly exists to demonstrate an abstract concept, at least not a story that you would read a second time. (Once you get it, you've got it: QED. Like a geometric proposition.)

So what we find is this: that what we have always known about fiction is still true. Details, specific images, metaphors that link up the senses to thought and feeling—that's the ticket to the reader's heart and head, to the reader's trust. Show, don't tell, the oldest "trick of the trade." It still works the special magic that enables us to see the usual in an unusual way in order to experience the usual profoundly.

I have stressed this point—or ramble—about current fiction because, as heartened as I am by the vitality and quality of so much that is written today, I am yet fearful that as more and more of the textures in our culture disappear, so too will those textures be less available to the young writers of the future. We have fewer and fewer neighborhoods full of conglomeration and bang. We have fewer and fewer family farms for kids to grow up on and then to draw upon when the time comes for them to write their novels. Our society does powerfully homogenize and blend. Sameness and similarity. The superhighways, Holiday Inn, McDonald's. Textural predictability. And TV is everywhere, right? Yes, but wrong, too!

If TV shows us a fictional farm, it is the Waltons' farm, one image of one farm to be shared by fifty million viewers, most of whom have never seen any kind of farm at all. Business, medicine, industry, law—rather than specify, TV does the opposite. TV "sees" an abstracted landscape created out of the simplest physical necessities of TV. Notice how most TV crime takes place in warm, outside weather, where it is always sunny and dry. Notice how many automobiles blow up in the desert or plumet off of spectacular cliffs. Notice how TV college professors live in those wonderful homes and have those lovely, oak-paneled offices. But it's not just TV. Abstraction is everywhere: the wax tomatoes sold in the supermarket or the often-spurious ideas about education and careers sold in the schools. The personas pandered in the clothing advertisements. But enough. I'm not here to get this far into this part of such a large topic. All I'm content to say is that the grit and sniff of life delights us, and there is less of it around these days and there will be less in days to come. That's a peril, because Abstraction is a poison, disastrous for a society or a writer. You can end up hating (and writing about) The Enemy but not individual people. You can take positions to The Poor but not toward individual families, all of whom are unhappy in their own unique way. Writers, especially younger writers, have to know the "danger" they run in our society at this time and guard themselves against it and write with their hands remembering the grain of wood or the dirt on potatoes in a time when so much is depicted as getting smoother and cleaner. And maybe sterile.

I have named no very contemporary names, given no specific titles. I accept the risk of my generalizations, but in this case I think that mentioning this author and that book isn't what I'm about. But let me make this point. In recent years there has been a hearty growth of interest in, a market for, the Informal or Familiar Essay. Not that the Essay was ever absent from the literary scene; think of its grand history—Hazlitt or

Emerson or E. B. White. Only now the Essay has a kind of prominence that it hasn't had for awhile. Edward Hoagland, Tom Wolfe, John McPhee, Paul Theroux, Russell Baker, Joan Didion, and suddenly many, many others. We've got the taste of the thing, you see. The delight in information itself, but more, the delight in information thought about, responded to, processed through a wondering sensibility. Has the Essay usurped the power of fiction, then, taken over the role of providing us our view of life's textures? Not likely, but its new presence does reveal our needs and tastes to ourselves.

OK, OK. A few names after all. But maybe surprisingly paradoxical ones. Think of the details and textures of Donald Barthelme or Robert Coover or Thomas Pynchon. Surprise indeed! But why so? Good writing is good writing, whether it is in the centrist tradition of Updike and Roth and Styron or at the "edges" of Barthelme and Coover and Pynchon. Joyce, for goodness sake!

Should I take the chance and be exactly specific after all? Why not? The kind of writing that I admire in itself and as an example of the textured strength central to all writing is represented by Douglas Unger's *Leaving the Land*. There! I've said it! May the Muses have mercy on my soul.

JOHN UPDIKE

Though the alleged minimalists—Carver, Beattie, Bobbie Ann Mason, Barthelme the Younger—get all the publicity these days, my heart still belongs to the old-guard maximalists, those who risk the onus of overdoing: Ozick, who lets her metaphors and fancy mind take her as far as they wantonly will; Barth, who pushed through on his impossibly tricky scheme in *Letters* and tested the will of even his most faithful readers; Roth, who in the face of all friendly advice runs his sexy, conscience-stricken, vociferous all-purpose hero through ever more ornate and obsessive paces; Salinger, who has taken nonpublishing to new heights of expressiveness; Oates, who publishes like crazy and can't ever get enough of fear and loathing in familiar surroundings; and (not to overdo) other hopeful and earnest intellectual children of the Fifties, raised on the Faerie Queene and the Fisher King, on brinkmanship by John Foster Dulles and big, big fins out of Detroit.

John Updike   photo by Dennis Chamberlin

I

ARTURO VIVANTE

I

Of the recent — this past year's — best-sellers, the only one I've been able to read in its entirety is Sue Miller's *The Good Mother* [1986]. At least there is some fire — in the form of voluptuous passion and love — in it. I've also admired a few of Tama Janowitz's stories — their whimsical, intimate quality; and Susan Daitch's novel *L. C.*— the faithfulness with which she traces the sentiments of a woman caught up in a revolution; and I found Edward Hoagland's novel *Seven Rivers West* rife with life. These are very different authors, however, and belong to no type. Perhaps the kind of writing that I'd be interested in reading more of is the novel of ideas, the *roman à thèse*. Certainly the kind I am *least* interested in reading is the fiction that, with physical action, tries to make up for the lack of an idea. But to get back to the novel of ideas, perhaps there hasn't been enough of that in recent and not-so-recent fiction. Perhaps writers pay too much heed to Joyce's precept that the fiction writer should stay behind the scenes paring his fingernails. Perhaps didacticism isn't as bad as critics say. After all, some of the greatest novelists — Melville, Tolstoy, D. H. Lawrence — indulged in it. They may not have been at their best in doing so, but they did have something of the preacher in them; it was a very essential part of their nature, and they'd hardly be recognizable without it.

Arturo Vivante

JON MANCHIP WHITE

As someone who is British, and whose career has been somewhat unusual, I need to express my opinions with a certain amount of circumspection; but there may be a point or two that I might usefully make.

A general point first.

While teaching fiction for ten years at the University of Tennessee, and for ten years before that at the University of Texas, I have always sought to encourage from students the widest possible variety of writing. For example, my current program offers, in addition to the usual core courses, courses and seminars in such topics as writing drama and screenplay, writing science fiction and fantasy, writing the detective and mystery story, and (a new departure) writing the supernatural and horror story.

I mention this because it seems to me that many writing programs tend to focus too narrowly on writing the mainstream or realistic type of novel or short story. This is a type that demands a maturity of approach and a practiced technique that adolescent or beginning writers can seldom, in the nature of things, command. A high proportion of them fail to write the mainstream story well, or even adequately, with the result that they become severely and often permanently discouraged, when all that has really happened is that they have failed to master a type of narrative for which they may have possessed no great facility in the first place. This need not have occurred had they been allowed to express themselves in some other genre which might have encouraged them to make use of a quality that most young people possess in abundance: the unfettered imagination. It thus seems to me that, by insisting on apprentice writers adhering too exclusively to a single literary form, many writing programs may be constricting what ought to be a free flow of talent. Perhaps we should bear in mind that probably nine out of ten of the country's coming writers will be the products of some writing program or other, or will have had significant contact with one. Nor is there any need to defend the respectability of those alternative forms I have mentioned (which in any case make up nine-tenths of contemporary reading matter). There is no need to apologize, for instance, in urging the claims of what James called "the dear old sacred terror," invaded though the field of supernatural writing has been in recent years by silly gross-out merchants. In America, in the nineteenth century alone, contributions to the genre were made by such writers as Brockden Brown,

Jon Manchip White

Poe, Irving, both the Hawthornes, Melville, Bierce, Wharton, Freeman, Glasgow, Gilman, and of course by James himself. Literary catholicity is surely a virtue that can contribute materially to the renewal of literature's pleasure and vitality.

Now (to come to more specific matters), there are also other forces that, it seems to me, might threaten the variety of writing that a healthy national literature ought to aim at. Here I must proceed warily, and perhaps only an outlander would have the temerity to aim a kick at such a sacred cow: but it does seem to me that, during the past forty years or so, the influence of one metropolitan magazine in particular has come to exercise an undue influence on American letters. It is a magazine that has published many outstanding pieces: but when one takes an overall view of the contents of magazines and journals in the 1920s, 1930s, and 1940s one becomes aware that in later years this publication has somehow helped to bring about a steady shrinkage and aridity in subject matter, coupled with a corresponding thinness and preciosity of style. One of its more curious achievements has been to induce an effect of gentrification even where experimental and avant-garde fiction are concerned. Even the liveliest pieces take on a musty tinge, wedged in between the arch cartoons and the ponderous articles on the origins of the Paraguayan nose-flute and fashions in facial hair in Eastern Rumelia. Worse, the magazine has managed to fob off its own preferred taste as the norm of a sizable portion of American writing, so that the fiction it offers has become the "official" fiction of other journals and of many writing departments. My own feeling is that American writing in general ought to look beyond this somewhat self-admiring model and aspire to something expressive of a far more daring range of subject matter. It is sad to see so many writers in the United States, of all places, writing as if they were citizens of Luxembourg or Lichtenstein.

Greatly daring, I will now turn ninety degrees and make something of the same complaint about much of the current writing in the American South, where I live and work. While I yield to no one in my admiration of Miss Welty, I wish she hadn't written that somewhat uncharacteristic story, "Why I Live at the P.O." Stories like that have had the unfortunate effect of spawning the sort of tepid and inbred kind of story in the South that the magazine I have just spoken of has fostered in the North. Too many Southern books and stories are now constructed according to what has become the safe and unenterprising formula of the "official" Southern story. Take a small Southern town, add a couple of quirky characters and a spot of branch water and shake them together into a cute and patronizing little anecdote. The blood, fear, cruelty, nobility, and squalor of the South have been filtered out. Walker Percy has remarked that he has never made use of any story told him while sitting on a stoop. An excellent prescription for a young Southern writer. The South deserves a Faulkner, a Caldwell, a Stribling, a Warren, an O'Connor, a Tate, a Lytle; it deserves a Baldwin, a Gaines, a Reed, a Young. Today it usually gets — what? Much of the literature of the modern South represents it as a gutless sort of place, where the writers of the Grit Lit. School perform a kind of inverted Uncle Tom for the benefit of the Yankees, huddling round the parish pump and creating a sort of Southern Cranford. American writers, whether of the South or North, oughtn't to be applauded for taking the easy option. Again, I am not pleading for any diminution of standards, but only for the recovery of a certain kind of robustness that I feel is still, in spite of shocks and setbacks, characteristic of the American spirit.

All this, of course, does a huge injustice to the army of American writers who are producing impressive work not only in the mainstream but in the wide range of genres that I have mentioned. In the South, for example, one has only to remember the splendid literary efflorescence that is characteristic to Texas. To all those writers, my profoundest apologies. They are the ones who recognize that America is a great and generous continent that ought to give birth to great and generous offspring.

End of sermon.

Amen.

ALLEN WIER

Considering the amount of talent, commitment, and plain hard work it takes to write well, all *good* writing is *deserving* of more attention and more readers. But there's no reason writers who produce good writing should *expect* more attention. The readership for good writing has always been small and seems likely to remain so. I'd be happy if good fiction (and, even, poetry) were a larger part of our popular culture, but I'm not miserable because it is not. The rewards of writing well will probably always be, primarily, intrinsic. I expect (I even hope) this is true when good fiction earns for its author rave reviews and fat royalty checks, as sometimes happens. At the same time, I have little regard for the notion that the general reading public cannot possibly appreciate good fiction.

Allen Wier

My mother is not a "literary" person but she reads a great many books, literary and popular. She reads poetry and fiction and all kinds of nonfiction. She appreciates and enjoys my work (not *solely*, she says, because her son is the author, and I believe her). Recently, my mother and I were talking about what makes a novel *good*. She asked me: "If you are a good writer—and I believe you are—why don't you write a well-written novel that you are proud of *and* that all my friends, ordinary readers, can really understand and enjoy?"

That is, I think, just the *kind* of fiction I would like to write.

I am drawn to fiction in which language becomes *a*ffective experience. I respond to textures and images and to the details and rhythms of a particular place, a particular voice. I like to be entertained, but sentences as well as story lines intrigue me. My list of favorite novelists includes the makers of many different *kinds* of novels. A good writer, I believe, responds to the different demands of many different stories; his or her sensibility hovers over and unites them, all kinds.

Talking about *kinds* of fiction can be fun so long as we don't take our categories too seriously. I'm glad so few good writers fit neatly beneath critical umbrellas. Recently I've been amazed at the variety of names I've seen classified as part of the so-called *minimalist movement* in contemporary fiction. I suspect some of these writers were surprised to find themselves in one another's company. Of course we all know to trust the tale not the teller (nor the editor, nor the critic); frequently a writer's work refuses to conform to its maker's (or reviewer's) notions.

Several years ago I first read the novels of Robbe-Grillet, which, in places, dazzled me. I admired certain cinematic effects, the glossy sheen or the jagged edge of surfaces, the play in point of view. Then I read his essays in *Towards a New Novel* (very readable and fun, I thought), but I had a hard time reconciling the aesthetics with the novels. Only in *Jealousy*, I thought, was technique fully integrated with raw material. The novels seemed to grow more from an impulse to make *criticism* than to make *fiction*. Because of that, I felt, Robbe-Grillet sometimes sacrificed fiction to a demonstration of aesthetic theories. Part of the pleasure in reading such a writer was in the eclecticism that freed me to appropriate any technique that might serve a particular moment in a particular work of my own.

I use the past tense to talk about my reactions to Robbe-Grillet because I'm not sure what my reactions would be today. When I'm asked, "Have you read *Jealousy*?" I can answer easily. But to, "What do you *think* of it?" I have to say what I *thought* of it, because as I change so do novels I have not reread. Fifteen years have passed since I read *Jealousy* and those years of living and writing would surely make the experience of reading *Jealousy* today different.

The kind of recent writing I'm especially interested in today is writing which indicates preoccupations I share with another writer. Such preoccupations may be as obvious as subject matter or as subtle as theme and technique. Right now, the end of February 1987, I'm well into a novel the elements of which have caused me to think about methods of storytelling—narrative stance, point of view, voice, and authority—and related methods of pacing—narrative drive and plotting different story lines. Because of my current fascinations, I have enjoyed recent novels that succeed (in different ways) with what I think of as a "panoramic" scope, such as Madison Smartt Bell's *Waiting for the End of the World*, Russell Banks's *Continental Drift*, and Edward Hoagland's *Seven Rivers West*. Because of the ways in which he reveals the indelibility of his voice, I am struck (again) by Wright Morris, this time in his recently published *Collected Stories*. Because I'm also interested, right now, in how a writer writes about love and marriage and divorce and the attendant joys and pains without falling victim to large clichés, I've been rereading the short stories of Andre Dubus.

My own work is not, of course, the only impetus to my reading. Sometimes I want to read only work that demonstrates concerns very different from my own. Sometimes what I'm working on has nothing to do with what I read. But seldom do I read a book because it is part of a trend. Even in Alabama, where I live, we hear about the latest literary fashions. But there may be less pressure here, so far from the center of publishing, to keep up with the trends. I don't want to ignore the merchandise, just the popular labels. Prevailing trends like prevailing winds are subject to sudden shifts, they come and they go. I'm suspicious of any writer who seems more committed to aesthetic theories than to the demands of each individual story or novel.

DARA WIER

We're surrounded by angels. Unravelling angels and angels of windknots, hungry angels and angels with thin closed mouths, angels of self, self-pity, self-consciousness, self-doubt, angels of truth and angels of deception, angels of courage and angels of cowardice, angels of fame and fortune, angels of bits and pieces and angels of systems, angels of sex, angels of where are we going, where have we gone. More angels than I can shake a stick at. In my first response to this question I'd written, "I'm a bovarist and like a book that consumes me. I like to know I'm in the hands of a writer on whom nothing is lost, who is fearless, smart, serious, and above and beyond the fray, whose sense of humor is tragic and whose sentences ride shotgun with angels." None of this I wish to take back, but all of it could stand annotation.

I'm a bovarist

Madame Bovary came into my hands long ago, before I'd written a single story, and before I'd been exposed (that is, my immune system was untested) to concepts or theories of aesthetic impressions. As have many poems, novels, stories, essays, musical compositions, songs, movies, sculptures, buildings, landscapes, photographs and human beings since, *Madame Bovary* changed my life. Flaubert offered me an invitation; I accepted it. While I was reading his book and for a few days afterward, I lived under Flaubert's spell. Everything and everybody I met registered a shade differently because of it. Degas's famous words, *"The artist does not draw what he sees but what he must make others see"* apply. I saw what I'd never seen before, as I'd never before seen.

*Dara Wier
photo by
Michael Pettit*

and like a book that consumes me.

Flaubert's book *consumed* me; self-consciousness was lost so that another's knowlege and conscience could be gained. To invert a commonplace of reading: "Read it. You'll love it. It's about someone unlike yourself." In mistaken attempts to cajole someone into reading, the operable phrases are *you'll identify with it* and *it's relevant to your situation.* I don't doubt or denigrate the value of art's commiserative benefits. Lord knows, sympathy, compassion, and empathy are necessary all around. I do distrust the aspect of limiting my worldliness to circumstances of my own sex, class, race, age, or region. At the same time I recognize occasions when self-consciousness, whether it be of self, sex, sexual preference, racial or economic heritage, age or homeland, is a necessity and a virtue.

Still I am cautioned by William James's examination of self-consciousness in *The Varieties of Religious Experience*: "Oh, this terrible, second me, always seated whilst the other is on foot, acting, living, suffering, bestirring itself. This second me that I have never been able to intoxicate, to make shed tears, or put to sleep. And how it looks into things, and how it mocks." Good books intoxicate me, make me shed tears, and sometimes, when I need their assistance, allow me to sleep.

I like to know I'm in the hands of a writer on whom nothing is lost,

It was William James's brother who wrote, "Try to be one of those on whom nothing is lost." No effort of time, intellect, or emotion would be wasted on one of these. Everything, the concrete and the abstract, and all things between would be saved. It was the first living writer I met who showed me Henry's sentence. I liked it then; I like it better now. Then I was eighteen and hoped to be given permission to take a poetry and fiction writing seminar at Louisiana State University. I was beside myself that I might be given credit for this work I did always anyway because I loved it. It seemed too reasonable, too lucky. As it turned out I was let in and the class was more than reasonable. I learned to read as a writer reads. I reckoned with exploded views of stories of all kinds. I saw the elements of style and composition, the parts that go into making fiction, separately, but *in positions indicating their proper relationships to the whole*. The teacher in this class, David Madden, never suggested by word or deed that I might be constrained or unduly shaped by Nature or my own or anyone else's nature. Nothing would be lost. But I would never again be shy with a book.

who is fearless, smart, serious and above and beyond the fray,

The fearless writers of my dreams say what is hard to say. Fearless in their styles, fearless with their subjects, they aren't constrained by tradition, habit, warnings, dogma, theory, marketplace, or favor, not even by their own desires. They don't lose courage because of fantasies of fame.

My colloquial *smart* needs to be far removed from definitions of both pain and fashion. I'm not looking for invented misery; there's plenty of real suffering around. I'm not looking for a neat, trim or elegant book— necessarily. I do like books which surprise me, turn my head and keep the pages turning. In *Art and Reality* Joyce Cary says:

> It is only in great art and the logic of the sub-conscious where judgment has become part of the individual emotional character that we move freely in a world which is at once concept and feeling, rational order and common emotion, in a dream which is truer than actual life and a reality which is only there made actual, complete and purposeful to our experience.

whose sense of humor is tragic

Who are these Chaplinesque characters? Who is so funny and so calamity prone? I've always felt uneasy in the presence of people who don't know when to laugh. So many of the fiction writers I admire open humor to view. Stanley Elkin, Philip O'Connor, R. H. W. Dillard, Milan Kundera, Margaret Atwood, Don Hendrie, Tony Ardizzone, these are a few.

and whose sentences ride shotgun with angels.
   I revere the sentence; I admire its paradoxical nature, its limpid qualities of predictability and inevitability, its availibility to how and what and why we think and to what's said. Gertrude Stein, Sherwood Anderson, Henry Miller, Flannery O'Connor, Nathanael West, their ways with the sentence, so singular, whimsical, unique.
   So there are many writers I admire. Now I want to ramble through a few of them, by no means all of them, and those whose books I've most recently read.
   Sometimes I feel as though I were born into a careening world slick with irony: plenty here, nothing there, imagination's pride of infinity measured against the facts' predictions of doom. I'm happy when I come upon a book in which there is no irony intended and none to be found. *Shoshone Mike*, Frank Bergon's first novel, is this sort of book. It's a masterpiece of no-irony, and its author has performed the difficult trick of self-effacement; graciously he appears to be nowhere to be found, his genius which, not ironically, is everywhere present is nowhere visible.
   And I admire Richard Ford's *The Sportswriter* and Don DeLillo's *White Noise*; I like Tobias Wolff's short stories and various works by Russell Banks. Louise Erdrich's and Paul Auster's novels make me look forward to reading their next.
   I've read all of Craig Nova's books: they are startlingly varied. When the surface is wild, some call it gothically loony, the underlying desire longs for sanity, serenity, calm, equamimity; when it's measured, citizenlike, almost tame, the underbelly threatens chaos and explosive justice. Nova seems to be a very good writer on both sides of this coin.
   Valerie Martin (*A Recent Martyr, The Consolation of Nature*) writes as if no one has ever spoken a relativistic word about morality, as if no one has ever questioned the necessity, much less the possibility, of Meaning. She sees a symbolic world and writes it with brains, grace, and courage.
   In his fourth novel, *The Year of Silence*, Madison Bell works around the edges, mirages, illusions, near-misses, fringes and margins of peripheral knowledge whose significance we need to know.
   In her recent collection of beautifully written stories (*Learning the Mother Tongue*) Cathryn Hankla writes, "The daughter was at school or perhaps not yet born. Or perhaps it would be a childless marriage

after all, who knew, who cared? For certainly, it would not last without fiction." Fiction is this essential. I couldn't do without it.

NANCY WILLARD

LETTER TO ACCOMPANY A GIFT OUTRIGHT

Dear David,

I might have given you something small and useful for your trip to Europe, like money, but I have decided to give you something large and awkward: five books. Homesickness strikes even the most ardent travelers, and when you feel it coming on you, open this parcel. I am sorry the parcel is so heavy, but I had to include *Sometimes a Great Notion.* After you've toted Ken Kesey's book across the Atlantic, you may agree with the reviewer who called it "elephantine," "a windy, detailed mock epic." I call it a large sprawling adventure story big enough to get happily lost in. American literature has had its share of elephantine books. Reading one that succeeds is like reading the Grand Canyon. Nobody who loves Mark Twain ever wished *Huckleberry Finn* a word shorter.

Song of Solomon is also heavy — the bookshop only carried the hardback — but not as cumbersome. I hope you'll read it aloud. This will take more time than your usual way of reading, but after you've set your watch back six hours you'll enjoy the way Toni Morrison takes time, takes it backward and forward like a shuttle in a loom, her sentences singing. When a good storyteller tells you the time, it turns into timelessness.

In case you don't have time to read large novels, I'm enclosing two collections of short stories, *The Little Disturbances of Man* and Eudora Welty's *Collected Stories.* I fear that the longer you stay away from America, the more you'll lose your ear for the fine shadings of humor in the conversations of the people you've grown up with. Take these two books, and you'll keep it intact. Grace Paley will help you take an interest in life, even in its most aggravating forms (lost tickets, broken glasses, broken promises). I wanted to give you Eudora Welty's essay, "Place in Fiction," but couldn't find it in the bookstore. I hope that leaving your country will sharpen your memory of all that's familiar and ordinary to you, like your mom and dad and your aunt Nancy, and I hope we shall cease to be ordinary the moment you've left us behind.

Nancy Willard
photo by
Eric Lindbloom

My fifth gift to you is *One Hundred Years of Solitude* — of course you know that American literature doesn't mean simply North America — because there are other ways of traveling through time and space than the ones you'll be using, and if you find yourself stranded in an airport that looks just like the airport you left, you'll want García Márquez to tell you: miracles are inseparable from the commonplace. They can happen at any time, in any place. You don't have to believe me. I'm giving you five writers who tell stories but not lies. You can take their word for it.

Love,

Aunt Nancy

HILMA WOLITZER

I'm pretty tired of the clamor surrounding the ubiquitous present tense, the use of the first person, and the postmodern mode. Some of the current, so-called minimalist writing — Deborah Eisenberg and Raymond Carver's, for instance — seems very rich and complex

Hilma Wolitzer

to me, and some other, more ornate and lyrical fiction is spare at heart, so I'll name names rather than try to provide categories or genres. Russell Banks is a writer I hope to read more of soon, and so are Richard Ford and Marilynne Robinson. They achieve a psychological reality that makes their stories organic to their characters, the way people's actual lives are. Richard Yates's bleak naturalism continues to engage my sympathy and admiration. Harold Brodkey makes me work hard through his convoluted prose for my pleasure, but the pleasure is real and astonishing. I always like reading Grace Paley, who tells the truth in a friendly, neighborhood voice, and no one, to my mind, is as hilarious and wrenching as Stanley Elkin. Poets like Denis Johnson bring their particular music to fiction without any sacrifice of its conventional delights. And Charles Johnson, Mary Hood, Daphne Merkin, and Chuck Wachtel all contribute to making the world new.

But maybe naming names wasn't such a good idea, after all — I've left out so many fine and diversified writers. I suppose there simply isn't a *kind* of writing I'd like to espouse or celebrate. It's the very variety of texture, sound, and content that most distinguishes contemporary American fiction.

JOSE YGLESIAS

I try to keep quiet. There is too much talk about literature. Still, I must not pass up any chance to urge on you the Harrison-Texas plays of Horton Foote, the Beulah quintet of Mary Lee Settle, and all the novels of William Wharton.

Jose Yglesias

THE ART OF
THE STORY

THE INFIDEL

LYNNE SHARON SCHWARTZ

I

Martin Solomon, the well-known painter whose recent work had been called, not entirely to his liking, "an anatomy of entropy," was standing in the bustling vastness of the New York Port Authority bus terminal, a suitcase dangling from one hand, a portfolio of drawings from the other, his raincoat slung over his shoulder. Reflexively, he scanned the crowd for the faces of interesting women, much as an engineer might note structural beams or an orthopedist curved spines. The terminal was undergoing dissection and reconstruction to keep up with modern times: sheets of plastic skirted raw masonite panels, and makeshift signs and arrows directed the dazed voyager. The usual melancholy of transience was heightened painfully; to Martin the place smelled of desperation, cried out to be left in peace. Martin too, though in transit between the arms of Paula, vacationing in Vermont, and Jess, in a SoHo loft, was in a state of solitary despair. In younger days, he had envisioned himself on these endless treks as a picaresque hero off to meet adventure. But tonight, with the rain battering at the bus windows, leaving a distorting sheen on the grey twilight landscape, he had felt himself an aging man burdened with luggage weightier each year, compelled to wander the earth homeless. There was still the house on the shore, but since Alice died it didn't feel like home.

"Men are incomplete," he had told Jess months ago. "They need women."

"The Infidel" appeared in *The Melting Pot and Other Subversive Stories* (New York: Harper & Row, 1987).

She had rolled her eyes. "Your originality is dazzling. Go on. You can be Sartre, I'll be Simone."

"Listen, my little sourball, I don't mean in all the ordinary ways, socially, sexually, emotionally . . . They need women psychically. Men are constructed incomplete."

She still looked dubious, hugging her knees to her chest in her big old armchair. She was small, with straight light hair that fell about her face, featherlike, and she was wearing a sweatshirt and blue jeans. She dressed only for gallery openings and meetings with editors. Jess looked like a charming student, but she was nearly forty. Martin was just stretching out a leg to nudge her gently, for she could flay him with words, then throw her arms around him and caress him to distraction, but her son Max came in. He was twelve and, like most people, adored Martin. "Wanna box?" he asked.

Martin leaped up and dashed the unruly grey hair off his face. Energy radiated from his big body as, hopping about, he aimed light punches at the boy's jaw. "Do it like I told you, keep alert, that's a boy. A killer. Going to be our next Muhammad Ali, eh, Jess?" He stole a quick glance at her. She had put her glasses back on and was studying the proofs of an article she had written about Duane Hanson, the sculptor whose clothed figures looked so authentic that real people came away feeling diminished.

"Uh-huh." She didn't look up.

Later, while Jess went out to a gallery, Martin made a stew, with Max's help. It had been raining that day too. He felt cozy, puttering around the kitchen with the boy, lovingly stirring the meat and vegetables, while outside the sky was grey with weeping. At last he held out a spoonful to Max. "Taste and see if it needs anything."

"It's great. But don't you feel kind of dumb wearing that apron?" It was Jess's, white with splashes of yellow flowers, a ruffle around the skirt.

"Dumb, why? I don't want to get my pants all dirty. Besides, it's pretty, isn't it?" Martin flicked the ruffle coyly and performed a few cancan steps, singing Offenbach heartily.

Max refused to join in. "Shit, you're weird, man!"

"Tough guy, eh?" He threw a few more punches, sending Max skittering and giggling around the room, till Jess returned and announced she was starving.

"How'd you learn to cook?" Max asked as he set the table. "Your mother make you?"

"My mother? She hardly cooked a decent meal in her life. If she even went to the grocery she had to lie down for an hour afterwards."

"Why, was she sick?"

"Hypochondria. The funny thing about it is you live a very long time. Everyone around you dies young, though, of exhaustion!"

"Oh Martin, cut it out, will you?" Jess called from across the room, pulling off her boots. "Max, I hope you never talk about me like that."

"Okay, forget it. Let's eat. Tell me about the show. What's the little motherfucker up to?"

"Well, he's still under the influence. Yours."

Martin smiled broadly, slapping his large hands on the table. "Good, good! Share and share alike."

In bed that night Jess said, "The way you talk about your mother. She's dead. Doesn't there come a time when you forgive people?"

"Forgive? Forgive is hard. But didn't I do everything a good son should, call her up, send her money, fly to Arizona every time she sneezed?" He reached out for her. "You're very tough, my love. Never let me off, do you?"

He thought even as he kissed her that he had never known a woman as relentless. She took his extravagant words literally, called him to account for every inconsistency, every hasty judgment. Jess thought words were permanent things solidly bonded to truth; holy objects to be used with scrupulous care. But Martin, who liked to be accommodating, spoke to serve the fleeting occasion. Words showered from him, Alice used to say, like puffs of dust rising around a genie. The image amused him. He could see the turban, the broad bare chest, the billowing trousers. But it was the springing from the bottle, he thought, that really attested to the powers of the genie. The dust was a by-product—pretty, but all for show.

"Am I that bad?" Jess said in his arms.

"Merciless."

"It's because I want you to be perfect."

"But I *am* perfect. I keep telling you."

"Show me."

He pulled her on top of him. Just before the climax there came a sinking feeling, his heavy history pressing down on him. His wife dead eight months, who had been barren, and Paula alone. He staved it off until the end. Then, defenseless, crushed, he rolled onto his side, away from Jess.

She drew him back, curled herself under his arm. "Don't go away like that. It's horrible. I'm not your mother, you know."

"I'm sorry. It's not that at all." He held her closer, though it took effort. His muscles felt like stone. "But don't you feel nice, Jess? Didn't you like it?" He made himself smile at her.

"That's hardly the issue, is it?"

"Look, it's been almost six years. You don't just drop someone after all that time, so long, ta-ta, cheerio, ho ho. She depends on me."

Jess pulled away and sat up. "Then why do you come here?"

"I come because I love you."

"No!"

"All right, no. Have it your way. I don't love you."

"No, no, you do love me."

"All right, so I love you."

"You know, Martin, I was a decent person before I got started with you. I was in good standing with myself. Go away, will you? I'll manage fine. Let's part friends."

"Ah, don't be cross, love. Come here. That's right. Tell me a fantasy and we'll do it."

"God, you're impossible! I don't want a fantasy. I like reality — have you heard of it?"

"Come on." He pulled her still closer, stroking in a teasing way. Despite his great weariness he had to be generous and selfless, yet again. Sacrifices were in order, to placate the gods. There was even a certain pleasure in renouncing the self, offering it as sacrifice. This is my body. Eat.

"Okay, baby, think of something — the most exciting, the most lewd, the most lascivious, the most erotic, the most outrageous, the most voluptuous, the most epicurean — "

"Oh, stop already, you nut!"

He had triumphed; she was laughing.

II

At twenty-five, Martin, in his romantic soul, viewed his continental trip as one of initiation, rather like the long, leisurely kind undertaken by sons of propertied British families in the nineteenth century, only Martin did not come from a great family and had to support himself with odd jobs. So much the better: he was nothing if not enterprising, and anyway, property was theft. In Paris, when he was not hauling crates of fruit or repairing the engines of Citroens, he divided his time among museums, painting, and women. Older women, for the most part. Girls were not as readily accessible to a foreigner. Older women whose husbands were preoccupied and lukewarm with middle age, women to whom a young and boundlessly energetic American artist was a morsel of exotica.

That ended, though, when he found Alice. She was a shy girl from a strict, well-to-do-family in Toronto, working for the overseas *Herald Tribune* and trying to perfect her French. She had little experience of men. As they sat in the Bois de Boulogne eating bread and cheese and olives and drinking wine, Martin wooed her with sweeping speeches. He disdained the surrealists, he thrilled to the Fauves and Matisse. Yes to Soutine and all feckless exiles. No to the sterilities of glass and steel, yes to the fecundities of Gaudí. His other passion was history, and his judgments ranged wide (he had read everything), though lingering as if nostalgic on the streak of revolutionary fervor of 1848. He called himself an anarchist. "A lawless man?" Alice laughed in delight. "Not at all! An Old Testament prophet, who bows to no authority but the ineffable! Squash the Philistines! Eisenhower! Cecil B. deMille! Coca Cola inundating the antique splendors of Europe!" Well-bred girls made the best audience. Martin pounded a fist on the grass, then sprang up to orate to the poplars. "We shall be drowned in another flood — Coke — for spiritual sloth. Where is the grandeur of mind that gave Samson back his strength? Man was born free, and everywhere he is in chains. So to speak. Life is beautiful, till we mar it by ugliness." He paused to breathe and offered a shy grin. "I was the valedictorian in high school."

When he returned to America he would paint enormous pictures, he told her, not flamboyant like himself, but pictures that showed the meditative, delicate soul within. He would transform the world by vision alone, he promised with a wink and a gleam: Martin was his own ironist. Modest, too, in his way. He did not tell her about the scholarships at Yale or the special attentions from the exalted painters there.

To eat, he would dig ditches if necessary. He was huge and had the energy of ten men — that much Alice could see for herself in the way he whisked her in and out of galleries and cafes and, finally, in his lavish love. She followed his lead down erotic byways querying, "Does everybody really do this?"

Martin too was entranced. He liked the slender toughness of her body, her chestnut hair drawn back in a ponytail showing the bare, clean lines of her face; more than that he liked her acuity, her ear alive to the slightest nuances of phrase, her rigor in choosing the precise word for her meaning. Sometimes, talking, she would pause for five or six seconds, her face suspended in calm, one hand open and outstretched as if the perfect word were a tactile thing drifting invisibly toward her; intriguing to him, what fevered activity must be hidden within, what flashes scurrying along the circuits of her brain. And still more, he liked the fact of her being—however minimally—foreign, Canadian, nurtured far from the tattered streets of Newark, where Martin's father had been a baker who died young. When Martin told her how relatives had taken him and his mother in, how his aunt had presided over the family candy store while his uncle took bets over the phone, Alice gaped like a schoolgirl. No room for a bulky boy in that apartment where his bed flipped out of a wall. No one had ever asked where he spent his time (the library, and when that closed, the streets), surely not his mother, staring at her blotchy ceiling. There was something crude and primitive and cobwebby and inarticulate about the life in those rooms, not the physical markings of poverty—he was no snob, he assured Alice—but the dismalness lodged in the woodwork. So he developed peripatetic habits; without a roof, he leaned up toward the light. For he earnestly believed life was beautiful. He had to. Could she see? Alice nodded urgently. The abundance he felt within, the very force of those longings bred from books and bleakness were proof enough. And here was Alice, with her reserve and elegance and precision. Class qualities, bred to deny easy access. Well, he would brook no such barriers.

There was no need to dig ditches. They came home and taught at universities, Alice in Romance Language departments and Martin in studio courses. Students loved him, especially when he marched at the head of their ranks protesting racism, and later, war. At rallies, after other speakers unreeled statistics of social injustice, it was Martin, scorning the microphone, who restored their spirits. However much they treasured their indignation, they must treasure their joy equally. He quoted Gramsci on the higher wisdom of optimism. Never cease believing that life was beautiful. After him came the singing.

He organized and exhorted in one university town after another. Alice wanted to settle in and take root; Martin was restless. Not your basic academic type, he told her. He bored easily.

"I see that. People and places both," she said. "You seem to riffle through them and throw them away like newspapers."

"Riffle. That's good, very good," said Martin. "Why don't you write a book instead of doing all those translations?"

They moved partly because administrations found the perils of Martin almost as great as the wonders. Folding her skirts neatly into a suitcase, Alice said, "Even if you're right, you don't have to reveal everything that's on your mind all of the time." That might be all very well for her, but Martin felt natural as a troublemaker, tilting at the status quo, forever urging the needs of blacks, artists, students, and above all, women, for he was an early and ardent champion of their cause. Someone had to do it, he argued. The students needed an example, and could she suggest anyone else among all those stodgy professors? She couldn't. There were days at a stretch so crowded with social agitation, he didn't even see Alice. The day he cast his spell over a townful of Republicans, making them march and even sing *"We Shall Overcome,"* he was so overcome he didn't notice she was not marching at his side.

Alice, tired of seeking new jobs, stopped teaching and devoted herself to translations of novels, at which she was excellent, the best translators being unobtrusive. Martin was proud of her success. His superior Alice. And yet, translations . . . Of course he did not hint at this to her. They were talking less about everything. When one of the French novels she translated, based on the life of the Renaissance poet Louise Labé, became a campus cult novel, it irked him that Alice won little glory. Who ever notices translators' names? He had to tell people. "Please don't make such a point of it," she said, driving home from a party at which he had thrust her forward and announced her credentials. "Why not? One of us around here might as well reap some rewards."

For his paintings wouldn't come right. Not bad, only just below first-rate, the most accursed kind of failure. It was tempting to blame the narrowness of the academic life, but he refused any cheap excuses: better painters taught.

Nor were there children. The doctors found nothing discernibly wrong with either of them. Martin in any case had already fathered a child, or had reason to believe he had, a couple of months before he met Alice. Giovanna, the woman's name was; till now he had all but forgotten. She had come with her three young children to visit parents in Florence and would return to a wealthy husband in Buenos Aires. On the eve of her departure she told him she might be pregnant.

"What do you mean, might? Don't you know?"

"Sometimes I'm a little late."

"How late now?"

"A few weeks."

"But—" Martin stammered. "But what will you do?"

"Un piccolo ricordo." A souvenir. She gave him a coquettish look. He could still remember her earrings, immense, pendulous, gold. He had suddenly found them revolting, but what could he do? She left no address—it was not something that could endure.

"Look here, Alice, we could adopt a baby. Six months later you'll be pregnant. That's what happens."

"Maybe later." She lost weight and grew quiet. Martin had never liked silence — it reminded him too much of his mother lying in that close room, or the dinners served on that oilcloth-covered table where the only sounds were biting and chewing and slurping and his uncle's pencil scratching at the racing form. So he filled their rented houses with students who buzzed around day and night. The more they buzzed, the quieter and more unobtrusive Alice grew, retreating to her study to work. But at some point the house would empty out.

"Talk to me."

"It's midnight. Aren't you talked out yet?" She was in bed with a book in a language he couldn't even recognize. Portuguese?

"But you haven't said a word to me all day."

"How could I? You're always surrounded."

Martin sat down at the edge of the bed and smiled, good-tempered as always. "I'm not surrounded now."

"I don't want the dregs."

Every two or three years she set herself to learning a new language — Greek, Russian, Serbo-Croatian. She wore earphones and listened to Berlitz-type dialogues on tape while she cooked dinner, now and then murmuring an odd bunch of syllables. "What are they saying that's so absorbing? You look spellbound," said Martin, tapping at her shoulder.

She turned off the tape. "What? Oh. Stop or I'll scream."

"What did I do! I asked you a simple question. Is it too much effort to answer? I mean, you're walking around here in another world, Alice."

"Stop or I'll scream. That's what it's saying. If you're alone and accosted in Athens."

The intervals at which she undertook these languages, Martin felt, were intervals at which she might have borne children. Or adopted children. But he could no longer mention such things. Now all her store of words was in foreign tongues. He felt faint with loneliness.

"Turn around, Alice. You're not really sleeping." She would let him make love to her, with never a sound, eyes closed. Mortifying. "Say something, goddammit," he once shouted. "Say you hate it, even!" His raised voice shocked him, but didn't seem to bother Alice in the least.

"What should I say? You just want company on your travels. It doesn't have to be me or anyone in particular. You could do it yourself and I could watch — it would be the same thing."

The injustice of it! To him, who sought only the perfect communion of spirits! She was deliberately withholding herself, refusing him what he needed. Just as his mother had done, but he had not succumbed then and wouldn't now. It all came clear: his work was failing because she was failing him. Women were the rich source, the spring, the indispensable path. Throughout history, Dante to Picasso . . . Poets were not mad when they wrote of their Muses.

Still, he was never unfaithful to Alice except in the abstract, though opportunities were near at hand. Students hovered close, hoping for a sign of his interest; a few were not content passively to hope and had to be gently deflected. Martin was surprised, since even in the abstract they were hardly the rich source he was after. Could it be that his exuberant hugs and kisses, the long conferences where he allowed them to expatiate on their private lives, the cups of coffee he offered not only at home but all over town, his letting his wild hair down at parties and dancing with the girls, even his occasional ribald remarks, were misinterpreted? Was he provocative, all unwittingly? The very notion disturbed his pride. Certainly no girl could ever claim his warmth had been anything but paternal, professorial. If he seemed more frankly *human* than the other teachers — well, it was his nature. Not for him that dry aloofness. He had never been an academic type.

It was no more than common courtesy to offer a girl a lift home after their weekly conference: she wasn't feeling well. As they pulled up in front of her house he saw she was weeping.

He put his arm around her shoulder. "What's troubling you?" It was too awful to speak of. Too embarrassing. Well, all right: she was pregnant.

Martin removed his arm, edged off a bit. "Uh, that's not unheard of. Is it someone you — "

"I went out with him a few times but I don't really want to see him any more."

"Well, in a college town like this I'm sure there are plenty of — "

"Oh, I couldn't do that. I'm Catholic."

"Catholic . . . I see. Look, don't despair. It'll work out somehow. Do your parents — "

"You don't understand! It's that . . . I mean . . ." She was hiding her face in her hands. "I'm still a virgin."

"Tracy, really. Catholic, all right, but there are limits . . . Aren't you getting a little carried away?"

"No, no," she managed to get out betweeen sobs. Her doctor had confirmed it. "It was very fast, do you know what I mean?"

"I think I can figure it out."

"The stuff travels, you know? It doesn't have to be really that near. Just sort of nearby . . . Oh, go ahead and laugh if you want. I know it must seem funny."

"No, I'm not laughing." He patted her hand, lying helpless in her lap. "It's just that it's . . . an unusual case."

"I need someone to help me." She looked at him beseechingly.

"Oh, my dear girl," said Martin after a considerable pause. "You don't really mean that."

"Why not? You always seemed to like me."

"Of course I like you, but . . ."

"Don't you see, I can't go through a whole pregnancy like this!" she cried.

He looked at her and stroked her arm. Paternally, he hoped. At this moment he could hardly distinguish. She put her hand on his knee.

"I've always liked you a lot, Martin."

He thought, while the hand inched up his leg, of the deprivation that had seeped into his life and what he had accepted docilely, so far. Help her. Wouldn't any man?

"Look, uh, Tracy, we'll have to talk this over. This is not just some casual thing." He put his own hand firmly over hers, to halt its progress. "Is anyone home now?"

Have your baby, Martin thought as he returned to his car an hour and a half later. I've cleared the way. First gently but efficiently to get the job done, and then more elaborately, so she might see what it was all about. He felt a trifle exploited, but bore that with patience. Women did, why shouldn't he? At least she was appreciative. So much so, that Martin had felt compelled to leave somewhat abruptly, declining her offer of a hamburger dinner. He drove a few blocks to the edge of town, stopped near a stand of maples ripe with the reds and golds of fall, and rested his head on the steering wheel to weep.

Absurd as it was, the singular event renewed him. He had not fathered a child this time, yet he had had some role in the mysterious process. He felt obscurely chosen, as if he were a larger-than-life character in an ambiguous myth. That winter he worked swiftly, with fresh energy and purpose. He was in his studio one afternoon when Alice interrupted to speak to him, which she rarely did. She had taken to wearing his old sweaters around the house, and her hair was very short now. He couldn't remember when she had cut it, before his encounter with Tracy or after.

"You don't look right. What's the matter?"

She said she had to have a hysterectomy.

Martin laid aside his brushes to listen. Finally he said, "Well, if it's necessary . . . Look, afterwards you'll be better than ever."

"How good is that?"

"Alice." He took her hand. They were sitting on tall stools side by side. "You know how good I think that is."

"We never had any children."

"It doesn't matter."

"You would have enjoyed them. Showing them off. You would have been a good father, too."

"I doubt it."

"Why? Look at you with the students."

"I probably would have suffocated them."

She stared at the floor. In profile, the lines of her face were still clean and young, after ten years. "Maybe. Well yes, I guess so."

She didn't have to agree so readily! "You would have revived them," he responded gallantly, then paused. "Why? Do I suffocate you?"

"I guess it's not your fault you're so large and . . ." Her hand was outstretched, palm up, but no word came. "Maybe any woman would be insufficient."

"Insufficient! You were all I ever wanted. And still."

"Mm-hm," she said abstractedly, and slid off the stool to look at the paintings. She had a new nervous gesture, he noticed, pushing her hair off her forehead with both hands, fingers outspread. "These new ones are good. Mysterious. Kind of like latter-day Madonnas, aren't they? They're better than anything you've done in years."

Martin grew hot. He realized he was blushing like a girl.

He understood women well enough to know it would be incumbent upon him, after the operation, to show her that it made no difference. Easy enough: to him it made no difference whatsoever; he harbored no old wives' superstitions. No, it was not the presence or absence of any organs that governed his desire, but that gradual shrinking of the spirit. In truth he felt more sorry for himself than for her. What was she losing but a mere lump of flesh? While he had given her his soul in trust, and instead of nurturing it she had starved it.

As he sat in the depressingly plastic waiting room with an atrocious painting of a dancing gypsy girl on the wall — what imbecile's idea to hang it in a hospital? — the idea that there could never be children now for him and Alice struck for the first time as a material reality. Nevermore. Like an attic door flying open, it released a rush of memory and speculation. What might it have been like, how might his life have gone, had he not met her at the American Library in Paris and been captivated by . . . what? By her appreciation of him. He thought of the women he had known during that boyish jaunt through Europe and before, back and back into the past like road markers sliding off a rearview mirror.

From the very beginning, with all the neighborhood girls he had managed to cajole into bed, he had been courtly and gallant, as courtly and gallant as a teenager from an inner-city slum could know how to be. Once, a girl cried out loud, gasping, and Martin stopped short in panic. Maybe he had hurt her, maybe there would be blood. "What is it!" "Oh God," she moaned. "Don't stop." That was how he learned that women might have a personal, noncharitable investment in sex. Once he knew, the fact and the lore surrounding it fascinated him. He was not shy about asking girls questions, and so became a virtuoso. It pleased him to please; it pleased him more to give help to the needy, to girls who had no idea what they were capable of, or to girls who knew but needed a little more time. Of his time and efforts he was unsparing.

How these needy girls had evolved into the sources of inspiration, how his exertions had become sacrificial offerings to the laps of goddesses, was a transubstantiation even Martin, with his vast learning, could not have explained. He only knew it had to do with art. And that Alice, more than any other, had offered the lure of transformation. He had first watched her bashful face pass through the stages of knowing to finally turn abandoned, and all the times he had made love to her since, or desired her only to be turned away, that progressive image had roused him. It was an image of incomparable voluptuousness, to which he was indispensable.

Now from all their straining nothing could ever spring, and as she lay being eviscerated he thought again that somewhere might be a child of his. Girl or boy? He hoped it was nothing like that lurid gypsy on the wall. The idea engendered no real curiosity or hope, though. What could he hope for? Rather, it opened on to a vista of possibilities — not only all the women there had been, but all the women there had not been, trailed by all the possible children. At every nerve-ending he sensed the abundance out in the broad world. The doctor who came to tell him Alice was stapled back together found Martin bemused, adrift in trancendent realms, like a youth who has heard the call of the spiritual life.

Still he strove to do what was right. When Alive came home he hovered over her like a mother, he brought her chocolate turtles and reassured her of his love.

"I know. I know you do," she said wanly. "I just want a little time to myself."

A few months passed. "Alice," he whispered, and caressed her as he used to. "Let it be over. It's long enough."

She felt limp in his arms, and distant. Unfair. Still, he groped for words befitting the occasion. "It's good to have you in my arms again."

"You look so sad," Alice said in her clever, doleful way. She stroked his hair, beginning to go grey. "My Knight of the Woeful Countenance."

"My Dulcinea," Martin replied obligingly, though as he said it he recognized she was hardly a Dulcinea. He was the street urchin her harmed eyes had once idealized. No wonder he was rejected.

The following month a critic saw his new work in a group show and singled it out. A gallery in New York was interested. As Martin looked his last at the two paintings bought by a nearby museum, it occurred to him that Tracy should be having her baby right around now. She had dropped out of school after Christmas and he had not seen her since. But he hoped all went well — he felt a familial concern. Before long there was a one-man show. He worked feverishly. He was thirty-six, not too old for a fresh start. He traveled, giving lectures, showing slides, showing himself. Everywhere he was such an excellent showman that even without the paintings his charm would have left indelible impressions. Happily, though, he was no charlatan but the genuine article: an artist, with an artistic temperament.

III

A new era dawned in which Martin became a personage. At each gallery opening, at each university he visited — those trips replete with parties and every variety of chicken dinner — was some woman he knew he might effortlessly possess, and often did, parched and deserving as he was. He was not without scruples or discrimination, would not become one of those middle-aged fools who break the hearts of mere children. They were all so skinny and boyish nowadays anyhow, besides which, a grown man could hardly talk to them. No, give him a mature woman with a fullness of spirit any day.

But he was ravaged by guilt. He thought of his marriage vows, his attachment to Alice, his dependence — for admittedly he was dependent. Was that a crime? She was, after all, his wife, and he needed her, when he returned from his wanderings, to greet him with her cool equanimity, to ask how things had gone at the shows or seminars, to sit up late over cups of honeyed tea, never commenting on his infidelities though it was hardly possible she could be ignorant. The enigma in this friendly civility — *did* she know, and if she knew how could she not speak? — kept him attached. So that with the others, after the first rush of arousal his spirit would falter. One of his great-grandfathers had been a rabbi back in the Ukraine, his mother had told him. He had always felt, *faute de mieux* a half-mystic connection to this rabbi — it was the closest thing to an artist his family had ever produced. Now Martin imagined he felt the genes of the rabbi stir within him in revolt and disgust, reminding him of what the decent life was. His spirit would falter, but luckily not his body. For was there not a morality to seduction too? Could one lure a stranger and then desert her midway? Manners were morals, and Martin was a lover of extensive courtesy, until he rolled away clutching a pillow, isolated in a fog of oppression.

When he had had his fill he resolved to give up these ways. This was not the man he was meant to be. Even his work, which by now was praised indiscriminately, seemed to him to have lost texture and to subsist on a surface brilliance. It was only love of a woman, of every plane and arc and fold of her body, every cranny of her spirit, that could open the subterranean chambers.

"Alice," he whispered in bed. "I'm going to change. It's not too late for us, is it? Say it's not."

"Of course it's too late. It's been too late for years." She closed her book, though.

"No! I've never loved anyone else." Moments passed. "You don't believe me, do you?"

"I don't know. Maybe. Why are you suddenly interested in me, Martin? Is the work not going well?" Her finger still marked her place.

"Interested? I've always been interested. You know I'm interested in everything in the world."

"Yes, and it's your world, isn't it, your little garden to drop in on now and then. It's all arbitrary with you. Like God. Who knows why he giveth and taketh away? But I'm not one of your creatures, you see."

He, playing God! When *he* was the humble supplicant, pleading for salvation at her hands! Yet her words did not pain him so much as that thorough calm. He had listened to similar complaints, but they were made in heat and truculence, and never so sharply formulated; he had to hand it to her for that, even as he lay stunned and aching.

"You don't even care any more, do you, Alice? . . . Do you? Tell me, for God's sake!"

She shut her eyes as if pained. "I have to get up early, a publisher's calling from Madrid."

Then he grasped it. She must have someone else, God knows for how long now. How had he never thought of it before? Occasionally some woman or other had asked about his wife. Do you have an "arrangement?" Does she have someone too? He had always said, with conviction, Oh no, she's very involved in her work. An extraordinary woman. Not once had he made a derogatory remark about Alice to any woman he slept with, or to anyone at all, for that matter. Such was his loyalty. While she, all along, like a snake in the grass . . . That she might prefer solitude he had managed to swallow. But this! Panic broke through his skin in a cold sweat and he pulled the blanket closer.

"Are you saying you want me to leave?"

"Not really. We get along all right. I like watching you, and you like to be watched."

His blood eased. She did need him. Maybe he was imagining it all, exaggerating as usual, yes. He could show her . . . Summoning his resources, like calling in the diverse troops, foot soldiers, light artillery, cavalry, Martin advanced with cunning on the supposedly impregnable Alice, first setting her book down on the night table, careful not to lose the place. Afterwards he held her close and murmured in her ear, "It isn't so, all you said, is it? Please." She appeared to be sleeping. Her lashes were glistening. A moment or two later she rolled over and curled up, her back turned.

IV

Martin's life became a quest for love. He bypassed ephemera with only a glimmer of regret, for he was pursuing something higher, spiritual. There was a French woman who taught chemistry at a private high school in New York City, where Martin now held a tenured position at the City University. Twice a week, on the days of his classes, he would spend the night at her Brooklyn Heights apartment and return to his house on Long Island the next morning. Françoise was a woman of firm and inflexible character: though she was divorced and had two children she struggled to support, she refused any help he offered. If he would divorce his wife and marry her . . . But this way, no, *merci*. He listened attentively, but Alice preyed on his mind. She was losing weight again and having dizzy spells. One does not desert a sick wife. He did not even need the genes of a rabbi to tell him that.

When he and Françoise made love, the image of Alice hovered over the bed. Françoise sensed her presence and could not abide it. Several times she actually stopped in the middle and fetched a pile of test papers to correct. At last, after almost a year, she declared she had to think of herself and her children, her future. Martin was dismayed that a woman he had chosen could be so pragmatic. She could not love him in "the old high way of love" (Yeats was Alice's favorite poet), where no obstacle could keep kindred souls apart.

"Well then . . .?" Françoise gave a shrug.

"But think," Martin pleaded, at his wit's end. "You're so logical and scientific. Measure. Which is greater for you in all this? The pleasure or the pain?"

She was a luscious, plump dark-haired woman with great green feline eyes. She was sitting cross-legged in her red-flowered armchair, wearing a black satin Chinese robe he had given her, her breasts spilling out the front. It flashed through Martin's mind that he must keep that image of her, in case it should be the last.

"The pain. I'm sorry."

He suspected he had not really been in love with her at all, for parting hurt less than he expected. Quite soon he was distracted by a woman he had noticed during the waning weeks of the Françoise era, a secretary in the admissions office at the university, also divorced, with three children. All the women he was drawn to, Martin couldn't help observing, were mothers. He liked visiting and finding the children rowdy and ubiquitous; as he bantered with them he grew excited by the prospect of soon snatching their mother away, locking the bedroom door against them and seeing her transform from mother to lover, possessing her in a way they would never know. The new woman, Peg, was not beautiful at all. She was tall and thin and moved gawkily — her jutting hips and elbows banging into furniture — and was the most sexually aggressive woman he had ever known. It was she who first suggested they have lunch, and in the restaurant pressed her leg against his. Martin could hardly believe it. His approaches were generally executed with a careful and gracious decorum. "You're far worse than I am," he moaned in bed. "Eat oysters," she advised. "You know what else might work? Sara Lee apple crumb." The latter she ate in bed, a habit he didn't care for. Alice never ate in bed, nor did she leave clumps of hair in the bathtub. Nonetheless something rapacious about Peg's lanky, small-breasted body made him avid. Together they would careen into a world where only flesh and sensation existed; all traces of who they were, and where, were forgotten.

But then at the awakening, the same oppression, the same withdrawal. Peg raged beside him, calling him names. Why did she even bother with him, he was only a stupid old clown who would soon be too feeble to hold a paint brush, not to mention screw. These were moments when he almost felt the pain was greater than the pleasure, and he understood, to some small degree, what Françoise had meant. At home in his studio, he labored over ungainly images of dislocation and imbalance. When critics called the work startling and original, he decided it was worth the torment.

He discovered she was unfaithful. She would bring home virtual strangers and not even bother to cover her tracks. "Why shouldn't I? What do you want me to do when you're with her — knit you a codpiece to keep it warm? You can drive a person insane, you know? All that wild talk about South Sea islands, then I don't hear from you for days."

"All right, all right, I'll tell her. Tomorrow."

But when he was away from Peg and could think clearly, he knew it would be foolhardy to leave Alice for a woman like that. She would betray him, she was mad; and when she tired of his body she would cast it aside the way she peeled her clothes in haste and kicked them across the floor.

After a year and a half she exchanged him for someone else. He was in physical agony, had never felt so battered and ready to die. Sexual memories taunted him like furies. Feverish, he thought of escaping into the depths of the Sound. Once he went so far as to drive his car to the water's edge, where he grew lost in dreams of his boyhood; when he awoke with a start he wondered why he was there, and drove home. Alice would find him huddled at the kitchen table and would stroke his hair, nearly gone over to grey now.

Months later, when it passed, he was empty and light-headed, as after a fast. He moved more slowly, his shoulders drooped, and he no longer searched for love. Still, there were women everywhere, and he would sit up talking in bed till the late hours, getting to know all about them — he continued to find so many so interesting.

He never stayed with them long; if he saw they were falling in love with him he extricated himself as best he could. With all his precautions, in some cases he left grief behind him, but what was he to do? He had not forced himself on them. Far from it. And maybe it was only right that a few should suffer, to offset in some small measure the suffering he had undergone at the hands of his mother, and Alice, and Peg, as if there were a great communal balance sheet of suffering to be rendered at the final judgment. Martin was not proud of such feelings, yet didn't the best of disciples sometimes doubt, or wish in vain that vengeance were theirs? Only the untried kept a pure faith.

Sometimes he would glimpse a woman on the street who reminded him of Peg, or of Alice in earlier days, and he felt such acute longing that he would have to follow her for several blocks. His heart fluttered, he stumbled with vertigo, fantasies roiled in his head. He never made any attempt to catch up or to speak, and later, sitting on a park bench to calm his blood, he would fear that he was in his dotage, though he was only forty-five.

Once, on the crowded steps of the Metropolitan Museum, he came face to face with an old lover. She was graciously polite, even warm, but Martin could tell she had not forgiven his defection. Was she one of those to whom he had sworn eternal friendship? If only he could remember exactly how he had dropped out of her life, he might say something mitigating or soothing, but alas . . . Everything else he remembered vividly. He remembered that though her manner was crisp and lively, in bed she was enchantingly languid. So often they were contrary to the way they appeared. Peg's public behavior was rather severe. Françoise, for all her luscious looks, tended to be phlegmatic, and his own proper Alice in her day, well. . . . All this was fascinating, but right now, of no avail. He knew this woman so well, her every expression and mood, the tone she used for each degree of personal connection, that he could have charted on a graph precisely where he stood in her feelings, precisely where the axis of love and the axis of resentment intersected. It was that very knowledge of her that she could not forgive, he well knew, a knowledge painstakingly acquired only to be interred. He sympathized with her veiled disgust; it disgusted him too, that glimpse of his heart as a rank, unvisited graveyard of intimate and varied data about women, once-precious relics, neglected and moldering.

V

When Martin returned from the upstate college where he met Paula — her dance troupe performed opposite the gallery showing his paintings — Alice told him about the lump in her breast. He was dazed by the rhythmic recurrence of events, life grinding in cycles (love, cancer) as though it had but a limited supply of plot. She had noticed it a while ago, she said, but had waited to speak until the doctor was sure. In a manner quite unlike her, hesitant and tremulous, she asked if he wanted to feel it. He didn't want to, but to refuse would be more horrible still. She opened her blouse and offered her breast, showing him the place. He felt it right away, like a berry deep in the flesh. His fingers recoiled but he forced his hand to remain. He was unsure what to do. He made a gesture like a caress. She stepped back and buttoned her blouse.

"God," he said. "Well, when?"

"Tomorrow."

"Tomorrow!"

The sooner the better. The doctor had urged an even earlier day, but she had not wanted to spoil his trip, or to shock him with a note in an empty house. Tears came to Martin's eyes as she recounted all this in her even way. Even, yet teetering on some brink. Martin led her to the sofa and they sat down. He realized that touch of her breast had been a farewell, and felt a surge of regret and loss. One flesh, the Bible said. Then shame crept over him. Men used the word "possess" for a woman's body, but ultimately . . . no. The word stood for all the advantages of possession, none of the liabilities. It would be her loss. He had not really possessed her in years, if ever. If they were truly one flesh he could feel the loss without shame at his feeling. Who was she, then? In one of those instants when reality threatens to appear as brutally as a graveyard lit by lightning, Martin strained to see her, huddled on the worn sofa, as a being distinct from himself, but it was too arduous. His imagination shrank back.

He turned with relief to a more practical thought, of Paula. He had promised to call her. Of course it would be out of the question to see her this week, perhaps for several weeks. And he felt a surge of regret and loss over that too, like a distorted echo.

Alice started to cry and Martin murmured the suitable words until she was calm again.

"Do you feel any pain? Do you want to lie down?"

"No, I feel all right. I'm hungry, but there's nothing around. I haven't shopped since you left."

"Let's go out to dinner. How's that?"

"Lobster."

"Terrific."

"My last meal. Don't they give condemned men whatever they want?" She tried to laugh.

"There'll be lots of lobsters in your future, you'll see. I'll even bring them to you in the hospital if you want. Remember last time I smuggled in a pizza? Nothing is more difficult to conceal than a pizza."

"Last time," she repeated. "What next? What can they take after this?"

"Oh Alice, don't think that way. Defy it. Go change and make yourself beautiful. Life is still good. It is!"

She smiled wryly, her cheeks damp with tears. "They're cutting off my breast and you're telling me life is beautiful. You really think so, don't you?"

He nodded gravely.

"You're lovable, you know. A lovable jerk."

He beamed like a small boy being appreciated, and for the moment he felt fulfilled again. This was the closest they had been in years. A bitter notion, but what was any pleasure without a dash of bitters? "No." He put his arms around her. He had almost forgotten the feel of her shoulders, square and firm. "Not a lovable jerk. A holy fool."

"Better stop while you're ahead, Martin. This is one show you can't steal."

Alice's recovery was slow. She shuffled groggily through the house in an old bathrobe, and could sit for hours over a jigsaw puzzle of a Rothko painting, adding four or five pieces a day. All the time Martin tended her, his thoughts kept straying to Paula.

She was a dancer. At the reception where they met she moved lithely through the crowd with a radiant calm. Martin saw her as a descendant of Isadora Duncan, only less dramatic, less self-important. He had not seen her perform, since he was at the time giving his own performance in the gallery, but he felt he knew exactly what she would be like. Watching her, he would know the long-awaited descent of peace.

He had told her all this in a late-night coffee shop, and she had smiled and said it was hard enough to do it, let alone theorize about it, but in any case it sounded lovely. She had crooked teeth, and with each smile they became more endearing; they gave her face an ingenuousness that made him want to protect and cherish her.

Martin did most of the talking that night. Painting was his life, he told her. As he spoke the words, he hoped they were true, for there was something about Paula that repelled myth making. No doubt his life might be viewed less favorably. Yet wasn't everything he had done ultimately in the service of art?

Paula mostly listened and nodded. She hadn't heard of him, she confessed, her blue eyes apologetic. She had so little time to keep up; dancing was terribly demanding, especially at her age. Thirty-seven. "A kid," Martin chuckled. That was ten years younger than he. Hardly indecent. She had danced ever since she was a child, she said. Halfway through college she left to get married, and soon after had a baby daughter. She had been very happy with her husband, a civil engineer, but he was killed in a plane crash five years ago. These facts she offered shyly, as if a famous artist might find them of scant interest.

Quite the contrary. He was glad she had never heard of him. He had had more than enough of those who had. He loved her single-mindedness, her instinctive dignity. Her happy marriage, that sweet bondage granted to only a few, drew his reverence. Beyond that, she was a mother, and he was enchanted by the tender way she spoke of her daughter, sixteen and a dancer too. Martin envisioned the daughter as a more innocent version of Paula, the same erect body, muscular yet soft and sinuous, the same lush fall of black hair with glossy bangs reaching to the eyebrows, the same olive skin and wide mouth.

"What's her name?"

"May."

"How lovely. I'd love to meet her."

Paula only smiled.

"Will I have a chance to, do you think? Will you invite me over so I can see where you live, what it's like, what you have hanging on your walls?"

"Oh," she said, abashed, "it's nothing special. Just the two of us in this four-room apartment, and we go about our business."

Martin was rapt.

"What about tomorrow? We can meet for breakfast and then take a walk. Are you leaving too? Maybe I can drive you back?"

Paula laughed at his grandiose gestures, his voice reverberating in the deserted place. "Thanks, but I have another performance tomorrow night. And I've got to get some rest." She stood up.

"Oh, I wish I could be there. But . . . I can't."

"I guess your wife is expecting you . . . Look, maybe we'd better say goodbye now. It's been a lovely evening."

"Nonsense! This is very important. Three-fifteen, my God! Come, I'll drive you to your place." He took her firmly by the arm. In front of the white clapboard inn they exchanged a long look, and he leaned over to kiss her lightly on the lips.

"Martin, you must meet people everywhere you go. I . . . I don't live like that."

"I know. I understand completely. That's why it's so wonderful. Till tomorrow. And sleep well."

He watched her walk up the flagstone path. In a filmy summer dress and sandals that laced around the ankles, she was like a mirage receding into the night.

The next morning they ambled on the outskirts of town, then kissed goodbye lightly again. He wouldn't disturb her stillness, not till they were both more than ready, when she would shed layers of calm like veils. He could practically see it, a mesmerizing dance. Underneath, perhaps even in the height of passion, there would be a still center: he would drink from it and be renewed. Saved. But first he would savor the desire, hold it on his fingertips like a bubble, in all its delicacy and iridescence.

After leaving her he sped south toward home and Alice, stirred by the poetry of his discretion. Yes, Paula was assuredly not the sort to be rushed. But Martin rarely rushed in any case; rather, he bided his time discreetly until he could be sure of a favorable response. Instinct always told him the moment. If instinct hung back he did not make the attempt. Or if he waited long and patiently enough, he might be relieved of the responsibility altogether—they did it. He was more sinned against than sinning, as it were. A few women had even kidded him about that diffidence. His interest, they said, was evident, but . . . "You force women into making the move for you, you big lazy lug." Valerie, he believed that was. "Ah no, love. I'm shy, underneath." "Shy! Don't make me laugh, Martin! You're a tease!" She was wrong. He *was* shy, somewhere inside. Paula would understand. Her appearing in his life could be a sign of grace, pointing the way to those hidden regions. Even in his paintings, there might come a hush, a reticence, all the epicurean joys of quietude. *Luxe, calme, et volupté.* Only Paula, alas, would not appreciate the allusion (as Alice immediately would).

He would revisit these thoughts over and over, like a child rereading a beloved book, while Alice slept heavily beside him. For months, till she recovered her strength, he mesmerized himself with anticipation of the new era.

The four-room apartment was nondescript, as he had been warned, but its plainness only made it a more perfect setting for Paula, who was unconscious of her great worth. Her daughter May also lived up to Martin's fantasies, a lissome girl who resembled her mother, though not quite so tall, a good girl in the old-fashioned way, well-mannered, who made her bed unasked and telephoned when she would be late.

"What a dream of a child. Do you think it's upbringing, or are some people just born serene?" Martin wanted to know.

"Born," Paula said. "I don't think I did anything special."

"You both have it and I don't."

"But you have your talent."

"Well, so do you."

"Performing isn't the same thing."

"Are you saying the artist has to be a tormented soul? That's a cliché, Paula. There were countless ones who weren't. Rubens, Van Dyck, Monet, Matisse. Duccio, I bet, was not tormented, but of course that was a different age. Lots of them were monks. Then again there's Vermeer—you'd never think it, would you? And Van Gogh."

Paula had drifted off to water her plants. Well, it didn't matter. He was getting to be an old bore anyway. She was so beautiful, wearing just an open long-sleeved man's shirt, and that curve of her wrist as she tilted the pitcher, nurturing . . . In the slant of buttery morning light on her head and shoulders, she looked like a Vermeer herself.

Twice a week, when he came to the city to teach, Martin would stay overnight with Paula, who rearranged classes and rehearsals to free the time for him. Those evenings he enjoyed the domesticity he had always dreamed of. Often they would all three be in the kitchen, fixing dinner or reading the paper or playing Hearts. May did her homework at the kitchen table — Martin was sure she enjoyed having a man around, poor kid, to have lost her father so young; now and then she would ask him for help with history or trigonometry, or for difficult words in the crossword puzzles to which she was addicted. He would think, This is real life. Ordinary family life. It even pleased him to be irritated by the way May peeled the Styrofoam off soda bottles, slowly, in long curling strips. But of course Paula was not his wife and May, however fond of her he grew, was not his child, and this was not his home. When Paula gave May grocery lists for the weekends — food to be eaten without him! — Martin suffered pangs of exclusion. May danced in a school production of *Carousel* one Saturday, and as she and Paula relived the evening at the dinner table, chortling over backstage anecdotes, he felt such a sense of emptiness he had to walk out of the room.

Paula had friends he had never even met. Martin would have loved to talk far into the night with a bunch of dancers — despite his grey hair and the wearied slump of his shoulders, he was still interested in everything. But she said their evenings together were precious, they had so little time. Finally she admitted she felt uncomfortable, being with a married man . . . She had never intended it. It was happening almost before she knew it. A married man with a sick wife, she added in a whisper.

"Please, my darling, don't torment yourself over it. It's not your doing. It has nothing to do with you."

"I don't see how you can divide things up like that. It has everything to do with me."

"If it weren't you it would be — " Martin stopped himself in chagrin.

She did not talk of giving him up, though. No question of that, by now. No question of Martin's leaving Alice either, nothing to be gnawed over and spit out, as in the era of Peg. Alice was not well. She had never regained her full strength after the operation, and though the doctors with their scans reassured her, Martin could see the wasting. If nothing else, he thought miserably, he had vision. Fading, she turned to him. Too late, she wanted to talk, to spend the time remaining with him. When, silently and hesitantly, she touched him in the night he made love to her, but what he had once yearned for he could do only with pity, and he felt wretched after. What she felt he never dared to ask.

How different from the quality of wonder and luminescence in his love for Paula! And yet the wonder appeared to exist by virtue of the desolation he felt with Alice, just as the wonder of light exists by virtue of darkness. Even at the extremes of pleasure, when all boundaries seemed to fall away, Martin sensed a pall of darkness. Another presence. He knew then that beyond their marriage, their history, and her illness, something adamant and irreducible soldered him to her. Once he had chosen her, and so he chose her still. To forsake her would be forsaking the rightness and power of his own will. That he could not do. That would be denial of his deepest self.

VI

There came a time when Alice needed radiation treatments. The same as five years ago, only worse: it had crept everywhere. This time she did not offer him her breast to feel for the lump. She sank into a solitude. Martin took her for the treatments and did everything there was to do for her, while she looked on mute. With her thinness, her eyes had beome amazingly large; he had the eerie feeling that they saw into him, tracking his every quiver. With contempt, he wondered? Or with pity. Longing, regret? Once, as they were returning from one of her treatments, he dropped his keys at the front door; the ring snapped and they lay scattered on the step, Paula's among them. As he knelt to gather them up he felt her looming above him, her eyes drilling into his bent back. "Why are you looking at me that way? What do you see? Are you thinking I'm clumsy?" "No," she said. "Not at all. I'm not looking at anything at all." It was true, he realized: she was not watching him, she hardly saw him, she had no further interest in him. It came over him with a deathly chill that he was not and had not been for a very long time the center of her life. The center of her life was herself, and she was watching inward.

When Alice died he called Paula and said, "I need to be alone for a while."

"I understand. Take all the time you need. I'm so sorry. Really, I am. I know what she meant to you."

How could she? It was such a secret, pernicious thing. He brooded on it as he stalked the empty house, not so much grieving as flagellating himself. Why had he not let her go when there was still time? She had not been strong enough to leave him—and in a fit of candor he cursed his power over women, wished it shorn away like Samson's—but he could have been strong enough to give her back her life. Instead . . . He tried to conjure scenes of their early days, to feel the balm of genuine regret, but the memories were static pictures, postcard views of Paris, refusing to come to life. There was nothing, nothing. It was all vanity. Even this self-loathing was vanity, for who was he to think of giving and withholding life?

After two weeks, for relief—even mortal sinners deserve some relief, Martin told himself—he went to Paula. They made love, and he wept. He stayed with her for a week: every night they made love and every night he wept, till it was clear he was trying even her saintliness, so he returned to his empty house. He fell into his old patterns, spending two evenings a week with Paula when he came to the city to teach. The rest of the time he worked. A fierce energy inflamed the paintings, a series of tangled bodies. He could hardly wait to finish each one, to see what he had done.

"What now, Martin?" Paula asked after a few months. It was late at night and they were sitting at her kitchen table, eating cherries. May was all grown and gone, twenty-one, living and dancing in San Francisco.

"What now, what?"

"Well, you're alone now."

"Not really alone." He reached over and stroked her cheek.

"You know what I mean."

"Yes, But I'm not ready to do anything yet."

"You're not ready?" She sat up straighter.

"No."

"I don't understand. I thought when . . . you know."

"I need some time, Paula. The work is going so well, I can't have any disruptions just at this point."

"Disruptions?" She leaned her head back, as if offering her throat to a blade.

"I'm sorry. My darling, you're everything to me. Don't you know that?" He leaned over to embrace her but she got up and walked away. "Don't. I can't bear it, Paula."

"Please don't touch me right now. Just leave me alone."

He stood by, pained and unable to help her. There was a little mound of cherry pits on the table. He cleared them away, then dried the dinner dishes and put them away, got into bed and lay in the dark by himself.

When they made love now, there was an absence. Alice had deserted him, and alone with Paula, he was bereft. Some nights when he stayed over, Martin simply lay wakeful, restless, ever so slightly bored. This was natural, he reasoned. Longtime lovers must have spells of boredom. He was fifty-one years old and entitled to a rest—God knows he had nothing to prove in that department. He watched old movies on television: *Now Voyager* he found comforting. Nor was there anything unnatural or clandestine anymore about their being together. The genes of the rabbi dozed in apathy, unperturbed by Bette Davis's tribulations. Yes, a perfectly ordinary situation.

There it was. In the dark middle of the night, with Paula's amiable body curled into his side, he confessed that this perfectly ordinary situation left him numb. To be compelling it wanted the dramatic context: the invisible audience, the betrayal, and the guilt.

Martin squeezed his eyes shut in dread. A vision of himself, such as the Spirit of Time Future brought to Scrooge, took shape in the dark: not dead but doddering, ludicrous, contemptible. He had loved—truly loved—Alice for ten years, Paula for five; soon two and a half, one and a quarter . . . geometric progressions were swift, he knew perspective. A week, a day, an hour. The nightmare vision sharpened. He saw himself as part of a relay race, a human baton. One after another, his exhausted partners passed him ever more frantically to fresh replacements and retired to observe from the sidelines. Only he was condemned to remain in the game until he dropped. He felt the abyss opening up, and his body gave a great shudder.

But as if somewhere the gods had a drop of mercy left for him (or were not quite finished with him yet), sleep came to his rescue. In the morning he felt better. He studied himself in the mirror, shaving: still presentable. Grey, but firm-fleshed. No jowls. Clear eyes. Thank heavens he was not a drinker—in a man his age it always showed. The terrors of the night evaporated in the steamy bathroom. He resolved, as soon as this group of paintings was done, to arrange somehow for him and Paula to live together. Or at least to spend more time with her.

He began, half-unawares, to stare at women on the street again, women of every age, class, race, and shape. When he was invited to parties or openings, he brought Paula along if she could make it—a new and unequivocal pleasure; but when she couldn't, he would strike up conversations with other attractive women. It was amusing to see if the old charm still worked, like digging out and oiling an old baseball glove. Only to stay in practice: use it or lose it, he remembered his uncle and his racetrack cronies joking, and at fifteen he had thought them pathetic. Since he disliked the chitchat of parties, he would invite these women off to a corner for a real talk, or out for a drink, away from the clamor. Once or twice dinner afterwards. But never anything more. Oh no, not again, he cautioned himself. Never mind ethics: it was simple self-perservation. He was, after all, merely satisfying a peculiar little need (less fortunate men were doomed to tie women up or dress them in leather — give thanks for small blessings), adding a little harmless spice to a life now so above reproach it was practically, well . . . bourgeois. And he was an artist, was he not?

At one of these gallery parties he was introduced to Jess. Martin had read her articles — she was one of the few decent art critics around.

"So you're Jess Masters! Let me tell you, I'm an admirer of yours. You're extraordinary! When are you going to cast that discriminating eye in my direction?"

"Your turn will come, no doubt," she said pleasantly, not visibly jarred.

Well, here was a woman!

They stood among a crush of bodies and voices. Martin bent closer and touched her arm.

"Look, let's go sit down over there. Okay? We have a lot to talk about." With her this was a risk, he knew. But she did follow him to a quiet nook, where soon they were arguing about de Kooning and everyone after, interrupting, piling challenges one over the other like zestful children piling hands. Her mind was fleet and keen, piercing impatiently through surfaces to the impulse beneath. It was not airy cleverness, either; she was fertile; she *knew* things. How long since he had talked excitedly like this, and to a woman! Martin felt a twinge of disloyalty. Of course he had learned so much from Paula, all about instinct and calm and the harmonious life, but . . . From Jess he was learning something tangible.

She was elegant at the gallery, in a sleek dark-green dress belted at the hip, glittering with chains and bracelets, so Martin was surprised, the first time he visited her SoHo loft, to find her girlish, in jeans and a navy-blue sweatshirt, and barefoot (narrow feet with a high arch, he noted; also Morton's syndrome, second toe longer than the big toe — this he had learned from Paula). The loft was filled with boys' paraphernalia — bat and glove, barbells, a bicycle; prints lined the walls; there were Indian rugs and large pillows, and on the butcher-block table, a bowl heaped with purple plums. Given her rigorous judgments, Martin had imagined her surroundings would be austere. That they were not suggested indistinct but intriguing possibilities. From behind a closed door came a thumping. "That's my son, Max. He's learning to play the drums.

I can ask him to stop if it bothers you. I'm inured." "No, no, that's quite all right."

As a rule Martin found his two days a week quite enough of New York. But to talk to Jess he made the trip. (The second time, he was stopped for speeding.) She loved to unravel everything dark and tangled in the light of reason, whether the subject was serious or the frivolous gossip they laughed over extravagantly. Often their thoughts traveled identical paths, all the same premises taken for granted. And Jess's enthusiasm — its particular mix of fervor and drollery — matched his own, so that listening to her mellow voice, Martin had the faintly delirious sensation of looking in a human mirror. On the street, she might suddenly stop walking midspeech, the pressure of an idea claiming all her physical energy. When he did this, Paula would wait in puzzlement or take his arm to get him moving again. Jess even hailed buses with his imperious gesture, as if commandeering them for her private use. At last he had met his match!

After about a month Martin invited her out one Saturday to see what he was working on. Paula was away on tour in North Carolina. Since Jess loved to eat he fussed over a lunch of steamed mussels and avocado salad — she always appeared so blithely self-sufficient, so little in need of anything he might offer. His efforts were rewarded. She said it was the first decent meal a man had made her in a long time, but added, lest he grow smug, that the competition was a sorry lot. After she looked at the paintings they walked along the beach. It was a warmish day in November. At the water's edge Martin showed off his skill at skipping stones, and they even tossed a ball back and forth for a while. To his relief, a flaw.

"You throw just like a woman, from the wrist. You're a sight."

"I know. I've been told before. It's hopeless."

"Nothing is hopeless. You just haven't been taught. Come here." He took her arm and made it circle in a wide arc. "Throw from the shoulder, with your whole weight behind it. The whole arm, don't be lazy. That's a girl. Push from the back."

She was an apt pupil. In a few minutes she was throwing yards farther. "Hey, I never could do that before. Thanks!"

Martin, exultant, gave her a quick, one-armed hug. "We'll make a *mensch* of you yet. Next time we bring along a bat."

Back at the house they had a drink — but only one, Jess said. She had to drive home.

"If you'd like to stay on a while," he said with hesitation, "we could go out to dinner later. There's a good lobster place nearby."

"That sounds lovely, but I can't. I promised to go with Max to see *Alien*."

They stared at each other, then burst out laughing. As she left, Martin gazed in through the window of her dilapidated yellow car. "Till next time."

"Good-bye, Martin. Thanks for everything." She zoomed off with an indecipherable grin.

He was confused. She had been in his house, they had had four hours together, and he had acted with a restraint that left him feeling musclebound. Jess must be baffled, if not laughing up her sleeve. It was Paula causing all this confusion. Must he deny himself for her sake? He had been denied so much already. . . .

He visited Jess a few days later. Paula was still away and Max was out at a drum lesson — quiet for once. She was fixing drinks, wearing her jeans and sweatshirt as usual, when he came up from behind and put his arms around her. She turned quickly but didn't retreat. Martin smiled and held her close for a richly triumphant moment before he kissed her. Jess looked more amused than aroused.

"Aha!" she said. "I had begun to wonder."

So she wanted a tone of comedy. Very well. "I'm a Jewish intellectual. I have to think things over." He kissed her again. She seemed to soften in his arms, and slipped her hand inside his shirt.

"And I thought maybe you just wanted an article out of me."

He drew back. "Good Lord! You didn't really think that *I—I* would see a woman for *that*!" He was genuinely appalled.

"I was only teasing, Martin." She reached her arms around his neck. "Resume what you were doing."

He had determined in advance not to let fogs of guilt plague him, but as they lay entwined afterwards he muttered, "Oh God, I can't do this."

"But you already did."

"I mean I'm incapable of this. I'm torn apart."

"You seemed capable enough. Are you allergic? Wait, I know. Anhedonism."

"This is no joke, Jess. Really." He told her about Paula. Naturally he had mentioned her before; he had — with a sickening sense of his own treachery — presented Paula as an old friend with whom he had a warm and intermittent sexual liaison. Now he winced at that version and gave her the truth.

"I see." She had moved across the bed as he spoke. "You might have thought of this before."

"I did! I agonized for weeks. Why do you think it took me so long to — "

"You might have thought of me, I mean. Or do you like having one in reserve? Like a backup system."

There was a long silence. Jess got out of bed and put her clothes on. "Let's eat something. I have a meat loaf."

While they ate they got into a heated discussion of the work of Gregson, a conceptual artist whose bare compositions Martin despised. Jess behaved as though they had never been in bed and Martin followed her lead. As he was leaving she relented and gave him an intimate grin. "I think I've figured out why women like you. They sense the presence of others. There's a feeling of camaraderie. Sisterhood." She kissed him with a gentle shove toward the door.

But he wouldn't keep away. He dreamed of spending the rest of his life with her (despite the pounding of the drums). It was inconceivable that his interest would flag — everything about them together was so right. Jess loved him too, she confessed. "And I hate it. You're part of someone else. This is disgusting. It reeks."

Hearing her lurch into despair, Martin felt tortured. He had done this to her, brought her down to his level. By possessing her he had shattered that splendid self-possession.

They dragged on through the bitter winter and into the spring. The pleasure, Martin assumed, must be greater than the pain. He taught Max how to box and cook and skip stones. Meanwhile he saw Paula as usual, but there were moments when he could not look at her face, whose serenity reproached him for the commotion he would soon cause. If she suspected, she said nothing. She was in Alice's place now, haunting Jess's bed, dimming his joys. Martin was worn out. He hadn't enough time for his work. Sometimes on awakening he wasn't sure which bed he was in. The flowered pillowcase he could glimpse from a slit in his eye, that was Paula's. The hard mattress on a wooden board — Jess's. And when his arms stretched out to empty space — his own, at home.

It could not continue. Surely he had learned something from Alice's slow death. He could redeem his life. "It's not fair," he told Jess in bed, one night late in June. "She needs me. That's all there is to it. I'll sacrifice myself."

"A martyr! What next?"

"Please be serious. You know I'm in torment."

"Yes, I know who you're sacrificing too. Okay, if she needs you then go to her. You're probably right. Here, put on your pants and go." She began tossing his clothes at him.

"I don't mean this minute. Jesus Christ, you're so literal." It was two-thirty in the morning. "I mean needs me in general."

"I don't understand in general. I only understand specific. If she needs you she needs you. Go. Here. Here's your socks, here's your shoes. Do you need a subway token? Oh, she's away, I forgot. Clever timing, Martin."

"Would you calm down? You're a hellion, do you know that? Get these shoes out of the bed, they're getting it filthy. I'm only trying to say, if Paula had any idea of this—"

"You bastard, of course she knows about it. You think she's dumb, don't you? With all your devotion, you ain't got no respect. Well listen, she's probably lying awake right now, knowing what you're doing. And take your hands off me, you don't have to do it while I talk about it! Big-shot stud! You complain about Gregson, so stingy in his work, but look at you! It's how you live! You think you love women, but all you really love is yourself, seeing yourself. My God, it's not even selfish. Without them you wouldn't have a self!"

"Stop, stop! I don't want to hear any more!" He rolled over with his face in the pillow and yearned for instant death. It would serve her right, too, a big hairy naked corpse in her bed.

"Listen," he said the next morning. "I was up all night thinking. I'm going to tell her this time." He had promised to spend a week with Paula in Vermont, where she had rented a cottage. May would be there too—her first trip East in a year. "When you see me next week I'll be finished and we can start leading a normal life."

Jess kept brushing her hair in front of the mirror with brisk strokes, as though she hadn't heard.

"What's the matter? Don't you believe me?"

"Whether I believe you or not is immaterial. Only don't come back here unless you've made your choice. I mean it." In the thick summer heat, Martin shivered.

VII

The rain was persistent. Martin sat down on a plastic chair in the terminal and watched people enter, dripping, shaking water from their umbrellas. Outside, it would be dark by now: in a few moments he would be out there hailing a taxi to Jess's. First he would rest for a while. It had been a trying week.

Not the first few days when, in glorious sunshine, the three of them had gone swimming and canoeing and, to indulge May, even ridden in a chairlift over the mountains. May's skin was sleekly tan now and she walked with an easy West Coast swing, yet from time to time the ingenuous child flickered behind the sophisticated manner. In the evenings they sat drinking tea while she regaled them with stories of her dancer friends in San Franciso. Paula listened proudly. Martin too, as if he had had a share in raising her. For hadn't he sat around the kitchen table helping her with logarithms, explaining articles in the newspaper, supplying words for the crossword puzzles? "Seven-letter novelist starting with D, author of *An American Tragedy?* . . . Nine letters, Martin, a prince of an anarchist, starting with K?" He had given more than she asked, supplied all the history. In a small way, he could claim she was his.

Caught up in the family, he almost forgot Jess. Or rather, her image performed an odd dance in his head. At night she receded nearly to the vanishing point, as he and Paula gloated over May and made love much as in the old days. Then in the morning she would loom very close and large. He put the ordeal off. This was a vacation, after all, the days long and full of light. He wished them longer, wished they would never end. If only it could be the present forever — Jess in abeyance far away, Paula contented, May young and eager, and he himself harming no one. But by the fifth day he was heavy with anxiety. He lay down after dinner and Paula came in to ask if he was feeling all right.

"Yes, fine."

"No, there's something. You might as well say it. I think I know, anyway."

"You do?"

"If it's all over, I wish you would tell me, Martin."

"What a thing to say! It's not all over. With us, it could never be that."

"But as far as, like, the day-to-day, it's over, right?"

"No. I just thought . . ." Martin paused because it hurt to breathe. The weight on his chest was crushing. He was too old for this, his heart . . . "I thought it might be best if we . . . saw each other a little less." It was out! he had done it! Immediately the pain in his chest eased.

"A little less?" said Paula in her serene way. "We don't see each other that much as it is. I don't really think I want that. I think I might want . . . well, more or nothing at all."

More . . . ? More he could not give her. But the prospect of nothing at all was suddenly devastating. How could he forsake her — she was a haven of peace, she was so familiar, she needed him. . . .

"I can't . . . I can't . . ." A strange and terrible thing was happening. He could locate no words. He couldn't locate a thought, a wish — there was only a dark clot in his head. Time stopped, leaving him wedged in its warp. When he tried to swallow, his mouth was as dry as a desert. An eyelid twitched. "I don't know. I can't — I don't want to end. . . . I can't face that."

"But Martin, it's not really fair, you know? Why should I live that way, when I know you're involved with someone else?"

He started to cry. "Don't do this to me!" It was all unexpected, all awry. "Please. Think it over."

For the first time since he had known her, she seemed quite without pity or solace. "I've thought and thought. I didn't like to say anything when I wasn't sure, but now . . . What do you expect me to do?"

"All right." He composed himself. "I understand your position. This is not the end, though. Not so fast. We'll have to talk about it in the city. Maybe I'll . . . I just don't know."

She didn't object when, hours later, in the middle of the night, he reached out for her. Martin tried to recover his old ardor. Maybe, in the end . . . But it was impossible: her responses were muted those last few days, her love-making elegiac.

She and May drove him to the bus when the week was out. Thoroughly exhausted, he said, "Thanks for having me up. I'll call as soon as you get back. When is that, the Monday after next? I'll be over." She sighed. "Call if you like. But I can't see how things will change." He couldn't pursue this with May standing there. It was too mortifying. "Good-bye, May darling. It's been marvelous seeing you. Drop me a line, don't forget." As he hugged her, May held herself rigid. That hurt.

Martin could envision exactly what awaited him at Jess's. After the pleasantries, dinner, maybe some fooling around with Max, maybe some art world gossip, sooner or later she would say, "Well . . . ?" His muscles went limp. No, he really wasn't up to it just yet. What sorts of men sit alone like this in bus terminals? he wondered. Frankly, right now he didn't especially desire either one of them. He desired only to be rid of his burdens, to slump over on the unyielding seat. No, he had to pull himself together. If he lived with Jess . . . But could he ever actually live with those drums? He was very fond of the kid, but six more years of drums? In earnest, if he lived with her, would he eventually grow tired of her unfailing brilliance, her energy so like his own, her trim body? And then what? He glanced around. Directly opposite him sat a soft, honey-skinned Indian woman in a sari, her shining hair pulled back in a knot, a red teardrop on her forehead. She must be around thirty-two or three, he imagined, and she was surrounded by four young children. The sari was something like the robes Madonnas wore. In fact the pattern the group of them made—the woman with her head tilted toward one child in particular—reminded him of one of Raphael's Madonnas. Where could she be going? There was only one large suitcase. Was her husband off buying the tickets or was she alone? And how did a sari work, anyhow? She had full curving lips. Martin smiled at her tentatively. Respectfully—he might have been smiling in appreciation of the children, as strangers do. Her eyes seemed to smile back, then she bent over the smallest girl, fixing the barrette in her hair. A dark man in a white shirt approached, holding a handful of tickets. The woman smiled a welcome while the children clustered around him.

Oh Martin, he thought, looking on at them, you are a sad case.

It was very unfair. He had served and worshiped all his life, while other men reaped the rewards. Nevertheless, one must go on. Take the next step, whatever that might be. He got up slowly, gathered his things, and headed for the exit. In a few minutes he would be at Jess's. It would be dry and warm, at least. She would be glad to see him, for a while, at least. He must remember what he used to tell his students, in the days of strife and idealism. (Of wine and roses.) No matter how great your anger at injustice, never let it embitter you. Don't lose your sense of joy. Remember that life is . . . But the word wouldn't come.

CHOWDER

STEPHEN DUNNING

The restaurant is narrow and deep. Brother's Cafe. I sit toward the back where it's darker. But I'm thinking more of noise than light. A crew is tearing up the street—jackhammers, picks, a small bulldozer.

There's a menu in th napkin holder. The girl who comes to take my order stands against the light. I can see her outline. She's slender, maybe twenty-five. "How do you read in this light?" I ask.

"It's terrible," she says. "It's so bad college kids come here to smooch."

It's been years since I heard anyone say *smooch*. I wish she wouldn't stand over my bald spot. "What's good?" I ask.

"Everything's ok. The kitchen's clean. We got almost everything." There are little shadows between the base of her neck and her collarbones.

"Say you and I were here on a date, what would you get?"

She laughs. "If we was here yesterday on our date, I'd order chowder. The boss buys plain chowder, like Stokely's—you know, like what you buy in regular stores?"

"Mrs. Somebody's chowder," I say. "My ma always said that's the best."

"Maybe. Anyway, Stanley the Cook adds a can of minced clams. Makes it chewy and nice."

"You talked me into it," I say. I'm self-conscious she's looking down where it's thin. "I'll take the chowder and a plain grilled cheese."

The waitress laughs again. "No, yesterday's chowder. If we was to have lunch *yesterday*."

"I know. I was just seeing if you was paying attention." Slipping into the other person's grammar is a salesman's trick.

"Well, today's French onion. It's ok. Stanley the Cook's heavy on the cheese. But I never get no compliments on the French onion."

"How's the juices?"

"The best," the waitress says. "Right out of the can. Never touched by human hand."

I like the way she talks back. "Ok then, the grilled cheese and a big tomato juice, ok? Maybe spice it up with some lemon?"

"I'll fix it up."

I nod and smile. "Good," I say. Maybe I'm having some luck. She has me in the palm of her hand. "Fix it up good, I'm a giant tipper."

"I'll bet. White ok on the cheese?"

"Perfect," I say. "My daddy always said you can spot all the roaches in white bread."

"Only if the light's good," she says, and laughs again. "I'll be back."

My eyes start seeing things once they get used to low light. What I look at most is a girl about twenty in a blue sweater. It looks like she has finished eating and is studying. Anyway, her chest is resting on the table top. I know she's aware of its being there. I asked Lola Ahrens once, like fifteen years ago. "Does a girl realize what she's doing when she rests her chest on a table?" Lola's the one girl in my whole life I would call a girl *friend*, not a girlfriend. I should have married Lola.

"Oh sure," she says. "Girls know. With boobs like mine, you're very aware."

The way I tell it you might think Lola is bragging on having a big chest. The truth is just the opposite. Her chest is about the size of mine, and I'm a normal male.

The light is ok, now. The girl in the blue sweater looks good, and I have this friendly waitress with a nice laugh. My job's looking better, too. Maybe my luck really has turned.

"Here's the juice," she says. I jerk my head like I've been asleep. Actually I've been watching the blue-sweater girl. "Knock, knock. Who's there? It's me, with the food." She puts down the juice and the plate.

"I was just doing my homework."

"Nice," the waitress says. "It's not you she's after, though. Check the guy near the phone."

I see the man she means. Or boy. I can't tell ages anymore. He seems to be waiting for a call. All three seem about the same age—the girl in the sweater, my waitress, the guy.

"What's wrong, is he blind? Lack of red blood cells?"

"Oh, he's all boy," she says. She pauses just a second. "He's my man. My live-in. He's going to see me through college once he's through. Anyway, he makes a move toward her, I kick his butt out."

I like getting in on her personal news. "Well, kick him out," I say. "You can move in with me. I already got me two goldfish and a stray cat."

"I just might do that," the waitress says, "now that we're so deep in this relationship of ours."

She doesn't ignore me from then on, but she's busy. Eight tables. The blue-sweatered girl and I are the only singles. My appointment is across town at two, so I eat pretty fast. My waitress comes by once. "Everything all right?"

"I know men who'd marry you for juice like that."

"Bring the next one right here," she says. "Especially if he's rich. Coffee?"

"Just the check, I guess," I say. "When you got time. You a big fan of MasterCard?"

That's another selling trick. I knew they took MasterCard from the sticker on the window. A good salesman gives people lots of chances to say yes. Also my boss loves it when my expenses come in on Master-Card. He hates little scraps all different sizes. "Sure, we take MasterCard," she says. "Didn't mean to neglect you. This place turns into a zoo around twelve."

"I know, I was watching you." I give her my plastic. "The guy in the green shirt wants to get something going with you."

She says, "Tell me something I don't know."

"You really hustle."

"Mind your mouth!" she says, and laughs. "I knew you was watching." She leaves with my MasterCard and the check. I think again of Lola. She said that women pretty much know what men are up to.

My waitress is back in a minute with the slips to sign. She holds out a ballpoint. "You're supposed to put your phone on, too. Come back sometime I'm not so busy, I'll treat you better."

"I got a pen. If I come back, what about your friend?"

She laughs. "I said I'd treat you better. *Better* don't mean bathtub privileges."

"I'll come back for Freddie the Cook's chowder recipe," I say. "Somehow I forgot to write it all down."

"Stanley the Cook," she says, and laughs.

The bill is three oh five. I add a buck to the slip, a big tip for me. The girl has gone into the kitchen. Instead of my phone number I write Ramada Inn. I wait a couple of seconds, but then take my copy, leave the others and the pen. The company hands out pens by the gross and tells us to leave them around. I leave them all over. The pen has the home office phone, for one thing. She can reach me there or at the Ramada, if she wants.

But I'm not holding my breath. Luck doesn't flipflop like a pancake. Recently, I was married seventeen days, total, to my former wife Sandy. While I'm on a trip, she splits, taking everything of value from our condo. I come home, she's gone. It's obvious she had help cleaning out the nest.

I've had mucho discussions about luck in general and my marriage in specific. Mostly in bars, but once in a while in a nice scene, like out walking with a woman. The best talk was in Galveston during our national sales convention. I was walking a gorgeous girl, Carol, out of our Cleveland office, one foggy night. Fog made it easy to talk. I got on to the question whether my Guinness-record marriage was good or bad luck.

You don't tell stories where you look like a jerk unless you feel good about the person you're with. I was quite hopeful about this Carol. Then while we're talking in the fog, arm in arm, she shoots me down with her answer on luck. "Tell me about luck," she says. "I married before I knew what I was doing. I was seventeen when I married that ape."

For an instant, in the fog, I didn't know how to take her. What ape? When I took her back to her room, she gave me her extension at work in Cleveland and said I could call her there. She wouldn't give me the number where she lived.

I usually work the topic of luck so I say I had good luck getting Sandy to marry me. I say, "Hey, we had a wonderful month, with the courtship and the seventeen days." Or, "How many marriages you know have even one good month?" But of course it was bad luck pure and simple when she and the guy she was running the scam with cleaned out the joint checking account, took the new TV, the stereo, the tapes I bought her, plus *my* tapes. That hurt. So did the good silverware serving fork and spoon Ma sent for the wedding, and my alligator shoes. Worse, she tousled my hair and pulled long hairs over the bald spot. "There's one," she said. "Oh, there's another. Oh, you still got lots of hair."

Now almost three months later I don't hold anything against Sandy. I can even laugh about the marriage, in a way. I do wonder how any man who loved her would let her get into bed with one guy after another before they cleaned him out. I mean, she didn't hold anything back. Of course I don't know she and her partner were lovers. Maybe they were all business. The point is, I am getting over Sandy, getting my self-confidence back. I can joke now about how I should have bought what

I sell. My line is electronic protection. Most of it protects against people breaking into buildings, stealing equipment. Cuts down theft and employee ripoff.

Except for missing out on the chowder, I'm having a dynamite day. I like the way my waitress looks and talks. She treats me like a person. And I'm hot! My first sale I'd counted on — our basic building protection package. About $4,400 net. The kicker is this guy Boomer buys the new computer package too. I hardly pay attention at first. I think, What's he talking about? In point of fact, I'm distracted by Boomer's hairpiece. I'll never wear a hairpiece unless I can get one that blends in better than his.

The computer package is there in our literature, of course. But until Boomer no one's taken it seriously. Boomer goes for it. That's $11,500. Figure me in for about eleven and a quarter percent against draw. Also, the day isn't over. At two I see a guy from Bradford Packaging across town. A salesman's dream. The guy I'm going to see has called the home office in response to a mailing. He knows exactly what he wants. All I do is write the order. Another six G's, or so. Merry Christmas.

I'm in and out of Bradford Packaging in forty-five minutes, the order signed, sealed and delivered. $5,800 and change. Ten days like today, I can fish the Bahamas the rest of the year. Maybe my waitress would eat a few clams in the Bahamas.

The Ramada where I'm staying is on the east side of town. I drive back the way I'd come, though, because it takes me past Brother's Cafe. My waitress let me know she had a boyfriend, but she was somewhat encouraging. What I mostly have in mind is someone nice to celebrate with.

I practice what I'll say. "Listen, I know where we can get us some chowder with live clams."

She'll laugh.

Then something like, "Look, I don't want to screw up anything important, but if you can have dinner I'd like that a lot."

Even if she says no, she can't be offended I ask.

My luck holds. When I get in front of Brother's, a Buick Skylark pulls out and I park. Twenty minutes on the meter, exactly in front of the door! When you're hot, you're hot.

Inside I stand for a minute to get the eyes halfway adjusted. "Table for one?" a woman says. There wasn't a hostess at lunch.

"Actually, I'm just looking for someone."
"One of our waitresses?"
"Yes, one who waited on me at lunch."
"Are you grilled cheese and juice? Mandy asked if you'd come back."
Mandy? Sandy, now Mandy. "Again?" I say.
"Did you have grilled cheese—"
"That's me."
"The girl's Mandy. She said if you came back after your pen I was to give you this." I can see the woman's face, now. She goes behind the cash register, bends over, then straightens and comes back. "Here." She hands me the company pen and a note.

"Well, listen. Thanks a lot," I say. "Can I give you a little something?"

I don't know whether she doesn't hear, or pretends not to. I must have insulted her dignity. I put the note in my coat and go outside.

The note doesn't start a fire in my pocket. I figure it will give a phone number and say something like, "I liked waiting on you. Call me, Mandy." I catch again on her name.

It's four-twenty. I decide to hit the Ramada, pour a little celebration drink of Jack Daniel's, and give Mandy not Sandy a call.

The ice machine outside my room is empty and dry. I cruise the halls until I find one that works. I fix the drink and read the note. It says,

> Dear grilled cheese and juice,
> Sorry if things I said gave you a wrong impression. You are friendly and funny. Come back some Tuesday, chowders on me. But Im true to my guy even if hes horny for other women.
>
> Mandy, from Brother's.
> PS If you got this you probably came back for me. Im sorry. Anyway heres your pen back. Thanks for the tip, Big Tipper.

I look into the mirror over the desk. I don't look too bad from the front. I toast my reflection, doing Bogey. "Here's looking at you, kid."

I swirl the drink, take a sip. "You look friendly. Not anyone I want to take home, but friendly." I'm actually talking out loud. "You got a great sense of humor."

I sip again. I'm not a big boozer. The Jack Daniel's is strong, but I love the taste.

I figure it's time for Plan B—take a shower, put on the rust sport coat, hit the lounge. Have a drink, maybe a conversation or two. Then a really nice dinner, to celebrate. *With* someone, if my luck holds.

A few years ago, when something big happened, I'd call Lola Ahrens and shoot the breeze. She's Lola Cawelti now. One night I call, her husband answers and asks who's calling. I give my name. He says if it's all the same to me, I can stop the long-distance calls to his wife.

Lola Cawelti. Doesn't that make you want to dance? I haven't called her since, but I still think about her. I should have married her. Her area's 714. If I get her number I can see for sure if my luck has changed. She could be home alone, or divorced. Her old man answers I can say, "Wrong number, hey, I'm sorry," and hang it up.

KEEPING ORDER

GLORIA WHELAN

The day before Mrs. Brady's annual tea for the residents of the Martha Mary home, Esther Birdwell, a retired teacher of domestic science, was praying earnestly for something she did not want. She was praying that the five harlots stay on at the Martha Mary Residence for Working and Retired Women so that they might be redeemed. Esther could not bring herself to refer to them as prostitutes, which had a job-oriented sound, something to be considered on high-school career day. She preferred the biblical word as a reminder of what the Lord expected of her: charity, forgiveness, and love—one thing more impossible than the next.

Esther rose from her knees. She knew what she must do, she must go to Sister Agnes and tell her of the sinful scheme she and some of the other residents had hatched. Still, she hesitated, looking about her room for some pretext to postpone facing Sister Agnes's anger. Esther's room was small and ugly with walls the soiled tan of potato skins. Her single window faced north and even on this bright April day was stingy with its light.

It was a room much like the one assigned to her when she had first moved into Martha Mary years before, the residence's first black woman. Esther, insisting upon her seniority, progressed to larger and larger rooms until she had achieved the luxury of two windows, enough space for a comfortable chair and even a closet with shelves. There were things at Martha Mary that made you feel warehoused: the rows of doors and mailboxes and shower stalls, the piles of trays and bins of silverware. Against all of that Esther had her room. When the sun came flooding in through the south-facing windows, touching her pale yellow walls and gilding everything she loved, it had buoyed her up like a sea filled with good salt.

Then the Director of the house, Sister Agnes, and the Board Chairman, Mrs. Brady, had decided to bring the harlots to Martha Mary. Mrs. Brady had called a meeting of the residents. Sitting next to Mrs. Brady, Sister Agnes — one of those charged women whose energy consumes flesh, leaving them thin but glowing — told the residents the Lord was bestowing upon them a great privilege.

Theresa Sullivan had whispered hopefully to Esther, "I'll bet they're going to let us have booze in our rooms." Esther knew better. Sister Agnes's idea of privilege ran to world hunger fasts when all the residents were urged to eat nothing for dinner but a bowl of rice. The endearing thing about Sister Agnes was that she was no saint. That is, she didn't have the courage of her convictions. The night of the fast she had invited all the residents down for a late snack of cocoa and peanut butter sandwiches.

Sister Agnes's privilege turned out to be the harlots. She referred to them as Five Troubled Girls but everyone knew what she meant. The Protestant residence hall down the street was taking in girls who were involved with drugs. Esther could imagine how gratifying it would be for Sister Agnes to announce to the director of the Protestant home, *We're* going to have *prostitutes*."

Lee Simon, who worked as a receptionist in a podiatrist's office and was considered the resident expert in medical matters, raised her hand and asked, "Will we be sharing bathrooms?"

Sister Agnes was no prude and knew what Lee was asking. "The girls will all have thorough physicals before they arrive here. If we can just give them enough love, I'm sure they won't go back to their old ways. We must keep in mind that living at Martha Mary is a condition of their parole. They'll have every reason to cooperate with us."

Theresa, who like Esther had achieved spacious quarters, said in a nervous voice, "What rooms are they moving into?"

Sister Agnes looked distressed. "Well, I'm not sure." She hesitated. "I know some of you are very attached to your rooms . . ."

Mrs. Brady, a little apprehensive, like someone giving a gift that might be the wrong size, interrupted Sister Agnes. "I'm going to be perfectly frank with all of you," she said. "The Board felt it would defeat our purpose to put the girls in the smallest and least desirable rooms. Their self-image is already poor. We want them to know they have our respect as well as our love." She had smiled out at the residents as though they were all part of a charming little conspiracy.

On the table in front of Mrs. Brady was her basket purse on which were painted replicas of the stores in the suburb of Colonial Heights where Mrs. Brady lived. Esther, a little overwrought by the announcement, wondered if there were a replica on the purse of the store where the purse was purchased, and in the window of the store, the purse, and on the purse . . .

Each year on the first Saturday afternoon in June the residents of Martha Mary were bused to Colonial Heights to visit the Brady home where fruit punch and little sandwiches were served to them and they were encouraged to stroll through the spacious rooms and gardens admiring, outdoors, the Brady's priceless iris collection and indoors, the priceless collection of French paperweights.

The residents were allowed to use the Brady powder room where paper towels with the Brady initials in gold were set out on the marble sink for their use. Occasionally one of the residents dried her hands on a piece of Kleenex and took home a paper towel in her purse as a memento. The sweeping stairway that led to the second floor and the more intimate Brady quarters was cordoned off with a pink ribbon. The residents never minded; it gave them something to speculate about on their way home.

Mrs. Brady, delighted to have so many women to whom she could give pleasure, was a gracious hostess. She would think with sadness of her guests returning to their dreary residence and some scheme would occur to her for refurbishing their visitor's lounge or she might resolve to have the piano in the recreation room tuned or a coffee machine installed.

On the day she announced to the women that the Five Troubled Girls were coming to live at Martha Mary, a similar feeling stole over her. Even as she was delivering her little speech, she was deciding the chairs in the cafeteria needed to be replaced, perhaps with bright plastic ones in cheerful colors. In this benevolent mood she was surprised then to look out at the faces of the residents and see dismay and anger. Hurriedly she said, "I want all of my good friends here to know the Board doesn't want to do anything behind your backs. That's why I'm having this meeting with you today. We want all of you to share in our decisions and we're certain you will welcome the opportunity to take these disadvantaged girls to your hearts. Remember we have the example of Our Lord who opened his arms to sinners. And whom among us would not admit to being a sinner? I hope you will look on these girls as a real challenge."

"I don't know that Our Lord ever *lived* with people like that," Theresa whispered.

"He certainly didn't share a bathroom with them." Lee looked at Esther who usually made their minds up for them.

"I don't suppose it will hurt us to do what we can to help," Esther said. You didn't teach school for forty years, as Esther had, without believing in amendment.

When the rooms were reapportioned Esther's had been among those to be given to one of The Girls. Had it been possible for a single black woman to find an inexpensive apartment in a decent part of the city, Esther would have considered moving. The residence hall was not all that desirable, located as it was in a deteriorating section of the city where many of the stores were boarded up and older women were preyed upon by muggers. The food was dismal — rubbery sausages in leaky nests of sauerkraut, weeks of fruit cocktail.

All the residents were required to take one meal a day in the cafeteria. Esther chose lunch. Making do with the snack kitchen's electric frying pan and toaster oven, she prepared her own dinners. From time to time she invited a friend to join her, perhaps for an omelet *fines herbs* with a nice salad. She would have loved to serve a little wine with her dinners but it was strictly forbidden to have spirits on the premises and Esther had survived her sixty-eight years, not all of them pleasant, by cleaving to firm principles and orderly ways. With laxness came clutter, wavering, despondency, and death.

In her years of teaching domestic science in an inner-city school, Esther had brought order into the disorganized lives of her students. Before her girls were allowed to pick up so much as a measuring spoon, they had to produce in their notebooks a letter-perfect copy of their recipe. The same notebooks held diagrams indicating the exact placement in the cupboards of every pot, pan, and mixing bowl. For many of the students these notebooks were their first hint of an alternative to havoc. Some of the girls learned to read while puzzling over directions for fettucini and quiche — Esther had taught thrift, but it was not a graceless thrift. She was sure none of *her* girls had ended up on the street.

With that in mind, she had approached Sister Agnes shortly after The Girls had arrived, offering to teach them cooking. She saw them, pencils at the ready, faces turned toward her, eager to be initiated into a world of rules. She would instruct them on the mysteries of keeping house; then they would find a house and keep it. Although Esther herself had never married, considering men by the time they came of marriageable age irremediable, these girls, she felt, could do worse.

Sister Agnes had been enthusiastic. A notice had been put in The Girls' mailboxes but when the hour came for the class and Esther was waiting in the residence kitchen with five notebooks she had bought with her own money, and before her, the ingredients for a gougère (believing they would appreciate the dramatic), no one had come. Finally Sister Agnes, looking in to see how things were going, expressed a polite interest in taking the class herself. She surprised Esther by turning out to be a competent cook. "My dad owned a bar and grill," Sister Agnes told her. "We all helped out."

The Girls had been at Martha Mary for three weeks when Lee Simon and Theresa Sullivan crowded into Esther's small room for tea. Theresa, who worked as a receptionist in a funeral home, had brought an arrangement of orange lillies for Esther, but their grandeur made Esther's dark room shabbier than ever. "Did you hear those tramps coming in at all hours last night?" Theresa had asked. "They were running up and down the halls at four in the morning, laughing and screaming. Why doesn't Sister Agnes get after them?"

"She's tried but it doesn't do any good," Esther said. "Haven't you noticed how much time she's spending in the chapel?" Some of the shine had gone out of Sister Agnes.

Lee said, "I haven't been able to have the children here since The Girls came." Lee had a number of nieces and nephews who enjoyed pounding on the piano in the recreation room and eating in the cafeteria, where they could pick out what they weren't supposed to have. "I don't care *what* Mrs. Brady told us. I'm afraid to let them use the bathrooms."

"I don't blame you. I hate to use them myself." Esther passed the macaroons she had baked earlier in the day. "They leave hair all over everything. The sinks are filthy and," she lowered her voice, "they don't flush."

"We saw your sign," Lee told Esther sympathetically. Esther's "Please Keep Things Clean" sign had been covered with lipsticked vulgarities. "I heard someone found a hypodermic syringe in one of the waste baskets."

"You can't tell me that isn't pot they're smoking, either. I can smell it." Esther had patrolled the school lavatories regularly and more than once had charged the boys' room in pursuit of an offender.

"That gold ring Mary Butler got when her mother died was stolen," Theresa said sadly. "Eleanor Wright's wallet disappeared out of her room, too."

"Everyone in the neighborhood knows we have women like that," Esther told them. "This used to be a respectable place to live."

"Who are those men in the big cars that come by for them? I saw the blonde getting into a Lincoln Continental with a . . ." Lee was about to say "a black man" but she remembered Esther in time and changed it to "a man in a green silk suit."

Esther never let things like that pass. "The *black* man was a pimp." The pimps made themselves at home in the visitors' lounge. Tall, thin, elegant men in bright colors with crested pompadours and long clawlike nails, they flocked in the lounge like exotic birds, directing indecent remarks to the residents and hustling The Girls out to waiting cars with proprietary fanny pats.

"Did you ever hear such language?" There had been late night caterwauling among The Girls and Lee had lain with her hands over her ears blocking out the graphic obscenities. "Why don't we tell the Board?"

"Some of us wrote Mrs. Brady but she just said we weren't doing enough to make them feel wanted." Esther had drafted the letter to the Board herself. "I wish she could have seen them in the cafeteria this noon." There was a strict prohibition against appearing in the dining room unless you were fully dressed, but Del, a bony horse-faced creature with hair the color of lemon marmalade, had wandered down for lunch in a filthy terrycloth robe. Behind her had come Bobby, a black woman at least six feet tall, looking in a red satin peignoir like a spreading conflagration. On her head was a wig which might have been a hibernating animal. Holding Bobby's hand was Dannette, a soft puffy girl with hair upholstered in pink foam curlers. She was wearing cowboy boots and a white lab coat over baby-doll pajamas. They paused, a bizarre tableau, at the entrance of the cafeteria. Bobby had grinned excessively. "Look at all these little ladies eatin' their lunch already. They be goin' to bed *real* early at night. The *good* girls, not like us."

In a fit of giggling the top of Danette's flimsy pajamas ditched its responsibility.

Bobby turned to her, "Cover yourself up, girl," she said sternly. "We gotta' behave like *ladies* here."

To protest this aberration, Esther had marched out of the dining room leaving her lunch half-finished, no hardship since they were having Spanish rice for the third time that week. Esther had been particularly furious at Bobby. Black women in the residence lived up to Esther's standards or received a visit from her which they never forgot.

And in fact after lunch Esther had marched up to Bobby's room, the room, as it happened, that had once been Esther's. She had knocked sharply. When Bobby opened the door Esther gasped — disorder everywhere: shoes strewn on the unmade bed, black net stockings draped over the lamp, dresser drawers leaking their embarrassing contents and under the bed....

"Honey, you be the cutest thing I ever see," Bobby had greeted her. "I noticed you right away when you was goin' into the shower with those little white rubber shoes on your feet. I got a auntie jus' like you. She say, 'Roberta, you gonna' come to no good.' I give her a microwave oven last Christmas and she wouldn't have it in her house. 'Where that money come from?' she ask me. She hurt my feelings sometimes but she be one wonderful person."

Esther interrupted her. "There are wine bottles under your bed." Esther was apalled that such a thing could happen in what she still considered to be her own room. "Drinking is strictly forbidden at Martha Mary."

"Don't you worry about us, honey. We know you sweet little ladies don't want us here. We be as anxious to get loose of this tightass place as you be to get us out. The probation officers, they *sentenced* us to this place. But you *know* we gonna' find a way to get out jus' as quick as we can."

What had shocked Esther the most was the discovery that Bobby did not consider living at Martha Mary a privilege.

Esther reported the visit to Theresa and Lee. "You should have seen my room," she moaned. "It was a pigsty."

"Wait until they turn up in Mrs. Brady's living room next week," Lee said with relish.

The invitations to the annual tea had appeared that morning in their mailboxes: "Mrs. Walter Brady requests the pleasure of the company of the Martha Mary residents on Thursday, June 10th, at half after three."

"You don't think Elizabeth Brady would allow those sluts in her *own* home? They didn't *get* an invitation," Theresa told them.

"How do you know?" Esther was deeply disappointed. Like Lee, she had been consoling herself with agreeable fantasies. If Mrs. Brady could just *see* The Girls, Esther was sure she'd have them out of Martha Mary in no time.

"Sister Agnes told me. I got there just after she put the invitations in the mailboxes and I noticed there weren't any in theirs. She said Mrs. Brady called her twice to explain the invitations were just for the 'regular residents' and not the 'new girls.' I could tell Sister didn't think that was right."

The three women fell into a rich silence. After a while Esther asked, "What time do they pick up their mail?"

"On their way down to lunch—breakfast, for them," Theresa answered.

"And Sister Agnes is down in the cafeteria then."

The two women nodded.

"There are five of them," Esther said. "Between us we've got three invitations. Where can we get two more?"

"Mary Butler on account of her gold ring," Lee said. "And Evelyn Palumbo. One of them tried to pick up her brother in the visitors' lounge."

"And Jean," Theresa added. "Bobby tried to pick *her* up."

"That's more than enough," Esther nibbled thoughtfully on a macaroon. It was good, really worth the trouble of toasting the almonds first, she decided.

The morning of the tea Esther had opened her Bible, as she did every morning of her life, to read a chapter or two. Right there in Matthew was the passage about the tax collectors and the prostitutes entering the kingdom of heaven before anyone else. Was the Lord trying to tell her something? Guilt overwhelmed Esther and she got down on her knees to pray that the harlots be allowed to remain at Martha Mary. The complaints about the harlots were true enough, but the day before Dannette had appeared in the dining room with a black eye and a reddish purple bruise on her cheek. Esther, who had never allowed herself to dwell on what the girls actually *did*, found herself having to admit there must be times when it was not pleasant for them. A few days after Esther's visit to Bobby's room, Bobby had knocked on her door. "I heard they turned you out of your room an' put me there. I tried to get you your room back, but that Sister Agnes, she set on killin' us with kindness. But don't you care, we're lookin' to get out first chance we see. Here's somethin' for you." Almost shyly Bobby handed Esther a bottle of expensive perfume. "It be delicate as shit, jus' like you."

Esther was going to refuse the perfume, but she recalled the story of Bobby's aunt and the microwave. Holding the perfume between two fingers, she thanked Bobby and hid the gift in the back of her closet.

It was not unlike teaching. You tried to remain objective, to keep a little distance between yourself and your students but as the term progressed, and in spite of yourself, you began to care first about one student then another and in no time you were lost.

Esther sought out Sister Agnes and confessed to having given The Girls invitations to the tea. "How are we going to keep them from coming with us?" she asked, expecting Sister Agnes's anger and worse, her disapproval.

Instead, Sister Agnes looked pained and said, "Something has happened. Dannette had a man in her room last night."

They exchanged looks. For different reasons Esther and Sister Agnes had kept out of the way of men. Now, after all, it was possible that even here at Martha Mary a man might appear in one's bedroom.

"I don't know but what you were quite right," Sister Agnes said, appearing more luminescent than she had in a long time, "to share your invitations. It was generous of you. I think the outing to the Brady's home will do us *all* good."

Esther saw there was to be war and that it would be a holy war.

As the women gathered in front of Martha Mary waiting to board the bus that would take them to Colonial Heights, their noses twitched in the soft spring air. June had breached the city. The smell of automobile exhaust was rich as roses. They stood in light spring suits and dresses, happy as schoolchildren who have taken off their winter coats and believe they will never have to put them on again. As they boarded the bus, Esther looked nervously around wondering where The Girls were; perhaps Sister Agnes had had second thoughts.

The bus door was closing with a hydraulic whoosh when a mélange of black leather, white boots, sequins, frizzled hair, short skirts, and see-through blouses emerged and ran toward the bus.

"They've put on their working clothes," Lee said, encouraged.

The Girls lined up on the back seat giggling and nudging one another like children on an outing. When the bus reached Colonial Heights they began to whisper among themselves. At the sight of the Brady's large home and expanse of green lawn the whispering intensified. They were the last to leave the bus and by the time they were strutting up the geranium-lined path, most of the residents were already in the Brady home. With mixed feelings Esther saw that Mrs. Brady was paralyzed by the sight of The Girls and would not have the presence of mind to shut the door in their faces. When Mrs. Brady was finally able to move she looked around for Sister Agnes and some explanation, but Sister Agnes had hurried into the Brady living room and hidden herself among the residents.

"Why don't we all go out into the garden?" Mrs. Brady managed. "It's such a lovely afternoon."

Once outside The Girls ran around the garden exclaiming over the irises which were at their peak. "Look here," Del giggled, "each flower's got its own name on a little stick. I gotta have some for my room." She broke off a bloom the colors of port wine and green grapes.

"No," Mrs. Brady's voice was shrill. "Please, it's taken years. We have to have the booms to hybridize. Wait!"

But The Girls were sweeping through the garden snatching at every flower they could get their hands on from the palest skim-milk blue to the darkest mahogany.

The residents, though horrified, stayed where they were.

Like beauty queens or presidents' wives, The Girls with their arms full of flowers wandered back through the French doors, Mrs. Brady at their heels. Bobby reached a long arm up to one of the lighted glass shelves where the paperweights were displayed. "These pretty glass rocks must cost you plenty?" But Mrs. Brady was in search of Sister Agnes. The Girls crowded around the paperweights and gazed wonderingly down into their kaleidoscope of colors. When the huddle broke up Dannette hoisted her purse strap farther up her shoulder to accommodate increased weight.

Mary Butler thought of her mother's gold ring lost to her forever. Eleanor Wright thought of her wallet with the only picture she had of the only man who had ever proposed to her. No one said a word.

"You all come and see this pretty pink ribbon they got wrapped 'round out here," Bobby called from the hallway. "Just like we gettin' the whole damn upstairs for a present."

As soon as she saw the ribbon stretched across the stairway from the newel post to the wainscoting, Dannette yanked at it, draping it around her hips and tying it in a bow. She did a few bumps and grinds and then ran up the stairs, the other girls skittering up behind her.

Mrs. Brady followed them calling, "I'm sorry, I'm afraid you can't go up there." But The Girls had disappeared into the bedrooms. Mrs. Brady screamed wildly down to the residents, "I could use some help up here!"

The residents sat on their chairs sipping punch and nibbling little cream cheese and chutney sandwiches. Esther thought the combination interesting but she gave poor marks to the cucumber sandwiches, which were soggy. "Should have buttered them first," she said to Lee. Overhead she could hear pleasurable cries of discovery.

July was always a quiet month at Martha Mary. Those who could escape the heat of the city did so. Esther didn't know anyone with a cottage on a lake or a place in the country but this year she didn't mind; she was back in her old room. The dirty fingerprints were scrubbed from the yellow walls. The floor was waxed. A freshly laundered and starched scarf covered the nail polish stains on the dresser. A cloud of Lysol hung reassuringly over the room. Streaming through the polished windows, the summer sun clung like a warm shawl to Esther's shoulders. She was pouring sherry for Lee and Theresa. With the sherry Esther served a small wedge of Brie and toasted water biscuits.

Theresa had brought a bouquet of yellow sweetheart roses garnished with tendrils of ivy. "The minute I saw it come in, I knew it would be perfect in your room," she told Esther. "I changed the water each day myself and kept them in the icebox at night—things spoil so fast there. She enjoyed bringing flowers from the funeral home. Once she got them outside they seemed to take on new life.

"Doesn't it feel funny having liquor in your room?" Lee asked.

"It's not liquor," Esther corrected her, "It's only fortified wine." Still

Esther had to admit Lee was right — it *was* against the rules. But Sister Agnes had been transferred and the new director, Sister Elizabeth, was away part of each day working in a real estate office. Although The Girls were gone, the residents no longer bothered to keep the bathrooms tidy. Some of them even appeared for breakfast in their bathrobes. Right this minute, Esther thought, feeling a chill in spite of the sun, she was breaking the Martha Mary rule about having spirits in your room. She reached for her sherry.

TAKES

STEPHEN DIXON

Man's waiting in the service elevator right next to the passenger elevator. Someone comes—a woman, hopefully a young one, through the front door or from one of the apartments upstairs or on this floor—he'll step out behind her with the knife, threaten her with it, take her in the automatic elevator rather than this hand-operated one to the top floor, walk her up to the roof, knife always on her throat, he always behind her and threatening softly but with a real scary tone in his voice, "One scream and I'll use it; make even a move from this knife or to see me and I'll kill you," take her to a good dark out-of-the-way spot on the roof—all depending what lights from the other buildings' windows are on it—rape her. She'll never see his face and his voice won't be his own. She doesn't put up a fuss, he'll leave her there gagged and tied up. He's scouted out the building. Not many tenants come in or leave their apartments this late, but it's worth the wait. Someone will come. Lots of single women in this neighborhood, so has to be a few in this building too. But on Saturday night, most, he bets, will be with men friends. One won't though and that's who.

Tenant on the eighth floor. Can't sleep. Something's up. Hasn't always been right when she thought something bad was going to happen, but enough times she has. It's not from any crazy imagination she's thinking this. The winos were really loud tonight. Few more bottles and things smashed on the street or whatever they're smashed against than usual too. And a couple more souped-up cars and motorcycles than she's used to racing past her building too. Why don't the police do something? If it's because they don't know of these things going on or they're too lazy to patrol or can't because of cutbacks, then why don't people call them more? This city. She turns the TV off. Get some sleep.

Young woman's mother in Connecticut. Thinking about her daughter. She went to New York to do graduate work in painting. Took an apartment with another young woman, a friend from college. But the building's bad. Filthy, poorly maintained, bell system that doesn't work; a firetrap, she's sure. Even if some of the neighborhood's okay, and some of the river buildings even elegant, and as co-ops or rented apartments, quite expensive, much of it's very bad. Welfare hotels. Cheap rooming houses. Awful looking men and women on the street day and night. Little park nearby where men drink and some dope and urinate in the open and make vulgar remarks to passing women and all sorts of other things. Beggars. In the *Times* she's read of break-ins and muggings and seen a city crime statistic chart that put her neighborhood near the top. Worried.

Man in a cab going across town. Should have got out of the cab and escorted her upstairs. Didn't like the looks of her building and block. But then he hardly knows her. She might have thought he was being funny in a way—forward, not funny. And he had this cab, was in it, did only promise to take her to the street door, or rather: just see, while he sat in the cab, she got inside that door, and then he might not have got another cab after he left her building or not so fast. Could have asked the cab to wait while he saw her to her apartment door. Now he thinks of it. But she said she'd be alright. He did ask. And he's sure that no matter how hard he insisted on taking her to her apartment door, she would have said no. *Still.*

Woman's in the lobby, presses the elevator button. Light above the elevator door says the car's on the top floor, the eighth. Slow elevator, takes days to get down. She doesn't like waiting in this creepy lobby. Anyway, her friend Jean will be upstairs and they can talk about tonight. The man she met. He was nice. Took her home in a cab, wouldn't let her share the fare with him. She wishes she had accepted his suggestion and let him walk her to her door. But then she would have had to invite him in. And offer him a coffee or a beer, when really all she wants to do, if Jean's up—she'll be up—is talk a little with her and go to sleep. Elevator's about here. It's here.

Man thinks now's the time. She's a good-looking one. Long legs, big ass. She'll screw well. He'll screw her well. He'll screw her till she cries for more, more. He steps out. She turns around. Knife's out. Damn, she saw him. "Don't say a word or I'll kill you right here." He gets behind her and puts the knife to her neck. Opens the elevator door, knife always against her neck. "We're going to the roof. I know this building. Don't say a word, make a peep—nothing—don't even sneak a look at me again or you're dead. I know how to get out of this building easily so I'll be out of here before you hit the ground. Now get in."

She gets in. She doesn't believe this. What should she do? This is a dream. A nightmare. It's the worst thing that's ever happened to her. Think, think. That knife. It pricks. They go up. He pressed eight. He said "roof." Maybe someone will stop the elevator on the fourth floor, fifth. There's only one outside button for each floor. No down and up buttons—just one, and if you press that button when you want to go down and the elevator's going up, it stops. Please. Someone.

It's too late to call her, her mother thinks. She'd like to. She wants very much to speak to Corinne, tell her how worried she is about her. Tell her that Dad and she will give her a hundred dollars a month extra to find a better building to live in. Two hundred. It'll be a sacrifice for them, but it just shows how anxious they are about where she's living now. If she's going to live in that city, she'll tell her, then it has to be on these terms. Of course she could say no, she likes where she's living now, took months to find and then paint and set up, doesn't want to take any more money from them than she already does and so on, and they really wouldn't be able to do anything about it. It's too late to call. But it's Saturday. She dials. Corinne's phone rings. If she answers it, or if Jean answers it—she hasn't once thought of Jean, for instance how she'd take to Corinne's parents' subsidizing most of their rent—she'll apologize for calling this late, but both will have to know she only has their best interests at heart. That's not enough. She slams down the receiver. She can wait till tomorrow? Has to, since Corinne will see her anxiety at this hour as bordering on mania. Just another nine or ten hours. Eleven's okay to call on Sundays for women that age. Even if they're with men friends who stayed the night, which, let's face it, could well be the case. She goes upstairs to wash up for bed. Her husband says from the bedroom "What've you been doing? I heard you slamming the phone down, picking it up, then slamming it again." "I only slammed it once. I was worried about Corinne. Worked it out in my head though, so it's now all okay."

Roommate at a party downtown. Wonders if Corinne's home by now. She's sure she's expecting her to be there when she gets home. Note she left will explain it or should. Something like "Aaron called. Sudden invite to big bash at a south of Soho artist's loft and wanted me to join him. I know. Swore I'd grind away at the books all weekend and maybe never see Aaron again, but what, dear, can I say?" They have a phone here? If so, she'll call Corinne and say she doubts she'll be coming home tonight, and she should try to do that before two. She's just about never seen or heard Corinne up after two. "Excuse me," to a woman she thinks is one of the three people giving the party, "but is there by any chance a phone in this place I may use?" "As long as it's not to out of town," the woman says. "Positively not." "Actually, if you're a good friend of either of the other hosts, you can make that call to as far west as Columbus, south as Washington, and as far north as Boston, let's say."

She's also a very pleasant girl, man in the cab thinks. Attractive. Even pretty. He'd definitely call her pretty, even beautiful in some ways, though he doubts a couple of his friends would. Still. And she had spark. Bright, besides. Far as he could make out, bright as any woman he's met in a year. He's definitely phoning her tomorrow. Monday night, not tomorrow. Doesn't want to appear too eager. Why not? She seemed like she'd like eagerness. Directed at her, but not just to score. She complained how most men she meets these days don't really care or get excited about anything but making money and getting ahead. Don't really read, don't think much about serious things, aren't interested in much art other than movies and music. She didn't say he was different but implied he was. She also gave him her phone number willingly enough. He likes her name. She seems to come from a good family: intelligent, moral, involved, well-off. He thinks she sort of took to him too. Maybe that's why he should act fast: so she doesn't forget why she was attracted to him, if she was. Tomorrow night. No, Monday's soon enough. He hopes she paints well. If she doesn't, he could always say at first—later he could level with her more—"Hell, what do I know?"

Top floor. Roof stairs and door. Always trying to get a look at him to see if he means it—seemed he did. Had one of the most maniacal faces she's ever seen, when she saw him just that one glimpse. Slim, young, smelly, wiry, ruthless, cagey-looking. He's crazy. He's going to kill her. If it was just robbery he would have taken the bag downstairs and fled. Knife isn't on her neck anymore. Rape and possibly kill her. She has to find a way to get away. She has to scream, run, kick, maybe on the roof. Now she's thinking. Roof, where there's space. Stairs he's got her trapped. This building's attached to the corner one and unless there's barbed wire or something separating the two roofs, she can make a run for it yelling all the time. Pick up a brick if they have one on the roof and he's cornered her against something like a wall or by a roof edge and throw it at him. Anything: teeth, knees and fists and then down a fire escape, but to escape. There's one that goes all the way past her bedroom window to the narrow alleyway on the ground floor. Corner building must have one too. If not, down her building's fire escape screaming, knocking, banging, breaking all the windows along the way if she has to till someone comes, wakes up, shouts, whatever, but helps chase the man away.

Tenant hears footsteps on the roof right above her. Who could be up there this hour? Trouble. Either some junkies got in the building or corner one next door and got to the roof that way and are shooting up. Or winos or runaways or just plain bums making a home for the night up there. Why can't it rain now or snow? Get them off. She just hopes the roof door's locked tight so they don't start walking down the building's stairs and making noise and throwing up in the hallways as happened a couple of times or trying all the doors. What else could it be up there but something awful? She hopes not someone forced to go for the worst of purposes. That's happened on one or two other buildings around here but never hers.

"Now you know what I want," the man says. "I want to screw you but I want it without holding the knife to your face. That way it'll be better for me and easier and quicker for you. Then if you're good to me and a good little girl all around and give no trouble I'll let you go. You're a real piece of ass, you know? I could tell right away you screw well and that you've screwed around a lot. You got the face for it. Saucy. Sexy. So, you going to do it like I say? You don't, you're dead."

"No, I don't want to do it with you," the woman says. And then louder: "Now let me alone. Let me get by you and downstairs. Now please — I'm asking — please!" He stabs her in the chest. She raises her arms. He stabs her several times. She goes down. She screams. She says "Help, I'm being murdered." He gets on one knee and stabs her where he thinks her heart is.

"Stop that, stop that," the tenant shouts out her window. "Whoever it is, leave that girl alone. Help, police, someone's killing someone upstairs! On the roof. Stop that, you butcher, stop that, stop!"

"Help me, I'm dying," the woman says. "Stupid bitch," the man says. He jumps up. Lights have gone on in some of the apartment windows in buildings that overlook the roof. "Shit," he says. "Hey you there," a man says from a window. "What is it, what's going on?" a man says from a window right next to that one. "I've called the police," a woman shouts from what seems like the building he's on. "They're coming. They're on their way. Everybody call to make sure they come. Girl, don't be afraid. They're coming. People from this building will be up there for you too." "Shit," he says and leaps over the low wall to get to the next building's fire escape.

Her mother thinks about the dream she just had. All the apartment buildings around hers were falling down, one after the other. She lives in a suburban townhouse and has never lived in anything but a private home, but in the dream she was in an apartment in a tall old apartment building in a large city that looked more European than American. The buildings collapsed straight down as if heavy explosives had been set off under them. For a while it seemed the window was a TV screen and she was watching the buildings fall in slow motion in a documentary. She was with her three daughters, all about four to eight years younger than they are now, and her husband and mother, who's dead. Then her building was falling. She held out her arms to her family and said, "Here, come into me." Her arms became progressively longer as each person came into her. She kissed their heads in a row—they were all as small as little children now—and started crying. Then they were at her family's gravesite behind her grandparents' farmhouse, burying her mother. "This proves life can go on," she said to her husband, daughters, and grandmother. She doesn't know what the last part of the dream means. There is no farmhouse or family gravesite. Her parents and grandparents are buried in three different enormous cemeteries. Where was her son in the dream? She gets out of bed, goes to the kitchen, writes down the dream and what she thinks the end of it means. "That everything will be OK with C (living in her city hovel)? That I really needn't be anxious about any of my kids or really about anything in life (how'd I come to that last conclusion?)? That if people stay in mind & memory (just about the same thing; I realize that) they're never really dead? That living, dying, illness, frailty, tragedy, mayhem, mishaps, madness, revolutions, terrorism (from inside & out), and the rest of it are all quite normal? (Was that all you were going to say?) That we're all basically entwined &— now stop all that; it was never in it. Then what? Time for God? Not at any price & why'd that idea pop in? (To interpret it theologically, that's all.) An important dream though, start to end, no matter what I don't make of it. Read all this back tomorrow. Underscore that: read, read! Maybe then."

    Her father can't sleep. He feels for his wife in bed. She left it before but is there now. "Hilda, you up? I can't sleep; want to talk." No answer or movement. Why'd she have to worry him so? Not that he can't handle it, but—He gets up, goes to the bathroom, drinks a glass of water. That was stupid. Meant to take two aspirins first. He gets the aspirins out of the medicine cabinet, puts them in his mouth and washes them down with another glass of water. Now he'll feel better. In about fifteen minutes. And his dreams are usually more vivid and peaceful in theme when he takes aspirins. His doctor thinks he should take an aspirin a night to reduce the fat or plaque on his blood vessel walls. He doesn't mind, especially for the side benefits of a more peaceful sleep and dreams, but usually forgets to.

    The woman's being treated by paramedics. She gives a description of her attacker and details of what happened. "Honestly, try not to talk," one of the paramedics says. "Yes, you probably shouldn't," a policeman says. She says "No, I want you to know what happened. If I go over it enough times, you'll get everything. I came into the building. We're still on my building?" "Yes, of course," the policeman says. "I meant, he didn't drag me over the parapet to the next building?" "If he did, he brought you back or you got back here on your own." "No, what am I talking about?" she says. "I came into the building. I'll proceed chronologically, no digressions. I came into the building." "I really don't want her talking," the paramedic says. "You heard him, Miss. Don't talk." "I came into the building. He was waiting for me in the service elevator. That elevator ought to be locked at night, not left open. People can hide there. I'm digressing, but so what? The lobby door should have a better lock. Anyone, with a little force, can push the door open when it's locked. The building should have better lights. Look at the lights when you leave in the lobby and hallways. Thirty watts, maybe. One to a hallway if you're lucky. There's a city law. My roommate's checked. She's studying to be a lawyer. Where is she?" "If you mean Miss Kantor," the policeman says, "she's not home. We've been inside your apartment. To look for your attacker. I hope you don't mind." "There's a city law saying the wattage should be higher, Jean said. Minimum of two lights too. In case one goes out. He had a long knife. Said he'd kill me unless. Well, he nearly did. Maybe he will have. No he won't. I should say that. No he won't." "You shouldn't say anything," the paramedic says. "This officer and I say *don't*." "But I wouldn't have sex with him. Why would I? It would have been worse than anything. He was filthy. A beast. A jungle. I thought I could escape on the roof. I should have tried to break away sooner. In the lobby. That way I would have had a chance. But I was so scared. I couldn't think. I got my wits about me going up the elevator. His knife seemed shined. Maybe he shines it with polish. He was sick enough. Maybe I should have let him do it. Screw me, he said. Maybe it would have been worth it, filth and all. When you can't do anything." "Now that's enough. Absolutely no more talk." "This has all been very valuable, Corinne," the policeman says, "but this man is right. Save your strength. I insist. For your own sake." "All right."

He's in a bar about ten blocks away having a beer and scotch. He got about twenty dollars from her bag. He's standing a man he just met to a drink. He says "Oh boy, did I have a good one tonight. Met a chickie on Broadway. She hadn't been laid for months. She just looked at me and said 'I'll give you twenty if you lay me in a basement I know of — it's the only place we can go. If you don't want to, just say so and I won't say another word about it.' No bullshit. Under a bus shelter. We were both waiting for the number four and she turns to me and says this. 'My husband's home,' she says. 'He never lays me. He likes men only now. You don't like men,' she says, 'do you? I hope not.' That's what she said. I told her I like women only. All parts of them, not just the ones that count. And I can do it all night. This is what I tell her. 'Or at least I used to. Now only half the night which is fine for most ladies, okay?' So we went to this basement. I was so hot by now I could have done it to her right on the street. She gave me the twenty. It was cozy down there. Even had a mattress and nice little table lamp on the floor. She took me into an alleyway and made me shut my eyes the last minute of walking so I wouldn't ever find the place alone. Even turned me all the way around a few times so I'd be all mixed up in my directions. I bet she did it with lots of guys down there. But twenty. For laying her. She was great. Clean. Wet. Smelled good. A Mother Earth, no Miss Twiggy. Big hips. Big tits. Big everything. I felt I was swimming in her. I would've paid her if I had a twenty and she asked. If I'd known how good she was, is what I meant, for I don't pay anyone for sex. Things are free now, free now, you don't have to pay. Women walking around without panties and bras, kids doing it before your eyes in cars—man, it's all over the place. But to get paid for it? Hey, I'll take it! But that was it. Twice. That was all she could take and to lay it on the line to you, me too. She was too much. She nearly killed me. Then we got dressed and left together and she made me shut my eyes again till we got into the street. She never gave me her name or phone number or address, but I bet she lives in that same building but higher up. You think she had a husband?" Other man raises his shoulders. "I don't. I think that's just her line so you don't think of going to her apartment right after to rob her. You know, some guys could just get her address from her bag while they're even balling her. 'If we meet, we meet,' she said when I said what about us doing this again sometime? 'You were the best,' was the last thing she said to me. Even if I wasn't, what do I care? All I know is she gave me a great time and made me twenty bills heavier."

The other man says "That's a fantastic story—unbeatable—I only wish it was me," and thinks if ever a guy was full of it, this one's it. He downs his drink, says "Got enough for a refill?—I'm a little low." "I think I can make it." "Thanks. I'm going to hit the pisser. Tell Rich for me to put a soda in back of mine this time," and goes to the men's room.

Her parents' phone rings. He looks at the clock. "Who can be calling so late? Probably a wrong number. You answer it, please, or just let it ring. I can't even move off the bed." Which one of her children? she thinks, going to the phone. It can't be anything but bad. It's rung too many times.

Her sister's sitting in a movie theater in Seattle. The phone's ringing in her apartment. Another sister's working in the sun on an archaeological dig in Egypt. This work is harder than she ever thought it would be, she thinks, and no fun. She wishes she was back home. Face it: she's homesick. She never would have believed it but she is. Her brother's sleeping in his college fraternity house. The person calling the house gets a recorded message that the phone's been temporarily disconnected.

The tenant leaves the building very early, says good morning to the policeman guarding the front door, asks how the girl is. "I haven't heard." "Do you know if they caught the man who did it yet?" "I don't think so." She goes to church, kneels, prays for the girl's life and that the man is caught and that the whole city becomes more peaceful again, at least as peaceful as it was about twenty years ago, but if only one prayer's answered then that the girl lives. She sits, covers her eyes with her hands, just let things come into her. It's quiet in here, she thinks. For now, this is the only place.

The man who took her home the night before gets up around nine, has coffee, goes out for the *Times* and a quart of milk and two bagels, dumps half the newspaper sections into a trash can, reads the front page of the news section as he walks home, reads the sports and book sections while having a toasted bagel and coffee at home, looks at his watch, nine forty-two, still much too early, slips in a tape cassette, does warm-up exercises, goes out for a six-mile or one-hour run, whichever comes first, comes back, did good time — must have been all the alcohol last night that gave him so much sugar — showers, shaves, checks the time, eleven thirty-eight, no, not yet; twelve, on Sunday, is really the earliest he can call someone he just met. If she worked as hard as she said she did this week — studying, painting, her waitress job every other weekday afternoon and all-day Saturday — she'll need a good ten-hour sleep. But once she gets up she'll probably need an hour just to get started. One. Call her at one.

THE ANVIL OF THE TIMES

RICHARD ELMAN

In the middle of the night the Vega family often heard strange loud cacophonies, as though metal were being tortured, or twisted. That was because they lived near a motor park where lorries battered by age and ill-use, as well as combat, were being readied to roll north toward the border and remove casualties from the struggle there to the nearby military hospital. The work went on night and day, and it was often said that the most creative geniuses of Nicaragua were all auto mechanics. One night, though, the urgency of what was being done to metal was piercing, exhausting. It sounded very much like sharp whining cries. Some new sort of lathe, they told themselves, was on line; and they hardly slept all night long.

The next morning they walked about as though enmeshed in cobwebs. The big lot with its sheds next door seemed strangely vacant. Patricio Vega felt so exhausted he did not go to work, but went off to the store to buy fresh milk for the children. While he was gone a party of Scandinavians arrived in an open jeep. They were from a certain international agency, intent on gauging living standards among the inhabitants of the Vegas' barrio. They were accompanied by a PR person from Managua. Could they come inside the house to talk?

Of course . . . Felicia Vega opened her door wide for the visitors. Her husband would be home soon. Wasn't he at work? She explained about last night and taking the day off and the government person frowned.

"How do you explain to these good people," he asked, "how you own your own house, feed your family, are clothed as well as anybody who is not an office worker, and your husband only goes to work when he pleases?"

"It's because we have always been good Nicaraguans," she smiled at him, waxily.

Just then Patricio appeared in the doorway: "Hola . . ."

He recognized the government man. "Aren't you the son of Andres Perra?"

"That sort of thing doesn't matter here any more," young Perra said. Their Scandinavian visitors looked a little downcast, but when they heard the coffee boiling they began to produce their soft pencils and questionnaires.

Young Perra told Patricio: "We're here to dispel some myths about life under the regime. I assume you will want to be cooperative."

"I'll be glad to tell the truth," Patricio said.

"He's a bit of a rascal," young Perra confided. "They all are. The children are our only hope."

"*Probablemente*," said a big Swede in Spanish.

Felicia Vega was noted throughout town for her custards which were said to be as sweet and rich as two weeks in Miami, but when she offered to serve some to her guests, along with their coffee, Patricio grew indignant. "Can't you tell what kind of men these are? They're snobs toward the likes of you and me . . ."

"I'm sure the Swedish gentlemen would love some custard," young Perra observed, "if it were hygienic."

"If it were not," Patricio said, "I would offer it to you. You could replace its scum with yours . . ."

"You are a fool to talk like that," Felicia said.

"Listen to your wife," young Perra added.

"Forgive me," he replied, with mock earnestness.

Patricio was a small dark intense man, with big eyes, and very shiny black hair. He seemed a man of strength, but was really a kind of intellectual: by days he worked at the refinery and evenings he took courses in French Literature and Philosophy at UNAM.

Nobody approved of his ambitions; nobody understood them. He was determined to be a "philosopher," and, though Marx was where he began, he was no longer a "Marxist." He called himself "post-Christian man."

Whenever he had words with a person in government, Patricio withdrew into a deep cauldron of philosophic silence. He could truly say no more for fear of becoming violent. "Even if you shut up nowadays," he reminded friends, "they know you are their enemy."

So it was much against his wishes that the wife of Patricio Vega went to her cold chest and removed the large bowl of milk custard and suddenly the small room was redolent with the smells of nutmeg and cinnamon. The Swedes all exclaimed at once, even before they'd been served, "Marvelous!"

"Our Nicaraguan cuisine is not to be denied," said young señor Perra.

"Indeed," said one aging Swede whose unruly blond hair had long since turned as white as flax.

More chairs were brought to the table and wooden spoons and earthenware bowls. A young Swede found his questionnaire and commenced to ask, "Do you believe living conditions are better or worse now than before?"

"I'll answer that," Patricio said. "They are clearly better now. Before we had no PR men on our hands. Now they cannot help but be better."

"He's known to be a wit," Perra said.

"Shut up. You are in my house." He turned to the Swedes. "Ask my wife how she likes standing in line hour after hour for pig shit."

"Some people expect us to make brassieres in the middle of a famine," young Perra mocked. He seemed a little flustered and, immediately, suggested that, after the visitors finished their custard, they should all go to a more interesting and cooperative household.

"These good people mean no harm," said an elderly balding Swede. "They simply need to speak out . . ."

"In the face of disaster," young Perra said, "that is not always our privilege. It's not always possible."

He insisted that the visitors leave immediately, and since they were, in fact, his guests they did as he bade them.

Making their goodbyes in the doorway, all the visitors must have felt they were betraying their own intentions in coming to Nicaragua, but they went anyway, feeling that to resist their guide would do little but provoke acrimony.

Just as they were going down the walk, the machine shop next door began to whine, and yammer, and shake. A high-pitched squeal issued forth. It seemed as though the Vegas' flimsy tin roof might come flying off at them.

"Our Revolution never sleeps," said their guide. "It never even takes a proper siesta."

"Heavens," the young Swede exclaimed.

"Surely not," his elder colleague responded with a joke. "It's just the roof."

The ground beneath them shook.

"The Gods must be very mad at us though," the older Swede added. From his tiny wooden verandah, Patricio Vega called out, "Now you know how we feel. Now you know . . ."

"Don't pay any attention to that troublemaker," young Perra said. Patricio replied, "He lives in a mansion in Altamira with the rest of his cell. They have a cook, and a VCR. While we . . ."

"Shut up," young Perra said.

"Now you know how we feel," Patricio added. "Now you finally know . . ."

The world beneath them shuddered one more time.

Young Perra shrugged: "With such roosters we make soup."

"With such oxen they govern," Patricio cried out. But the Swedes were already seated in their jeep and driving off into the dust of the long hot afternoon.

TURNABOUT

RICHARD ELMAN

      The informer was called a patriot by everybody except the people who knew him best in his own neighborhood; they called him, simply, "The Ear." This insult was double because that was what informers were called during the hated years of the Tyranny. Those days of intimidation were said to be long over. Jesús Galabos's neighbors, nevertheless, liked to point out he was a member of the CDN, and was only doing his duty when reporting bits and pieces of unruly speech and behavior to his contact in the Ministry of the Interior. It wasn't like the old days really: those people had been so depraved.
    Jesús was a small, dark man with overeager brown eyes which stared constantly out at the world from beneath his great-domed bald head. He was perhaps the only person in his barrio who'd lived in the hated USA. So he would say he knew all its vices and evils. Galabos had made his living once as a shrimp fisherman in Puerto Peñasco, Sonora, and then, for a while, he was a "coyote," ferrying aliens across the border from Mexicali for a good price and, as often as not, bringing them to the Border Patrol.
    "They don't love brown people in the States. They don't love anybody but the rich. I did what I was paid to do, and the Border Patrol also paid, from time to time."
    He was sixty. He looked both wizened and sleek, as fit as a man of only fifty perhaps. His wife, who knew all his habits, lived with him but would not "cohabit," under the instructions of her priest. All his life he'd been a hungry man and even when he had taken pains to satisfy that hunger it still gnawed at him. So now he'd chosen to work for the State which, alone, in Nicaragua could sate his needs.
    He found he was surprised when the lives of his neighbors were affected by the things he told his contacts. People were suddenly prey to his whims: a printer had his hours changed; a housewife was disciplined

for claiming more household members than she had; a brewery worker was accused of malingering. And so on. He visited his slanders, without prejudice, on everybody alike.

So many things like that were happening to the friends and neighbors of Galabos that people started to shun him, and he had to go further afield to supply his weekly quota of "antisocial behavior." He did so, nevertheless, out of a feeling of near omnipotence. Never before had he seemed so much the master over others, and consequently over himself. To himself he was "Muy Estimado Commandante," though in fact he was just another humble servant.

One day he went to call at noontime at the house of an old *cumpa*, Juan Kino. When he climbed the rickety porch steps and peered in through the window of the front room, he saw Kino's pretty wife Linda, naked, beneath the dark thrusting hairy body of a thickset man who was definitely not Juan. Galabos backed away and thanked his stars he'd been quiet, discreet. He would put the matter to the back of his mind. But that Sunday afternoon at the Star Bar he found himself telling the incident to his handler whom he couldn't help noticing was also dark and thickset, with a wiry full beard, like Fidel's.

"Adultery in the front room. Only fancy," the man said. "Did you see the fellow's face?"

"I'm not sure," Galabos said.

"Do you think you could identify him?"

"Surely," he replied. "that will never be necessary. It was only sin."

"I asked you a question," his handler insisted. Sternly. And his eyes blinked hard. "Well?"

"Surely no," Galabos lied. "Surely I could be mistaken and all that . . ."

"We shall see . . ."

The man from the Ministry scribbled something in his little note pad. "We lie for so many different reasons we never understand the reasons why we lie," he said, and dismissed Jesús, urging him to be more diligent, and truthful.

Jesús went away with small trepidations. A few days later, he was told he was going to be disciplined for filing "untruthful reports." "It's too late in life for this," he said.

"It's a mistake to think," Jesús reflected, in his new job in a flour warehouse, "that by admitting to lies we are being truthful."

HISTORY BY NARRATION

KYNA TAYLOR

There is fifteen years between my mother and her sister. And in all the years of my life, my mother would not let me speak at great length with my aunt, for fear that she would corrupt me. Mom says that her life, that their lives, are rooted in a different and darker world that has nothing to do with me. But I tell her that if I am to know the story of my bones, I must begin at the beginning. "Bone-tales," my aunt calls her narrative. She begins at the beginning.

When I was a child, I lived on a poor dirt farm with my family. I call it a dirt farm because that's all we had — a few chickens, a couple cows, and a whole lot of dirt. Dirt for miles. Lord, you could look in any direction and all you could see from one corner of your eye to the other was flat land and dirt. Maybe it wasn't all that bad. Dirt could go from light brown to dark brown. But it could drive you crazy, all that unbroken brown rubbing against the sky.

The banks sold us that dirt for every penny my Poppa had. He said it beat sharecropping in West Texas. My father lied some, but maybe sharecropping is worse than getting swallowed by dirt. There were a few shacks like ours on the plains, separated by about two hundred yards, along with a few fences to keep in the cows and some blades of grass. There were barns to house the chickens. But that's all we could grow on that dirt: shacks and black people. Everything faded to a uniform brown.

The world was so flat we could see a storm heading for us before it came within a hundred miles of our yard fence. Way off in the distance my sisters and I would watch the black clouds pile on each other as the wind blew, until the ones on top fell over and went under the ones on the bottom, making the whole heap roll. Sometimes it would take all day for that wheel to crank on to us. Sometimes all that blackness would eat the plain like a thing alive. And when it was grey between the black and the brown we knew that a hundred miles away all that dirt was turning to mud. Until that wet beast ate our farm, our skies were blue.

Yes, I lived during the Depression. And let me tell you, the Depression was when a lot of white folks got real poor real quick. I suppose it's possible that some of our people got hurt by it, but none of the black folks I knew even flinched. Try pinching a dead man to see if he'll hop around and cry "Ouch!" For us, going from poor to poorer was so short a trip that no one even noticed the ride. None of the banks tried to take away our land. Hell, who would want to deal with a bunch of desperate and irate Negroes with a marked taste for shotguns? Dirt can be had anywhere without a fraction of that trouble.

One night after a ring dance at Peterson's barn, Timmy Jacobson and I crept into an old smokehouse to drink the latest batch from my father's still. Timmy was so big he had to duck past the hooks dangling from the ceiling, designed to hold cow rib cages and such. In the lantern's light I noticed that some hooks were crusted over with dried blood gone black. I didn't like the place. Old man Peterson hung himself on one of the hooks when his wife left him. I thought the place was haunted. But the grain was good and Timmy was better and I was sure the ghost would let us be.

Next month when I told Timmy that my cycle was late, he didn't even blink. He wanted to do right by me and went looking for a wedding ring. I didn't feel like doing right by Timmy so I went looking for the midwife. She gave me some foul-smelling brew to bring it off and I spent the day in bed. I remember that I had dreams of worms like green syrup slipping into my belly — my woman's belly — to eat at the little nit that grew there. I watched my Momma die to give little Sharon to my father. And just who was Timmy Jacobson to be worth all that? What man's nit is worth all that?

My grandfather, Elizah, liked to see God everywhere. If God wasn't in Elizah's shack by Elizah's black stove, then God was not home. And when God wasn't sitting in His throne in that decrepit shack, then God was always looking into it from the sky above. Elizah would point to a corner of the ceiling and shout, "Do you see it? God's eye peeking in on us?" I could always talk him into telling me about God's eyelashes; Grandpa said they were black and fluffy, as if they were made of the storm couds that roared over the plains in the summertime. I still wish I had seen those lashes.

One day, Elizah and God must have had a falling out. Old Pop grabbed his shotgun that bright morning and blew a hole into the ceiling where God's eye had blinked. But God is persistent and before you could sigh twice that eye had appeared in a different part of the old man's roof. So God kept looking and Elizah kept shooting until there was no part of that ceiling that wasn't peppered with buckshot. Elizah had just run out of his homemade shells and was throwing old bits of tire rubber (which he kept for emergencies) into the air when the Almighty, probably in a huff, took the hint and left the crazy old fool. The light streaming through the new air holes in that roof made some kind of effect, with all those tiny sunbeams bouncing off an old man's shiny pate. Everyone on the plains laughed. And so did I. But I took Elizah's shotgun just in case I started to look divine.

Sharon caught a cold and died. Just like that. No doctor with a housenote would step foot on our porch, the hospitals wouldn't take us back then, and medicine never came our way. We were dropping as fast as we were birthing and it took every root-worker and midwife to ease our way into one or the other. When my mother was pregnant with my last little sister, the root-woman says to her, "Don't name that baby, Ann."

And Momma says, "I name all my babies. Her name is Sharon."

And the root-woman says, "Names are for the living. Death is about that little one."

And Momma says, "I haven't sent one of my children to sweet Jesus without a name. When God calls her, he'll call her by her name. Sharon."

So God called Momma and God called Sharon and they rest in the churchyard with all our other little ones. The ones who caught a fever and died, who caught a chill and died, who were born jaundiced or starved in the womb and died. They went all kinds of ways. And with them went their mothers sometimes. The plains people used to say that Sadie, the root-woman, would whisper the names of all the dead women and children into a magical glass jar. One day, when the wind and the blowing dirt had washed the names from the stones by the church, someone would open that jar and go mad with hearing how many souls we had lost.

I was about eighteen years old when I went to New Orleans to shake the dirt out of my shoes. The men there were so bold and dashing: dark grey zoot suits flowing over their graceful forms, bright silk shirts, and those cool felt hats perched on their processed heads. Sometimes they wore jewelry, bright gold halos to strong black hands. I don't quite recall what the women were wearing, except that when I got my outfit, gold and glittery and loose all over, I lost all the money I made clearing tables at The Lion's Den. We all wore knives, we women. We had sheaths just below our right hips holding sharp, slim stilettos. The girls at the club had to teach me how to use it—we didn't need knives to play in the dirt back home.

If you were real pretty back then, you could hook yourself a bandleader, or maybe the head of a jazz quartet. I was never more than plain, handsome if you were especially kind and the light was good, so the best I could manage was a devilish piano-man from Grand Coteau. That boy worked well with his fingers. His hair was never out of place. Slim, wiry, and dartlike, he reminded me of the stiletto I had wrapped around my thigh. Behind his piano he would kiss and coo until the house would shake and everyone would swear that he was the best. Five hours later, not one of those people could remember his name. Neither could I, so I called him Daddy. Daddy had lead shoes when it came to money, always on the verge of sinking for good. He never really went under. But after a life's worth of struggle, he never got much more than his upper lip above the water.

Jonathan Barnes, the man who owned The Den, had two sons go to the war. He thought it was a big honor. They put all our black men in their own regiments, separated from the white soldiers. I thought it was a damned clever way to destroy some of our best. The white man is no fool and has more schemes for erasing people running around in his fevered brain than the swamp has snakes slithering through the water. He asked me what I thought about those damn Germans and all our black heroes fighting together. I told him it was a crock of nonsense: why should our boys die in a dispute between a bunch of white folks? He told me that women just didn't understand and never will.

When his boys died, one near Alsace and the other in Italy, Barnes didn't feel like doing much of anything anymore. Didn't want his friends, didn't want his business, didn't feel like booking bands and stopping brawls and writing the cash totals in the back of his Bible. I told him that those boys had it good. There's a hell of difference between dying quickly in a magical-sounding place like Alsace and crawling to some marshy place of the bayou to die like an animal. Barnes just shook his head. "Dead is dead," he muttered and gave me the Bible and The Lion's Den. It was the first lucky break for me in all my twenty-five years.

It was the tail end of a marshy summer night when I looked into the mirror and stared at an old woman. The years hardly make a sound when they stomp you, face and body, and make the soul start dreaming about crossing rivers on a tiny raft of red and yellow roses. Then come those days when you are surprised to see yourself alive at all in the morning. So I give your mother a call and I say, "Lillian, I'm feeling pretty old."

And she says, "I bet you look it too."

And I say, "Did they teach you anything up at the college other than how to be stuck up and persnickety? Something useful, like how to keep time from sitting in my joints and making them creak every time the clouds roll in?"

And she says, "No, nothing like that. But I'll send you my daughter and she might know."

And I say, "Well send her down, then."

And she says, "Alright. But if you try to teach her how to screw two men at the same time like you tried to teach me, I'll kill you, Rue."

She likes to call me that. Rue. Don't even think of calling me that. Use the name my mother gave me. And whisper it in a jar when I am gone. My name is Elizabeth.

THE FIRST TIME AVA SAW ANGELO NAKED

EUGENE MIRABELLI

The first time Ava saw Angelo naked was on their wedding night—11 May 1860—when he strode into their bedroom, accidently revealing to her startled eyes that from the waist down he had the hindquarters of a horse. Now Angelo was no brute. He was a miller and this was in his house in Carco, Sicily. He had knocked gently and he had thought he heard her whisper *Come in,* but when he opened the door the room was ablaze with candles and Ava was still on her knees in prayer at the bedside. She lifted her head and saw—Angelo was wearing only the fancy shirt he had married in—saw those supreme flanks, hocks, fetlocks, and horny-soled feet. The blood drained from her face. For a moment she wavered and flickered, then she murmured the last words of her Hail Mary, blessed herself and stood up. "Amen," Angelo said, taking her cool hand in his. "I have something to tell you."

"Your legs—" she began.

"Remember," Angelo broke in. "God created horses, too. In fact, horses are among the most noble of God's creatures. Horses aren't soaked in blood. They don't have fangs or claws. They don't kill and they don't eat other horses. Horses are peaceful, more peaceful than men, not cowardly like sheep or stupid like oxen, but serene and powerful. God created horses just to show us what He could do in the way of power and beauty, and when He finished, He admired His handiwork. He admires horses. Horses have strength and grace and intelligence, horses have courage and endurance, horses have fidelity. Besids, I'm not wholly, not—

"Your bottom half—" she began again.

"There've been other unions, but they were horrible mismatches and produced mongrel beasts. Harpies, manticores, bull-headed minotaurs. Only Chiron, the centaur, was a scholar and teacher. Besides, as I said—"

"Your *thing*—" she began once more.

"Don't let the great size frighten you." His voice was gentle, almost complacent.

"A *horse*?" she asked, astounded.

"A stallion," he said. He was quite frank about it. Sicily was a beautiful land where strange and terrible things happened every day of the week.

"I will not bed down with a horse!" Ava snatched her hand from his and ran around to the far side of the bed and stood there, watching him.

"It's been a long day and we're both tired," Angelo said, keeping quite still so as not to frighten her.

"So?"

"And when we're tired we should go to sleep."

"I'm never going to sleep. Certainly not with you," she said, her voice trembling.

"You look so fierce," Angelo remarked, simply to make her feel better. He had begun to stroll very slowly down the room on his side of the bed. "You look—"

"*Not tonight, not tomorrow night, not ever!*"

"Wild," he continued. "Like an animal. I like that, of course. An animal." He paused at the foot of the bed and smiled at her. "You are a magnificent woman."

Ava had almost started to say someting but now she hesitated, her lips still parted, distracted by what he had just said.

"A splendid woman," he continued. "It's hard to believe that when I first saw you your legs were so thin I thought they would snap in two. You were always running after your aunt and everywhere she went you would follow her, trotting after her like a foal."

"Because I was ten years old," she protested.

"And now you are a woman of seventeen with beautiful teeth and strong round arms. And, I suppose, study legs. We will be *superb* at making love."

Ava clapped her hands over her ears.

Angelo laughed. He praised her hair—told her it shimmered like a river at midnight—then he spoke quietly about her luminous eyes, her gleaming shoulders something, her something breasts, and so on downward, dropping his voice softer and softer, so that Ava who had opened her fingers just a bit to hear him had to open them more and still more until, straining to catch his last words, she forgot herself and said, "What? What flower?—Stop! Don't come any closer!"

"Calm yourself," Angelo said. He seated himself on the low chest which stood against the wall by the foot of the bed. "How long do you plan to stand over there?" he asked.

"As long as I want to."

"Of course. But why not sit on the bed? Filomena scented the sheets with lavender, just for us."

Ava seated herself guardedly on the edge of the bed, watching him all the time.

"This is a pretty room, isnt' it?" he said, looking around. "I whitewashed it myself a week ago." In fact, it was a pretty room. In addition to the bed there was a low dresser, a rush-bottomed chair, and in the space between two shuttered windows there was a washstand with an oval mirror hung above it. Angelo said, "The candles look nice, too. I didn't expect you to light them all at once, but they do look nice. Like a church at High Mass. Maybe that's why I'm so sleepy. Church always makes me sleepy," he confessed. "Or maybe it's my age. I'm no child and at my age—"

"What are you doing?" Ava cried, jumping up.

"I'm unbuttoning my shirt. I'm going to bed."

"Bed? What bed? Stop!"

But Angelo was already on his feet, rampant, and now he threw off his shirt, letting it billow onto the chair, and there he stood naked while a dozen shadows of him reared and plunged on the whitewashed wall at his back. Ava had started to cover her eyes but it was too late. Now she simply looked at him and the candle flames grew calm again and the shadows grew still. His flesh was a rich chestnut color and his hair was black—black on his head, black in his beard, black everywhere. His shoulders gleamed, at the base of his throat there was a little hollow filled with golden shadow and on his chest the pattern of hair spread like the wings of a crow. His navel was deep and dark, his legs—ah, those splendid stallion legs—his flanks so smoothly muscled that as he walked the flesh shimmered, and the short downy hairs on his rump, the curling hairs on his thighs, the tassellike hairs on his fetlocks, all sparkled like coal, and in the center, of course, as if the darkness of night had taken beastly shape—But Angelo was blowing out the candles one by one and it was becoming harder to see. He stopped when there was only the solitary chamberstick burning on the chest of drawers. Then he leapt into bed, stacked two pillows behind his back and sat with the sheets pulled to his chest. He looked at Ava. "I'm going to sleep," he said.

"I'm not sleepy."

"Would you like to rest on top of the covers?"

She came and sat on the edge of the bed, her back to him.

"Give me your hand," he said.

"What are you going to do?" she asked, half turning.

"I'm going to sit here like we used to sit on the bench in your aunt's garden. What did we ever do there? Now give me your hand."

"All right," she said. She lay back on the covers against him and got comfortable. "But don't try to reason with me," she added.

"Of course not." He put his arms about her and took her hands. "Now that we're married, there's a secret I can tell you."

"I already know your secret," she said.

"Now listen. This is what you don't know. When a man of my kind, a man of my nature—when a man who is part stallion makes love to a woman, she inherits three gifts."

"Everything I ever inherited is in that ugly chest."

"These gifts come because he makes love to her. They come with his lovemaking, with his—" Angelo hesitated, hunting for the proper word.

"What three gifts?"

"Her childbirths will be easy, her milk will be sweet, and she will be beautiful forever."

"Angelo, you liar." She laughed.

"These talents will be yours by nature," he continued, undeflected. "And they'll be passed on to our daughters and their daughters, too, if we make love often enough."

"And the boys? What would they inherit?"

"My sons will be like me, of course." His breath was soft behind her ear. He went on talking in a voice gentle and resonant and even dreamy, speaking of his father and mother and the village where they lay, which was deep in the heart of Sicily, and in the hour or so that followed he told about those spirits hidden in the hills and fields around the village, told about the patron saints and beasts and, while his voice grew even sleepier, he talked about his relatives, not all of whom were horses, for one was a famous tree and another was a rock and there was an aunt—

"Yes?" Ava said, turning to him. "Go on. I'm listening."

But Angelo was asleep. She turned all the way around and crept cautiously over the covers to study his face: his beard, his lips, the hard wrinkles at the corner of his eyes. *A handsome man*, she thought. His breathing was deep and slow, for he was fast asleep, but the guttering candle made the shadows on his face waver as if he were stirring and about to wake up. So Ava lay on the covers and listened to his soft, slow breathing and watched the candle flicker out and strove to keep awake.

Angelo awoke early and found Ava sleeping like a statue at his side atop the bed covers. He gazed at her in the milky light, at her flushed cheeks and parted lips—how young she was!—cautiously lifted his hand to caress her, but changed his mind and slipped softly out of bed. In the dim hall he pulled on his workpants and boots, then groped his way down the dark stairs to wash in the courtyard. He hoped that a brisk walk on the hills would relieve the painful energy compressed in his legs, his thighs. He pulled on his shirt and flung open the gate and abruptly a horse and rider materialized out of the grey air. "He has landed," the rider told him.

"Ah!" Angelo said.

"Yesterday at Marsala."

Angelo wheeled and ran back into the courtyard, pounded once on the stable door, once on the kitchen door, then clattered up the stairway to his bedroom. "Garibaldi has landed at Marsala and I'm going to join him!" he cried, throwing off his shirt. Ava reached for the latch on the window shutters, staring at him. Angelo sat on the bed to pull off his boots and pants, then flung on his wedding shirt and strode out to the hall. He returned clothed in the fancy shirt and his best pair of velveteen pants. "I have waited all my life for this," he said, pulling on his boots. He crossed the room to Ava who stood by the open window, still staring at him. "You're crazy," she said soberly. Angelo took both her hands in his and kissed her lips. "Remember that I love you," he told her.

"Garibaldi is an animal, a beast," she said, her voice rising.

He laughed. "Then he has come to the right place."

"We will die," she wailed.

"We have always died. But today you should be singing."

Ava wrenched her hands from his and began to beat her fists on his chest, shouting "Go, go, go, go, go —" She had broken into sobs.

"I have never been so happy," he said, putting his arms around his sturdy young woman who wept for him.

Angelo kissed the crown of her head and rushed down the stairway to the dining room. There he tossed back the lid of a black oak chest, peeled away the linens and flannels and came up with an antique bird gun, then he strode into the yard, pulling a heavy pistol from under the big flower pot by the door, and was shouting *Filomena*, as he crossed to the stable where the boy had saddled the gelding. He mounted, took the bundle of food which Filomena handed up to him — leftovers from the wedding wrapped in oilcloth — and went out through the gate at a canter, leaving the boy at the stable door, Filomena in the middle of the yard, his uncles and half-brothers asleep indoors, and his virgin bride face down on her bed, beating her pillow.

Garibaldi had landed on the western shore of Sicily and everyone knew what he had come to do. He was a simple man with a simple desire. He would drive the King's troops first from that great island and then from the Kingdom of Naples and the forlorn southern peninsula, so that these lands could join with those in the north and become one Italy, a single nation as it had been ages ago. The King had 24,864 well-equipped troops waiting in Sicily. Garibaldi had come ashore with only 1,000 volunteers, some in red shirts and others in street clothes, and for guns they had junk — antique smoothbore muskets, one hundred Enfield rifles and five ancient cannons without gun carriages. At dawn the next morning he walked his patched-together army inland through seas of green corn and beans to Rampagallo, and the following day he trudged with them past silvery groves of olive trees up to the sunbaked highlands of Salemi. They spent the night in Salemi, some in houses and others in monasteries and still others under tents in the orchards outside. The next day their numbers increased a bit as volunteer *squadre* came up from the countryside, armed with flintlocks or pruning hooks, and somewhere among them was Angelo, Angelo Cavallú, *our* Angelo. He was dusty, for his horse had collapsed of exhaustion and Angelo had trotted over the hills and into town on his own two feet. That afternoon he saw Garibaldi dismount, stroll across a corner of the piazza and pass through a doorway: a pleasant-looking man with a rich honey-color beard, clothed in a loose red shirt — a man who moved with the effortless grace of an animal. Garibaldi was content at that moment, for he had just ridden in from a survey of the ground along the road to Palermo and now he was going to study a big map of Sicily which one of his officers had found. That night, when he folded the map and went to bed, rain had begun to fall, but when he awoke at three the next morning the rain had ceased and it was beautiful. He pulled on his pants, drank a cup of coffee, called in his officers, told them what he planned to do and sent them to rouse his little army. He had been walking up and down the room and now he burst into song. Here was a fifty-three-year-old man about to attack an army of vastly superior numbers in a battle in which defeat meant death and he sang like a lover going to meet his mistress, because he was about to have his heart's desire.

    That morning Angelo marched with the *squadre* down the road and through a valley where everyone bought oranges and lemons, then they left the road and trudged up a stony hillside. From the top of their bald hill they looked across a shallow valley to a steeper, terraced hill on top of which brightly uniformed troops were gathered in squares — there and there and there and there and over there. They were too many. Angelo's disheartened *squadre*, which had never been in a battle before, drifted quietly off to the side to watch how it was done. Over there, General

Sforza ordered his trumpets to sound and ranks of identical soldiers began to step down the hill, to wade across the stream at the bottom and mount toward the volunteers, firing as they came. Over here, a bugler blew that fancy musical reveille which Garibaldi loved so much and a handful of his skirmishers began to fire at the oncoming troops. Of their own accord, the rest of Garibaldi's men, who had been sitting on the stony rubbish high on the hill, stood up — men in red shirts, men in street jackets, some even in top hats — and now they were running down at the troops in a burst of musketry. Angelo galloped after them. The Garibaldini drove the army back across the stream and part way up the terraced hillside. Then everything slowed. The afternoon grew slack and there was only the irregular clatter of gunfire, or once in a while the top of the enemy hill blossomed into white puffs of smoke and cannonballs shrieked past, and the sun roamed aimlessly overhead. It grew hot, terribly hot. Every so often Garibaldi's red-shirts were driven down, or they climbed even farther up, but their numbers always diminished and now there were not so many — in fact, there were only a few hundred crouched on the steep hillside, pressed together here and there beneath the ragged terraces. Angelo sat with his shoulder against his own bit of loose stone wall, sucking the juice from his last orange, and he peered higher up the hill to where Garibaldi huddled with his bare sword and a crowd of his outlandish army. The terrace wall they clung to was nearest the summit and royalist troops were firing volley after volley down on them, even throwing rocks. *He is a lion,* thought Angelo, *but I am only part of a horse and maybe not the best part at that. What do we do now?* A rock hit Garibaldi on the back and he stood up, his sword flashing. His men stood up beside him. Now Garibaldi was climbing the terrace, his men were climbing the terrace. They were rising up everywhere on the hillside, rising and climbing through the ragged noise, crawling higher and higher, clawing up over the last heap of stones into a hazy white smoke filled with crackling gunfire and screams. Then there was the long hilltop slanting off and royalist troops running away, streaming down and away to the valleys, fleeing.

Angelo marched here and there and elsewhere with Garibaldi for two weeks while the old fox outwitted the king's generals and drove the royal army from Sicily, then Angelo walked home. He wore a stained slouch hat and such tattered velveteen that when he turned in at the gate only his dog, Micu, recognized who it was, circling him and barking excitedly and leaping while Filomena and the boy stared. His bride cried, "Angelo!" from an upstairs window, "Angelo!" from the doorway, "Angelo!" as she threw her arms around his neck. He kissed her forehead and each cheek and said, "Tell Filomena to start heating water because I am going to take a long, long bath."

In the house they poured pots of steaming water into the copper tub which Angelo had dragged to the side of the bed. Ava laid out the towels, brush and soap on the table between the windows and turned to go, but Angelo took her wrist in one hand and gently closed the door with his other. Without a word he shed his shirt, pulled off his boots and stepped out of his pants. Ava stood at the window, staring out, and heard his gasp as he lowered himself into the scalding water.

"I cannot wash my own back," he said in a reasonable voice.

Ava turned hesitantly, a light flush on her cheeks, and took the soap and brush from the table and knelt behind his back. She lifted a cupped handful of water and let it trickle onto his shoulder, then another handful and another and one more. She dipped the soap into the water and slid it tenderly all the way across his back from the tip of one shoulder to the tip of the other. "Ah, that's good," Angelo murmured. Ava pressed her wet palm to his warm back and rubbed in a circle, making suds. "The first time I saw Garibaldi I was so close I could have reached out and touched him," he told her. "He's an old man, older than I am, but he moves very lightly, like an animal.—Would you like me to tell you what I've been doing for two weeks?" Ava dipped the soap into the water and swept it up and down his marvelous, silken back, enjoying herself. "Yes. Tell me," she said absently.

Later, when he had finished with his stories and his bath, Angelo stepped from the tub, letting the water sluice from him in streams as if he were a mountain, then he toweled himself dry and fell asleep in his bed for a day and a night. He dreamed. Maybe the dreams came from his aching muscles or the marrow of his bones or maybe they came from his blood, which was, after all, the mingled blood of men and beasts, of Siculi and Greeks, Romans, Carthaginians, Byzantines, Arabs, Jews, Normans, Spaniards: pure Sicilian blood. Occasionally his magnificent legs twitched and he gave a deep resonant groan, because he was dreaming not only his own story but the cruel three-thousand-year history of all Sicily. He was having a nightmare. At last he awoke and in the pale blue dawn he found Ava sleeping at his side, on top of the covers, an arm flung over her head and her hair spread loose upon the pillow.

He kissed her lips. Before she could rub the sleep from her eyes, Angelo said, "Come with me. I'll show you the world in the morning." He began to open the shutters. Ava stood there in her white chemise and watched him as the room filled up with light. She wanted to look at those equine hindquarters, those powerful flanks and long shins, wanted to see the dark whorls of hair on his chest, the satin nap on his underbelly, his black pouch and stallion thing. His flesh was the color of bronze and smooth beneath her fingertips as a chestnut fresh from its hull. Suddenly he knelt and scooped up the hem of her chemise, standing and lifting it so rapidly that she barely had time to raise her arms before the garment was unfurling in air, falling into a shadowy corner of the room. He put a warm hand on her haunch and when she lowered her eyes he kissed the nape of her neck. Now he whispered a few words in her ear and she tossed her head back, laughing. Who knows what happened next? Her births were always easy, her milk was always sweet, and she remained beautiful into old age. Their daughters inherited these traits. Their sons had legs like their father.

MEL'S BACK

WANDA HAYNES FRIES

Mel had just turned off the shower when he hears Evelyn rattling in the kitchen. He slides the glass door open, stepping onto the bath mat. With the heel of his hand, he wipes a circle in the steam on the mirror. He slept last night in the cab of his semi. The hot water has eased the stiffness from his joints, erased the grit from his face. While he shaves the scent of bacon tracks him down the narrow hall.

Evelyn smiles as he comes barefoot into the kitchen. He's naked from the waist up, the hair on his chest still damp. He drapes a pink towel across the back of a dinette chair, and, turning it to face him, straddles it.

"Hello, stranger," she says, striking a can of biscuits against the edge of the counter to pop it open. "What brings you through this time?"

"Got a load of lumber to haul to Neon. I got in around two."

She's used to him dropping in. He got into the habit while their sons were still at home. But even now that both boys are grown-up and gone, he still rolls in every few months to see how she is.

Books and papers clutter the table. At forty, Evelyn has gone back to college for a ministerial degree. ("Don't surprise me none," Mel's mother said when she heard. "Scratch most any preacher and you find somebody who used to be a drunk.") A red-bound book called *Strategies in Counseling* lies open on page seventy. When Mel picks it up, he sees notes scattered down the margin in Evelyn's looping hand.

He lays the book face down. "How's school?"

"It's all right." She dumps frozen orange juice into a plastic pitcher. Her hands are big and brown, the nails chewed into the quicks. "I'm tired of doing fourteen things at once, but I ought to finish next year."

On the ledge at the base of the window, Evelyn's grey-striped tomcat sleeps in the sun. Mel gets up to scratch it behind the ears, but when he touches it, it arches its back and leaps down. "I can't believe it's this built-up out here," he says, looking out the window at the trailers that stud what used to be pastureland. Their green metal siding glitters like cheap jewelry in a green felt case.

He takes a fork and wiggles bacon around in the pan. Over the sizzle of grease, he asks her if she's heard from the boys.

"Wayne called last week. He's working at the Corvette plant. Ben's reenlisted. He's put in for Germany. Says he wants to see the world. But I don't know about it, Mel. I keep having nightmares about them shipping off to Nicaragua or the Middle East. I wish he'd have just come on home."

"And do what? It's dead around here."

Because of the mess on the table, they eat in the living room. They sit on the sofa, balancing their plates on their laps. Mel studies her face in silence. Without makeup, her dark hair loose and falling to the center of her back, he thinks she still looks like a girl. He wonders if her chambray shirt belongs to one of his sons or if an old lover left it behind.

Evelyn smiles when he takes the plates to the kitchen, running water over them before the egg yolk has a chance to dry. The clutter of the house always bothered him when they were married. Now it seems familiar, comfortable.

"Remember how we used to fight because you left dishes piled up all over the house?" he asks her.

"It wasn't just dishes. I left cigarettes burning in ashtrays, my clothes wherever they happened to drop. You got to admit, the place was a pigsty."

"Sounds like grounds for divorce to me," he says. But the joke falls flat and she looks away.

They both know that wasn't why he left her. His brother told him more than once, straight out, that everybody in the county knew how Evelyn spent her nights when Mel was on the road. He spent a long time thinking about that, trying to picture her drunk and naked in another man's arms. But it made him feel like somebody trapped at the bottom of a river, the water filling his lungs up, pushing out the air. For months he wouldn't even ask her about it. He dreaded what she might say.

As he watches her scour dried egg from the bottom of the skillet, his arm touching hers, Mel wishes he could ask her why it took her so long to pull herself together, why she had to hurt him so bad to do it, why she had to hurt herself. But before he can even frame the question, the pan disappears under the rinse water and comes up clean.

They spend the day like married people. Evelyn types a paper for her

Monday class. Mel changes the oil in his truck. That afternoon they see a Dirty Harry movie. Every time Clint Eastwood narrows his eyes and peers down the barrel of a gun, Evelyn hides her eyes against Mel's sleeve. When they go out for pizza, she tries to pay half, but Mel snatches the ticket away. "Now you're being ridiculous. Who paid for breakfast?"

That evening they play five-hundred rummy and she beats him. It tickles him to watch the pleasure she gets out of winning. She keeps a poker face through each hand, but he figures he should catch her sooner or later with a bundle. She won't lay her spreads down as she gets them, but holds onto each card, picking up his discards with a sly smile. To go out, she lays her whole hand down at once, as though she's playing gin.

"Don't gloat, Evelyn," he says, tallying up the final score. He stacks the cards neatly, then tosses them onto the coffee table where they spew out again. He looks at her left hand, which rests palm down on the arm of the sofa. "Do you ever miss being married?"

"To you or to Jake?"

"Either. No. Me, I guess."

"Sometimes. But I don't know if I could go back to living with somebody again."

"It sure is odd, you making a preacher."

"It isn't really, is it?" She lifts her iced tea, and, with her sleeve, wipes away the ring of moisture underneath the glass. "You always said I was looking for something, you just didn't know what. Maybe I've finally found it."

"You used to scare me, some of the places you looked. I never knew how to protect you. I never knew what you wanted me to do."

"I know it." She pushes her hair behind her ear. An earring glitters like a goldfish swimming into the light. "I didn't know what I wanted you to do, either."

Mel settles back on the plaid sofa. Evelyn stays on the floor. His knee rests in the space between her shoulder blades. "We used to have a lot of fun," he says. "Remember when we took that old Corvair cross-country and had to hitchhike home?"

"I knew it wouldn't make it, but I didn't want to tell you. I was afraid you'd say we couldn't go."

"Why didn't you do things like that after I left?"

"I don't know. Maybe I didn't need to anymore."

Through the open window he smells honeysuckles, hears distant cars swish by like satin dresses over crinolines. He remembers Evelyn all dressed up for their senior prom. She'd tucked a red carnation behind her ear, and under her pale-pink lipstick, her smile was almost white.

Mel lifts her hair, seeing her like the double exposure of a slide, the woman sitting in front of him, the girl pausing in the doorway, ready to leave them both behind. He sits up and leans to kiss her neck. With his hand under her chin, he nudges her face around.

She stirs, but instead of turning toward him, she moves away. She reaches to the floor for a basket of silk flowers, a Mother's Day gift from Wayne. She places it in the center of the table carefully, as though she is planting it in concrete, where it can never again be moved. She starts to say something, falters, tries again. "You're just tired, Mel. And feeling lonesome. I'm not even the same person anymore. It'd be like making love to a ghost."

He leaves the next morning while she sleeps. He puts a note on the television, along with some money he knows she needs but probably won't spend. By nine he's dropped his lumber, and by early afternoon, he's headed southwest out of Louisville with a new load.

On I-24 he picks up a girl who says she's thumbing to St. Louis. She has long blonde hair, and even under layers and layers of makeup, her face looks young. They don't look a thing like each other, but something about the way she tilts her head when she climbs into the truck reminds him of Evelyn.

"Hello, little darling," he says, watching her settle into the seat. Between the hem of her cropped T-shirt and her low-slung jeans, her navel dimples up at him like a second smile. "Aren't you a little young to be hitching rides?"

She shrugs and takes out a cigarette. Without offering Mel one, she drops the package back into her canvas bag. When he has pulled back onto the highway, Mel tries again. "I'm serious. Don't you ever watch the news? All kinds of lunatics prowl these highways just looking for sweet young things like you."

She's crawled into the truck as easily as if she's known him all her life. Now she gazes unconcerned across fields that flatten steadily as the land stretches west. She answers him without bothering to turn around. "I'm careful. Won't nobody bother you if you're careful."

Mel studies the brown ridge of bone at the center of her narrow back. Last month he had coffee with a state trooper in a truck stop just west of Cookeville, Tennessee. The trooper said that a few days before, he and his partner had found a young girl in a ditch off the interstate, her chest plugged like a watermelon, semen flaked on her thin white thighs.

Mel wants to give this information to the girl as a piece of evidence, to make her understand that some time she might have to pay for taking all these chances, that the world isn't always as safe as it seems.

But her tanned back silences him, and he sighs. "Well, little darling," he says, checking his rearview mirror before he steers into the passing lane. "If St. Louis is as far as you're going, at least this one time, you've got me to take you safely all the way."

HERE AT THE STARLIGHT MOTEL

ANDREA BARRETT

I had to leave ten bucks at the front desk before the clerk would turn on the phone.

"I'm just making a local call," I said. "Just one."

He picked at his nails and said. "Those are the rules. If you've got a credit card I'll take that instead." Then he smiled, knowing I hadn't checked in under my name.

I gave him the money, which left me with four dollars and a little change. Then I called Robbie Calkins's house in Chesterfield for the first time ever. He gave me his number early on, just for an emergency; I wouldn't have called except I knew his wife was gone.

"Just come for a drink," I said. "I'm at the motel." I could hear his daughters playing near the phone and his mother-in-law screeching at them. I knew he had to be going crazy.

"Well . . ." he said. He waffled a bit and then he came — he always does. He doesn't have the willpower God gave a goat. Which isn't to say he doesn't have other things. He's brown-eyed and big: six foot three, two-thirty or so, and running a little to fat, which I never liked in a man but didn't much mind in him. He has beautiful hands, and a smile that says everything's easy. And although he's only twenty-eight, not much older than me, he has a wife and three kids and a beat-up car with a baby seat in the back. He has responsibilities.

He didn't say about those until later. I didn't know — until I finished school and went to work in the office at the fertilizer plant in Leverett, I only went out with single men. I was fine, and then Robbie transferred in from the plant, took over a desk, and flirted with me more than any single man I knew. Robbie made my breath stop the day he first walked in and everyday afterwards; Robbie teased me until I kissed him in a parking lot one night and came here to the Starlight Motel with him another. Once we were here, he talked to me until I fell in love and couldn't stop listening, and when I did the world went black and grey on me like an old TV show not worth watching. He's been my lover, on and off, for ten months.

When I hung up, I hid the rum and the radio, the Doritos and magic markers; combed my hair and changed my shirt. I got ready for Robbie like I always had, but when he opened the door I saw right through him. I looked at him and saw the doorframe, dark sky, the champagne bottle he carried. He didn't block out the rest of the world the way he used to, and that made me think I had a chance. He was just a shadow, standing there as stiffly as if he'd never opened a motel room before to find me inside.

"Room sixty-three," he said, and smiled the smile he used whenever we'd broken up and he wanted to come back. He wore a pink shirt I'd always loved, possibly to please me. "Were we here before?"

"Sometime in August," I said. "Remember the smell?"

The last time we'd had this room, the Slukarskis's were spreading manure in their celery fields in Sunderland, across the river. We had the windows open and the room smelled like a barn. We've smelled everything here, from every window: cucumbers rotting, apples, asparagus in June. The Starlight Motel is on Hadley's commercial road where it cuts through the rich river land, and we've steamed up almost every room in it. I know all of them. This one has the flowered bedspreads, the broken towel rack, the bug-eyed kitten pictures on the walls. The drawings I've tacked up all over change the room a little; Robbie's mouth popped open when he came in and saw them.

"Jesus," he said. "What've you been doing here?"

"Nothing," I told him. "Just killing time. My landlord found roaches in the house and made us all move out for a couple of days so he could spray."

I made that up. I came here Monday, after Robbie called me at work to tell me Amy had been born. When we hung up I quit my job at the plant, went home to Chesterfield and packed a bag, and came here to get rid of him. But I knew if I said bugs, that's what he'd believe. He's never been curious, never wanted any more of me than I chose to give. He would have taken less if he'd known how.

"I thought we'd celebrate," he said, holding up the bottle. He drifted near one wall to peek at the drawings.

I said, "There's a glass in the bathroom," and he moved away.

When he came back he sat on the bed and popped the cork. "To Amy!" he said, clinking his glass against mine.

"To Amy!" I responded.

Amy's his newest daughter, the excuse he's used for months to pull away. Now that she's here he acts happy because he has to, because he can't remember I saw his face when he first found out Lisa was pregnant and broke up with me. He had two other daughters, no money, a too-small house in Chesterfield, and me; it wasn't a great time for him to have another kid.

"I can't see you anymore," he'd said to me then. "Lisa needs me, and I love messing around with you but it's just messing around. I have responsibilities."

Only a fool would have taken him back after that; I took him back three times and don't even know why, except that being with him was like smoking, hard to quit even after it stopped being fun.

Robbie took his shoes off and stretched out, careful not to touch me, and since we were in one of our stages of just being friends I didn't touch him. I've always had to read his mind. I passed him a joint, and he chattered the way he always does when we haven't slept together for awhile. Whenever he decides we shouldn't be lovers anymore, he talks to me like he doesn't have another friend in the world, like we have something in common besides going to bed. He does that until he's talked his way into touching me again. I listened and looked at the drawings I'd tacked to the walls. They made me feel like in the old days, before he took all the little things away.

"Lisa started getting pains on Sunday night," he said. "So I called the doctor, but he said to wait until they came closer together and come in then."

He told me all about the pains, never asking why my walls were covered with magic-marker drawings. He never wonders; he's not in love. His world is solid and all of a piece and nothing like mine, and the worst he ever gets is wistful for the apple farm where he grew up. His biggest talent is for liking what is. Mine is, maybe, for loving what isn't, and that's no talent but just something to shed. I should have done it way before. I came here on Monday with some clothes, some rum, a little money, a few joints rolled in a plastic bag, my phony ten-dollar Walkman, and no plan except to stop seeing him; I closed the curtains, covered my head, and slept. The next day I went to the McDonald's north of here for breakfast. I wore my phony Walkman and got Christmas carols even on the rock station, Christmas being right around the bend.

"Egg McMuffin," I told the waitress. "Coffee, extra cream."

"Hash browns?" she bellowed, thinking she had to scream at me because of the headphones. They used to yell at me like that at work, when I started wearing the radio after Robbie first dumped me. It kept me from hearing him on the phone.

"No, thanks," I told her. I ate by the window and tried to remember things I used to like to do. I couldn't think of anything.

"I took her to the hospital then, anyway," Robbie said. "And it's a good thing, because we hadn't been there an hour before she really got cooking. They had to call her doctor in from rounds."

"Really?" I said. I knew how to humor him, like I knew from listening to him how babies were born, what little girls do, what it's like to marry your high-school honey too young.

Wednesday, I went to the Rite-Aid for some matches. A big display of Diet Coke towered near the door; cases of bottles, cheap. I bought a case and picked up some nail polish, because I felt like drinking rum-and-Diet-Cokes and doing my toes. Not much, I admit, but at least I felt like something. Near the nail polish was a stack of fat manila drawing pads that reminded me of school, and I liked the way they looked so I bought three. I bought some magic markers too, sixteen colors packed in a plastic envelope. It started to snow before I was done, and I stopped the car on the way back and watched the fields turn white. I used to like the snow.

When I got back here I made myself a drink and then opened the markers and took out the first four: black, blue, silver, grey. I didn't know until I started that I was going to draw the stars, the water, and the bridge. I drew them the way they were our first night here, when we stayed so late. We were giddy from too much wine, sore from too much messing around; we'd wandered out back to the creek and the footbridge that crossed it. The sky was very black and crammed with stars. We stood on the bridge and looked for the Milky Way, but we didn't know where to look or what to look for.

Robbie waved his hand and said, "Look, Diane—the Big Dipper."

I looked and thought I saw it. "What's that?" I asked, pointing to another group of stars.

"I don't know," he said. "It looks like a bear."

"Like a bear with a broken leg, maybe."

We laughed and then stood for an hour, naming the rest of the sky.

"Barn Owl," he pointed out. "Bicycle, Lizard, Apple Tree."

"Miner," I showed him. "With Headlamp. Cat, Cow."

"Swallow," he said.

I sat on the four-inch railing that guarded the bridge and leaned back into his arms, drawing my feet up so there was only him between the water and me. He made a move to tip me over and I let myself go.

He caught me, of course. "You're so trusting," he said. I am. He tipped me over and over again and still I didn't resist, and we made love on the planks of the bridge and then went back to our cars. He went home to Lisa and I went home alone, in such a fog I could hardly see.

I drew the stars silver in jet-black sky, the bridge black and grey, the river black and blue. I drew them just exactly as they were, not like I saw them that night when I couldn't see anything, but like they were before I fell in love. On the bridge I drew a pair of shoes I'd lost that evening, when Robbie had carried me down the outside stairs so my thin blue heels wouldn't stick in the metal grids. My shoes fell off, but before I lost them, I'd had this one clear minute when he was just a hot body I'd slept with and I still had a chance. Somewhere between losing my shoes and naming the stars I fell in love: bump, thumpety-thump, like falling down stairs, and after that I never saw him again the way he really was.

"Amy popped out in ten minutes. What a screamer!" Robbie said. "You should have seen her." Like I would want to see. I was surprised he hadn't brought me baby pictures. He loosened his tie, and unbuttoned his shirt partway. I poured him more champagne.

After I drew the stars I wanted to use some other colors, so I drew the cows the way they were the morning we met before work in a field at the edge of the river. The cold had made mist in the willows, and some cows who had wandered down to drink drifted in and out of the mist and rubbed against us as if we were cows too. Robbie, behind me, let out a loud cow noise and scared me so badly I jumped back into his arms. When he did it again the cows answered back, lifting their big slow heads from the water as if they were singing. One sang out, and then another, then several sang together; then they stopped and moved so close I was scared they'd crush our feet. They let us through quietly when we left for work, and when Robbie drove here to the Starlight Motel I followed him and we called in sick and stayed all day.

We always had that—after cows, after work, after almost anything. I guess you always do, but I wanted something more and didn't know what. He'd told me over and over again he'd never leave his wife, and I said, "Fine," but never looked ahead because there wasn't anything there. I looked for little things, instead. When we left for work at night, I looked for morning. When we left our room here, I looked for the time we'd come back. When he talked to me, and then was quiet, I waited for him to talk again. I didn't know what else to want. I'd forgotten everything.

I drew the cows brown, like big brown dogs. The mist I drew yellow, with the sun shining through. Willow trees I drew lacy green, bark brown, river blue. I didn't draw Robbie and I didn't draw me. I drew what was there before we made it into background. I drew with my headphones on and listened to Christmas carols. "Silent Night" reminded me of stars: I wedged the star picture in the mirror and admired it. I leaned the cows against the back of the chair. I fixed another rum-and-Diet-Coke — I'd been drinking all day but wasn't drunk and listened as a choir of little boys' voices brought me peace on earth, good will to men, joy to the world. "And this shall be a sign," they sang. The things I'd drawn were road signs I hadn't seen until I drew them — Go Slow, Stop, Do Not Pass. Robbie had made me blind.

He told me how Sarah and Emily had helped him decorate the baby's new room. "I made it from a closet," he said. "The room, I mean. And the girls drew pictures with crayons and we hung them up all over. It looks funny — sort of like in here."

He scanned the drawings on the walls, but they weren't signs for him and didn't mean anything. All they did was remind him of his daughters. Maybe that's all I ever did. He says his oldest daughter and I both resemble deer.

"I didn't know you could draw," he said. "That's neat." He might not have been so pleased if he knew the drawings were the way I'd learned to see him again like he was before I draped him in my dreams.

I liked the drawings I did Wednesday so much that I woke Thursday full of energy and went back to the Rite-Aid for some thumbtacks. I picked up breakfast at McDonald's, came back and hung the drawings, and smoked a joint. When I bit into the Egg McMuffin, I thought of the egg at my sister's house, where I went for a week the first time Robbie dumped me. Mary Ann, my oldest niece, was soaking a chicken egg in vinegar for some science project. All week we watched the acid eat away the shell; when we took the egg out the shell was gone and the insides jiggled, held only by a membrane. In the light the yolk bobbed dreamily around, and I threw up when I touched it. I thought I was pregnant — I'd seen Lisa, hugely pregnant, on the street in Chesterfield, and the next thing I knew my breasts swelled and I puffed up. I cried and craved strange foods at night and missed two periods, but it was all just my body's joke, its way of saying what an asshole I was.

I put down my breakfast and drew the soft membrane, the cloudy white, the sunny yellow yolk. And then I kept on drawing, whatever I could think of. I drew the tobacco fields across the river, the way they looked the time Robbie first came back. I didn't draw him, but I drew the acres of white gauze shading the plants, the poles suspending the gauze, the green leaves underneath. I drew tractors in other fields. I drew my desk at work, my sister, my friends, my cat. I drew a coffee cup. I drew all I'd lost since I first slept with Robbie, when I started seeing the world through grey Vaseline. I used every color I had.

Robbie paused for a minute and I knew I should say something. "I'm glad things are going so well," I said.

I wasn't paying much attention, but I figured that would cover whatever he was talking about. He was just a stranger by then, slightly drunk, lying next to me in bed; what I'd always been for him but never seen. He unbuttoned the rest of his shirt but still didn't touch me. I lit the joint again and passed it after a tiny puff. There wasn't any point in getting high.

Robbie talked about his wife some more, but he was flushed and horny and drunk and high, forgetting his lines. When I whispered, "Make love to me?" and touched his ear, I knew he wouldn't say no. He was counting on me to fill the gap, knowing he wouldn't get any at home for six weeks. I know Robbie. I knew he wanted me to want him the way I used to, wanted to make me crazy at his touch.

"Well," he whispered. "Maybe one last time." He'd said that so often he didn't believe it anymore.

I let him touch me and take off my clothes; he had to take his off himself. When he started in with his standard tricks I waited to see if the drawings would vanish and the room grow grey, but nothing happened. His fingers reminded me of celery, his smell of fresh-turned fields. Dried bugs jumped in the ceiling light when he moved hard, and I found that by folding two parts of the bedspread together I could turn two anemones into a rose. I let him heave and toss and sweat and try to make me come, and I just lay there, just a body. A cold fuck is what he's always wanted, no emotions, no strings. I gave him snow. I've always liked the snow.

He lifted his head above me and flicked away a drop of sweat. "What's the matter?" he said. "Don't you want me?"

I did, but just to feel what it was like not to want him. I touched his back, amazed to find it only flesh.

When he finished he dressed quietly and left; I didn't have to say I wouldn't see him anymore. I made myself a drink and drew his head the way it looked when he was going out the door; I drew the door. And then I went outside and sat on the stairs. Across the river the snow swept over the fields and piled at the feet of the odd trees left standing here and there. My hands were freezing, but I thought I smelled seeds coming up underneath.

THE PROFESSION OF LETTERS

THREE UNFLATTERING APPRAISALS

THE LITERARY LIFE: A PORTFOLIO

M. G. LORD

*M. G. Lord
photo by
Sylvia Plachy*

THE LITERARY LIFE: A PORTFOLIO | 333

THE STAR SYSTEM: A JEREMIAD

GEORGE GARRETT

I would much rather not be talking about this. Because if I do and if I tell the truth, as I perceive and feel it, I am bound to offend many and probably annoy all the rest. But I will do it. For reasons which may become clear as we go along. Maybe so.

Let me say, here and now, that I am going to abide by the general ground rules and will be dealing, more or less strictly, with the limited world of American fiction. But please bear in mind that I see fiction as a living part of a living Literature; and that includes all of us and all the going forms of contemporary writing — poetry, drama, nonfiction, essays, even criticism, journalism old and new, what-have-you; and, as well, must include all of the known and going forms of narrative including (yes) film, TV, radio, and, by all means, the "interactive" computer narratives which are coming along these days. It is a serious flaw of the American literary mind-set which allows us (all too often) to pretend that all of these things are not closely related, are not always interwoven in a single, if not quite seamless whole. Or maybe it is not mind-set. Maybe it is (as I think in my more cynical mode) a deliberate pretense on the part of self-serving parties and practitioners to keep, dog fashion, the limits of their little territory somehow defined and exclusive. I blame part of it on the Iowa Workshop which insisted on the separation of the poets and the fiction writers. For its own purposes. Not everybody has followed that design, and it certainly is not the only way to go; but it has been hugely influential and advantageous, too, to those who followed faithfully. Time, most of history, certainly *all* literary history up through Dryden and, I would argue, on through the Augustan Age in England, is on my side. There were always hierarchies of forms, allowing for an interchange, an *intercourse* between critical thinking and popular practice and fashion. But, truly, we find ourselves well into the eighteenth century before some chaps begin to separate poetry and prose or to separate poetry from other forms of discourse merely by the fact that it may be in verse. In terms that Aristotle and John Dryden, and most likely Fielding and Swift and Pope would have understood and acknowledged as *given*, Faulkner, Joyce, Woolf, Mann, and Proust were poets in every way and every bit as much as, say, Eliot, Pound, Yeats, Williams, Moore, Stevens, Frost, etc. Indeed, the former had a certain critical edge because their poetry comes in the shape and form of fully realized fable rather than in evocative fragments. Moreover, and I do believe Aristotle and Dryden and all the others in between and some pretty good ones later, too, would have to allow for the fact that other even more widely influential fabulists, let us say Fellini, Kurosawa, and Bergman, are by definition poets of the highest order. What I am saying—and no fooling—is that when it comes to poetry, you can have your Plumly and I'll take Proust, thank you. You take Mark Strand (poetry and prose) and I'll take Thomas Mann, if you please. Dave Smith is to be measured not against the examples of James Dickey or even the magnificently versatile Robert Penn Warren, but, rather, against Faulkner at his finest.

I am only kidding to the extent that (as you see) I don't really believe at all in the favorite American literary parlor game of literary *ranking*. I am just arguing that all our literature is part of a wholeness which (for whatever reasons) we sometimes choose to forget. I confess that I once used the same argument, allowing all our literary creators to claim the name of poets, in a discussion with Donald Justice. Whose answer was that of the active generation surely James Merrill could, under the best classical standards, take his place alongside the great Masters. Maybe so. . . .

Am I being too cranky and pedantic? Well, after all, I finally got my Ph.D. last year, after thirty years; and, in the time that may be left to me, maybe I ought to be allowed to make up for lost time and sound as academic as I please. But not for long.

You need to know a little bit more about me to evaluate my point of view. I am a witness here, but I am not a disinterested one. There are a few facts which may be pertinent. I started reading and writing before I could actually do either. That is, I was regularly *read to*, by my father and my mother and by others in the family, before I was well out of the crib. For richer and for poorer, we lived in a house with (as it turned out, when my father died and we sold the house and counted them) many thousands of books. Everybody read and everybody wrote, too. Before we *learned how to write*, we dictated our stories and poems and plays to those who did. And there were always some writers in the family, some pretty good ones on both sides. (So? There were also a dancer, a musician, a PGA golfer, soldiers, and sailors. A little of everything.) By habit and example we learned to be, I hope, *open* to almost everything without being entirely undiscriminating. There was room, among the many mansions of the heaven of literature, for Shakespeare and Kipling and Dickens and Stevenson, for Hemingway and Sinclair Lewis, for the *Harvard Classics* and the Hardy Boys, for *Don Quixote* and *Don Sturdy and the Temple of Gold*. I read all the time, then, and I still do. And after I became a teacher and then later a certified (by finally being published) writer, I did not put away childish things, but just added to them. I have for thirty-some years judged countless contests and grant applications and prizes. And I have edited poetry and fiction, too, for various magazines and presses. And I have reviewed books all the time, individually and in clusters for chronicle reviews and in mountainous caches, over the last few years, for the annual "Year In Fiction" essay for the *Dictionary of Literary Biography Yearbook* where in ten or twelve thousand words I try to do my best to report on a calendar year's worth of American Fiction. At this time I am still doing at least some of all of it. And I think it would be perfectly safe to say that I read more fiction, at all stages of its development, than anybody else in this country. And in terms of published books, you cannot convince me that I do not read more novels and story collections than the entire professional staffs of the *New York Times* (Sunday and daily) and the *Washington Post* (ditto) put together. Add on, say, *Vanity Fair, New York*, and the *Village Voice*. And I am not a bona fide speed-reader, either. Not such an outrageous claim. You will surely have noticed that they review pretty much the same books. And close readers will also have noted the irrefutable internal evidence that they read each other's stuff, reviews, pretty closely, too. And *really* close readers will notice how phrases on book jackets, inevitably and slightly translated, reappear in their reviews. Now. You can argue *selectivity* all you want to. I'll give you some points on that one, but will argue back that a true and honest selectivity would not produce such *uniformity* of agreement in various places as to which books are worthy of attention and which are not. I would also argue that, for these professional book arbiters, by the time they have taken care of their friends and enemies and have paid off professional obligations of one kind and another to publishers, selection has been greatly simplified. Of course I can't claim, and I don't, to *know* as much as they do, collectively or individually. And I remain helplessly dependent on them for *information*, if not for judgment or wisdom. Anyway, by all rights, I ought to have a sense of what is going on. And I simply do not And that is the one and only thing I am absolutely sure of.

You want to know something? I will bet you good money that I read more short stories in any given year, in magazines and book collections, as well as in manuscript, then Shannon Ravenel or William Abrahams. But they have the answers every year (though I read *them*, too, and notice that they are not overburdened with memory of their earlier certainties and that their answers tend to change as the years go on and by). I am sorry I don't have many answers. I envy their scope, authority and confidence. They have strategic points of view. I am down in the trenches. A literary grunt with a limited view of shell bursts, flares, and rusty barbwire. And I claim to be a writer, too. Oh, if I only had good sense, I would try to be a lot more like Faulkner in this matter. I saw him once, at a polite distance in Princeton. While I stood there, a hotshot New York editor came up and gave him a new novel that he thought Faulkner would really enjoy. And Mr. Faulkner (somewhat to my surprise) thanked him kindly for the book, but added that he probably would never get around to reading it. "These days," he said, stuffing his pipe, "I only have time for the Old Verities."

God, I wish I had spent as much time on the Old Verities as on the many ways and means of contemporary American fiction, fine and dandy as it is! Of course, as I gather from his family and friends, Faulkner was, as ever, half kidding. He read everything he could get hold of. All the time. An old friend of his told me once, "He would read matchbox covers and cereal boxes if there was nothing else." In that sense a kindred spirit. . . .

Something more before we get down to what the middle-aged survivors of the 1960s used to call the nitty-gritty. (I wonder if guys like Daniel Ellsberg and his celebrated psychiatrist still use expressions like that.) Not only do I not have a good sense of the Big Picture, but also, try as I will, I *miss things*. Lots of things. It has become, over the years, a kind of a desperate game, trying *not* to let anything escape my attention, slip through the cracks, as they keep on saying. Well, truth is that I don't even come close. And unlike the *Times* and *Post* people, in the anarchy of my effort, I sometimes even forget the work of my friends. Example: to my everlasting shame, I read and greatly valued (I even wrote a blurb for the book jacket) and then just plain *forgot!* for "The Year In Fiction," one of the better novels of 1985, *Scorpio Rising*, by R. G. Vliet. Russ Vliet was a poet and fiction writer I much admired. I just forgot. . . .

Point one, then. There is so much being done that it is easy to overlook a lot of it; and, in truth, a whole lot of very good fiction is overlooked each and every year.

It is my best and considered judgment that American fiction is, overall, a reflection of American life and society; that our fiction is large, very large both in sheer numbers, *quantity* of production, and in its wild variety of forms. Like our great country, it's seething with diversity, wild with plurality. There are dozens and dozens of good — and I mean very good — writers, a crowd, a multitude, of them. Even within the limited parameters of my aesthetic tastes. Or yours. Look, I may think minimalism, as a *program*, sucks. I may think of smartass metafiction as a social disease. But I am continually surprised and delighted and (all right) instructed by superb writers who do nothing else but minimal and smartass. The basic rule of thumb is that the more open and supple you allow yourself to be, the more of them (good writers) there are to be found out there. And you know what? I think this situation is purely and simply wonderful. If you like to read fiction, if you really enjoy it, it is a great time to be alive. Now, of course, it may be somewhat inconvenient for those folks who make their livings by generalizing all about the contemporary literary scene and its trends; I mean professional critics and reviewers and their academic accomplices, the specialists in contemporary literature (of one kind or another) who, together with (yes!) the writers they bet on and praise, have a vested interest, the most obvious kind of *self-interest*, in maintaining their own arbitrary status quo, their artificially created Establishment. Artificial? Pray remember we are talking about "serious" fiction, mostly. Serious fiction has no establishment based on *sales*. Unless you want to quibble about hundreds (in a nation of millions). And do not forget the publishers, large and small, who must use the distortions of the Establishment to simplify their difficult tasks and to (pardon the expression) maximize their slim profits or, anyway, (again, please) minimize their losses.

I am here saying (yes) that in our time the Establishment, in none of its loosely collusive and more or less related forms, is not honestly representative of what is really going on in American fiction, day in and day out. I am also trying to imply that to the extent that they know better, those who help to maintain, preserve, protect and defend the Establishment are dishonest people. And those in the Establishment who *don't* know better are too ignorant and stupid to be believed.

Take your pick, members-in-good-standing of the Literary Establishment, in my book you are either liars or dupes. No, I'm only hurrahing you. What I'm *really* saying is that you, O judges and salesmen and hypocrite readers and writers!, are really just like all the rest of us. Caught up in the System.

There are really no officers in the army of Contemporary Lit. We are all grunts.

Point two, then. The Star System, which works for journalists, professors, critics and reviewers, publishers, foundations, and, don't forget, the Stars too, has no real basis whatsoever in fact or in truth. The Star System is about as applicable to our real life and times as, say, Courtly Love in the Age of AIDS or the Feudal System in the Era of Affirmative Action.

The Literary Star System *may* (I will allow only for the possibility) be a necessary and relatively efficient way to deal with the literature of the past, especially of the remote past. But the closer we get to the present, the greater the distortion of both facts and truth, and the greater the extent of the injustice.

Stars—and you know who you are, O Voices of Your Generation, Spokespersons for Decades, and so, alas, do we—I am not saying you aren't good. Am not even saying you are not all you are cracked up to be. I am saying—and you will be hard-pressed to prove otherwise; you will have to read at least as much as I do and know a little bit more; and you don't; and you won't—you are not head and shoulders better than many, many, many living and working American writers. And you know it. No matter how many times you read your happy press clippings, you can't get rid of your doubts. (Poets are the worst about this. Some of my poet friends and colleagues get, *really!*, instant facial tics and migraine headaches if I merely mention the names of poets whom they haven't heard of. A powerful weapon. Fun, too. Reader, do you remember James Dickey, in various places, insisting that we are the only intelligent life in the Universe? It would be unbearable to him, and us too for different reasons, to discover another James Dickey out there somewhere banging out anapests and three-stress lines).

Names? You want names, of course. Examples from the world of American fiction. Well, you won't get them from me. They know who they are. And you know who they are. Any recently published anthology (anthologies are the Rogues' Galleries of our time) will tell you. And one thing about the Stars that I have noticed. No matter how they got to be Stars, by hook or crook, they don't *stay* where they are by being anything else than *ruthless*, ruthlessly self-serving, invincibly ignorant of anything going on outside the castle walls. Merciless folk. Note how they want and get full credit for every little half-assed act of generosity they perform. They want not only to be deeply admired, but also well remembered. And like the legendary Elephant, they never forget.

I may be (and proud of it, too) an advocate and mediator for the literary peasants, but I have also been amongst the Stars, here and there — completely by accident of course — on panels and committees and so forth and so on. And I can report to you that (in my best judgment) most literary Stars are shamelessly mean-spirited and vindictive and utterly self-serving. And, as far as I can tell, with only a shred, call it a fig leaf, of moral rectitude. You will surmise that I really don't *like* them very much. True enough, but irrelevant. I love my family and friends. I have a large family and lots of friends. Socializing with Literary Stars has never been my idea of an upscale experience. Tell you the truth, I can't figure out how they can stand each other's dreary company. Only excuse I can see for it is that, like some corrupt Renaissance Court, they can't afford to let each other out of sight for a moment. Let that, the company of each other, be their reward.

Do you think I am being pretty silly, foolish? Well, here is the text for this sermon. You did notice that my rhetoric here is the rhetoric of preaching. Which is as good as any other, as long as everybody understands it. My text comes from St. Paul's first epistle to the proud and worldly wise congregation in Corinth. "Where is the wise? Where is the disputer of this world? Hath not God made foolish the wisdom of this world?" (I Corinthians 20).

If you can't stand preaching, we can always be political. Why not?

I speak here on their behalf, the working majority. They are, here and now, my constituency. The truth is that, just like the Society at large, our literature is much more democratic than any of the existing Star Systems will allow. You know what? In terms of quality, I can in a matter of minutes put together an anthology of American story-writers, writers you have never heard of, that will be in every way and by any standard as good as the finest collection of Stars you can assemble.

A few years ago, as an exercise, I used to get each of my creative writing students to take a single year in the 1920s or 1930s or early 1940s and read straight through the *New York Times*, Sunday and daily, and the *Herald Tribune*, for book reviews and for literary news. Then to come and to report to us as to how, say, 1929 *saw itself*. Next step was to compare and contrast that vision with the later judgment of the literary histories.

This exercise taught a lot of different things. One good one was humility. O Stars, cultivate a little humility and you will be stronger and better for the experience! Of course, it indicated that even in this self-conscious and manipulative century, characteristics which may be as commonplace as (and not unrelated to) our merciless savagery, tacit and active, with each other at all levels, even here, in the good old twentieth century, there have been huge discrepancies between reality and status quo.

I remember once, in the late 1950s, trying this selfsame argument out, in terms of poetry, with Stanley Kunitz. (It was in a restaurant in Middletown, Connecticut, Stanley, in case you have forgotten. Refresh your memory.) And you shrugged off my arguments, Stanley, with an example. "If Robert Frost came along now," you said, "we would surely recognize him." Brash and sassy and full of bile and irony, I said, "Yes, sir, I reckon you would recognize Robert Frost. We have certainly come that far." Second time around, do you get what I was saying? Somebody else at the table, I think it was my old friend Dick Wilbur, allowed as how *in this age* no talent could go undiscovered and unrewarded for long. He seemed mildly wistful that this was so. Never again would there be exciting and happy posthumous discoveries. Somebody else (who? I wish I could remember) jumped in and went too far, too, claiming that even poverty had finally disappeared. Soon there would be nobody left to feel sorry for. We laughed. What else? This was, after all, the late and high 1950s. Everybody was still reading John Kenneth Galbraith. *Assured of certain certainties,* as Eliot wrote once. . . .

What am I getting at here? I am saying that there are no *real* Stars in American fiction these days. Stars are few and we are many. And from experience, the experience of reading not writing, not as one among the many, permit me to assert that, by and large, the many are very good. It is wonderfully exciting and rewarding to be a reader of American fiction in this day and age. We have so many exciting and rewarding writers. Young ones and old ones. This, the active and visible presence of the elders in our literary culture may be, ironically, the *newest* distinction of our time. May be, after all, its finest and most distinguishing characteristic. Writers of every race, creed, color, country of national origin, sexual preference, etc. American, myself, for as long as any white folks have been here, American, then, to my genetic code and the marrow of my bones, I can be pardoned for wishing that our wondrous plurality extended beyond political and social life to include our literature, itself, as an honest and accurately reflective part of the vital national debates going on. But to have worthwhile debates you have to have more than one side, more than one self-serving point of view, and maybe even a little passion, also. Our Stars, and the Establishment of which they are ornaments, have too much to lose to be real and serious participants in our political and social life beyond the most reflexive, simpleminded, and stereotypical levels. Truth is, they have even less to contribute than the Rock Stars so many of them yearn to become.

What's to be done about all this, if anything? Maybe nothing. Too many people, including many of the new and younger writers, read much too little. They don't even have time for the Old Verities. They just barely have time for the Stars. So, in the end, the Star System may finally come in the future to be as real as it is false now as a model and description of the present. So relax, Stars. Posterity will probably take care of you, will preserve the reputations you have acquired, if not earned. One way or the other. No controlling *that*, you know. The future may find all of us to have been foolish and far from relevant to anything that matters to them. My own experience with history and historians teaches me that they will not settle for, not without interrogation and inquisition, the official, the Establishment view of things.

Meantime what is there for us to do, those locked and lost in the present (though not without good memory or solid knowledge, not without a *past*, then), who care at all about American fiction? We are appalled (I speak for my constituents, both readers and writers) at the *waste* involved. Waste, including deadly toxic waste, is such a commonplace of contemporary American life. Why and how should literature be spared? So many worthy talents that are lost to us by the waste of the System. But those who survive the school of hard knocks and the great shrugs of indifference (may I, with mild pride, count myself among them?) are tough, hardened. Are not likely to cease and desist in the face of indifference, even rejection. And we need not, shall not cease in the effort, as readers, to seek and find new and worthy writers. Discovery is still a real possibility. And even though people, including writers, appear to be reading less and less, there are more and more literary magazines (coming and going) and presses, places for good writers to appear and to be discovered.

As for the Stars, I believe they are safe enough from any serious literary revolution. We already had one, right after World War II, a revolution which, among other things, raised unknowns like Faulkner and Fitzgerald to the status of Stars in our firmament. And it is already late in this tedious and terrible century, too late for much beyond the usual decadence to come to pass. And, anyway, I can't think of any century which has witnessed more than one serious literary revolution. Thus our Stars will go on being Stars. Happily ever after.

There is one thing we could do, maybe ought to do. In fairness (never mind *justice*) we are entitled to ask more of them. They should be held, feet to the fire, to the highest standards imaginable. Damn near absolute standards. For instance, the contemporary southern writer (even the achievements of the late Flannery O'Connor) *should* now be measured against the standards of William Faulkner. Our poets should not be allowed to measure themselves against, just for example, Mark Strand and Charles Simic. Compare and contrast them to Chaucer, Shakespeare, Milton, and Byron. See what I mean? And our Stars should never— ever—be permitted to have it both ways. They may not be our lucky lords and leaders and yet, at one and the same time, lay claim upon a common bond they share with us, the many, the unwashed, the majority. They are not just Folks. Never can be any more. And, beyond that, we should agree that no one in the Literary Establishment need be trusted. For trust, unlike so many other things, must be earned.

SHORT STORIES ARE NOT REAL LIFE

DAVID R. SLAVITT

So, I'm teaching.

I wanted to teach, but it is nothing like what I thought it would be. It isn't that coming in from the forbidding cold of the literary marketplace.[1] It is only a different kind of cold. I ought to have known, but then one never knows . . .

That's one of the main differences between literature and life. Literature is what you can make up, while life is the correction, what actually happens. Better writers than I have demonstrated their utter inability to live any more shrewdly than ordinary nonwriting mortals. But that is, as they say, another story.

What I imagined, I suppose I may as well confess, is some glossy advertisement of myself in tweeds, strolling about the gracious lawns of this ivied bastion of learning and civility. I wear the tweeds all right, but I feel like an impostor because my students and my colleagues are outfitted as urban guerillas. And I spend almost as much time on the train or the bus as I do on the campus. The bus takes only half an hour longer and saves me ten dollars on each round trip. On the other hand, the bus takes me into the Port Authority Terminal and subjects me to that terrible walk from Eighth Avenue to Times Square on Forty-second Street.

On one of the marquees, last week: *The Pink Clam.*

If I were a better person, I wouldn't notice such things, or not so much as I do.

But that distressing block isn't any worse than the subway ride I have to take either way. *Apprenda Inglés.* Or, on the adjoining placard, *Apprenda terror.* They've got a selection of killers, rapists, and brutalizers for whom the police are looking, and they're willing to pop for a hundred dollars for information leading to the arrest and conviction etc. etc.

---

1. A reference to the annual publication of the R. R. Bowker Co.

Only a hundred? Is violence that common, that cheap?

But this isn't what you want to hear. This is your standard urban complaint and has nothing to do with life at the university (except of course that it does). I come out of the subway entrance after all, and pass through the tall and guarded gates of the university into a world that is supposed to be better and safer and isn't at all. I go to the building where I'm supposed to have my conferences, and I get into an elevator which is painfully slow and . . . ugly. Sixteen thousand dollars a year they charge these kids, and the elevator looks as though it were from some project in an East Harlem slum. Its door takes an actual ninety seconds to close. The metal wall panels were in need of painting ten years ago and the plastic shield over the fluorescent light has been removed, broken or stolen, so that there is a hideous glare. People in the elevator look in that terrible light as if they have some disease.

The bullpen in which I have these conferences is also awful, full of discarded typewriters on which people have left notes saying, "Broken. Dangerous. Do not use!" Most of the chairs are covered in leatherette and seem to be from dinette sets that have been broken up in domestic tragedies I don't choose to imagine. My little cubicle has one of those chairs, less extensively slashed than many, a wooden chair that I use, and an ugly wooden desk with two drawers, one locked and the other unclosable. In the unclosable drawer, one of my colleagues has stored a bottle of Almaden burgundy.

I guess it could be worse—M/D 20/20, or Night Train, maybe.

What this large room looks like is the city room of some foreign language newspaper on either the day before or maybe the day after its bankruptcy.

I sit here, in my little cubicle, waiting for students to show up for their conferences. I will read their short stories. I will try not to let on that I don't much like short stories. But Ignoto and Ungar[2] teach the poetry courses, and novels are long and cumbersome and strenuous, which is another reason for my wanting to teach. Short stories are what's left. Short stories are what you can read aloud in class and then talk about for an hour or so. Which is what I do.

But what difference does it make? I mean, when I think about what I'm doing, teaching writing to young men and women, I have the nagging feeling that I'm probably doing them harm. It's like teaching them

---

2. Ignoto, Italian for unknown, but there is a possible reference to David Ignatow, a poet on the faculty of the Columbia University College of General Studies Writing Program. Ungar is probably imaginary.

to go over Niagara Falls in a barrel. I never wanted any of my children to write. Why, then, should I encourage these kids? (I tell myself that it's very unlikely that any of them will actually succeed or persevere in the attempt . . . but that is not exactly soothing to my ruffled moral sense.)

On the bus into the City this afternoon, I was reading the *TLS*[3] and Robin Buss[4] wrote, "The novelist (or, for that matter, the writer on natural history) elaborates a context; the short-story writer highlights, and by lifting something—an incident, a character—and making an entity of it, implies its extensions." Not bad, you know! It was in his (or her?) discussion of a book of Daniel Boulanger's stories called *Les noces du merle*. I am unlikely to read this book. It's in French, a language I do not speak or even read very well, despite the certification of this very university that I am proficient in the *langue*. Not at all. I have looked up *merle*, and I'm able to report that it is a blackbird or perhaps a water ouzel, but why a blackbird (or water ouzel) should be getting married beats the hell out of me.

But Mr./Mrs./Miss/Ms. Buss is on the right route there, I thought, being, myself, on a Greyhound and not too happy about it. In the seat behind me, a schizophrenic was muttering and crooning to himself, which wouldn't have been so bad if he hadn't occasionally surfaced into a kind of sense, addressing some denizen of his memory or nightmares and articulating all too clearly, "Come on, bitch, where's the money. Give me the money, bitch! The money. The money, bitch."

A black man in his early forties, I'd guess. And distressingly, the bus was full so there was no possibility of moving away from him, not for me nor for the woman in the seat beside him, also black and quite uncomfortable. She had a hat with cherries on the brim, and she had a Bible on her lap which she clutched either for divine protection or else to use as a weapon if it should come to that.

And what did I do? Nothing, of course. I mean, I thought of going up front to report to the driver that there was this raving lunatic on the bus, but what could the driver have done? Put him off, somewhere in the middle of the New Jersey Turnpike and leave him to wander in traffic? The woman with the Bible was free to complain herself if she chose to do so. I had no more reason to interfere than anyone else. And I was

---

3. The (London) *Times Literary Supplement*.

4. A reviewer for the *TLS*, not identified but perhaps related to John Butt, lecturer in Spanish at King's College, and Colin Russ, lecturer in German at the University of Kent, both of whom appear in the same issue (October 4, 1985).

correct, I think. We got to New York anyway, and no harm was done. Or no new harm, I should say.

But Buss was correct. Novelists build contexts, while short story writers work by synecdoche,[5] isolating and then implying some nimbus of meanings. It's a magic trick, really, a razzle-dazzle performance.

I open the school paper and read yet another account of a piece of distressing violence, some female undergraduate who accepted the offer from a young man wearing a college sweatshirt to help her carry her groceries from the supermarket back to her dorm. And of course she got attacked, tied up with wire, and her roommates were tied up . . .

I throw the paper away and open my briefcase, drawing out the brown Manila envelope in which the short stories of my students are mixed in with departmental directives and printouts from the registrar's office which are inaccurate and out of date. I fish out one of the stories and read it.

There's a girl waking up and the man with whom she spent the night is gone. His clothes are gone. But as she goes into the bathroom, she finds that the toilet seat has been left up. For a paragraph of fine writing, she looks in the mirror and considers her naked body.

Is this the writer's body? Is this a piece of literary exhibitionism? It is silly to suppose that the speaker in a short story has any particular relationship to the writer, but then these are students and they may not know that rule. The odds are that this is all true, that this happened more or less the way it is written down. And if I have connected the name on the first page to the right face — and body — then the description is probably accurate, even to the large pink areolas.

The story is about the relationship of this girl and Hilda, her college friend who is now married and divorced and has a three-year-old-son. They were roommates back in school, and they had a set of signals they used when one of them wanted the room to herself for a few hours if she had a date she was thinking about going to bed with. Now there is friction because the protagonist lives by herself and enjoys her freedom while Hilda has the kid to worry about. The protagonist baby-sits willingly enough, but Hilda is jealous. The wrinkle in the story is that Hilda is somewhat repressed and can't admit, even to herself, that she's jealous of the sexual freedom of her former roommate. What comes out, instead, is a weird and unpleasant jealousy of the friendship between the child and the narrator.

Not bad, really. It could be cut a little, here and there, but the basic

---

5. The figure of speech in which a narrower term of reference is used for a wider one.

structure is sound and the writing is efficient and graceful most of the time. A little flowery? But that could perfectly well be the character who's thinking and speaking this way. Certainly, it's good enough to use in class. What I usually do is bring something along to talk about if there isn't anything from the work of the students that we can discuss.

John Leonard[6] passes by on the way to his cubicle which is just beyond mine and we exchange greetings. His left arm is in a sling and I ask him who beat him up. I'm making a joke, but it turns out that he really was beaten up. In the subway, on the way up to school a week ago, he saw a young woman being roughed up by a gang of four or five toughs and he tried to stop them. They turned on him and bounced him around, literally and very hard, actually cracking his shoulder blade.

"On the way to school?" I ask.

He nods, smiling ruefully.

"I mean . . . in the afternoon?"

"That's right."

What can I say? I tell him I'm glad he's alive.

"Me, too," he says, and he goes on toward his cubby.

I'm distressed, of course, for his sake, but for mine as well. After all, that's the subway I take. I'd told myself that for little old ladies at three in the morning, there was a certain risk, but for someone like me, six feet tall and hefty, at rush hour . . .

But would I have done what he did? I was at less risk on the bus, but then so was the woman the schizophrenic was bothering. It is an uncomfortable question, and either way I decide, I lose — on the grounds of cowardice or folly. Before I make my choice, my first student appears. Or, not so fast. An ex-student, as he announces himself.

He's something of a wreck already, a tall, shaggy kid with bad skin and a diamond stud earring on the lobe of one ear. He had shown me a competent if repellent story about young men and women in the East Village living in squalor and doing drugs, and there was a peculiar Raymond Carver[7] trendiness to the way he described his people and the things that happened to them, all with a weird flatness that a psychiatrist would call a lack of affect. And there was also a disturbing authority in the way he described his hero kicking off his shoe, removing his sock, and using it as a tourniquet so he could inject heroin into a vein.

The writer has come by to say he can't make the class. At first, I think

---

6. Former book reviewer and columnist for *the New York Times* and a member of the Columbia University College of General Studies faculty.

7. Author of *Cathedral,* Knopf, 1983.

that he means this evening's class, but he means the whole course. A conflict? Or is he dropping out of school entirely? He is unforthcoming and almost provocatively vague, but it was thoughtful of him to drop by and let me know. Otherwise, I'd have worried about him.

I will worry about him anyway.

He leaves and the author of the story about the woman with the lovers and the jealous friend peeps around the partition. Yes, I'd remembered the right one, with the terrific complexion. And the pink areolas, too, I suppose. We discuss the story. Apparently, I've got it wrong, was too quick in my reading, or too jangled. The mother really is jealous of the relationship between her friend and her little boy. I suggest that this is unlikely, but that the unlikeliness is possibly useful for her. She can rewrite to make her story into something like the one I thought I'd read. And she can further complicate it by admitting a little jealousy on the part of her narrator toward the friend who has a child while she doesn't. Just a line somewhere, about how her clock is running. "She must be in her late twenties?" I ask.

The writer is in her late twenties. She nods, yes.

"Well, you'll think about it," I tell her. "Or we'll see what the class has to say. You don't mind if we do this in class?"

She doesn't mind. But she blushes. Stage fright? Or the business about the pink nipples?

She could omit that sentence, of course. But I can't tell her that. I couldn't tell the driver about the lunatic, and I couldn't have protected the girl in the subway.

Why Almaden? Why not whiskey in a flask? It's something to consider—not to leave in the desk drawer, but to carry in my briefcase, along with the Manila envelope.

I tell her that I think she's doing pretty well and that I'll see her in class in fifteen minutes or so.

She leaves and another young woman is waiting to see me. She doesn't have anything to show me.

"Oh?" I ask. Usually, if they don't have anything, they just don't show up for conferences.

"It's been kind of a bad week," she says. And gradually she lets me know that she had to move into a different apartment because somebody broke into the place she lived in before. "And, well, it was . . . very bad."

"You're all right, aren't you?"

"I am now. I was in the hospital for a couple of days."

"You were attacked?" I ask, concerned but also thinking that this is crazy. All this in one day?

But she's nodding, yes. Does she want to talk about it? Does she want not to talk about it? I don't want to pry. I tell her, of course, that she can take her time and do something later on, when she's up to it. It isn't a weekly performance, after all. Anybody who could write good stuff every week, reliably, wouldn't need the course.

I tell her to take it easy and ask if there's anything I can do. She shakes her head, but she smiles, acknowledging my good will.

We walk together across the campus to the classroom building. Small talk is not exactly appropriate so I don't even try. I'm thinking that there's a Cheever story I've got in my bag that has a couple of nice moves in it. We can talk about that one. But I'm also thinking that this is a terrible day and wouldn't fit into the conventions of short fiction. Too many coincidences. Too much, too much . . .

The class goes pretty much the way I expect, only we get the beginnings of a new story one of the young men has been toying with. He wants to see whether there are possibilities he hasn't thought about. What catches my attention is that he's got footnotes throughout the story. It's an odd stylistic thing to do, and I ask about it. The only stories he's read are from *The Norton Anthology of Short Fiction*,[8] and he thinks all stories are set up this way.

I explain that this isn't necessarily so and show him the Cheever book that has stories without footnotes. On the other hand, I find myself entertained by the idea. Why shouldn't stories have footnotes? At the very least, they could be the parsley that decorates the platter and gives a certain authority to the *presentation*. Or a nice looniness.

Or innocence, which, on a day like this, seems particularly precious.

When the class is over, I put myself together, stuff the new material into my briefcase, and head toward 116th Street. Two of the students tag along with me, either in friendliness or because we are safer in a group. One of the students, a dark, rather chunky, but carefully groomed young woman, tells me about an episode last term when several members of one of her classes went together to the West End Bar for a few drinks. She left the bar a little before ten, went down into the 116th Street subway station, and got on a train. At 110th Street, two thugs got on and sat down near her, which wasn't in itself anything really alarming. She only began to worry when they got off at 34th Street, followed her to the ticket window of the Long Island Railroad, listened while she bought a ticket to Babylon, and then bought tickets to Babylon for themselves.

Now she was scared. She spoke to one of the trainmen and told him

---

8. Edited by R. V. Cassill, 1978, W. W. Norton & Co., New York.

about the two young men who were following her. He asked her where she was going, and she showed him her ticket. He told her not to worry and said he'd call the police. She got onto the train and waited, but no police showed up. The train pulled out, and the two young men were right there in the back of the car. They pulled into Babylon and she got out, and they got out, and she began to walk faster, and they began to walk faster, and then a police car pulled up. The trainman had called the police after all, the Babylon police, of course, and they were just pulling into the station to meet the train. The two thuggy guys ran off, but it was a near thing. If those cops had been only a minute or two later than they were, or if the trainman hadn't been so obliging as to make the call . . .

"Are you taking the subway?" she asks.

"Yes, but not just yet. There's a book I want to get and I haven't had anything to eat."

There is an uncertain moment. I consider inviting the two of them to join me, but on the other hand, there are two of them, and I suppose they'll be safe enough, at least while they are together. Later on, the dangers will be greater. Besides, I really want to be alone. There is a Chinese restaurant down at 110th Street I like to go to that one of my students told me about. It was closed down by the Board of Health for rats and has since reopened, but as the student said, that's a kind of recommendation. In the other Chinese restaurants around 110th Street, you have no idea how long it has been since the exterminator showed up or how many rats are running free. Besides, this one has a bar and I can get a gin on the rocks, or even two, to cut through the accumulated residue of the day's dreariness. I like the Chinese place. The tables are close together and one can eavesdrop, which is better than trying to read without spilling soy sauce on the book. And there is something reassuring and steadying about the Chinese waiters, fugitives from one great civilization and witnesses to the collapse of another, hustling pots of tea and platters of food when they have to, but mostly sitting around the large round table in the back, talking among themselves, laughing occasionally but mostly demonstrating an elegant ruefulness — which is, after all, what most short stories leave you with, isn't it? "Araby" or "I'm a Fool" or "The Lady with the Pet Dog"[9] all come to a conclusion that would produce the expression and physical attitude of any of those waiters.

I drink my gin and wait for my hot and sour soup and beef lo mein. I also listen to a couple at the next table, very intense, probably graduate

---

9. Stories by James Joyce, Sherwood Anderson, and Anton Chekhov, respectively.

students. Or he is, anyway. He is wearing a denim jacket over a black T-shirt, jeans, and work boots. She is in a voluminous skirt and a tight black sweater. Nice figure. Hair almost black. A complexion that is smooth but running to olive, so that, presumably, her areolas are more brown than pink. The two of them are going through some crisis so serious that they can hardly talk about it. They do the things that people in short stories do, or people in short stories written by students — twiddling spoons and chopsticks, staring into a teacup as she is doing, or at the ceiling as if some answer might emerge there or at least the next line of dialogue, which is what he is doing. It is tempting to imagine him storming out of the restaurant. And she has no money, not a dime, and is embarrassed, but I come to her rescue, offering at least to lend her the money, which requires her to tell me her name and address. It is not hard to leap ahead, as I have been trying to get my students to do, leaving out the predictable and obvious details, the dumb novelistic information about how to dial telephone calls or put tokens in turnstiles, and arrive at her apartment, modest but neat and, as a matter of personal preference and to avoid the cliché, devoid of insect life. Her areolas are, indeed, a lovely mocha, and her clam a glistening healthy pink.

Nonsense. No such thing is likely to happen.

More likely is that they will leave together while I go alone down into the 110th Street station, to get mugged by those toughs who are still there, frustrated after their attempt on my student that took them all the way out to Babylon and more dangerous than ever. My briefcase stolen, and my wallet and my watch. My shoulder blade cracked like John Leonard's. I'll be lucky to get away with my life.

And what happens? What happens? It's a vulgar and gossipy question that a poet doesn't have to answer and that a novelist addresses in a very secondary way. But in a short story, we know that something is going to happen. We can tell, because we know that there's only a page or two left in the text, that a resolution is upon us of one kind or another. A moment of re-vision in which the writer makes his move. It can be some dumb piece of cuteness like "The Gift of the Magi"[10] or it can be exquisite and perverse, a switch on our expectations that some sudden reversal is about to be effected, some transformation somehow imposed.

I am not set upon or mugged. I get back down to Times Square and across to the Port Authority Bus Terminal, make my way through the pimps and grifters and derelicts and schizophrenics. I don't see my friend from earlier in the day, but if I were to loiter a little and if my hearing

---

10. Short story by O. Henry (William Sidney Porter).

were more acute, I have no doubt but that I'd be able to pick up the phrase that must be floating through the air, "Where's the money, bitch? Come on, bitch, the money!"

Without untoward incident, I board the bus and am even lucky enough to have two seats to myself so that I can doze on the way home. It is an uneasy sleep, the kind that would surely occasion a paragraph or two of dream material if life were a short story. But it isn't. Because I am on the bus, I remember the Buss piece in the *TLS* and how novelists elaborate a context. Novelists and writers on natural history, I think it was, but then novelists are natural historians, whichever way you want to take that phrase. And life is not just sensations and assaults but a context, or a set of them actually. Natural and unnatural histories. I am physically uncomfortable, gritty and exhausted after a trip into the city, but I have survived it and I will return to my house, drink a glass of soda water, let the dog run in the yard, go into my study where my wife will have put my mail on my desk, and then into the bedroom. She'll be asleep but she'll know I'm home, and I'll get undressed as quietly as I can and get into bed beside her. I'll feel the warmth of her body, and the context of our lives will cover us like the blanket, with warmth and weight as if it were a physical object.

I have not been seduced. I have not seduced anyone. I have not been robbed or assaulted. Those are, like short stories, abrupt violations of life, and on the unreal island now behind me there is no way of distinguishing between the normal and the abnormal, the real and the unreal, or the text and the footnotes for that matter. And I am not immune to these possibilities of dramatic reversal and loss. Nobody is. But my life is in that study and that bedroom. It is my childhood, that you don't know about, and my parents' dreams for me, and mine for my children and grandchildren. None of that kind of thing is of interest to the writers of short stories.

The surrealist lights of the Bayonne refineries that I can see through the bus window look like a monstrous city, devoid of life but — obviously — full of energy, tanks of it, rows of gleaming pipes alive with it. There is a cracking tower with a pulsing plume of flame. One hardly needs to invent dream scenes; they leap out from all sides, or, as here, slip by at dizzying speed. I close my eyes but don't sleep. Instead, I think of my students, sad and brave, more or less blessed or afflicted with talents for writing and living. At the moment, they are occupied with short stories and experiences, but some day they may go on to novels and lives.

Which will be, I hope, mostly dull and mostly happy.

FORMS AND THEMES OF CONTEMPORARY FICTION

SPIRIT OF QUEST IN CONTEMPORARY AMERICAN LETTERS

IHAB HASSAN

My subject is quest in contemporary American letters. In quest, a person, most often a man, increasingly a woman, invites risk. Selves at Risk: the phrase reminds us that if the self is a fiction as contemporary literary theory claims, it is a fiction more effective, more durable, than all the theories that proclaim it so. Call it an eidolon, blooded, sweaty, and rank with the rage of history.

Still, you may ask: Quest? Adventure, in the fading glare of our century? In this era of satellites and supersonic jets, of the ubiquitous McDonald's and pervasive Panasonic? In our coddled jacuzzi culture, our cybernetic, if not quite cyborg, society of acronyms and first names, where acedia measures lives between hype and fix? Indeed, the very name of quest may strike some as quaint, lacking as it does deconstructionist brio, feminist bravura, or Marxist glitz.

Yet the spirit of quest endures, unquavering, with stiff upper lip. It endures, moreover, confident of its future and proud of its largely British pedigree. From rain forests, across oceans, steppes, savannahs, saharas, to the peaks of the Andes or Himalayas, men and increasingly women still test the limits of human existence. They test spirit, flesh, marrow in a timeless quest for adventure, for meaning really, beyond civilization, at the razor edge of mortality. And they return, with sun-cracked skin and gazes honed on horizons, to tell the tale.

Indeed, adventurers can be eloquent, even loquacious. I must, therefore, limit myself here to contemporary American prose writers whose work absorbs the traditional form of quest, adventure, and autobiog-

---

A shorter version of this essay appeared in *Contemporary American Fiction*, edited by Malcolm Bradbury and Sigmund Ro (London: Edward Arnold, 1987); and some passages appear in *Selves at Risk* (Madison: University of Wisconsin Press, 1990).

raphy into an impure genre. And I must address mainly one large, perhaps overweaning, query: what kind of symbolic option does this genre provide at the present time? The question is best grasped in three of its constituent parts, namely: (a) What are the *literary* features of the genre? (b) What is its *historical* motive in the American experience? and, above all, (c) What does the genre finally reveal about *individuals*, their *society*, the *geopolitical* conditions of our world?

I

The literary genre in which autobiography, adventure, and quest meet remains mapless—henceforth, I'll simply call it quest or adventure interchangeably. It draws on a capacious realm of experience, which we can try gradually to imagine, if not to define.

Consider autobiography first, now furiously rife. Why this greed for self-witness? Perhaps because we live in a self-regarding age; perhaps because through autobiography we deny the obsolescence of the self in mass society; perhaps because we lack consensus in our values, and so must ground our deepest articulations on the self, on death itself, the invisible ground of every autobiography. But perhaps, too, we choose autobiography because it expresses all the ambiguities of our postmodern culture.

Autobiography is, of course, literature itself, the impulse of a living subject to testify in writing, as the Greek etymology of the word proves. But in the current climate of our ironic self-awareness, autobiography loses its innocence; it becomes the vehicle for our epistemic evasions, our social and psychic vexations. The innate contradictions of autobiography emerge to confirm the cunning of our knowledge. This is evident in the questions that theoreticians of autobiography now ask. For instance:

1. Can a life ever be translated into words? Is there no irreconcilable tension between word and deed? Was John or Goethe right about "the beginning," the priority of the Logos or *die Tat*?
2. Can a life still in progress—the dead don't write autobiographies, they only have biographies written about them—ever grasp or understand itself? Isn't autobiography doubly partial, twice biased, in the sense of being both personal and incomplete, partisan and fragmentary?

3. Can we ever distinguish between fact and fiction in autobiography, any more than we can in our media? Isn't memory sister to imagination, kin to nostalgia or self-deceit?
4. Isn't autobiography, therefore, itself a quest rather than the record of a quest, a labor of self-creation no less than of self-cognizance or expression?
5. And doesn't this quest, this labor of self-creation, in turn affect the real, living, dying subject? Put another way, isn't autobiography shifty in that a first person present (I, now) pretends to be a third person past (he/she, then), and in the process alters both persons' characters?
6. To that extent, isn't all autobiography both an act of dying (pretending to round off one's life in writing) and also a wager on immortality (aspiring to remembrance through print)? Isn't it a counterfeit ending as well as a pseudo-eternity?
7. Lastly, how does autobiography transform the most private confession — from Augustine through Rousseau to Elizabeth Taylor, say — into public expression? Doesn't autobiography, however prurient or idiosyncratic, offer us the best mirror of a society, even of an epoch?

These conundrums of autobiography betray our graphomania, betray also denser imbrications of culture. Still, all these difficulties fail to inhibit the primal powers of adventure and quest. For if autobiography is the central impulse of literature, adventure and quest both revert to myth, which prefigures literature and still breathes life into all its shapes. Originally, adventure and quest related to such mythic narratives as the shamanistic flight, the hero's night journey, his trials in search of ultimate knowledge. Later, these narratives provided the structures and archetypes of epic, romance, and novel. To this day, they inform the Gothic novel, science fiction, the detective story, all manner of travel and action tales, which find rich analogues in the *Mahābhārata* or the *Gilgamesh*.

Yet raw action is not really their point. In the most resonant adventures we find a spiritual element, a mystic or ontic affirmation, a sense of the sacred that confirms the order of Creation. As Paul Zweig remarks in his book *The Adventurer*: "The gleams of intensity which invest [these moments of being] have an otherworldly quality, as if a man's duel with risk were not a 'vocation' at all, but a plunge into essential experience. . . . Adventure stories transpose our dalliance with risk into a sustained vision."

We can suppose, then, that autobiography, adventure, and quest coalesce in a contemporary genre that conveys both the perplexities of the postmodern condition and the ancient, visionary powers of myth. This genre, defying any comfortable distinction between fiction and fact, employs the sophisticated resources of narrative to raise fundamental problems of human existence, problems personal, social, metaphysical; for, as Walter Benjamin saw, storytelling, woven in the fabric of life and death, becomes wisdom itself. At its center stands the "hero with a thousand faces," an ontological voyager, a doer, prophet, and overreacher, at once an alien and founder of cities, another version of our selves. Yet as a literary form, the genre also hints its own abolition — in death, in silence, in extreme spiritual risk, in all those final conditions that make literature superfluous.

II

But it is time now to engage the second question, regarding quest in its historical assumptions, its American milieu. Certain commonplaces of criticism reverberate still in our minds. American literature, critics have said, is largely autobiographical, a literature of the Self, from Poe's Arthur Gordon Pym through Melville's Ishmael, Twain's Huck Finn, and Whitman's Myself, to Salinger's Holden Caulfield or Bellow's Augie March. It is also, we are often told, a symbolic, visionary literature, less social than metaphysical, with a prepossession for myth and romance. Its bias is for innocence, evasion, solitude, wonder, as the titles of even scholarly books intimate: *The American Adam, The Imperial Self, The Reign of Wonder, The Virgin Land, A World Elsewhere, Radical Innocence.* Finally, it is a literature, though Adamic, of extremity, of intense and brooding modernity, as D. H. Lawrence insisted.

Such enduring critical commonplaces confirm quest in the American grain. The quest moved west, absorbing that dire and dazzling energy Europeans expended in their colonial empires. It found in the wilderness its need for *otherness*, found its motives in the eternal search of misfits, outlaws, scalawags, crackpots, vagrants, visionaries, individualists of every stripe, for something they could hardly name: El Dorado, the New Jerusalem, the Earthly Paradise, the Last Frontier. "Philobats" (walkers on their toes), as Gert Raeithel argues in his psychohistory of *voluntary* American immigrants, they formed weak attachments to objects, persons, places; they relished movement, exposure, transgressive fantasies. Yet Americans could no more exempt themselves from history than from power or desire. Their quests, therefore, reveal certain social attitudes, historical patterns, that we also need to ponder.

Here Martin Green's *The Great American Adventure* proves pertinent. Green reviews classic adventures, from Cooper to Mailer, and discerns in them particular features — and I would say manners. These include a pagan, anti-intellectual, antipacifist outlook; a masculinist, often misogynist, stance; a concept of manhood linked to nationalism, patriotism, America's Manifest Destiny; and a strong sense of caste, if not class, led by military aristocrats *and* democratic woodsmen (hunters, trappers, Indian fighters) who magnificently possess the frontier virtues of valor, self-reliance, knowledge of the wilderness, and, above all, a rude *ecological ethic.*

In any event, though adventure became secular in the last century, possibly anti-Christian, it often took a spiritual, even mystic, turn. As Green says: "Although hunting is an activity of the aristomilitary caste, being a hunter in the American sense is in some ways not a caste activity, in that it takes place in a non-social space, outside the frontier of society. . . . Just for that reason, however, it represents more vividly the sacramental function of the man of violence. . . . Thus, if the hunter fails to represent the social aspect of caste, he nonetheless represents its religious aspect vividly." The religion in question is, I believe, "natural," the kind we sometimes see shimmer through the paintings of Thomas Cole, Frederick Edwin Church, Winslow Homer, or Albert Pinkham Ryder.

Spirit was never stranger to violence, of course, the violence of nature first, the sacramental violence also of the hunter or primitive warrior who breaks the taboo against killing on behalf of his tribe. Indeed, some historians of the American frontier have come to consider the notion of "sacramental violence" as crux. Thus, for instance, Richard Slotkin claims that "the myth of regeneration through violence became the structuring metaphor of the American experience." He continues, "An American hero is the lover of the spirit of the wilderness, and his acts of love and sacred affirmation are acts of violence against that spirit and her avatars."

We can plausibly surmise, then, that the historic experience of America proved singularly congenial to the spirit of quest. That experience provided an alternative to colonialism *within* the boundaries of the continental United States itself, provided a dramatic encounter between Self and Other that became, through dime novels and Hollywood movies, an international myth — the myth of the Indian, the myth of Frontier and Wild West. It is as if the "complex fate" of which Henry James spoke at the turn of our century really entailed, more than a confrontation between Europe and America, a spiritual adventure into the uncharted wilderness of both the New World and of the Old Adam, Caliban, whom Lawrence derisively invoked:

> Ca Ca Caliban
> Get a new master, be a new man.

III

This brings me to my third and central question, concerning quest as an intelligent mirror of our epoch. For in quest, I would claim, contemporary reality—personal or collective—finds a critique more stringent, certainly more felt, than many so-called radical critiques now provide.

We can commence with the solitary adventurer. What impels him or her to risk or seek? No single answer will do. Adventurers have adduced rage, boredom, loss, maladaptation, whim, curiosity, rivalry, fame, the need to experience extremity and intensify existence, the lure of things difficult and strange, the urge to confront death and master, if only for an instant, their own fate. Their motives may be ultimately, as we have seen, ontological: some profound affirmation, self-renewal, under the aspects of *both* harmony and strain, surrender and defiance. In quest or adventure, the self opens, becoming everything that it is not, opens for an instant to the light.

But quests also retreat from the light, and darkness and dread crowd their path. For every Conquistador of the Spirit, there is an Aguirre, Wrath of God; for every metaphysical Columbus, an Ahab, striking the sun, or a Kurtz, mouthing horror on all fours. Nor is the impediment to quest always demonic. Memory may cast its shadow, inescapable shadow of our past. "Once *more* [italics mine] on my adventure brave and new," cries the poet (Browning), and in that cry we hear both presage and remembrance. Yet *again*, the seeker starts. Is his quest, then, merely an invitation to rehearsal? Italo Calvino writes this about his errant compatriot:

> Marco Polo imagined answering that the more one was lost in unfamiliar quarters of distant cities, the more one understood the other cities he had crossed to arrive there; and he retraced the stages of his journeys, and he came to know the port from which

he had set sail, and the familiar places of his youth, and the surroundings of home, and a little square of Venice where he had gamboled as a child.

At this point Kublai Khan interrupted him or imagined interrupting him, or Marco Polo imagined himself interrupted, with a question such as: "You advance always with your head turned back?" or "Is what you see always behind you?" or rather, "Does your journey take place only in the past?"

Thus, in some journeys at least, the past seems to await us at the only destination we *can* reach, making every quest an elegy to its own hope.

This past, though, is not petrified in regret; it is what we come to *understand* as our past, a kind of retroactive winning through. For seekers do change when they seek more than change. No one saw this better than Eliot in the Christian transfigurations of the great *Quartets*. Hear now the voice descanting in the rigging of a windblown ship:

> "Fare forward, you who think that you are voyaging;
> You are not those who saw the harbour
> Receding, or those who will disembark.
> Here between the hither and the farther shore
> While time is withdrawn, consider the future
> And the past with an equal mind. . . .
>   O voyagers, O seamen,
> You who come to port, and you whose bodies
> Will suffer the trial and judgement of the sea,
> Or whatever event, this is your real destination."

Such solitary intuitions, however, scarcely exhaust the motives of quest. Men also venture in exclusionary groups—from the Argonauts to the Magnificent Seven—finding in male brotherhoods of risk alternatives to societies they disavow. Often, they elude their own sahib-kind, drawn to "natives," perhaps erotically, in associations that racism, or simply difference, may subtly excite. Often, they themselves "go native," repugning a life they perceive as vapid, sated, noxious, a delirium of boredom and high-tech genocide. In short, they flee the contemporary world, flee Western history, hoping to discover another time in another place. Their journeys are as much judgments on occidental reality as essays in utopia.

Yet the best among them also realize that their intrusions on a primitive "paradise" alter it; their acts of exploration change the land they explore. Contemptuous of power, they themselves become its reluctant agents. Thus organized quest leads easily to conquest; we call it imperialism, colonialism. This has prompted Salman Rushdie to quip, "Adventure and politics are best kept apart, rather like uranium and plutonium." The advice is apt though rarely practical; for nuclear politics now permeates the most isolate enterprise, spreading our disease.

Here we touch on something strange: I call it the adventurer's "wound." Frequently this is a literal, if obscure, infection, a mysterious disease like the Grail King's. Herman Melville suffers it in *Typee*, Francis Parkman in *The Oregon Trail*, Ernest Hemingway in *The Green Hills of Africa*. They all endure some debility, some "pathetic" (the word is Melville's) flaw, a failure in their pampered immune systems. It is as if, in each seeker, two organic as well as cultural orders struggle more than meet. Call them Self and Other; call them the West and all *its* Others, those people it has discovered and deformed in the name of modernization. Thus "the wound," secret agon of the blood, throbs also with the drama of colonial contamination. Is this the wound of postwar history, the revenge of the repressed, on an earth caught between enforced planetization and virulent retribalization?

Yet "the wound" is not only external, a gash in history, cicatrix of cultures. "The wound" is also in the traveler's mind, in his divided consciousness, his alienated state. It is in his ambitious gaze, a gaze without innocence, sometimes panoptic, at once wounded and wounding. Encroaching on primal societies, the explorer finds, indeed *brings*, a serpent in every "paradise" — which always, I nearly said already, has serpents of another kind. Being human, he disturbs the pleroma of existence. Being, in addition, an occidental seeker, a *writer*, he disrupts that pleroma even more. Is this what the "pathetic flaw" of the scribbling adventurer means?

Note, though, who writes, who speaks. It is not the wilderness nor its aborigines. Note who ventures and seeks. It is not the "native." In the Middle Ages, Arabs raided the earth, roamed the seas, and Ibn Battuta exceeded Marco Polo in reach. In the fourteenth century, Ottomans looked on northern Europe much as Europeans were later to look on the Americas, rich and heathen lands fit only for conquest. But it was really with European Renaissance voyagers, in "search of Christians and spice," that natives became "natives" precisely because they remained where they had been born. They were discovered; like children, they were not meant to be heard, only seen. The winsome Bushmen and gentle Tasaday may have perfected an irenic mode of life. But they have not traveled far from the Kalahari Desert or rainforests of Mindanao — nor far from the Stone Age. It took another kind of curiosity, drive, aggression, ingenuity, restlessness, to "speak" them so that we could all hear. And as Western explorers spoke them, everyone heard, everyone changed.

Protest against this "imperialist discourse" has resounded in critiques, ranging from Frantz Fanon's *The Wretched of the Earth* to Edward Said's *Orientalism*. Nor is Western humanism itself spared, which Sartre exorbitantly calls, in his introduction to Fanon, "an ideology of lies and pillage, an alibi of aggression." Fanon himself clarifies best the sinister exchanges between colonizer and colonized. If the former resorts to the vocabulary of the bestiary (speaking the native in "zoologicial terms"), the latter ends by introjecting the values of his speaker. Even the native intellectual, Fanon grieves, "throws himself greedily upon Western culture." "He will not be content to know Rabelais and Diderot, Shakespeare and Edgar Allan Poe; he will bind them to his intelligence as closely as possible." I need not stress, a quarter of a century after the publication of *Les damnés de la terre* (1961), how prophetic Fanon's vision has proven, and also how warped by its own extremity.

There is less violence in Said's view, if not less predilection. The "Orient," he argues, is a European invention, a form of cultural and political production. Moreover, "European culture gained in strength and identity by setting itself off against the Orient as a sort of surrogate and even underground self"; and it universalized the claims of its history as the only World History. Said then reminds us that Flaubert *could* represent the courtesan Kuchuk Hanem in his memoirs of Egypt; *she* had no means to represent herself. Nor, I might add, has anyone of us who lacks the power to roil history. But was it power alone, the power bequeathed to him by Napoleon, Champollion, and Jean-Baptiste-Joseph Fourier, that permitted Flaubert to "speak" Kuchuk Hanem? In 1846, Flaubert made this entry in another journal that Said does not quote:

> Amongst those who go to sea there are the navigators who discover new worlds, adding continents to the earth and stars to the heavens: they are the masters, the great, the eternally splendid. . . . I am the obscure and patient pearl-fisherman who dives into the deepest waters and comes up with empty hands and a blue face. Some fatal attraction draws me down into the abysses of thought, down to those innermost recesses which never cease to fascinate the strong.

Here, I suggest, is the trace of an inner stance, of some wilful personal choice to which Flaubert's privileged discourse owes more than we admit.

The point requires that I return to it by another way. No doubt, the West has constituted, often controlled, its Other by the institutions of Orientalism. But such institutions are not unique to the West. Said ignores a tradition of Counter-Orientalism, a popular "Occidentalism" so to speak, rather contemptuous of "infidel and uncircumcised" Europeans. Coincidentally, another scholar, also named Said, Quadi of the Moslem City of Toledo, wrote in 1068 about northern European barbarians, "more like beasts than men," who lack any "keenness of understanding and clarity of intelligence, and are overcome by ignorance and apathy." Conceivably, Edward Said ignores this tradition of reverse discrimination because it has proven, until quite recently, impotent, unable to trans-late, carry itself over, in an effective ideological discourse of its own.

But why? Why did the "infidel" and "barbarous" West possess that historical power? Why was it able, since the Age of Exploration, to impose its will on so many others? What induced those explorations in the first place, the urge for adventure and quest? Why did the Occident develop the discipline of Orientalism while the Orient lacked, until the mid-nineteenth century, any sustained scholarship about the Occident, any grammar or lexicon of a European language? To answer simply by invoking science, technology, or sea power is to beg one renitent question with another.

Such questions may seem indelicate — or perhaps merely delicate. Certainly, I have no confident answers to offer, only meditated guesses. Let us suppose that a set of circumstances arose in Europe, by accident and design, by everything that still defies historical explanation. Among these circumstances I want to count diverse factors: geography, mercantilism, secularization, an idea of progress, scientific detachment, individual rights, some political freedoms, a certain fluidity in class structures. I want to count also personal qualities: will, consequence, self-reliance, a transgressive (or innovative) urge, that inner stance Flaubert revealed a moment ago. Could these factors begin to explain the ascendancy of the West in the last three centuries?

But my task, finally, is not to second-guess the inequities of history, only to comprehend the motives of its seekers. Certainly the latter exhibit an independent attitude. Emerson put it more forcibly:

> A man should learn to detect and watch that gleam of light which flashes across his mind from within, more than the lustre of the firmament of bards and sages. . . . I shun father and mother and wife and brother when my genius calls me. I would write on the lintels of the door-post, *Whim*. I hope it is somewhat better than whim at last, but we cannot spend the day in explanation. Expect me not to show cause why I seek.

Something of that Emersonian Whim is at the bottom of all quest, I think. But something else, too, that Emerson neglects: a Wound. For the adventurer/seeker is a Westerner, scion of the rich of the earth, drawn to the wretched by a vision they may find sentimental or absurd. Though he may be neither soldier nor colonizer, domination no less than quest is the motive of his history and its deep wound. But this is also the wound from which history, planetized history, flows, sometimes suppurates. His flight from modernity cannot avail, not his search for lost innocence, nor his nostalgia for otherness. His yearnings for desolations of sand and snow, in Arabia or Antarctica, lead him to an abandoned Coke bottle that rules space even more than Stevens's jar ever ruled the hills of Tennessee. Yet his will, malaise, disequilibrium, some radical whim or wound or asymmetry in his being, has made the world we know.

IV

All I have said is prelusive to exemplary texts of contemporary quest. Such texts, fiction and nonfiction, could be ascribed to Michael Arlen, John Barth, Saul Bellow, Paul Bowles, Eleanor Clark, James Dickey, Joan Didion, Edward Hoagland, Norman Mailer, Peter Matthiessen, John McPhee, Robert Stone, Paul Theroux, Paul Zweig. But now I have space to cite only a few instances of the genre, wherein autobiography, quest, and adventure so freely mingle in examples of selves, of American selves, at risk.

Bellow had never traveled in Africa when he wrote *Henderson the Rain King* (1959), possibly his best novel, no more than Defoe had visited the Americas when he wrote *Robinson Crusoe*. Bellow's book, we know, is a romance of ideas, a quest for reality, full of ordeals, meditations, initiations, and rituals in the midst of a mythic Africa. Its hero, Henderson, who speaks in the first person, is big, rich, and puissant, though past middle age, with a face "like an unfinished church," a truly exceptional "amalgam of vehement forces."

But Henderson's own heroes are not simply adventurers. They are men of universal service, like Albert Schweitzer and Wilfred Grenfell; they seek to *give*. For Henderson has grown weary of the voice within him that always clamors: "I want, I want, I want"; he wants now to conjugate it: "I want, you want, she wants." In the end, we know, he goes back to study medicine at the age of fifty-five. Before that, though, he must find his truth, which always comes to him in blows; he must overcome his guilt, fear of death, and ravening desires.

The search takes him, at *whim*, to the Dark Continent. This is not only an exotic and distant place; not only the land we exploit or colonize; but also the space where we meet our darker self or double. There Henderson's bungling adventures lead him finally to a kind of terrible clarity, terrible and tranquil at the same time. Like Daniel, he enters a lioness' den, and lives deeply in her mysterious presence; an avoider all his life, he tries to become like her, "unavoidable." He enters Being, which alone enables Love, and learns to move with the rhythms of things — no more *grun-tu-molani*, as huge Queen Willatale enjoins him, no "more rage for life." Thus he comes at last to fulfill a proverb he once read in his father's library, which has haunted him throughout his existence, "The forgiveness of sins is perpetual and righteousness first is not required."

Quest, here, requires temporary exile from civilization, with all its clutter and distractions. Quest also compels Henderson to desert Lily, his second wife, and the only person with whom he has a vital, struggling relation. Hence the recurrent prophecy from the Book of Daniel, "They shall drive you from among men, and thy dwelling shall be with the beasts of the field." But this archetypal movement into the wilderness must complete itself in a return. Having learned self-acceptance, having slain the mythic monsters within him and overcome his own death, death frozen like the huge eye of an octopus, the hero goes back to society. Thus Bellow encompasses both "Africa" and "America," nature and civilization, though he leaves us no doubt which in the end is wiser — the colonized, so to speak, becomes moral colonizer. Thus, too, he shows that the garrulous, querulous, greedy "I" can learn to calm itself. Here is the climactic passage in the lioness' den:

> The odor was blinding, for here, near the door where the air was trapped, it stank radiantly. From this darkness came the face of the lioness, wrinkling, with her whiskers like the thinnest spindles scratched with a diamond on the surface of a glass. She allowed the king to fondle her, but passed by him to examine me, coming round with those clear circles of inhuman wrath, convex, brown, and pure, rings of black light within them. Between her mouth and nostrils a line divided her lip, like the waist of the hourglass, expanding into the muzzle. She sniffed my feet, working her way to the crotch once more and causing my parts to hide in my belly as best they could. She next put her head into my armpit and purred with such tremendous vibration it made my head buzz like a kettle.
>
> Dahfu whispered, "She likes you. Oh, I am glad. I am enthusiastic. I am so proud of both of you. Are you afraid?"

Here Henderson's wound—not literal though deep enough—begins to heal. At least, so Henderson tells us in a fiction no less open or whimsical than life.

Bellow's Africa, of course, is not Conrad's, not Fanon's. It rather shares the eerie, spiritual space of Cooper's prairie, Poe's Antarctica, Melville's Pacific, even if politics can be read into any space. Nor are Henderson's African tutors—Prince Itelo, Queen Willatale, King Dahfu—but ideal figures of ideological instruction. Nor, again, is Henderson's guide, Romilayu, but a device for the seeker's own gargantuan, sometimes maudlin, and always errant needs. Still, Bellow manages to bring history and mystery to a romance wherein cultures collide in the clang of passions, tang of words, more than in any anthropological fact.

Norman Mailer's *Why Are We in Vietnam?* (1967) is even more ambiguous as a fiction. Despite the title, the novel concerns Vietnam only tangentially. Ostensibly, the book relates a rousing hunt for grizzly in the Brooks Range of Alaska. Actually, it renders the initiation of a sixteen-year-old Texan, called D.J., into the violence within him and around him, a quest for manhood and identity which will permit him to confront the war in Vietnam two years later.

D.J. is, of course, in the tradition of questing, adolescent heroes—Huck Finn (Twain), Henry Fleming (Crane), Nick Adams (Hemingway), Ike McCaslin (Faulkner), Holden Caulfield (Salinger)—whose initiation into reality also provides a critique of American society. Thus, in the remote wilderness of Alaska, under the Aurora Borealis, D.J. learns something about the betrayals of his father, the corruptions of America, the merciless laws of nature, the love and fear he harbors toward his friend, Tex—learns, above all, something about the intractable mystery of existence. Love, Power, Knowledge, Magic, Nature, and Death are all intimately bound; when their vital relations decay, we enter the universe of waste: cancer, excrement, money, Vietnam.

Once again, the hero learns from a beast. Here is the message in the grizzly's dying eyes:

> At twenty feet away, D.J.'s little cool began to evaporate. Yeah, that beast was huge and then huge again, and he was still alive—his eyes looked right at D.J.'s like wise old gorilla eyes, and then they turned gold brown and red like the sky seen through a ruby crystal ball, eyes were transparent, and D.J. looked . . . and something in that grizzer's eyes locked into his, a message, fellow, an intelligence of something very fine and very far away, just about as intelligent and wicked and merry as any sharp light D.J. had ever seen in any Texan's eyes any time (or overseas around the world) those eyes

were telling him something, singeing him, branding some part of D.J.'s future, and then the reflection of a shattering message from the shattered internal organs of that bear came twisting through his eyes in a gale of pain, and the head went up, and the bear now too weak to stand up, the jaws worked the pain.

As in Bellow's novel, so in Mailer's, social criticism blends easily into the metaphysics of quest. Mailer's satire of America — this "sweet beauteous land" which has allowed plastic to enter its soul (materialism) and bureaucratic violence to shape its policy (Vietnam) — can be savage as well as obscene. No one, nothing, is spared in the "United Greedies of America," as its messages collect nightly in the EMF of the North Pole, and an "hour before sunrise" begins "to smog the predawning air with their psychic glug, glut and exudations, not to mention all the funeral parlors cooling out in the premature morn. . . ." In the end, though, Mailer slyly introduces a radical uncertainty into his account. We never really know who tells the story: D.J., the white, athletic son of Dallas millionaires, or some "mad genius spade" up in Harlem, a crippled disk jockey? Who speaks for America? Mailer will not say, though clearly his prose sings, no less a critique of America than a paean to it. Or is the whole book, this breezy, hip, sarcastic, poetic "I," the voice of some demiurge, more beast than man, yet immaterial enough to speak its warning to the whole world, not just about Vietnam, through the Aurora Borealis?

In contrast to Bellow's and Mailer's fictions, James Dickey's *Deliverance* (1970) seems less a quest than a brutal tale of survival. The reader may wonder: Deliverance from what? From moral complacencies, social pieties, perhaps from civilization itself? The clues are scattered, and in one place they become nearly explicit. Making love to his wife on the morning of his fateful adventure, the narrator, Ed Gentry, imagines — he is on the whole steady, unimaginative — the golden eye of a girl, a studio model: "The gold eye shone, not with the practicality of sex, so necessary to its survival, but the promise of it that promised other things, another life, deliverance." Another life, deliverance: there lies the book's knot which links its two heroes, Ed Gentry and Lewis Medlock, doubles.

Ed — all are called by their first names — is practical and forthright, given to task at hand, as Lewis is visionary. Lewis seeks immortality and learns finally to settle for death. Meantime he trains himself implacably, trains his instincts, will, and powerful body, to survive an atomic holocaust in the Georgia woods. He insists on turning the canoe trip of four urban businessmen into a moral, a life principle, a way, a provocation to everything Western civilization has achieved in three thousand years.

He wants to recover something absolutely essential, and in doing so perform some superhuman feat that beggars eternity. But Lewis breaks his leg early on the trip — again that wound — and it is Ed who pulls the survivors through, after two murders and one death by drowning.

The scene is perfectly set for the encounter between nature and civilization, instinct and law, *within* the West itself. An entire region of the north Georgia wilderness is about to drown, turned into a serviceable lake. The Cahulawassee River, with its horrendously beautiful whitewater rapids, must vanish. Ageless cemeteries of hillbillies must be moved to higher ground. Marinas and real estate developments will appear on the dammed lake. On the eve of their departure, the four white, married, middle-class men pore over a colored map of the region, intuiting the secret harmonies of the land, thinking that, henceforth, a fragment of the American wilderness will survive only in archives and the failing memories of old woodsmen.

Excepting Lewis, though, these businessmen are unfit to venture; they have learned to meet existence mainly on legal, domestic, or social terms. Still, they sense obscurely an alternative to their humdrum lives. "Up yonder," as Lewis tells them, life *demands* to be taken on other terms. This they discover in scene after harrowing scene, in encounters with the stupendous force of nature (the rapids) and malevolence of man (hillbilly outlaws). Yet, too, they experience a strange happiness at the heart of violence. Three of them survive, irrevocably altered.

Dickey's novel is a masterpiece in the poetry of action and menace. Relentlessly, it renders, in a prose at once tight, elusive, and earthy, the atavism and terror of two autumn days in the Georgia woods. The book spares us no detail in the struggle of life for itself. But the book also reveals instants of subtle intimacy, moments of pure being. Having climbed, with bare hands, the sheer face of a gorge to kill a man at daybreak, Ed suddenly exclaims:

> What a view. *What* a view. But I had my eyes closed. The river was running in my mind, and I raised my lids and saw exactly what had been the image of my thought. For a second I did not know what I was seeing and what I was imagining; there was such an utter sameness that it didn't matter; both were the river. It spread there eternally, the moon so huge on it that it hurt the eyes, and the mind, too, flinched like an eye. What? I said. Where? There was nowhere but here. Who, though? Unknown. Where can I start? . . . What a view I said again. The river was blank and mindless with beauty. It was the most glorious thing I had ever seen. But it was not seeing, really. For once it was not just seeing. It was

beholding. I *beheld* the river in its icy pit of brightness, in its far-below sound and indifference, in its large coil and tiny points and flashes of the moon, in its long sinuous form, in its uncomprehending consequence. What was there?

Perhaps this is the selflessness of every mountaineer, every adventurer, at his moment of truth, healing all wounds.

Dickey prefixes an epigraph from George Bataille, which proposes a "principle of insufficiency" at the base of human existence. The radical lack may underlie all life *as perceived by human beings*. Something is always buried, hidden, lost to us: murdered bodies lying under forest leaves, the forest itself flooded beneath a lake, hillbillies invisible, colonized within their own state, some part of our own nature, concealed and irreclaimable. Ed and Lewis — Ed *becomes* Lewis — manage to discover this perilous part of existence, and manage through great pain to reclaim it. But they must also face the ordinary world again, which Ed sees, at the end, in the image of a policeman: "When we reached town he [the policeman] went into a cafe and made a couple of calls. It frightened me some to watch him talk through the tripled glass — windshield, plate glass, and phone booth — for it made me feel caught in the whole vast, inexorable web of modern communication." The feeling passes, for Ed possesses the river permanently: "Now it ran nowhere but in my head, but there it ran as though immortally." So ends his quest.

The transition from fiction to nonfiction seems almost imperceptible: the next two works share so many assumptions with the first three. Perhaps the authorial voice in the novels is less meddlesome; perhaps their interest in narrative, character, dialogue is more vivid or intense. Perhaps their imaginative freedom, a gaiety of reality, is more consciously felt. But these are matters of degree, conveyed in nuance more than informal definition. In all, quest takes the language of the self to task and witness, and words walk in the shadow of death.

John McPhee's *Coming Into the Country* (1978) takes us to Alaska again, this time under the aspect of fact. As a reporter, an inspired essayist really, McPhee speaks in his own voice and gives us a luxuriance of precise detail, naming every flower, shrub, tree, bird, and beast in "the last American frontier." Yet the book often reads like a fable or romance because its characters are haunted by a dream of freedom, a stubborn intuition of possibility.

The Alaskan settlers — not the ones who go to make big bucks on the oil pipeline or a killing in real estate — all want space, independence, a chance to prove their worth. They seek a meaning in life, to which money, power, possessions, and celebrity are irrelevant. They want to live off the land, under the most exigent conditions, survive like Indian or Eskimo. They want to learn something about the final truths which civilization masks or distorts.

Their character, then, is solitary, anarchic, antiauthoritarian: no State or Federal interference, please! They are not socialists, not feminists, not joiners of any kind. But they obey the ecological ethic, without sentimentality or abstraction, like Cooper's Leatherstocking. Ecology? It is "something eating something all the time out there," the wife of a settler says — but eating out of need, without malice or waste. The voices of these uncommon men and women deserve to be heard in their own timbre:

> I want to change myself thoroughly "from a professional into a bum" — to learn to trap, to handle dogs and sleds, to net fish. . . . It isn't easy to lower your income and raise your independence. . . . I've had to work twice as hard as most people.

> I wanted to get away from paying taxes to support something I didn't believe in, to get away from big business, to get away from a place where you can't be sure of anything you hear or anything you read.

> The czars exiled misfits to Siberia. The Soviets do that, too. . . . Alaskans are inheritors of determinative genes that took people out of Europe to the New World. [We're] doers. [We] don't destroy, we build.

> The bush is so far beyond what anybody has been taught. The religious power is here beyond all training. There are forces here that a lot of people don't know exist.

> Life and death are not a duality. They're just simply here — life, death — in the all-pervading mesh that holds things together.

Does it all seem too literary? These pioneers, many of them college graduates, are articulate. McPhee himself joins them, drawn by their fierce vision. He knows that in their demesne, the grizzly stands as a symbol of freedom, the totem of all natural men who accept the rules of the wilderness, survival, death. (Like Faulkner's Ike McCaslin or Mailer's D.J., McPhee doesn't carry a gun to see the grizzly.) But McPhee is also sufficiently clear-eyed to perceive their ineluctable contradictions. For the Alaskans end by reproducing the same conflicts they presume to leave behind them. They bring with them alcoholism, envy, wife-stealing, even murder. And they dramatize the acute political dilemmas of our world in the four-way struggles between Federal Government, the State of Alaska, Corporate Enterprise, and the Individual, struggles that bush planes and snowmobiles carry to them at the edge of the Arctic.

In short, *Coming Into the Country* conveys tensions within both the Individual and American society—Freedom vs. Equality, Progress vs. Conservation, Libertarianism vs. Liberalism, State vs. Federal rights— tensions that even the immense Alaskan wilderness cannot resolve, dissolve. But the book also captures another persistent motive of the American Dream, the spirit of quest, an anarchic, quasi-religious impulse, still vibrant, still unappeased, in the space of that Dream.

The space of Peter Matthiessen's quest, in *The Snow Leopard* (1978), is Nepal's Inner Dolpo, specifically the Crystal Monastery at Shey Gompa, which you can find on a map of the region. There, Matthiessen hopes to track the rare, nearly invisible, snow leopard. The animal becomes a symbol of spiritual knowledge or attainment, though Matthiessen never manages to see it. His Zen teacher had warned him, before starting, in New York, "Do not expect too much": that is, "You may not be ready yet to see the leopard." But in Zen, the admonition could also be taken to mean: to see or not see the leopard is the same, *satori* simply comes.

Matthiessen begins his journey in a troubled state. His young, beautiful wife, Deborah, from whom he is about to be divorced, suddenly dies of cancer, leaving him a young son. The widower resolves to undergo the perilous journey nonetheless, as if to cleanse himself, come to terms with his guilt or pain, his wound. He gives us, in diary form, the record of his two-month mountain trek to the holy Crystal Monastery in the company of a professional biologist, George Schaller—who *does* see the leopard—as well as various Himalayan tribesmen and Sherpa guides.

The journey proceeds in several symbolic dimensions: horizontal (from Kathmandu to the Crystal Mountain), vertical (from valleys through mountain passes to unassailable peaks), temporal (present to past and back), cultural (West to East), generic (alternating between the forms of autobiography and didactic essay), and spiritual, a "journey of the heart," toward enlightenment. The diary itself appears as a continuous dialogue of heterocosms, straining for peace between the One and the Many in all their manifestations.

This symbolic journey, however, is not without afflictions. It confronts Matthiessen with the obdurate vanity of the self, its voracity, its tenacious fear of death. The journey also puts him in constant interactions with "natives," including porters, villagers, monks, lamas, Sherpas, who form a tacit hierarchic system—lamas and Sherpas at the top, precisely because they are the most loyal, brave, cheerful, and selfless. In them, he finds a tacit critique of his own society, its "corrosive money rot," its "retreat from wonder," its "proliferations without joy." Thus, indirectly, Matthiessen comments on race, sex, drugs, violence, illusion in America, with particular reference to the culture of the sixties, seen now from the austere, wholly essential perspective of the Himalayas. And he reveals the inexpugnable colonialism (Western) and caste prejudice (Asian) all around him.

How spiritually successful, finally, is this quest which subsumes the spirit of so many other quests? True to its moment, it seems ruled by ambiguities. Matthiessen relapses frequently into black moods; when he reaches the remote Crystal Monastery, he finds it empty; he never glimpses the snow leopard; he even begins to suspect that the willed act of searching may preclude the finding; and he worries that entrusting his experiences to the written word may falsify them irrevocably. Finally, in Patan, after the journey's end, he awaits Tukten—his favorite rogue or trickster porter—at a Buddhist monastery in vain. Sometimes, even, Matthiessen wonders if he has not been spared "the desolation of success." On the last day, he sees his face in the mirror: "In the gaunt, brown face in the mirror—unseen since last September—the blue eyes in a monkish skull seem eerily clear, but this is the face of a man I do not know."

That stranger's face, of course, is the face behind every human face, a face in and out of time. For even in the high, sublunary landscape of the Dolpo, where lungs gasp with each breath and life itself seems but a thin stain on eternity, history obtrudes. The wounded, whimsical, Western seeker finds himself always *in* the world, *between* two worlds. All around him, the evidence of poverty is excruciating, and dogs must eat human excrement. As Matthiessen puts it, "Confronted with the pain of Asia, one cannot look and cannot turn away." This may be the penultimate word on the interface between certain cultures, an interface that only the transfigured Bodhisattva can face as he willingly reenters the wheels of incarnation. As for the rest of us, the ultimate word may be intermittment, inconclusive quest, pain.

V

Quests, indeed, have no conclusion—that's the start of mine. They are extreme enactments of our fate in the universe.

Everything is gathered in them, from personal whim or wound to geopolitics, from the mythic experience of America to the factitiousness of Western societies, from narrative genre to the nature of ultimate reality. As a symbolic option in the contemporary world, quests recover something essential in human life, sometimes in encounters with animals (lion, grizzly, leopard), often in encounters between cultures, almost always in encounters with nature. However ravaging or equivocal, quests somehow pluck the nerve of existence; they dispel the amnesia and anesthesia, the complacent nihilism, of our cosseted lives. And they do so nowhere more vividly than in contemporary American and British letters.

More probably, they simply yield an indefectible perception of an individual alone, edging cultures, hedging histories, acting riskily on a vision of himself, or herself, and the world, a perception that, from our best selves, speaks to all.

CONTEMPORARY FICTION AND POPULAR CULTURE

CONSTANCE PIERCE

One of the most favored conventions of current fiction is reference to popular culture, especially to the entertainment media. Here are excerpts from the openings to several recent stories, randomly gathered:

> She loves movies, she loves Clint Eastwood, now what if *he* came in the Outlet Mall right now and walked over to her and said Excuse me ma'am, I need a king-size bedspread in a Western decor?
> (Lee Smith, "The Interpretation of Dreams")

> . . . my eye was on our waiter, a boy who looked like Timothy Hutton.
> (Merrill Joan Gerber, "Hairdos")

> They met after a rock concert.
> (Mary Hood, "Hindsight")

> The preacher emcee, trailing the long cord of his microphone, moves with slow-motion bounces, as though trying to get the feel of the astronaut's walk on the moon. The preacher has on a pink plaid jacket, and because the TV color isn't tuned properly, his face is the same bright shade.
> (Bobbie Ann Mason, "The Climber")

Often the references are to the technology involved:

> On way home bought Ramona fur wrap, Olga bracelet, Lorenzo Walkman.
> (Irvin Faust, "Year of the Hot Jock")

> On the VCR James Bond was in bed with a girl with auburn hair.
> (Rachel Pastan, "The Road to New Orleans")

Perhaps more often, the writer takes a backward look, alluding to the popular culture of another era:

> Every Southern town had one, and ours was no exception. One year, my sister and I had an after-school routine that included watching the Mouseketeers on TV.
> (Greg Johnson, "Crazy Ladies")

> It's steamy hot and the radio's loud. Fifties stuff: shoop, shoop, dee doo, waa-oo, my babee left me.
> (Bob Shacochis, "Hot Day on the Gold Coast")

Either way, the effect is contemporary—up-to-the minute and state-of-the-art, or up-to-the minute in evoking the nostalgia said to be our current affliction.

That these are openings tells us that in some way the popular culture trope is strategic. Contemporary readers are a weary lot, fatigued with high art and the timeless aims of so much modernism, suspicious that many writers are "out of it"—that is to say, out of the mass trends that infuse most of American life. Immediately recognizable pop references provide a way for writers to declare contemporaneity, to announce that they are not-modern—though modernists from Scott Fitzgerald to the Dadaists were fascinated by the popular culture of their own time. It is the specific, time-bound reference that promises to deliver on at least part of Fitzgerald's famous pronouncement, "An author ought to write for the youth of his own generation, the critics of the next, and the schoolmasters of ever afterward." The youth of America might well see itself exhorted to read a story that opens with references to VCRs and Walkmans and pop-chart songs, or even the "fifties stuff" they know so well from "Happy Days" and golden-oldies broadcasts all across the land. But so will older readers eager to know about the milieu inhabited by their children, or eager for a glimpse or strain from those happy or unhappy days of their receded youth, with its rituals of radio and mouseketeer watching, old-style rock 'n' roll, the movies, and ads and brand names of defunct products. Ads and brand names, because popular culture seems to be everything the mass of Americans partakes of with enthusiasm, from the TV news, to shopping malls and T-shirts, to commentary on popular culture. Writers who "open" with these allusions promise, up-front, to tell us something about the implications of this culture in our emotional and notional lives—or in our national life.[1] At the least, they promise to animate the moment of reading with the vitality and spirit of the beloved or arresting bit of pop consumption.

As for the critics of the next generation, the phenomenon as a whole should provide enough to remark on; the schoolmasters of "ever afterward" should be kept busy with explanatory footnotes, unless by then everyone is a pop historian. Though this kind of reference to the contemporary cannot hope to compel in the same immediate way when it becomes a reference to history, our fascination with, and access to, the whole history of electronic entertainments would seem self-perpetuating, and so what looks like a trend may well turn out to be a staple. In fact, a look backward to John Dos Passos's *USA*, or Robert Coates's *The Eater of Darkness*, or Fitzgerald's detailing of the "Jazz Age," or any number of early-century works reveals a continuity, a hint that what we're experiencing is less a trend than a tradition.

But contemporary writers have good uses for pop culture besides currency in the marketplace of the new. A quick reference can locate the story in time, tell something immediately significant about a character, and enliven the surface of the narrative. It can also be a necessary hoodwinking to draw a reluctant reader into a time and subject that might ordinarily be resisted. Here is Alice Munro's opening to "The Moon in the Orange Street Skating Rink," which will be a story of old people, much of it set in the not-too-recent past:

> Sam got a surprise, walking into Callie's variety store. He had expected a clutter of groceries, cheap bits and pieces, a stale smell, maybe faded tinsel ropes, old overlooked Christmas decorations. Instead, he found a place mostly taken up with video games. Hand-lettered signs in red and blue crayon warned against alcohol, fighting, loitering, and swearing. The store was full of jittery electronic noise and flashing light and menacing, modern-day, oddly shaved and painted children. But behind the counter was Callie, quite painted up herself, under a pinkish-blond wig. She was reading a paperback. . . . *My Love Where the High Winds Blow*, by Veronica Gray.

And in our new nostalgia for the slightly old, does anything fetch us into Joan Chase's recondite *During the Reign of the Queen of Persia* more than the reference in the first sentence to "barns advertising Mail Pouch in frayed and faded postings?" This is an advertisement itself advertised all across the nation by a Charles Kuralt "On the Road" segment, a sign for which the reading public has already been prepared. It is therefore capable, in one deft stroke, of enveloping a reader in a reassuring atmospheric. (That is not to say that there aren't barns with Mail Pouch signs all across Ohio, as Chase describes, even now.)

These would all seem to be legitimate strategies, if they are always strategies, given the pop reality of contemporary life and what writers are up against in their bid for readers — as is the current practice of making epigraphs from rock lyrics instead of from older literary texts, the Bible, or Greek and Latin writings. There is also the ultimate opening: a title such as *Bobby's Girl, A Piece of My Heart, Track of My Tears* (continuing in the tradition of Faulkner's *That Evening Sun*, etc.). These parallel recent movie titles — *Blue Velvet, Stand By Me, Baby, It's You* — and more problematically, the ineluctable use of oldie-but-goody come ons in TV ads.

The question of appropriation is bound to come up when we consider how writers use popular culture, even when we're willing to believe that most writers are working in good faith. The low grumbling about contemporary fiction in book reviews and the mass-distributed magazines still interested in fiction frequently takes a quick swipe at the pop convention. And it's true that such references allow writers, so marginal in America anyway, to borrow some of the vitality of the mass-disseminated entertainments with which they can never quite hope to compete. Readers are most dissatisfied with this move, though, when it seems vampirish — a cool draining off of peasant blood to replenish a languishing aristocrat, if you will. In other words, when the writer has no use for pop references but to present himself as "pop" or "authentic" and nonliterary — that is, when they seem especially calculated to hook a ready sensibility, as sexual and violent passages rendered in unnecessary detail once did, and no doubt can still do. When the references seem to employ no principle of selection that serves the story as a story, the reader might rightly feel manipulated — but even so, being manipulated this way can be fun. For that matter, who doesn't love the raisins dancing to "I Heard It Through the Grapevine" on the TV raisin ad? Fiction brimming with well-detailed popular culture titillates in a way that many readers do not object to in the least, even when they're aware of the strategic quality of the references.

As for the readers who do mind, who expect something more from fiction than a mere replication of the signs and sounds that already batter our minds and senses every day of the year, inescapably, the gratuitous (and maybe the ungratuitous) references to popular culture seem to be an irritating tic.

But if popular culture is inescapable, wouldn't all fiction interested in the culture as we experience it or in creating realistic settings and characters be obliged to use such references? Wouldn't a fictional world devoid of popular signs and entertainments seem, by now, preternaturally unreal?

There's something to this, but it's also a well-known point within the theory of rhetoric that references, either iconographic or linguistically set, as in titles or lyrics, will take on metaphoric weight, perhaps out of proportion to what the writer or artist has in mind. Since metaphor is more or less a habit of mind by now, these references perhaps seem automatically unreal, metaphoric. This is all very complicated. Can there even be such a thing as "mere replication" of the outward signs of our culture when details shift so readily to metaphor? Won't even the pop-culture reference used in utter bad faith quickly become an emblematic of the story's truth, a "message"? There is something titillating in the metaphor itself, something that suggests but doesn't quite take responsibility for what it suggest—something that vaguely (or even pointedly) "shows," or "half-tells." It's likely that the writer's penchant for suggestiveness, as much as anything else, is what disgruntles many readers, or at least the ones who want to *know* and despair of the writer's ever quite telling. That the writer has held out such a tantalizing bit of bait as the media culture or "our times," or even our old lives as rock 'n' rollers—and not delivered: this might have a particular power to disgruntle.

Not that there aren't plenty of writers who do deliver, including most of those I've already cited, but in different ways and amounts. When Jayne Anne Phillips opens "Home" with the mother referring to network anchormen familiarly by their first names, it says worlds about the woman's insularity, and it locates a revealing habit shared by many Americans. As we watch the daughter try to find an easy way to visit in her mother's household before going back out into a less-contained world, it is just this set of references that underscores how many of us have internalized a version of "the outside world" by a wholehearted acceptance of its media emissaries. "Walter" on the lips of the mother (aging, single-minded, divorced, a recent mastectomy a figurative reinforcing all the ways she is "cut off") makes poignant and informative, in one quick move, a contemporary condition. It also updates a traditional literary fascination with exile and alienation, wherein the very agents who convince us we are in-the-know and therefore in the world are known to be infinitely distant from us, our "relations" only a one-way closed-circuit effect.

By the same token, Shacochis's "shoop shoop, dee doo, waa—" economically defines the space the reader is to settle into to read "Hot Day on the Gold Coast," and it gives crucial information about its narrator, who has "forgotten the words." Another story in the same collection of stories set in the Caribbean gains affectiveness and informative context from an epigraph taken from a Bob Marley song. In fact, most all of the writers mentioned so far select their bits of pop culture for interest and for their figurative potential in the story being told, for their "telling" aspect.

The fiction that shows *and* tells something informative (not merely suggestive or vaguely damning) about the ways that our experience — right here, right now — is derived from and co-opted by popular culture can be fascinating reading. This is to say, by now, fiction about experience co-opted by the culture of commerce, with few of the early-century's fine discriminations between culture and commerce. The best fiction dealing with the subject offers the public dimension and the public domination of what passes for private experience — and this fiction puts the lie to another bit of grumbling about contemporary writing, that it is insular and concerned with private life in a very narrow way.

Bobbie Ann Mason's work is worth discussing at some length. In dealing with the "junk mind" of the young protagonist in *In Country*, it is almost as if this writer has brought a Stephen King setting inside a head — littered with Burger King wrappers, flashing with the evening news, raging with fads and pop lyrics, its most serious decisions shaped by sitcom reruns and the top stories of the hour. It is, excruciatingly, a real setting too, Main Street USA (the King version in its focus and selection is only the clearer comparison). How like ours is this teenager's mental terrain. Whatever else we have in our heads, we've also a vast dumping ground where rinds and shards of popular culture accrue in an ever-growing heap. That reviewers of *In Country* condescend to this character, and to Mason for having created her, is truly astounding.

These bits of input from popular culture from the Mason character's sense of her self, the reality that circumscribes and determines her modes of operation in everything from decorating her body to staging and acting out a dark night of history, in a Vietnamese jungle popularly imagined.

In the stories in *Shiloh*, Mason works a consistent metaphor: the layering-over of Appalachian culture (our national "authentic" culture, but surely something else for natives of the region) by popular-commercial culture, transforming a people as developers transform the landscape. In these painful stories with their bits of comic relief, none of the characters can get near what "they" might want; they respond instead to the messages , electronic and otherwise, from the culture at large and they seek to satisfy inchoate desires in very meticulous, but probably unrelated ways. Norma Jean Moffitt in the title story wants "something" (mobility? a divorce? relief from her infantalizing, scourging mother? absolution for the baby that died silently while she watched a drive-in movie?), but what she does to move toward this something is to work out, join the fitness craze.

It is language, the speech of a "region" that stretches coast to coast and is more class-specific than geographically determined, which doesn't get much changed or co-opted in Mason's fiction. Her dialogue, in perfect pitch, persists as a speech of the people, something that our pop culture of fads, products, make-work, dope, TV, rock music and all the other phenomena touched on in "Shiloh" cannot quite "impact."

Mason's work, to use a current buzz word, resonates with the implications of popular artifacts and entertainments, constructing not so much a "case" against mass culture as a picture of its interconnections and pervasive power, and the limits of that power too. She is really quite precise about who is doing what to whom and how, and she does it by references that strike each other glancing blows, producing small sparks of illumination. Another contemporary writer who achieves something like this using the same kinds of references is Brett Easton Ellis, but how differently he proceeds!

The biggest sound-and-light show to come down the pike lately is Ellis's *Less Than Zero*, almost as painful on our eyes and ears as it is numbing on the narrator's. The novel is a kind of rewriting or updating of Fitzgerald's *Gatsby*, its East and West conflated by the pop culture they share, its eyes of T. J. Eckleburg the red and blue lenses of Elvis Costello's glasses, reposing against his white, white skin. Ellis is a chronicler of the Rock Age, and his novel has—literally—on almost every page, a reference to a record or celebrity or MTV video or *People* or a billboard or T-shirt sign; this amassed detail tells how very much more full our lives have come to be with pop culture since Fitzgerald chronicled his Age with a few well-placed billboards and popular songs of the time.

This enormous presence of pop detail in Ellis's otherwise spare novel (spare in its prose, its characters and events) overwhelms everything else to become the main subject matter and central metaphor, and eventually the thing that the novel indicts—for Ellis's novel implies, tonally and structurally, that along with bad parents and the flight of the old values, rock music and celebrity culture are to blame for the chilled-out narrator Clay's clay-feet and for the general grimness of the hyper-lit-up landscape he describes and its interior correlative. Ellis chooses again and again the songs ("Teenage Enema Nurses in Bondage," "Sex and Dying in High Society," etc.) that, in their titles alone, will speak a certain species of degeneration, of narrative event ("New Kid in Town," "Somebody Got Murdered"), of character type ("L.A. Woman") and character motivation (from "New Kid" to "I Wanna Be Worlds Away"). When the distracted, business-obsessed father gets together with his son, Ellis portrays the man's inadequacy by having him play "a Bob Seger tape as if this were some sort of . . . communication." Clay's lost innocence comes to him in a quick memory of "Itsy Bitsy Spider" and "Little White Duck"—"songs I forgot existed"—while the grandparents' generation, idealized by Clay, is compromised by its taste for Frank Sinatra and its unremitting and dangerous innocence ("Sunny Side of the Street" is the grandmother's special song). These fight for impact among references to other entertainments—"Alien," "Another World," "Donkey Kong"—whose names speak as a truncated, pointed chorus, interpreting all the way just how uncannily our popular culture can speak the truth of things. This is underlain with the unvoiced but blaring message of the novel, that pop culture has created, and been created by, a monster of deadening commerce.

Business and its many connections, or "gonnegtions," as Meyer Wolfsheim would have said, was Fitzgerald's theme, and Ellis dutifully sees it through here, even beyond the replicated allusions to the products of commercial culture connecting with the bodies of zombie rich kids in a Village of the Damned, every parent a West Egger. Beyond the T-shirts and the Walkman "phones" and all the ways pop consumerism penetrates the orifices and veins of American youth, the book is full of pimps and dope dealers and movie moguls, and it all works together to put the lie to any illusions we might have of popular culture being a great equalizer, however much it binds us notionally. Sitting in Fatburger with a friend, the room suffused with Joan Jett and the Blackhearts' "Crimson and Clover", Clay narrates:

> I stare at the walls and listen to the words, *Crimson and clover, over and over and over and over . . .* " I suddenly get thirsty, but I don't want to go up to the counter and order anything because there's this fat, sad-faced Japanese girl taking orders and this security guard leaning against another yellow wall in back, eyeing everyone suspiciously, and Trent is still staring at my Fatburger with this amazed look on his face and there's this guy in a red shirt with long stringy hair, pretending to be playing the guitar and mouthing the words in the booth next to ours.

While the same music circulates through the brains of American teenagers, the gulf of class is as wide as ever, just as the gulf of race is—so clear later on in the book when the rich kids in their advertising T-shirts encounter a "Fuckin' Spic" in his advertising T-shirt.

The closure to this supremely moral fiction returns to a song, and Clay gives us his last word before he lights out for some impossible Territory (one that is not, in some way, Los Angeles):

> There was a song I heard when I was in Los Angeles by a local group. The song was called "Los Angeles" and the words and images were so harsh and bitter that the song would reverberate in my mind for days. The images, I later found out, were personal and no one I knew shared them . . . Images so violent and malicious that they seemed to be my only point of reference for a long time afterwards.

Less Than Zero argues that if there is a place to escape American culture, it is in the private interpretations of it, formed in the kinds of images it has already given us. This novel's references accumulate in a view and a theory of the place of pop commerce in our lives, and it is itself a display of where the quick "words and images" of pop have led some of us: to the place where every word says more than it seems to, and every sign is a sign of something else.

It is not just the obvious imposition of popular-commercial culture on our lives that some of our most interesting fiction now explores, but rather that imposition's invisible or near-invisible aspects. In the end it's probably not enough to have our fascination with pop culture merely piqued, yet again, in fiction, a form of discourse capable of so much more. To know this fascination, in its elusive workings, is to know ourselves in a profound way, and some of us want to know very specifically: about our happy conflation of entertainment and advertising, about what we can learn of our intracultural differences in how different ones of us receive and use pop culture, about its special effects on our minds and hearts. Writers so inclined have important work to do with, and within, this pervasive tangle. The problem they may encounter is that the convention that can still say "come hither" could begin to glaze over the interests of more readers, producing fatigue. But maybe not. Pop culture is a constant in our lives, but an ever-shifting presence, too, with new products and technologies coming along all the time to fascinate us. Its significances are hinted, ever-more abundantly, just in their names and physical features, and these compel all of us susceptible to contemporary life and market strategies, all of us who fancy ourselves students or armchair critics of pop and Americana. Popular culture will probably survive as a literary convention, in spite of having become obvious as a literary convention — just as nature has.

NOTE

1. Or perhaps our regional lives. In spite of random gathering, many of the writers cited here are Southerners. It is as if Southern writers are at once mesmerized and repelled by mall cutlure and the pop entertainments that have finally brought them into the American mainstream, muting their cultural differences while exploiting regional clichés. On the one hand, what a boon to be "with it" as soon as the rest of the nation is with something, after all those decades of being thought backward, lagging behind in consumer tastes. On the other, Southern writers are clearly disturbed by the loss of difference and by the crockpot mush into which every American can seem to be melting at last.

SPEAKING A WORD FOR NATURE

SCOTT RUSSELL SANDERS

Why is so much recent American fiction so barren? Putting the question more honestly, why do I find myself reading fewer contemporary novels and stories each year, and why do I so often feel that the work most celebrated by literary mavens (both avant-garde and establishment) is the shallowest? What is missing? Clearly there is no lack of verbal skill, nor of ingenuity in the use of forms. And there is no shortage of writers: if you pause in the checkout line at the supermarket, the clerk is likely to drag his manuscript from under the counter and ask your opinion. It is as though we had an ever-growing corps of wizards concocting weaker and weaker spells.

To suggest what is missing, I begin with a passage from D. H. Lawrence's essay about Thomas Hardy. Lawrence argued that the controlling element in *The Return of the Native* is not the human action, but the setting where that action takes place, the wasteland of Egdon Heath:

> What is the real stuff of tragedy in the book? It is the Heath. It is the primitive, primal earth, where the instinctive life heaves up. . . . Here is the deep, black source from whence all these little contents of lives are drawn.

Lawrence went on to generalize:

> This is a constant revelation in Hardy's novels: that there exists a great background, vital and vivid, which matters more than the people who move upon it. Against the background of dark, passionate Egdon, of the leafy, sappy passion and sentiment of the woodlands, of the unfathomed stars, is drawn the lesser scheme of lives. . . . The vast, unexplored morality of life itself, what we call the immorality of nature, surrounds us in its eternal incomprehensibility, and in its midst goes on the little human morality play, . . . seriously, portentously, till some one of the protagonists chances to look out of the charmed circle . . . into the wilderness raging around.[1]

All fiction is a drawing of charmed circles, since we can write about only a piece of the world. Within that circle, language shines meaning onto every whisper, every gesture and object. All the while, beyond that circle, the universe cycles on. Much contemporary fiction seems to me barren in part because it draws such tiny, cautious circles, in part because it pretends that nothing lies beyond its timid boundaries. Such fiction treats some "little human morality play" as the whole of reality, and never turns outward to acknowledge the "wilderness raging round." And by wilderness I mean quite literally the untrammeled being of nature, which might include—depending on where you look—a woods, a river, an alien planet, the genetic code, a cloud of subatomic particles, or a cluster of galaxies. What is missing from much recent fiction, I feel, is any sense of nature, any acknowledgment of a nonhuman context.

While Lawrence's account seems to me largely true of Hardy, it does not apply to the mainstream of British fiction. In the work of British novelists from Defoe and Fielding through Austen, Dickens, George Eliot, Joyce, and Woolf, up to contemporaries such as Margaret Drabble and Anthony Powell, the social realm—the human morality play—is a far more powerful presence than nature. What Lawrence wrote about Hardy applies more widely and deeply, in fact, to American literature. Hardy glimpsed "the primitive, primal earth" in Dorset, and Wordsworth searched for it in the Lake District, and Lawrence himself found remnants of it amid the coalfields of the industrial Midlands. But these were pockets of wildness surrounded by a domesticated landscape. In America, by contrast, until well into this century—and even, in some desert and mountainous places, still today—writers have not had to hunt for wildness. For over three centuries, from the time of William Bradford in Plymouth Plantation to William Faulkner in Mississippi, when our writers looked outward from the circle of human activity, they could not help but see "the wilderness raging round." Our feelings toward this wild arena have shifted back and forth between a sense of revulsion as in Bradford and a sense of reverence as in Faulkner; but what has been constant through all except the last few decades of our history is the potent fact of the wilderness itself. Again and again in the great works of American literature, the human world is set against the overarching background of nature. As in Hardy's novels, this landscape is no mere scenery, no flimsy stage set, but rather the energizing *medium* from which human lives emerge and by which those lives are bounded and measured.

Soon after writing his essay on Hardy, Lawrence undertook a study of American literature, attracted by the same quality he had identified in *The Return of the Native*. In the works of Melville, Cooper, Hawthorne, Crèvecoeur, and Thoreau he found a divided consciousness: on the surface they were concerned with the human world, with towns and ships and cultivated land, with households and the spiderwebs of families; but underneath they were haunted by nature. Thus Melville seemed to Lawrence "more spell-bound by the strange slidings and collidings of Matter than by the things men do." Cooper sentimentalized the New York frontier in his Leatherstocking tales, yet wildness kept breaking through. This divided consciousness arose, Lawrence argued, because in America "there is too much menace in the landscape."[2]

By the time his *Studies in Classic American Literature* appeared, Lawrence had moved to a ranch in New Mexico, and he could write from direct experience that, "when one comes to America, one finds . . . there is always a certain slightly devilish resistance in the . . . landscape."[3] In *St. Mawr* (1925), a short novel written during his American stay, the heroine flees from England, where every scrap of country has been "humanized, occupied by the human claim"; and she settles as Lawrence did on a mountain overlooking the desert. Here she "felt a certain latent holiness in the very atmosphere, . . . such as she had never felt in Europe, or in the East. . . . The landscape lived, and lived as the world of the gods, unsullied and unconcerned. . . . Man did not exist for it."[4] Something like Lawrence's awestruck encounter with the American landscape has been recorded time and again in our literature. By sampling this tradition, we can see more vividly the sort of nature-awareness that has largely disappeared from contemporary fiction.

Lawrence's response to the land as holy, as a source of meaning and energy, while it is an ancient view among Indians, is a fairly recent view for white people. The earliest responses to the wilderness were typically those of horror and revulsion. Here, for example, is William Bradford, writing some time after 1620 about the Pilgrims' first impression of their new land:

> [W]hat could they see but a hideous and desolate wilderness, full of wild beasts and wild men. . . . [W]hich way soever they turned their eyes (save upward to the heavens) they could have little solace or content in respect of any outward objects. . . . [A]ll things stand upon them with a weatherbeaten face, and the whole country, full of woods and thickets, represented a wild and savage hue. If they looked behind them, there was the mighty ocean which they had passed and was now a main bar and gulf to separate them from all the civil parts of the world.[5]

One feels that in Bradford's devout eyes the wilderness was, if anything, more certain a presence than heaven itself. Merely because a writer is overwhelmingly *aware* of the American landscape, however, is no guarantee that he or she will know what to make of it. None of the intellectual gear that Bradford had carried with him from "the civil parts of the world," least of all his Puritan theology, had equipped him to see this New World with any clarity. Like many who followed in his religious tradition, including Hawthorne two centuries later, Bradford looked at the wilderness and saw the *un*holy, the *dis*ordered. It was all a menacing blur.

Since the time of Bradford, many of our writers — reluctant or unable to invent a fresh language of nature — have tried to squeeze American landscape into a European frame. Washington Irving, for example, taking a tour of the prairies in 1835 shortly after his return from a stay in Europe, described the Oklahoma frontier in terms of classical mythology, royal gardens, and French and Dutch painting. He laid out the countryside as if on canvas, with dark bands of trees or prairie in the foreground, lighter river valley or hills in the middle ground, and hazy sky in the distance, the whole suffused, as he remarked at one point, with "the golden tone of one of the landscapes of Claude Lorraine." The western forests reminded him of Gothic cathedrals, "those vast and venerable piles, and the sound of the wind sweeping through them supplie[d] the deep breathings of the organ." Later in his account of the frontier expedition, Irving made his Old World frame explicit:

> The prairies bordering on the rivers are always varied in this way with woodland, so beautifully interspersed as to appear to have been laid out by the hand of taste; and they only want here and there a village spire, the battlements of a castle, or the turrets of an old family mansion rising from among the trees, to rival the most ornamented scenery of Europe.[6]

The "hand of taste" is evident here and throughout *A Tour on the Prairies*, rearranging the rude Oklahoma countryside to make it more nearly conform to the landscape of England or France.

Irving was only one in a long line of American writers who gazed at the wild countryside and regretted the absence of human "ornament." Even so keen an observer of our landscape as Thomas Cole voiced a complaint similar to Irving's after returning (in 1832) from his own European sojourn: "Although American scenery is often so fine, we feel the want of associations such as cling to scenes in the old world. Simple nature is not quite sufficient. We want human interest, incident and action to render the effect of landscape complete."[7] Half a century later, in a notorious essay on Hawthorne, Henry James listed all the ornaments that were missing from the American scene. It is a long list, including castles and kings. By comparison with the Old World, the New had little to offer except raw nature. And James had no more idea than Bradford what to make of a wild landscape. He felt at ease only in Europe, where nature had long since been cut into a human quilt. Still today, although young writers may no longer feel compelled to live in Paris or London, most who grow up in the backwoods or on the prairies — in Oklahoma, say, or Indiana — eventually pack their bags and head for the cities of the East Coast or the West, as if the land in between were too poor to support crops of fiction.

While some writers were trying to squeeze New World landscapes into Old World frames, others tried to discover a fresh way of seeing the "primitive, primal earth" that was laid bare in America. One of the earliest inventors of this homegrown vision was William Bartram, the vagabond naturalist, who gazed at the American countryside on the eve of the Revolution. Here is Bartram, camped in a Florida swamp:

> The verges and islets of the lagoon were elegantly embellished with flowering plants and shrubs; the laughing coots with wings half spread were tripping over the little coves, and hiding themselves in the tufts of grass; young broods of the painted summer teal, skimming the surface of the waters, and following the watchful parent unconscious of danger, were frequently surprised by the voracious trout; and he, in turn, as often by the subtle greedy alligator. Behold him rushing forth from the flags and reeds. His enormous body swells. His plaited tail brandished high, floats upon the lake. The waters like a cataract descend from his opening jaws. Clouds of smoke issue from his dilated nostrils. The earth trembles with his thunder.[8]

Darwin would not have had much to teach this intrepid naturalist on the subject of violence in nature. Despite these dragonlike alligators with their smoking nostrils, Bartram stuck around long enough to explore the swamps. Everywhere on his travels he learned what he could of the Indians, plants, soil, and beasts. He was helping, in fact, to invent scientific observation, a way of seeing and speaking of nature as separate, orderly, obeying its own laws. He treated the lagoons and rivers and forests through which he traveled as a sequence of habitats, although of course he did not use that newfangled word.

The works of Bartram circulated widely in Europe, where a new generation of writers, including Wordsworth, Coleridge, and Chateaubriand, feeling encumbered by civilization, were eager for these glimpses of wild and wondrous territory. What often happened to American literary landscapes when they were transported across the ocean may be suggested by looking at Chateaubriand's New World romance, *Atala* (1801). Unlike most European Romantics, Chateaubriand actually traveled to America, spending the winter of 1791–1792 in upstate New York. Not content to write about the landscape he had actually seen, however, he borrowed heavily from Bartram's *Travels* and from his own fancy to produce descriptions such as this one, of the Mississippi River:

> [W]hile the middle current sweeps the dead pines and oaks to the sea, one can see, on the side currents, floating isles of pistia and water lilies, whose pinkish yellow flowers, rising like little banners, are carried along the river banks. Green serpents, blue herons, pink flamingoes, young crocodiles sail like passengers on the flower-ships, and the colony, unfolding its golden sails to the wind, lazily drifts into some hidden bend of the river.[9]

The bend must have been very well hidden, since no other traveler on the Mississippi has ever discovered a scene remotely like that one. Along those fabulous shores, the Frenchman noted mountains, Indian pyramids, caribou, bears drunk on grapes, and snakes that disguised themselves as vines to catch birds. While Bartram was given to exaggeration, especially in the vicinity of alligators, he always checked his enthusiasm against what his eyes were telling him; Chateaubriand suffered no such inhibitions.

Like Lawrence and many other European writers, Chateaubriand was lured to America by the very qualities in our landscape that drove Cooper, Irving, and James to Europe. This contrary movement has been going on now for two centuries. I imagine that right this minute, in the air over the Atlantic, jumbo jets are crossing paths, the eastbound ones carrying Americans to Europe in search of castles and gravestones, the westbound ones carrying Europeans to America in search of redwoods and waterfalls.

Emerson had a look at landscapes on both sides of the ocean, and decided that the native variety was the one best suited to his imagination. His *Nature* (1836) seems to me still the most eloquent manifesto for a way of seeing appropriate to the New World setting. In the essay he urged American writers to cast off the conventions of thought inherited from Europe, that stuffy old wardrobe of hand-me-down ideas, and "to look at the world with new eyes." But how? By turning away from "the artificial and curtailed life of cities" and going back to the source of all thought and language, to nature itself:

> Hundreds of writers may be found in every long-civilized nation, who for a short time believe, and make others believe, that they see and utter truths, who do not of themselves clothe one thought in its natural garment, but who feed unconsciously on the language created by the primary writers of the country, those, namely, who hold primarily on nature. But wise men pierce this rotten diction and fasten words again to visible things.[10]

This advice is easier to accept than to apply, as Emerson's own verbal landscapes demonstrate. In *Nature* itself, whenever he began to fasten words onto visible things — seeing, for instance, "The leafless trees become spires of flame in the sunset, with the blue east for their background, and the stars of the dead calices of flowers, and every withered stem and stubble rimed with frost", — he interrupted himself to ask a question or to drag in some of that discarded European baggage: "What was it that nature would say? Was there no meaning in the live repose of the valley behind the mill, and which Homer or Shakespeare could not reform for me in words?"[11] Listening for what nature had to say, Emerson was always a little too eager to hear the cultural mutterings of his own well-stocked mind, and thus his landscapes are less substantial than those drawn by many of the writers who followed his precepts — including, most famously, Thoreau.

However much we might quarrel about who belongs on the short list of primary writers — those who renew our language and vision by fastening words to nature — I hope we would agree to include the name of Thoreau. His descriptions of the Concord River, the Maine woods, Cape Cod, and Walden Pond are among the most vigorous and penetrating accounts of our landscape ever written. One of his prime motives for undertaking the experiment in living beside Walden Pond was to train himself to *see*: "It is something to be able to paint a particular picture, or to carve a statue, and so to make a few objects beautiful; but it is far more glorious to carve and paint the very atmosphere and medium through which we look." In passage after passage of *Walden*, Thoreau portrayed a dynamic nature — frozen sand melting and sliding down the railroad embankment, ice breaking up on the pond, geese circling overhead and muskrats burrowing underfoot. Watching this energetic landscape was his chief business:

> Sometimes, in a summer morning, having taken my accustomed bath, I sat in my sunny doorway from sunrise till noon, rapt in a revery, amidst the pines and hickories and sumachs, in undisturbed solitude and stillness, while the birds sang around or flitted

noiseless through the house, until by the sun falling in at my west window, or the noise of some traveller's wagon on the distant highway, I was reminded of the lapse of time. I grew in those seasons like corn in the night, and they were far better than any work of the hands would have been.[12]

Thoreau situated himself *within* nature, and drew upon all the senses — he devoted an entire chapter to sounds, for example — to convey what was going on around him in the green world. The forces at work in pond and forest he found also at work in himself. An entry in his journal catches this feeling memorably, "A writer, a man writing, is the scribe of all nature; he is the corn and the grass and the atmosphere writing."[13]

In Thoreau we find no conflict between the scientist's method of close, reasoned observation and the poet's free play of imagination. Since Thoreau's time, however, as the products of reason have come to dominate and efface the natural landscape, writers have found it more and more difficult to combine these two ways of seeing. In *Life on the Mississippi* (1883), for example, Samuel Clemens wrote about having to learn every mile of the shifting river by heart. He studied hard, and eventually became a professor of the river, but at a price:

> Now when I had mastered the language of this water and had come to know every trifling feature that bordered the great river as familiarly as I knew the letters of the alphabet, I had made a valuable acquisition. But I had lost something, too. I had lost something which could never be restored to me while I lived. All the grace, the beauty, the poetry had gone out of the majestic river![14]

However, we can see from *Huckleberry Finn* (1884), published one year after *Life on the Mississippi*, that he was in fact able to fuse an adult's rational knowledge and a child's fresh emotion in his vision of the river. Here is Huck, for example, watching the sun rise over the Mississippi:

> The first thing to see, looking away over the water, was a kind of dull line — that was the woods on t'other side — you couldn't make nothing else out; then a pale place in the sky; then more paleness, spreading around; then the river softened up, away off, and warn't black any more, but gray; . . . and you see the mist curl up off of the water, and the east reddens up, and the river, and you make out a log cabin in the edge of the woods . . . ; then the nice breeze springs up, and comes fanning you from over there, so cool and fresh, and sweet to smell, on account of the woods and the flowers; . . . and next you've got the full day, and everything smiling in the sun, and the song-birds just going it![15]

To sustain the vision of nature unsullied, Clemens had to push his narrative back into the time of his own childhood, some forty years earlier.

Faulkner did something similar in his short novel, *The Bear* (1942). Although written near the beginning of World War II, it deals with events from a time sixty years earlier, when patches of wilderness still lingered in Mississippi. In order to see Old Ben, the fabled bear, Faulkner's young hero must leave behind his gun, his compass, his watch, every mechanical contrivance, and yield himself to the woods. At length he is granted his vision:

> Then he saw the bear. It did not emerge, appear: it was just there, immobile, fixed in the green and windless noon's hot dappling, not as big as he had dreamed it but as big as he had expected, bigger, dimensionless against the dappled obscurity, looking at him. Then it moved. It crossed the glade without haste, walking for an instant into the sun's full glare and out of it, and stopped again and looked back at him across one shoulder. Then it was gone. It didn't walk into the woods. It faded, sank back into the wilderness without motion as he had watched a fish, a huge old bass, sink back into the dark depths of its pool and vanish without even any movement of its fins.[16]

In the course of the novel Old Ben is killed, the last of the half-Indian hunters dies, and the stand of virgin timber is sold to lumber companies and invaded by railroads and whittled away by the surrounding farms. Faulkner was concerned in *The Bear* not so much with the conflict between reason and imagination in our ways of seeing nature, as with reason's wholesale assault upon nature itself. His fable reminds us that, in a little over a century, our wilderness continent was transformed into one of the most highly industrialized landscapes in the world.

And thus we come, by way of a far-too-sketchy history, to our own time. In an age of strip mines, nuclear plants, urban sprawl, interstate highways, factory farms, chemical dumps, mass extinction of plant and animal species, oil spills, and "development" of the few remaining scraps of wilderness, many of us have come to view our situation in a manner exactly contrary to that of William Bradford. The landscapes that we ourselves have fashioned often appear "hideous and desolate." We can no longer cut ourselves off from the "civil parts of the world," however much we might wish to.

What has become of nature in recent American writing? A decent answer would be far longer than this entire essay, and even then could only touch on a few literary landscapes—Wendell Berry's Kentucky, say, and Eudora Welty's Mississippi, the Roanoke Valley of Annie Dillard, Edward Hoagland's Vermont, John McPhee's Alaska, Thomas McGuane's Montana, the deserts of Edward Abbey and Barry Lopez, the alien planets of Ursula Le Guin, the Africa and Nepal of Peter Matthiessen, the great plains of N. Scott Momaday and Wright Morris, the fabulous Antarctic of John Calvin Batchelor and the Central American jungle of Paul Theroux, the microscopic arenas of Lewis Thomas. All of these writers seek to understand our life as continuous with the life of nature; they project "the little human morality play" against the "wilderness raging round."

Notice that most of them work outside the braided literary currents that critics, reviewers, and publishers regard as the "mainstream" of contemporary fiction. They work in the essay (Abbey, Lopez, Hoagland, McPhee, Dillard, Thomas); in science fiction or fantasy or fable (all of Le Guin, Batchelor's *The Birth of the People's Republic of Antarctica*, Theroux's *Mosquito Coast*); in travel writing (Matthiessen, Theroux); or in "regional" fiction (meaning, so far as I can tell, fiction set in a recognizable landscape that is not a city: Berry, Welty).

Consider one brief example that stands for a larger pattern. Bobbie Ann Mason's *Shiloh & Other Stories* and the revision of Wendell Berry's *A Place on Earth* came out within a year of one another (1982 and 1983, respectively). Both are set in western Kentucky; both dwell on the breakup of rural lifeways. For Mason, nature supplies an occasional metaphor to illustrate a character's dilemma—a tulip tree cut down when it was about to bloom, a rabbit with crushed legs on the highway—exactly as K-Mart or Cat Chow or the Phil Donahue Show supply analogues. For Berry, no matter how much the land has been neglected or abused, no matter how ignorant of their environment people may have become, nature is the medium in which life transpires, a prime source of values and meaning and purpose. Whereas *Shiloh & Other Stories* was widely praised and imitated and briskly sold, *A Place on Earth*—a far more searching and eloquent book—was generally neglected; when reviewed at all, it was treated as an old-fashioned view of an out-of-the-way place.

That a deep awareness of nature has been largely excluded from "mainstream" fiction is a measure of the narrowing and trivialization of that fashionable current. It is also, of course, and more dangerously, a measure of a shared blindness in the culture at large. Not long ago, while camping in the Great Smoky Mountains, I had a nightmare glimpse of the modern reader. It was late one afternoon in May, the air sweet and mild. I left my tent and crossed the parking lot of the campground on my way to a cliff, where I planned to sit with my legs dangling over the brink and stare out across the westward mountains at the sunset. Already the sky was throbbing with color and the birds were settling down for their evening song. The wind smelled of pines. Near the center of the parking lot, as far as possible from the encircling trees, a huge camping van squatted. There were chocks under the tires, but the motor was running. The air-conditioner gave a high frantic squeal. The van had enough windows for a hothouse, but every one was curtained, even the windshield. Lights glowed around the edges and threw yellow slashes onto the blacktop. What could keep the passengers shut up inside that box on such an afternoon, in such a place? Passing by, I saw through a gap in the curtains a family clustered in front of a television as if in front of a glowing hearth, and I heard the unmistakable banshee cry of Tarzan, King of the Apes.

Whenever I am feeling gloomy about the prospects of making nature *present* to contemporary readers, I think of those campers. They had driven their rolling house to a mountaintop overlooking an awesome sweep of land, and had parked there, with engine running and curtains drawn, to watch a movie starring an Olympic swimmer playing an English lord swinging through a Hollywood jungle. If the Great Smoky Mountains could not lure them from their box, how could words on a page ever stir them? Could such people be made to see, through stories, where it is we actually dwell, what sort of ship we ride through space?

Of course, readers have always been willing to pull on their mental boots and journey to places in books they would never think of visiting in the flesh. Millions have read *Walden* and *Life on the Mississippi*, yet how many have built a hut in the woods or rafted down a river? What is new about contemporary readers is not their preference for an indoor life, but how far indoors they are able to retreat and how long they are able to stay there. The boxes that shut us off from nature have become more perfect, more powerful, from all-electric mansions in the suburbs to glass towers in the city, from space shuttles to shopping malls. Today, the typical adult reader leaves a humming house in the morning, drives an air-conditioned car to a sealed office, works eight hours under fluorescent lights, stops on the way home at night to buy dyed vegetables and frozen meat wrapped in plastic, enters the house through the garage and locks the door. Except for lawns, which are fertilized and purified to an eerie shade of green, and a smoky sky, and a potted plant or two, everything this reader sees all day has been made by human beings. Only the body itself stubbornly upholds the claims of biology, and even this biological datum our reader treats with chemicals designed to improve or delay the workings of nature.

Reading this account, perhaps with a canoe strapped to the roof of your car and a compass dangling by a thong around your neck, you may scuff your boots on the floor, impatient with my dark picture. But, with all due respect, I think my campers watching a Tarzan movie in their van are more typical of the age than are the regulars on the Aubudon bird count. Despite the sale of recreational gear and the traffic jams in National Parks, I believe that, on the whole, Americans today have less direct experience of nature than at any time in our history. I am not talking about occasional visits to the woods or zoo, as one might visit Grandmother in the country, but of day-to-day living contact with the organic world.

You can see this ignorance of land and landscape illustrated in the stylish fiction of our time. Read Raymond Carver's collection *What We Talk About When We Talk About Love* (1981), for example, and, aside from references to fish, deer, and geese as prey, here is the most elaborate account of nature you will find, "A big moon was laid over the mountains that went around the city. It was a white moon and covered with scars."[17] (Read, for an instructive contrast, Thomas McGuane's *Nobody's Angel*, also published in 1981, which opens with the line, "You would have to care about the country," and over which the Montana landscape presides.) In Don DeLillo's *White Noise* [1984] — the most honored novel of 1985 — the only time you are reminded that anything exists beyond the human realm is when his characters pause on the expressway to watch a sunset, and even the sunset interests them only because a release of toxic gases from a nearby plant has poisoned it into technicolor. (For a contrast to *White Noise*, read Ursula Le Guin's novel of the same year, *Always Coming Home*, which summons up an entire culture and cosmology governed by the most intricate and lively understanding of nature.)

Sample the novels and stories published in America today, and in the opening pages you are likely to find yourself trapped inside a room — a kitchen, perhaps, or a psychiatrist's office, a bedroom, a bar, a motel — with characters talking. When they pause in their talk, it is usually to shift into another room, where they raise their voices once again. Some might say it is inevitable that our fiction should have such an indoor cast, given that we live in an age and a place dominated by cities; inevitable that characters should display such ignorance of nature, given the shabby way we treat the environment. Of course DeLillo, Carver, Mason and their less able imitators are reporting on our condition: surrounded by artifacts of our own making, engulfed by human racket, illiterate in the language of the cosmos. But durable art, art that matters, has never merely reproduced the superficial consciousness of an age. Cervantes did not limit himself to the platitudes of feudalism, nor Melville to Puritanism, nor Faulkner to racism, nor García Márquez to nationalism and capitalism. They quarreled with the dominant ways of seeing, and in that quarreling with the actual they enlarged our vision of the possible.

However accurately it reflects the surface of our times, fiction that never looks beyond the human realm is profoundly false, and therefore pathological. No matter how urban our experience, no matter how oblivious we may be toward nature, we are nonetheless animals, two-legged sacks of meat and blood and bone dependent on the whole living planet for our survival. Our outbreathings still flow through the pores of trees, our food still grows in dirt, our bodies decay. Of course, of course: we all nod our heads in agreement. The gospel of ecology has become an *intellectual* commonplace. But it is not yet an *emotional* one. For most of us, most of the time, nature appears framed in a window or a video screen or inside the borders of a photograph. We do not feel the organic web passing through our guts, as it truly does. While our theories of nature have become wiser, our experience of nature has become shallower. And true fiction operates at a level deeper than shared intellectual slogans. Thus, any writer who sees the world in ecological perspective faces a hard problem: how, despite the perfection of our technological boxes, to make us feel the ache and tug of that organic web passing through us, how to *situate* the lives of characters — and therefore of readers — in nature.

How we inhabit the planet is intimately connected to how we imagine the land and its creatures. In the history of American writing about landscape, we read in brief the history of our thinking about nature and our place in the natural order. Time and again, inherited ways of seeing have given way before the powerful influence of the New World landscape. If such a revolution in vision is to occur in our time, writers will have to free themselves from human enclosures, and go outside to study the green world. It may seem quaint, in the age of megalopolis, to write about wilderness or about life on farms and in small towns; and it may seem escapist to write about distant planets where the environment shapes every human gesture; but such writing seems to me the most engaged and forward-looking we have. If we are to survive, we must look outward from the charmed circle of our own works, to the stupendous theater where our tiny, brief play goes on.

NOTES

1. "Study of Thomas Hardy," *Phoenix: The Posthumous Papers of D. H. Lawrence* (London: Heinemann, 1936), pp. 415, 419.
2. *Studies in Classic American Literature* (1924; reprinted London: Mercury Books, 1965), pp. 138, 48.
3. Ibid., pp. 52-53.
4. *St Mawr* (1925; reprinted and bound with *The Virgin and the Gypsy*, Harmondsworth, England: Penguin, 1950), pp. 109, 147.
5. *Of Plymouth Plantation*, Book 1, Chapter 9 (written 1630-50; first published 1856; reprinted in Sculley Bradley et. al., eds., *The American Tradition in Literature*, Vol. 1, 3d ed.; New York: Norton, 1967), p. 19.
6. *A Tour on the Prairies* (1835), in William Kelly, ed., *Selected Writings of Washington Irving* (New York: Modern Library, 1984), pp. 462, 436, 495.
7. Quoted in Roderick Nash, *Wilderness and the American Mind* (rev. ed., New Haven: Yale University Press, 1973), p. 80.
8. *Travels of William Bartram* (1791), ed. Mark Van Doren (New York: Dover, n.d.), p. 115.
9. *Atala* (1801), trans. Walter J. Cobb (New York: New American Library, 1961), p. 16.
10. *Nature* (1836; reprinted in Sculley Bradley et. al., eds., *The American Tradition in Literature*, Vol. 1, 3d ed.; New York: Norton, 1967), pp. 1075-76.
11. Ibid., pp. 1069-70.
12. *Walden*, ed. J. Lyndon Shanley (Princeton University Press, 1973), pp. 90, 111.
13. *H. D. Thoreau: A Writer's Journal*, ed. Laurence Stapleton (New York: Dover, 1960), p. 66.
14. *Life on the Mississippi*, in Guy Cardwell, ed., *Mark Twain: Mississippi Writings* (New York: Library of America, 1982), p. 284.
15. *Huckleberry Finn*, in Guy Cardwell, ed., *Mark Twain: Mississippi Writings* (New York: Library of America, 1982), pp. 740-741.
16. *The Bear*, in *Three Famous Short Novels* (New York: Vintage, 1961), pp. 202-3.
17. *What We Talk About When We Talk About Love* (New York: Knopf, 1981), p. 31.

THE AGRARIAN IMPULSE IN CONTEMPORARY AMERICAN FICTION

GREGORY L. MORRIS

Every few years this country experiences a revival of interest in, and concern for, the agricultural way of life, that vague and shimmering ideal practiced by an ever-diminishing number of Americans. The agrarian existence has always been a part of our national consciousness, and the economic upheavals that regularly beset the rural sector bring with them a resurfacing from this consciousness of a primitivist myth.

William Adams has recently and convincingly argued that the American agrarian myth, far from being moribund, is still a vital element of our national imagination: "That . . . the symbolic matrix of farm, family, and independence remains compelling and perhaps formative, is suggested by the waves of public emotion set loose in the current controversy over the fate of small farmers." Using the spate of "farm films" that emerged in the past three or four years as examples, Adams maintains that the contemporary resurrection of the agrarian myth, despite the "disintegration" of the literal truth from which that myth springs, reveals as much about our *political* imagination as it does about our historical imagination. There is, Adams writes:

> A profound affinity between [President] Reagan's appeal to rural tradition and the radical or populist pastoralism informing these particular movies. For the radical imagination, the struggle of small farmers against the monstrous and blind forces of the market and corporate interests is a vast metaphor, a way of imagining our own political circumstances. It appeals precisely because it is so clear and, in a mythical sense, so familiar: power against powerlessness, the big against the small, dependence against independence. From the traditional, conservative side, which Reagan attempts to represent, something similar is at stake. If American society and culture

are changing too quickly, and if traditional political identities are threatened by such changes, then it makes sense to call for a return to older and safer understandings and values. The changes are not real, the president's pastoralism suggests; they will disappear if we recover a more traditional sense of what it means to be an American. Political differences notwithstanding, the deeper unity here is the displacement of powerlessness and confusion onto myth, a displacement which resolves in symbolic and illusory form things we cannot express, let alone resolve, in more rooted forms of language and action.[1]

Art, in the particular case of American cinema, has reacted to a political situation by acting to mitigate the ineffectuality of a people (the reality) through the reexpression of, at best, a semieffectual belief (the myth).

What has gone unnoticed, I think, amidst all the hubbub of publicity and politics, is the steady, quiet, and responsible working of the contemporary fiction writer within the tradition of agrarian myth and art. Fascination with the agrarian ethic has long been a part of the American literary imagination, and today a number of this country's best fiction writers (in fact, some of its best and often *younger* fiction writers) have turned away from that popular modernist setting, the City, and toward the perennial locus of farm and fields. Moreover, there is nothing modish, nothing reflexive, about this phenomenon; the contemporary writer creates not so much from a fashionable *response* as from an inherent and timeless concern for the agrarian way of life.

Just what that way of life consists of is the subject of the first section of this essay, for in order to understand the fiction one must first understand the specific belief from which that fiction springs. The sections following that analysis offer observations on general characteristics of agrarian fiction and fiction writers in the 1980s, and then a more detailed analysis of the quality and character of some of that fiction.

I

American agrarianism in our time is a complicated weave of economic, political, and ethical belief. In fact, agrarianism has evolved into what Don Paarlberg has called "agricultural fundamentalism," a term which suggests the profundity of such a faith. While composed of many tenets, this creed is held together by an overriding conviction that "farming is not only a business but a way of life."[2] And how very much is left to implication in the phrase, "a way of life"—certainly far more than an agricultural economist might admit. (As an exercise, read Wendell Berry after reading Luther Tweeten.) To lead an agrarian way of life is to observe, in varying degrees, a whole web of relationships, to move within a world where private responsibilities are freighted with greater consequences.

Locked at the center of this belief is the invariable sense of *place*: the land and the landscape, the physical presence of earth and rock and water and sky, the elements of wind and rain and flood and hail and snow, the natural curses of weed and locust and drought, the squareness of barn and house, the hot and cold solidity of machine, of tractor and plow and harvester, the fleshly pulse of horse's flank and cow's womb. The reality of place, of farm, is inescapable, and characters in agrarian fiction are measured by the depth of their connection to this sense of place.

The quality of this connection is especially important to agrarian fundamentalist belief, which invests the land with specific imaginative qualities—qualities of poetry and spirit and myth. The land is poetry in its abundance, its fruitfulness, its unpredictability and mystery. The land is spirit in its ineffable connection with the sacred; the land sustains both the physical and the mystical needs of those who work it, redeems them, bestows upon them a sort of secular, earned grace. The land is myth in its broad cycles of beginnings and endings, of plantings and harvestings. The extent to which the farmer (or writer) gives up his or her imagination to these qualities defines the limits of his or her agrarian belief.

These qualities of poetry, spirit, and myth are significantly coupled with—are in fact dependent upon—an equally powerful sense of time. Farm existence, perhaps more than any other lifestyle, is bounded immediately and recognizably by time: the daily cycle of the sun's rise and fall, and the routine of the day's labor; the annual cycle of season's change, and the subsequent routine of season-specific labor; the perpetual cycle of animal birth and life and death. And within it all, the timelessness of the land, its seeming infinitude and invincibility, its deathlessness. Time allows for the overwhelming sense of continuity that links past, present, and future in the agricultural fundamentalist way of belief. Ties of blood and name and memory and land string themselves through the fluidity of time, and characters are judged by their acknowledgment, or denial, of these ties.

The land, as I've said, bestows its own brand of grace upon the farmer. And this grace is an earned grace. Grace and blessing and redemption come through a right relationship with the land — more specifically, through a right *working* relationship with the land. The relationship is direct, immediate: to farm is to work. The relationship is participatory, not spectatorial. Moreover, labor in its purest, clearest, most right-minded form is an act of salvation. As we'll see, rightful work possesses value, is precious in and of itself. Rightful work describes a proper relationship between laborer and land; the work-act transforms itself into a "dance," an unconsciously choreographed movement of man and tool and earth that releases the poetry inherent in flesh and soil.

But the individual is only part of a larger human community, perhaps of larger separate communities. There exists the immediate community of family, of blood tie, and the extended community of town or village or region, of fellow farmers, fellow workers, fellow "dancers." Fidelity to these communities is essential. Again, denial and acknowledgment determine the quality of one's communal allegiance. Severance from the community — whether self-imposed or exercised upon the individual — comes traumatically and with powerful moral resonance.

The agrarian Self, then, becomes a composite of these relationships with land, time, labor, and community. Part of the agrarian tradition in fiction describes, or celebrates, a Self redeemed by land and by labor on the land, and by the specific life lived upon the farm. Another part of this tradition imagines a Self redeemed privately, independent of rural influences. Yet another part of this tradition, a bleaker part, pictures a Self left unredeemed, the forces of land and work and kinship ineffectual. The contemporary writers considered here explore the full range of this tradition, their fiction celebrating, mourning, or sometimes damning a way of life and those who follow it.

Observation: Not surprisingly, a good number of those contemporary writers working within the agrarian tradition have emerged from, and/or persist in, an agrarian lifestyle. Some kind of connection with such a life is vital; "genuine farm fiction" must be written by genuine farm-nurtured or farm-natured people. Few things are more embarrassing than a writer raised far from the farm trying to fake the "physical details" of everyday farm life. No one who hasn't treated sheep for soremouth, for example, could describe the process as Douglas Unger does in *Leaving the Land:*

> Her lamb nuzzled at my pantleg. It butted me once. It sucked at the crease in the seat of my jeans. I grabbed it up and straddled it. I looked at its mouth. There was a crust of scabs on its lips and gums from the soremouth disease. After giving the lamb a worm-

ing pellet, I pulled my knife out of its scabbard. I lifted its head and spent a while scraping the scabs on its lips and gums open with the knifeblade, slitting the gums a little with the sharp point, blood trickling from its mouth. I pulled out a squeeze bottle of iodine and covered the open wounds. That way, the lamb's mouth wouldn't close up with soremouth and it would grow. I squeezed alcohol over the knifeblade and wiped it off on my jeans.[3]

Or consider this passage on the birthing of pigs, from Jim Heynen's *You Know What Is Right*:

The boys liked to watch pigs being born. Drying them off in the straw. Putting them next to the sow's teats. Watching them discover the little world of the farrowing pen. But after a while the boys would get tired of this and go off to do something else.

Except for the youngest boy. He liked to stick around by himself. When the other boys left, he leaned down and put his face close to the sow. Now that there was no one there to laugh at him. This way he could hear the pig coming and when it was born his face was right over the newborn. He quickly put his eye over the eye of the little pig. When it opened its eye, the first thing it saw was the boy's eye, only an inch or two away from its own.[4]

Such realistic detail is purchased with experience, past or present. Writers like Unger, Heynen, Wendell Berry, Janet Kauffman, William Kittredge, Will Weaver—all share personal connections with farming and the agricultural way of life, having been born into farming families. Berry, Kauffman, Weaver, and Gretel Ehrlich now work their own operations, laboring as both artist and farmer/rancher.

One might argue, in fact, that the most successful agrarian fiction— and more important, the most successful *fiction*—is produced by those writers most actively involved in the routine of farming. The degree of authenticity and poetry corresponds to the degree of intimacy with the way of life described in the fiction. These authors uniquely possess the firsthand knowledge to reveal the profound and visceral connections of all animate nature, and surely that is an enduring function of great literature, going all the way back to the modes of pastoral and georgic in the classical period.

(For the sake of contrast, one might look at those writers who *employ* the farming life in their fiction, but who have not actually lived in that milieu. A writer like Nicholas Delbanco, for example, who uses the agrarian vision to partially inform his significant thematic concerns in "The Sherbrookes Trilogy," who comes to the tradition with a particularly urban and urbane sensibility—the Vermont gentleman farmer. Or a writer like Ron Hansen, whose roots and birth are in farm country—Nebraska—but who makes only occasional use of that connection.)

Many of these writers announced their loyalties with their first published book of fiction. Unger, Kauffman, Ehrlich, Weaver, Joan Chase, C. J. Hribal, Anderson Ferrell, and Alfred Alcorn all published first novels or first story collections that, in one way or another, worked within this agrarian tradition. Chase, Hribal, Ehrlich, Ferrell, Weaver, and Alcorn have yet to follow up with a second book, offering no indication of where they might be headed thematically. Unger, in *El Yanqui*, deliberately shifted his locale and his concern, setting his novel in Argentina and turning to matters of political and moral conscience (though Unger does include a brief section set in the *pampas*, giving us at least a taste of Argentine ranchlife). Only Janet Kauffman has followed her first effort with a second book in the same vein, or at least a work that uses an agricultural environment for its landscape. Obviously, then, one of the important questions concerns the likelihood and viability of a sustained agrarian tradition in American fiction of the 1980s. So far, only Wendell Berry has consistently and devoutly steeped his fiction in the world of the American farmer.

Observation: As in the past, contemporary agrarian fiction tends to be very region-conscious, with particular regions closely tied to agrarian concerns. The South, with its own Agrarian school in the 1920s and 1930s, presently is represented by the writing of Berry, Anderson Ferrell, the late Breece D'J Pancake, and to some extent Bobbie Ann Mason and Leigh Allison Wilson. The Northeast, which lacks a solid agrarian tradition, has had writers like Delbanco and Alcorn and Carolyn Chute using bits of that tradition to color their work, and in the case of Chute to darken their work; while in the Northwest most recently Ken Kesey has visited and departed the world of the farm in *The Demon Box* (note the photograph of the author atop his tractor, the Merry Prankster turned Earth Father). Appropriately enough, though, the most vital and concerted and, in some ways, the most technically interesting work has originated in the American heartland, whose durable agrarian tradition makes it a fertile source for contemporary work in this vein. In the High Plains, writers like William Kittredge and Gretel Ehrlich, writing respectively of Montana and Wyoming, have studied the agrarian ethic as it applies to the ranch; Douglas Unger, writing of South Dakota, has studied the loss and attempted reclamation of a farming way of life in that region between 1930 and 1970; and Louise Erdrich, in *Love Medicine*, has touched upon a tribal ethic within the farming country of North Dakota. In the

Central Plains, meanwhile, Ron Hansen and Wright Morris are writing of Nebraska; Jim Heynen writing (it would seem) of Iowa; C. J. Hribal and Will Weaver working out of, and in, Minnesota; Joan Chase and Philip O'Connor writing of northern Ohio, and Janet Kauffman of Michigan. (Kauffman, in her recent novel *Collaborators*, straddles the regional fence in writing of her home state of Pennsylvania.)

Observation: While contemporary agrarian fiction is regional-minded, it is not particularly political-minded. Most recent farm fiction, in fact, is noticeably apolitical, assuming a preexistent political problem and working within or around it. Art absorbs and overshadows any specific political or economic program. When politics does figure into the fiction, it does so in minor ways. Agribusiness, vertical integration, and overextension sometimes exert themselves as economic forces within the fiction, but such elements are never the main concern of the writer. Rather than attempt a political or economic critique of the farm crisis (of whatever year), the contemporary storyteller focuses on the effect of such forces upon the character and soul of the people who work the land; if those writers offer any type of statement, it is a statement upon the changing *way of life* of these people. Most often in contemporary farm fiction politics takes the form of selling, or the possibility of selling, the family farm. Almost always it is the farm-widow who is left to decide the fate of land and life and family legacy. In the stories of C. J. Hribal's *Matty's Heart*, in Philip F. O'Connor's novella *Ohio Woman*, and in *Leaving the Land*, widows and mothers choose to retain the land and the long-held inheritance of farm and family; in Joan Chase's *During the Reign of the Queen of Persia*, in Wright Morris's *Plains Song*, and in Breece D'J Pancake's story "Trilobites," the farm is released, given up in exchange for a new way of life, with only faint hints at damnation or praise. Retention of the land implies the retention of the agrarian Self, of a specific landlocked spirit; relinquishment of the land implies escape, a movement away from a life disillusioned and toward a life reillusioned.

Observation: Despite their use of a conservative belief-system, most contemporary agrarian fiction writers are effectively experimental in their technique. There is nothing timid or backward, for example, about the narrative risk in *Leaving the Land*, a novel halved in time and voice, its two parts narrated by mother and son. Just as experimental is the technique of *During the Reign of the Queen of Persia*, where the narrative voice seems both anonymous and identifiable, both distanced from, and involved in, the events it so artfully describes. Nor is the voice of Kauffman's *Collaborators* the naive and immature voice of a woman-remembering-the-girl; indeed, the language spoken by that voice is strikingly, sometimes chillingly poetic, idiomatic, even eccentric in its daring use of the vernacular. And the multivoiced narrative of Erdrich's *Love Medicine* is as radical and successful as any avowedly experimental fiction. In short, form in contemporary agrarian fiction seems to reflect a progressive change in the function of that fiction, sometimes outdistancing the belief, generally carrying that belief with it.

II

A survey of dominant motifs of agrarian fiction surely must begin with the seasonal cycle. Time is measured by seasons marked in remembrance, and by the events caught within the limits of those seasons. So that when Ben Alton sifts through the past and its darkness, in William Kittredge's story, "Thirty-Four Seasons of Winter," he does so by matching the memory with the season and its labor:

> Ben Alton remembered years in terms of winter. Summers all ran together, each like the last, heat and baled hay and dust. "That was '59," he'd say. "The year I wintered in California." He'd be remembering manure-slick alleys of a feedlot outside Manteca, a flat horizon and constant rain.
> Or flood years. "March of '64, when the levees went." Or open winters. "We fed cattle the whole of February in our short-sleeves. For Old Man Swarthout." And then he'd be sad. "One week Art helped. We was done every day by noon and drunk by three." Sad because Art was his step-brother and dead, and because there'd been nothing but hate between them when Art was killed.[5]

And in Janet Kauffman's story "Chickens," time and spirit seem out of kilter until a tornado comes and sets things right again: "I felt better than usual about the animals, nature back in season as it seemed to be." With the alternation of seasons comes the consoling order of sowing and harvest, and care for the animals—all interactive labor appropriate to the country.

Common, too, in contemporary farm fiction is the conventional contrast between country and city, the assumed innocence and simplicity of rural life juxtaposed with the sophisticated and vaguely corrupted life of the town. In *Leaving the Land*, the town of Nowell becomes for a younger Marge Hogan a symbol of her despair and failure, her useless search for a lover:

> The years immediately following the war were fertile for weeds. There was a kind of plague of them. The white fluff seeds of the Canadian thistle and of the milkweed and dogbane filled the air like an invasion of tiny white parachutes. Hot winds swirled them through the streets so thickly that Marge gave up trying to pick them off her dress. She walked down the main street of Nowell, collecting seeds.
> She hated this town. She hated the way the sun blinded her, glaring off the white abode storefronts. She passed the high square wooden false front of the Baker Hotel and gazed up at five dark windows, one with an old white head leaning on the sill next to a box of withering geraniums. Clumps of cheat grass made a shambles of the sidewalk as they broke through the concrete and spilled in wild tufts toward the curb. Weeds scratched at her ankles as she walked. Sharp seeds prickled under the collar of her dress. She would have to comb them out of her hair like wedding rice.
> *White*, she thought, *white* . . . [3].

The barrenness and sterility that mark the town at the novel's beginning return at the end to exert their claim: "This town is like a sprawling, ragged, sagging heap, washed by fifteen seasons of winter to the same shade of gray as a pile of old barn boards" [195]. Here, the senses of time and place commingle, turning the landscape of the town into part of nature's leavings, a remnant of years of winter's wear.

For many writers, the town functions as the locus of community, a place made for reunion, gathering, the singing of the several agrarian voices. Unger's Nowell, C. J. Hribal's Augsbury, Wright Morris's Battle Creek — all serve to pull together those discrete farm worlds into occasional units. But nowhere does community exert so strong an influence as in Wendell Berry's Port William books. Just as the town serves the needs of the greater farm community, so do more specific parts of that town identify themselves as centers for the Port William Membership, a group of men who sustain the mythic, mystical spirit of the immediate landscape; barbershop, general store, graveyard — all become meeting places for the intimate community-within-a-community of the Membership. When one renounces one's place in that community, he or she forfeits an almost secret emotional connection with the profounder life of the town. In "It Wasn't Me," Clara Beechum (daughter of Old Jack Beechum, most ancient of the Membership) returns to Port William with her banker-husband Glad Pettit, to sell the Beechum place after Old Jack dies. Just the idea of selling the land, of denying the relation of place and past, is enough to distance the Pettits from the community of which Clara was once (by blood) a member. The Pettits do not "inhabit the world" any longer, have returned as aliens to the communal ties of custom and kin: "The letter in the notebook [Old Jack's notebook] was written in a language the Pettits did not speak; they had forgot the tongue in which an old man might cry out from his grave in love and in defense of a possibility no longer his own in this world."[6] As long as that language remains vital, spoken and understood, the community survives; when that language is lost or given away, as in *Leaving the Land*, the community fails and falls into bleak silence.

These lapses into silence, these failures and fallings, have in fact come to mark the differences in the types of agrarian fiction currently being written. Indeed, failure — its degree, its variety, its scale — seems to characterize most of today's farm fiction, just as it seems to figure generally in so much of today's serious fiction. What distinguishes the species of failure in agrarian fiction is its breadth; whereas much of contemporary fiction details (*over*details?) the disintegration of the Self, of the I, contemporary farm fiction moves from the failure of the individual to the failure of a vision — or at least to degrees of failure of that vision.

For example, there are writers who highlight the violence and brutality of an agrarian life. Gretel Ehrlich, in her *Wyoming Stories*, portrays a ranch-and-cattle life that carries a nasty edge to it: cockfights, drunkenness, long solitary hours, memories of death. Similarly, William Kittredge, in the stories in *We Are Not in This Together*, maps out an agrarian world marked by violence — gunshot wounds frozen over with ice, stomachs ripped apart by bears. It is a world in which the Self — the authentic Self — resides in the past and in memory, or in imagination and dream. Kittredge articulates a strong sense of place, but the holiness of that place is often violated by the vicious actions of the men who inhabit the landscape. In "The Soap Bear," for example, a murderer stalks a lone rural couple. The description here plays upon the terror of rural life:

> On Christmas day, spooning oyster dressing out of their turkey, just the two of them because there hadn't been any children — she didn't want children growing up in a sheriff's house was her excuse for having her tubes tied off — she started talking about a song she heard on the radio, a song called "Satan's Jewel Crown." Doris said it made her think about those people out there who were courting the devil by cutting the tongues and privates out of dead cows and leaving the rest. She said the song made her sad because no one ever offered to ruin her life . . . [41].

Violence here evokes failure — marital failure, personal failure. A similar description is offered in Ron Hansen's story "True Romance," where a Nebraska farm becomes the backdrop for perverse violence (the same sort of stock mutilation) and failure (the reality of infidelity posed against the fantasy of soap-opera television "romance"). Love is brutalized, eviscerated like the cattle left dead in the fields.

The same sort of grotesqueness and horror shadow the work of Breece D'J Pancake, whose stories of rural West Virginia crackle with dark varieties of violence and despair. In "Time and Again," for instance, an old man runs a snowplow along the roads that snake the mountainsides, an act that clarifies and, in a way, makes safe the lives of strangers. Yet behind that act lurks the ironic and utter viciousness of the same man's secret life wherein human beings — a wife, bludgeoned hitchhikers — are literally fed to the appetites of hogs.

More significant, though, than the violence of Pancake's world is the desperation that eventually drives the young from the land. Most of the farms in Pancake's stories are failed or failing, and most of the men find themselves impelled by the need to escape a doomed landscape. Even when the farm is clean and vital and shows evidence of right and appropriate care, the need to escape overtakes the need to remain. In Pancake's West Virginia, the agrarian vision is an extinct vision, killed off by the forces of geography and pain and failure; and the individual Self flees to escape a similar extinction.

Another motif worth noting is the ambiguous position of the matriarch in agrarian fiction. The matriarch sustains the work ethic but also rebels inwardly against the "generative" qualities of her biological condition which subject her to patriarchal control, and this rebellion is inherited by her daughters with often fatal results. Wright Morris and Joan Chase are especially adept at studying the psychological hardships of farm women during a time of crisis. Morris's *Plains Song* is the long recollection of Cora Atkins, a hardworking settler of the Nebraska plains and matriarch to a family of strong and disparate women:

> There are women who like to work but do not know how, and women who hate work who push themselves to exhaustion, hardly knowing and never learning that work, in itself, is gratifying. That work was never done reassured Cora. She knew how to work, and asked only that she work to an end.[7]

But there is another kind of "work" to which Cora must reconcile herself, that of sex and childbearing, and it is *this* labor that haunts Cora, and that in the following vision drives a wedge between subsequent generations of her family:

The summer chores were demanding, each day long and exhausting, but never long enough for her to catch up. Too tired to sleep, she would sometimes rise from bed and go below to sit in her rocker. In the moonlight the white trim on the barn's doors and windows stood free of the barn, and seemed to come toward her. It was eerie what she saw, or thought she saw, one night. Her husband, Emerson, moving like a sleepwalker, came down the stair and passed unseeing before her, crossing the yard to the privy, where he sat with the door open, his legs white as paint. On his way back he paused to dip water from the pail and take several deep swallows, his Adam's apple pumping. . . . He had belched, then said, "What a woman needs is one thing, but what a farm needs is another." She had been too startled to reply. He spoke as if he saw her right there before him, at the door to the porch. . . . Somewhere in the barn, or behind it, she heard the moaning caterwauling of the cats. Their piercing ear-splitting shrieks no longer dismayed her. How well she had come to understand it! Nothing known to her had proved to be both so bizarre and so repugnant as the act of procreation, but she understood that it was essential to its great burden of meaning. In the wild, cats shrieked. In the bedroom Cora had bitten through her hand to the bone. Dimly she gathered that Emerson, in speaking as he did, wanted her to know that she had failed him. What a farm needed was sons. She had borne a daughter, to be fed and clothed, then offered on the marriage market. Who would be there to run the farm as they grew old? Nothing in Emerson's nature assured her that he would not repeat the first experience, but the passage of time, the consoling rut of habit, had dulled the terror and anxiety she had once felt. [35–36].

The ambiguity of Cora's sexual nature—sex as a practical necessity, sex as emotional expression—becomes almost a genetic trait passed along to the women in Cora's family. As those women drift farther apart from each other and from the woman who is the emotional center of the family, the familial connections weaken; and as those familial connections fail, so fail the connections with the past, with the farm, with the specific agrarian vision by which Cora lived out her life. Like Willa Cather, Morris concerns himself with the American prairie farmwoman, but Morris pushes beyond the dreamily suggestive sexuality of a woman like Alexandra Bergson in *O Pioneers!*; Morris allows Cora Atkins to suspect her very humanity as circumstances conspire to pervert it.

Similarly, Joan Chase's *During the Reign of the Queen of Persia* examines the slow decline of a family into separateness, three generations of women drifting toward fragmentation. The grandmother, widowed, eagerly awaits the selling and abandonment of the family farm; her daughters fall into death and failure; and her granddaughters show the frightening legacies of their mothers and aunts. The past becomes a record of emotional barrenness and cruelty; sex, for the grandmother, is a punishment inflicted upon her by her husband, is a need she can neither feel nor understand:

> Married, they moved into rooms up over a store on the town's one street and in the secret dark Jacob touched her and moved himself in her, and though she got accustomed to it, a part of her was more aggravated by his touch than satisfied, and then it came to seem more invasion than touch, his need something he took care of, quick and by dark, by daylight no trace left, as though it had never happened between them. Lil felt resentment rising in her; his tacit denial shamed her, convinced her that he felt he stole something from her, was taking without asking. Every night, nearly, he turned to her and held her against him while, rapid and brutish, he moved in her. She began to be sick to her stomach nearly all day long. Afraid that it was a baby coming, dreading it, she lay under his heaviness, which blocked out any trace of light, and thought: Soon I'll be dead.[8]

This aversion and dread, this sense of the male as outsider and "provocateur," is passed along to Lil's daughters, who themselves become victims of failed or fearsome marriages. Chase takes us through several consciousnesses, letting us watch the family's disintegration from several perspectives. When one of the daughters weakens and eventually is overcome by sickness and death, the family veers momentarily toward a spiritual sense of home and place and community. There is talk of "radical forgiveness," of "miracles," of "the resurrection of forgotten love." But the distance between generations is too great—as the farm is sold off or burned away in fire, the last connection with the past vanishes; the family flies apart, their only hope that the barn-burning might purify their past, cauterize the wounds of death and attempted death. When the farm is lost, so is the familial center and any sense of rootedness and continuity: events drive the family into the modern world.

Not all contemporary agrarian visions deny the redemptive spirit of the agrarian ethic. Louise Erdrich, for instance, in *Love Medicine*, paints a desolate picture of a rural, semiagricultural North Dakota that has fallen under the weight of its past. The land, while only partly responsive to the people who till it, still holds a certain magic, a certain spirituality; part of that spirituality derives from the tribal belief in the land's holiness. Families split apart, grow weird and profane, yet still manage to redeem the occasional lost soul. That "love medicine" is potent, particularly among Erdrich's strange, mystical women. The women stay with the land, seeking not escape but acceptance and reconciliation. Erdrich's vision is peculiarly Native American, and the persistence of this ancient culture represents a significant variation on the "white" agrarian tradition. One can't help but notice, however, that Erdrich's second novel, *The Beet Queen*, moves to a North Dakota town for its locale, and that the mystical fields fade to a dreary backdrop, a vista glimpsed from a passing car: "With the air cooling on and the vents and windows shut, we were enclosed. The fields spread, dry and failed, between Blue Mound and Argus. Dust rode on the horizon in buffeting shapes. The drought had turned the landscape a uniform white-brown. But all of that was outside our vehicle."[9]

Will Weaver's *Red Earth, White Earth*, too, is influenced by the Native American tradition, though Weaver takes a very different approach. *Red Earth, White Earth* describes the breakup of family and farm, and the return of the absent son to the land. Guy Pehrsson's return is complicated by the web of relationships developed since his leaving, a web that includes his mother and Guy's blood-friend from childhood, Tom Little Wolf, a Flatwater Indian and an Indian activist. Weaver works through Pehrsson's past, detailing the influence of Indian legend and spirit upon Pehrsson's imagination. Guy's perspective upon the land—the town of White Earth, the Pehrsson family farm—is divided, informed by both the Indian sense of spirit and the traditional American farm consciousness.

Part of the consciousness involves Pehrsson's own sense of the familial and regional past, an understanding of "the old blood":

> The old blood was a river from the red lake of the heart that flowed into the past. The river started wide in the present; his father, grandfather, and himself, three generations of living men, formed a wide breach in time. Beyond Helmer, into the fourth generation and further back, the river narrowed. Beyond Helmer were shadowy photographs of big men and long-skirted women beside sagged cabins. Beyond photographs were only images, memory. A tall man with blue eyes and great hands . . . a woman with red hair. But all of them were men and women who worked the land. If right now he spaded up a hole and put in his hand, in the cool earth he could feel them shifting, turning; hear them whispering to him; feel the pull of their fingers on his.[10]

But Pehrsson's separation from the land separates him also from that connection of "old blood." So the old struggle renews itself, the struggle to reestablish a link to the past and to the land.

Weaver points out that this severance is a natural part of farm life, almost a willed distancing of farmer from community or from nonfarmer: "His hayhouse. The woods and fields. Tractors and farming always far from the buildings or the road. Always he had used these things to distance himself from people. Most farmers did that. . . . They chose land over people." [226] Weaver here argues against the agrarian insistence upon community; his farmer chooses isolation and silence. And that silence, too, is a product of the land's character and force: "As he spoke he suddenly felt the great weight of the land all around him. . . . He suddenly understood that farmers spoke in short sentences or none at all because the land weighed down their voices. The land took away speech because it was always bigger than words to describe it. The land had no need for words" [144]. So much for the agrarian evocation of the land's presence: the land demands silence. And ultimately the land claims that silence — Tom Little Wolf dead, a victim of "overdreaming," Guy Pehrsson and his mother retreating to California, leaving the farm to his father. Reclamation of past and land fails, as if politics were too strong a medicine for matters of spirit and desire.

III

In this final section of the essay I would like to focus, all too briefly, on three remarkable writers — Douglas Unger, Janet Kauffman, and Wendell Berry — who have successfully absorbed and integrated the motifs described in the previous section. The centrality of agrarian fiction depends on the vital presence of writers as skilled and wise as these three; they provide test cases of the viability of a fictional mode both hallowed and endangered.

In *Leaving the Land*, Douglas Unger accepts and develops certain tenets of the agrarian creed, while showing too the ways in which that creed has failed or been made to fail. Very strong in Unger's novel is the sense of place, the farmstead both a workplace and a homeplace, invested with a history both familial and geological. The rightly run farm is a place of health and well-being; work is a restorative, an elixir. Good work, soulful work, is a pattern of rhythms, a dance (as it is repeatedly figured in agrarian literature) among men, machines, and land. Work becomes an expression of harmonies, of movements and sentiments synchronized:

> Ben Hogan worked. He worked and never slowed. . . . He milked in the barn. He leaned his head against the cow's flank and bellowed with some old song in his mind, or with pieces of many old songs

that he strung together. His hands squeezed and pulled in rhythm to that horrendous hour or so of out-of-tune yodeling. . . . When Marge watched him build a fenceline, it was like watching a dance. He dug holes with a double-bladed shovel. He lifted the blades up and pumped them down into the ground, spilling the earth in a pile beside the hole in the upswing, never breaking his rhythm, never stopping despite the sun that made him glisten with sweat [9–10].

The sense of place and the potency of work are significant elements in this novel, for both act to redeem the main characters, Marge Hogan and her son Kurt. Both the Hogan family farm and the small town of Nowell, South Dakota, are squeezed by the external economic pressures of corporate agriculture and of vertically integrated farming systems. The town gives in, goes dry, loses its sense of being and of place, becomes a sort of reliquary. The Hogan farm fails as well, but it remains the *Hogan* farm; there are offers to buy the farm, chances to renounce title and history, but the family — and in the end Marge especially — clings to the land (not *their* land — the land is never owned, just worked). When Kurt returns to his hometown one Christmas, after an escape to college and to sea (an odd and curious thing how so many agrarian characters seek the ocean when they escape), he returns with a conscious desire to maintain his severance from the farm. But the spirits of family and land are too strong, too persuasive — even in the bleak landscape of failure and ruin, the essential holiness of the soil wrenches denial into acceptance. As Kurt labors at a small sheep operation, watching the workings of corporate farming in the fields at the edge of his vision, he turns cynical and embraces the ethos of escape: "What matter if a whole style of life was gone? . . . There was little beauty to it. . . . There was only sweat, and maybe a certain sense of unspeakable smallness in my soul in that of all the generations behind me, of all the lost tribes of my forefathers who had dug potatoes, milked cows, sown grain, picked fruit from primeval gardens, it had all come down to me in a knowledge I only wished to lose" [248].

The son replicates the desire of the mother-as-girl: Marge Hogan too sought escape when young from the farm and its way of life, sought to "leave the land," but she stayed on and came to work fiercely for the keeping of that farm if not for its way of life. Her struggle has left her empty, exhausted, a part of the general human wreckage: "I'm tired of feeding my body. I'm tired of putting my body to bed, tired of getting my body up in the morning. And work . . . I'm so sick of work I don't know what to do. I'm tired of seeing, breathing, feeling, everything. I want something better." [275–276] Yet within the depleted flesh still burns a remnant of spirit, some part of her in touch with the vaguely holy. And it is this remnant of spirit that Marge passes along to her son, just as she passes on the deed to the homeplace. Kurt turns his vision to the past, recollecting the labors of his grandfather and men like him, and arrives at part of the knowledge transmitted through spirit and family and land, the knowledge that he had formerly wished to lose: "But I knew what they were here for. It was like a secret now, an all-but-unobtainable secret once a wisdom strong enough to move whole tribes across mountains. . . . It was the knowledge of his generation that if at first you don't succeed at life, you can always learn to plow. I thought, *There must be other secrets now and I don't know them.*" [277] Knowledge, family, the homeplace, all are reclaimed; the present reconnects with the past, acknowledging the lapse or the refiguring of the ethos, but declaring the vitality and need of such an ethos. The spirit moves again across the land and within those in touch with the land — Kurt kneels to pray, loses the words, but affirms the sentiment and essence of his prayer.

A vision more artistically, philosophically, and psychologically complex is that of Janet Kauffman in *Places in the World a Woman Could Walk* (a collection of stories) and *Collaborators* (a novel). Kauffman is interested in women — generally women who work farms — and the ways in which that work shapes their bodies, their spirits, and especially their language. Labor, true to the agrarian belief, hardens and cleanses the body; labor signals worth, value, promise, and points toward the integrated ("whole") soul; labor strips people of their pretensions, lays bare the neutrality of the work-chastened flesh, and invests their language with a lean kind of poetry. Kauffman's farmwomen are powerful, "muscled," full of spirit, and given to vision — like Mrs. Bagnoli (in the story "Patriotic"), crackerjack tractor driver, "known . . . as the woman whose husband survived eight hours in a moving cement mixer":

> It doesn't take long to see that Mrs. Bagnoli is a purposeful, serious-minded woman. It's clear she commands a world-view. Small things fall away. She sits up on the blue cusion seat, her back straight, her neck like a fine stalk, very slender and pearly above the black collar of the blouse. Her hair rises and rises, then falls in sprays. She doesn't look left or right, and — as soon as the clutch is released — we *glide*, around the barn, cutting right from the lane to make a path through the weed field.[11]

Women "sail," move with grace and clarity when freed of man's "interference" ("Your farmers, my darling, pressure-hosing all their machinery — *they* are the interference. But a woman! A woman belongs to the planet!") Fluidity and force are especially important to Kauffman's women, whose men so often desert or, when they remain, brutalize these women.

Important to these women too is the sense of place. The impress of the World is upon them, around them—they hunt for a place in that World to "walk," to move upon the earth in search of "proofs" of the world's real way. Walking becomes a form of coming or leaving, and of knowing. Women walk their regions (Michigan, Pennsylvania) and their farms to acquaint themselves with the world and with themselves.

In *Collaborators*, Kauffman pursues the nature of womanhood and of the special relationships among women (woman-woman, mother-daughter), within the landscape of a Pennsylvania tobacco farm. Here again the agrarian elements shape the fiction: place is at the novel's heart, so that when the daughter, Andrea Doria, seeks escape and solitude she goes—she *walks*—to the "center" of her world:

> And so I walked off and walked down the middle row of the tobacco field, as I often did, and sat down in the center of the field, under the green roof of the tallest plants. The leaves spread out, tented, over my head, and the heated air felt as smooth as a liquid on my face. I crossed my legs and sat like a foreigner, just fine.[12]

Labor becomes a metaphor for the relationship between family members, the love and effort in "taking down" the tobacco suggestive of the same sort of "collaboration" and even at times the distance between daughter, son, father, and mother. The rhythms and the balance of the dance emerge in the work-effort, choreographed as if by nature: "We move like a circus troupe, climbing, balancing on the rails, tossing whatever we have, one to the other, a precision routine that is silent except for the rustle of leaves, somebody's coughing, and once in a while a cue, or encouragement— Hold it, Dovie; or, Okay, here we go" [42-43]. Time is measured by the seasonal labor of planting, nurturing, harvesting, curing—the cycle of agricultural life.

Against this cyclical, predictable, regular way of life—or outward life—Kauffman sets the intricate and stormy inward life of a mother and that mother's attempt to instruct her daughter in the ways of the world and the uses of language. The mother stays with the farm, with her husband, with her family; her best friend breaks loose, "kicks herself out": "She said she had already figured out how to survive without holding tobacco in her arm like an offering every September" [47]. And so the mother works to reconcile these varied allegiances, becomes a "collaborator": "Collaboration, subterfuge. That is a decent living, my mother claims. Mingle, subvert. Float, dive. She juggles her favorite words" [41]. But death, the ultimate subversion, takes the mother (and her words), after she endures a painful recovery into voice and spirit following a stroke. Her lesson to the daughter is a strategy in survival, in "witnessing" the small miracles and grace-giving moments of a sometimes brutal world. Labor and language, the well-muscled spirit—these are the tools in Kauffman's world, the means to an expression of her vision.

Clearly the most authentic, most consistent evocation of this agrarian vision, though, appears in the work of Wendell Berry. Known mostly for poetry and essays that celebrate—and sometimes eulogize—a specifically rural, farming way of life, Berry has also translated that vision and voice into fiction. For the last thirty years he has chronicled the ways and workings of the town of Port William, Kentucky, a fictional rendering of Berry's own hometown of Port Royal, where he continues to live and write and farm. This Port William cycle consists of four works of fiction: *Nathan Coulter, A Place on Earth, The Memory of Old Jack,* and *The Wild Birds: Six Stories of the Port William Membership.* (All but the last title are novels; the first two books on this list were originally published in the 1960s but were later revised and republished in 1985 and 1983, respectively. I exclude from this list Berry's long dramatic poem "The Bringer of Water" because of its form, although it too deals with the Port William story.) Taken together, these books tell the history of this Kentucky farmtown and its farmpeople, and in the process offer a significant and telling transformation of the agrarian myth into actual practice.

At the center of this cycle is the community—an intimate community—of men and women (though Berry, unlike many contemporary agrarian writers, focuses on men) who work and farm and sustain the memory and spirit of their shared "place on earth." Thus, the Port William *Membership.* The community of town is essentially an extension of the community-in-miniature of the family, that web of blood-kin and personal relation that gives a person a history.

That community, of course, resides within a specific place—region, town, farm—and for Berry, place defines character and labor. Berry writes of rural Kentucky, of bottomland and hillside farms that run beside the Kentucky River. Place means land, and a man's moral, right relation to that land. As one of the "members," Mat Feltner, recollects saying to the son now believed killed in World War II, "A man's life is always dealing with permanence— . . . the most dangerous kind of irresponsibility is to think of your doings as temporary. . . . What you do on the earth, the earth makes permanent."[13] The land, and what one does to the land, remains long after men and women who live and work on it. The land is inherited, cared for; the right-minded, right-sighted farmer keeps the land as a steward. The farmers whose vision is clouded, bent, deflected, sees the land from the mistaken perspective of possession; thus Old Jack Beechum, most ancient of the membership, recalls his misapprehension of the land's purpose when young and full of desire:

> What he had in his mind now as he sat and thought, or walked the lengths of afternoons and thought, or worked and thought, was more land. He wanted more land. A man falling in his own esteem needs more ground under his feet; to stand again he may need the whole world for a foothold. His thoughts now ranged over the resources within his boundaries, and over the possibilities that lay outside them, seeking the terms of some new balance. His mind played over and over again the airy drama of ambition: how to use what he had to get what he wanted — a strange and difficult undertaking for him, who until then had wanted only what he had. Once he had hungered for the life his place could be made to yield. Now he would ask it to yield another place, at what expense to itself and to him, he could not then have guessed.[14]

Possession, acquisition, exploitation: all are wrong ways of perceiving, understanding the relationship of man and the earth upon which he walks and plants and harvests.

This sense of rightness pervades Berry's fiction. Berry suggests an intuitive moral relationship between the elements of the planet, a sort of natural harmony disrupted by the wrong-headed and clumsy interference of man. Rightful work becomes, as it does in other agrarian fictions we've examined, a dance, a smooth meshing of muscle and iron and spirit; when that right work is perverted by man's willfulness, the dance turns awkward. Thus, in *The Memory of Old Jack*, Jack and his hired man begin in harmony: "They might work closely together for half a day without speaking, cooperating like the two hands of a single body, anticipating each other's moves like partners in a dance. . . . At times in the heat and striving of some hard day their eyes would meet and acknowledge the strange grace of their labor" [78]. The "dance of good labor" is redemptive, expressive of the spiritual relationship between man and earth that feeds the agrarian vision. Right work bestows grace. When that relationship goes sour, however, when the rhythms collapse, the dance grows troubled: "There came between them in the third year, not an open break, never a disagreement that either of them could have stated, but a disharmony, a withdrawal from the center of their agreement. There began to be a roughening, an imprecision, in their teamwork that made them conscious and resentful of their dependence on each other" [80]. Fluidity gives way to coarseness; anger and discordancy banish grace temporarily, the land robbed for the moment of its potential for holiness.

Such relationships are significant, for they allow people in the present to connect with people in the past, to tap into the current of time and spirit that flows through all things, that is the essence of place and time and work. In the story, "It Wasn't Me," the town's lawyer, a man sensitive to the nature of his world, watches Elton Penn (the new owner-steward of the Beechum place when Old Jack dies, the proper owner, the new member) work his land and horses, and finds himself lost in this rich, peculiar, near-sacred essence:

> Elton was working a team of black Percherons. He had them stepping, urging them and himself, and yet there was an appearance of ease in their work that to Wheeler bespoke the accomplishment of the workman: the horses were fitted and harnessed and hitched right; the plow was running right.
>
> Having already stopped his car, Wheeler turned off the engine, and in the quiet that followed, in which he could hear the wind, he sat and looked. Watching Elton, he might, he felt, have been watching his own father as a young man, or Old Jack himself as a young man. He realized, as he had not done before, how it had been with them. He felt himself in the presence of a rare and passionate excellence belonging to his history and his country, and he was moved. He sat there a long time, watching, forgetting the year he was in [*Wild Birds*, 71].

Within such a system of harmonies and relationship, death too becomes part of the synchronous movement of man and time. Death serves to clarify one's nature and one's place in the ongoing scheme of things. In "The Boundary," Mat Feltner slides toward darkness as he walks the limits of his farm before his death. As he approaches that double boundary of land *and* time, he comes to recognize the immediacy and primacy of his life's beneficence:

> He gives no more regard to death or to the dead. The dead do not appear again. Now he is walking in this world, walking in time, going home. A shadowless love moves him now, not his, but a love that he belongs to, as he belongs to the place and to the light over it. He is thinking of Margaret and of all that his plighting with her had led to. He is thinking of the membership of the fields that he has belonged to all his life, and will belong to while he breathes, and afterward. He is thinking of the living ones of that membership—at work today in the fields that the dead were at work in before them.
>
> "I am blessed," he thinks. "I am blessed," [*Wild Birds*, 96].

And through the course of the Port William cycle, we witness the natural and right decline *and* replenishment of the Membership, new and younger men moving in to replace the absent, to assume the ritual-dance of labor of those lost to time and death. So that when Virgil Feltner is lost to the war, Nathan Coulter — narrator and protagonist of the first book of the cycle — moves in years later to take Virgil's place, marrying his widow, becoming the stepfather to the child yet unborn when Virgil left for that alien place. And when Mat Feltner dies, his grandson (in "That Distant Land") takes his place in that "membership of the fields," joining in the resumption of work that transforms itself into a ceremony of remembrance. And in "The Wild Birds," another of the Membership provides in his will for the man who *might* be his son, leaving him land and a presumed place in the membership, doing justice to family and land and community.

Actions in Berry's agrarian world are always defined by their propriety, their integrity, their fidelity to the guiding ethos. People work to "come through," to endure, to make a passage onto some kind of personal *and* communal peace or grace. More than any other agrarian fiction writer, Berry *sings* his personal vision; the rhythms of his prose are the rhythms of the land he so carefully and passionately celebrates; the voice is the voice of the poet, both praising and mourning a way of life and the people who have traced that way of life in their private, very significant histories.

NOTES

1. William Adams, "Natural Virtue: Symbol and Imagination in the American Farm Crisis," *Georgia Review* 39 (1985), pp. 711-12.
2. Don Paarlberg, *American Farm Policy: A Case Study of Centralized Decision-Making* (New York: John Wiley, 1964), p. 3.
3. Douglas Unger, *Leaving the Land* (New York: Harper & Row, 1984), p. 247.
4. Jim Heynen, *You Know What Is Right* (San Francisco: North Point Press, 1985), pp. 3-4.
5. William Kittredge, *We Are Not in This Together* (Port Townsend, Wash.: Graywolf Press, 1984), p. 17.
6. Wendell Berry, *The Wild Birds: Six Stories of the Port William Membership* (San Francisco: North Point Press, 1986), p. 51.
7. Wright Morris, *Plains Song* (New York: Harper & Row, 1980), p. 19.
8. Joan Chase, *During the Reign of the Queen of Persia* (New York: Harper & Row, 1983), p. 75.
9. Louise Erdrich, *The Beet Queen* (Henry Holt, 1986), p. 294.
10. Will Weaver, *Red Earth, White Earth* (New York: Simon & Schuster, 1986), p. 165.
11. Janet Kauffman, *Places in the World a Woman Could Walk* (New York: Knopf, 1984), p. 55.
12. Idem, *Collaborators* (New York: Knopf, 1986), p. 102.
13. Wendell Berry, *A Place on Earth* (rev. ed., San Francisco: North Point Press, 1983), p. 176.
14. Idem, *The Memory of Old Jack* (New York: Harcourt Brace Jovanovich, 1974), pp. 66-67.

THE LOST TRIBE OF AMERICAN FICTION

PAUL WEST

Sometimes the game we play with literature interests us more than literature itself, especially if we are French and so assume from the outset that an idea about a book is always more interesting than the book itself. In this country, not that long ago, there was a good deal of earnest but glib talk about the dead or dying novel. Had the novel served its purpose? Had it revealed its all? Had it met its match, ousted by the culture of the cathode-ray tube? Or was it in a slump, like lyric poetry before Wyatt and Surrey, like science fiction before Einstein and Heisenberg? Was it a Lazarus or a Nero? Or, rather than picking up its bed and walking again, or fiddling while civilization flamed out, was it terminally discredited, like the idea of phlogiston?

It must have been fun to toy with these random hypotheses, to draft obituary while wondering, ever so faintly, why no one talks about the dead or dying *poem*. Fun, but foolish, inasmuch as no one had ever defined what the novel was or is. How could anything that various be dead? Like the corpse of Emiliano Zapata, it was everywhere and nowhere. Like the corpse of Eva Perón in an unpublished novel of Julio Cortázar, it was burgeoning mightily underneath all of Latin America, ready to surface in that ancient horror mode: the living dead. Its possible origin went back to Longus and Thomas Nashe, Lucian and Homer. It was, turn and turn about, romance, epic, fable, history, anthropology, sociology, a chart of manners, a graph of social climb, likely to beget as many hybrids as Polonius, in *Hamlet*, attempting permutations of the literary modes—"tragical-comical-historical-pastoral—"and then seeming to give up with his "scene individable, or poem unlimited." All or nothing. It was bound to provoke self-mocking definitions such as "a prose fiction of a certain length having something wrong with it," which is as useful as a shoehorn made of sheep's liver. If you couldn't pin the pesky thing down, you could at least back away from it wittily, as if you had encountered a genie from outer space.

Since then we have had the rise and fall of the French New Novel, an ostensibly plotless, characterless, unpsychological mode based on doting, almost philatelical observation; the rise and slight fall of Latin American Magic predicated on only a sampler of that continent's modern fiction; and the so-called nonfiction novel, from Truman Capote's *In Cold Blood* to Beryl Bainbridge's *Young Adolf*, in which we meet young Adolf Hitler in darkest Liverpool. We have also seen the reworking of traditional texts, such as Frederick Busch's *The Mutual Friend*, told by Dolby, the factotum of Charles Dickens's last years, and Walter Abish's assemblages of sentences appropriated from works in print, named by Joseph Pestino "The Bartlett Appropriation School of Text Construction." We may be forgiven if, confronted with this on top of what the novel became in the eighteenth and nineteenth centuries, we conclude that the novel is as mutable and various as cancer, though mostly less deadly. There it is, in the heads of thousands upon thousands of readers and living practitioners, blundering or fidgeting forward, making you wonder if indeed the thing has a life of its own, a destiny to which it has been called by a force or forces unknown. (By *it* I intend a longish prose fiction substantial enough to be bound separately as a book.) Perhaps it even has a special drive within it, urging it on toward fulfillment: a goal we can only guess at as, maybe, a short text denuded of everything inessential, resembling crystals in a crucible, or a lethal prodigy of verbal fusion, bound for saftey's sake in the lead of which pencils used to be made. Indeed, trying to envision the next phase or the terminus of the novel is a fictional enterprise in its own right, and the right use of the novel form over the next fifteen years may well be the fingering of the novel's future, a whole series of prophetic demonstrations predicated on almost three centuries of its entrails, a triumph of frenzied self-appraisal done by master craftsmen while the hacks, still twiddling around with plain novels about plain folks, in a style whose poverty masquerades as pregnant discipline, look only to write within the expectations of the reading public, who purchase novels with much the same arm motion as they lift up pounds of margarine. For every discovery, every innovation, there will be a thousand banal returns to the fold.

I myself do not believe in such givens as the inevitable novel, decreed from on high by some Calvinistic trinity made up of E. M. Forster, Georg Lukács, and Alain Robbe-Grillet (bewitching as I find the third's little book of essays, *For a New Novel*). A genre, a form, lives only in the heads and at the mercy of those who use it. *For a New Novel* spawned no school, except perhaps a school of critics, and clashed with Robbe-Grillet's own novel-writing practices. And *Finnegans Wake*, sublimely imitable as it is, generated no school of imitators, but has remained a combination of Taj Mahal and dead end. Not even the majestic exhortations of William Gass (*Fiction and the Figures of Life*) or the moralistic tootings of John Gardner have had that much effect, except as late vindications of what stylists or homilists have done already. The whole thing is more or less random, which is perhaps why critics try to tidy things up. My own version comes close to that of Sir James Jeans, the doyen of science popularizers, who many years ago in *The Mysterious Universe* talked of a room full of radium atoms, all of them identical, to just one of whom each year, for reasons unknown, came atomic death, regular as clockwork (as we used to say). Out of the cascade of potentials drops this norm, more predictable than what will come next into my own head, or into those at present blank pages of the history of the novel form.

Maybe, as some have suggested, texts write themselves, using authors as their vehicle, and breed among themselves, using the authorial imagination as a bedsheet, in a kind of backstairs promiscuity. Even as I write this, Mrs. Gaskell's *Cranford*, which I dipped into last week, is working on me subliminally, most of all some phrase about being possessed by Amazons. Let it. Reciprocal seepage is out of the question; we can't influence *Cranford* any more, but we can modify its image, and we do each time we read the book, each time we surrender to it and let it influence us in a thousand ways we could never pick apart.

Influence apart, though, the fascinating thing is how the novel evolves, much as astronomy or metallurgy has evolved. I ought to know better, perhaps, but I dote on the idea that the form in which I have now made a dozen forays can be made to yield this or that result, with almost no-holds-barred, as if it were plasticine, or a geranium being made to make a vertical U-turn along a wire frame. Like the sonnet, the essay, the soliloquy, it is there for use: malleable, adaptable, open to experiment as the codified embodiments of music were open to Schoenberg, Cage, the young Copland. You do not hear this kind of thing from the mercantile novelists, or indeed the mercantile composers, but you do hear it, beginning maybe as a whine or a whimper of hubristic aspiration, and then you hear something more assured as the novelist-composer (call him Marcel Woolf-Mann) contemplates the shapeability and the rigors of the medium, open before him or her like the continents of Cathay or Ind. My own view is more that of a vacancy perceived, as when a lodger has moved out, say, and the room is mine to do over as

I think fit. You can be haunted, and persuaded, by the ghosts of forerunners, but you have to remind yourself of how much you inherit that they did not have, in science, history, and the sheer simple accumulation of their own artifacts, to be ignored or built upon.

Expressed in greater detail, this means that we have the gorgeous images of Jupiter and Saturn from Voyager flybys, history-repeating-itself with new variations in Vietnam, the bizarre verbal and structural experiments of Raymond Roussel, the oneiric wasteland of self-abuse dreamed up by Jean Genet, the blustering monologues in the fiction of Djuna Barnes. And, on a perhaps less illustrious plane, we know that Rimbaud could have added jet lag to his recipe for garbling the mind, and that the man in Xenophon who rightly (if redundantly) cried out *"thalassa!"* when he saw the sea, might have been moved even more had he known that the chemical makeup of ocean saltwater matches that of our cardiac cells, where sodium and potassium are king. It is possible, of course, to ignore what goes on around us, but such an attitude ill-fits those who wish to create the future; they end up, like so many novelists in our time, re-creating the past, yet wanting huzzahs for doing so. My own view would be that, cognizantly immersed, we doggy-paddle forward to the next rough epiphany: nearer than ever to seeing the edge of the expanding universe, yet awfully far away, which means there is still room to imagine something without being corrected by the Jet Propulsion Laboratory in Pasadena, whose name itself comes from an earlier era.

Of course, trying to create the future of the novel is only a fancy way of saying trying to write our next few novels; but the fateful aura abides of experimenting until something already there in the matrix of life pops into view for the first time. In other words, penicillin, the quark, the monopole were there all the time, or much of it. On the other hand, can we say that the interior monologue or stream of consciousness was built into the matrix, before Édouard Dujardin "discovered" it in 1887? I hasten to add that I mean the literary technique so-called, since consciousness itself may be thought of not so much as streaming as of bouncing about, almost like jazz, as the astronomer Eddington said. Where the monologic jazz was before we hit on it is hard to say, especially if you think that there would have been no *Ulysses*, and no Joycean prose, without James Joyce. One is entitled to wonder if aesthetic experiment is freeer than its scientific counterpart. Is there a true distinction between what was latent but unfound and what was unfound because no one had invented it? In Latin, *invent* means to *come upon* something that is in your way, but the something was there all the time, whereas the artist puts it there. Archimedes exclaiming his *Eureka!* (I have found it!) has not invented the twelve-tone scale or the clerihew. Or anything else.

In this sense, the imaginer experiments with himself, herself, and not with the givens of the physical life, imagining the imagination into being, whereas the scientist finds what he is going to find by imagining it. Notice too how the artist uses the word *artifact* to mean work of art, whereas to the scientist the word means an undesirable accidental flaw. Perhaps this is why scientists have no patience with complex metaphor, since their "coming-upon" things is different from that of artists. The scientist could no more devise a future for the novel than a novelist could produce the unified-field theory. We tend to think that, because artist and scientist overlap, they work in the same way, whereas the one deals with conjuring, the other with laws. When, some years back, I published a novel called *Gala*, in which I used a framework based on the genetic alphabet, all but one of the scientists I knew were bemused. But I was glad to have used a scientific finding as an aesthetic discipline, and my schematic delighted the formalist in me because, for example, it was rooted in nature, whereas the various rhyme schemes of the sonnet are not. I had a cosmic inevitability which added emotional weight to my narrative. Mostly, however, such abstruse patterns go unnoticed, or, if noticed, go unhailed; the scientist doesn't want the facts turned into a novel, and the novelist by and large can't see the cosmic force of a recondite natural pattern. Hidden form, as Holst once said, is mere refrigeration; even so, as a hidden constraint, it constrains the artist, and that may be all he or she is looking for, like Raymond Roussel shaping a novel outward from one central pun which you may never detect. Not all hair shirts are visible.

Look now at the novel, with a mere nine years to go before the end of the century. In all its varieties, it hangs in still. Bruised, broken, stunted, it has evolved without being much seen to have done so, mainly because critics are poorly read. In fact, the good old-fashioned novel has died repeatedly through the century, from body blows struck by Joyce, Beckett, Queneau, Cortázar, and others. It has lived on in the hands of literary taxidermists, of course, but effectively it was blown up before 1950, to take a handy date. When Joyce exclaimed that the rampaging Nazis should leave Czechoslovakia alone and read *Finnegans Wake*, he meant, I think, that the *Blitzkrieg* that mattered, the one against orthodox novels, was already over; the novel was a blown-up city and wide open to reconstruction. Of course. Since then, we have been building with the wreckage as best we can, building newer houses of words from older ones, trying to find, as Beckett puts it, a form that will accommodate the mess. Not long ago, in a speech of welcome aimed at the Spanish novelist, Juan Goytisolo, at the Spanish Institute in New York City, I came up with the phrase "The Lost Tribe," meaning, perhaps in some forlorn echo of a Conan Doyle adventure novel, those who were busy picking up the pieces: after Joyce, after the French New Novel, after the novel of black humor (which tried to find wrong only with society what is wrong with life), what was left? Beckett had given a lead in *Watt*, written while he was picking potatoes in hiding from the Gestapo in France, and John Hawkes had actually discussed trying to create the future. It was clear, at least to some of us, that the most-touted American novelists of the sixties and seventies had changed the novel little and had left America snoozing amid tame, palatable books while the rest of the world forged ahead.

The tribe were recognizable names—Abish, Connell, Davenport, Dillard (Richard), Federman, Gass, Nemerov, Hawkes, Nova, Purdy, Sontag, West, White—but they did not add up to a movement, each one doing a different thing for special reasons. What they had in common, at least in retrospect, was a desire to rehabilitate the novel form, perhaps to Europeanize it, to reveal it to American readers as not the final version of anything but a volatile entity capable of subtle construction and inventive deployment. Not a formulaic thing at all, and certainly light years away from mere sociology, but another form of *art*—a word that few American novelists care to use about what they do, as if art were a somehow retrograde thing, somewhere between lunacy and impetigo. I once told a scientist that the artist really wanted to make something perfect, and he scoffed, but not ironically, "Is that *all*?" Well, the First Cause did not accomplish it in the fateful seven days, so I don't see why humbler artists should not drive themselves mad with the vision of it. Another scientist, in fact Hans Bethe who figured out on a train how the sun works, said a more enlightening thing. I'd told him how, to help with the writing of *Gala*, which was a "walk" through the northern Milky Way, I'd built a model of the Galaxy in my basement. He paused, then said, "A *working* model?" At that moment he was entertaining a fiction, indulging the novelist, to be sure, but also letting himself hope a little. After all, so long as there's a reader, or a novelist willing to reread, a novel itself is a working model of some world or other, and what is a particle accelerator if not that? Models minify gigantic dreams.

Anyone hunting a basis for a late-century fictional *Poetics* would do well to examine the essays of the novelists named above, especially those of Abish, Davenport, and Sontag, whose lengthy "Against Interpretation" meets some writings of my own about Thomas De Quincey's term *involute*—a compound experience incapable of being deciphered and therefore the raw material of many a deliberately manufactured literary enigma such as you find strewn through, say, Beckett's trilogy: *Molloy, Malone Dies, The Unnameable*. That would be the local basis, anyway. Farther afield, but available in translation, there are the so-called Morelliana, the aphorisms of a failed novelist Morelli which Julio Cortázar appended to *Hopscotch*, the novel with appended optional chapters too. Morelli cannot write the supernovel he has in mind, but he can theorize about it almost voluptuously, all the way from the crazy logic he calls "lo(co)gic" and his view of the novel as a *liber fulguralis* (a lightning bolt) to something he calls anthropophany—the showing forth of humanity in a novel that, appropriately enough, seems to abandon the dualisms and the deceits denounced by Alain Robbe-Grillet in *For a New Novel*. Morelli is a figure of parody, but I found on teaching *Hopscotch* that students warmed to his theories rather than to the novel itself: a sad but indicative finding; people want to know what's going on, what the intellectual landscape contains.

It contains not only the idea that the word *text* is perfectly adequate, since it means something woven, but also the bolder idea that the Western novelist is not necessarily obligated to any orthodoxy, any more than the Latin American novelist, poised between voodoo and tyranny, is obliged to the novel of Europe or North America. This means that the novel, far from being hidebound, as the bookstore chains would like it to be, qualifies for a term that André Gide came up with: *disponible*, meaning at its own disposal, to which you might add Paul Valéry's own bit of jargon: *implex*, for awareness made maximal. For those who need one, and they seem to be many, it would not be hard to assemble a little catechism for the novel-to-come, or for the future novel already dispersedly here. As always the jargon is arch, awkward, and inadequate, but it embodies close-ups that carry a whole climate with them, of divergent critical thinking about the novel by its current practitioners. *Erotics of reading. Involute. Lo(co)gic. Liber fulguralis. Anthropophany. Text. Disponibility. Implex.* Buzzwords all, they have the charm of horseflies laid out on a window sill. Even so, if I had room and time, I would add Nathalie Sarraute's "suspicion," for the disabused frame of mind in which the modern reader regards the all-knowingness of the old novel, and "sub-conversation," her version of Valéry Larbaud's "the very first spurting of thought." Then I would bring in the notion, for which there is no ready-made word, of composition: the novelist *composes* the novel as if it were a symphony, shifting large masses around like tectonic plates, in the fashion of Mario Vargas Llosa, and grooming stylistic detail as if each word were a tiny drama, each phrase a potential *Lohengrin*. I suppose that is part of the (to play the game a moment) disponible implex, or the available max. As I say, these terms come from practitioners whose immediate aim was never the creation of suave technical argot, and you have to take them as impatient gestures, impromptu asides, semirational sparks from within the psychoanalysis of fire.

Other things to think about, whether you are writing or trying to fathom those who do, include the increasing problem: Where is the narrative voice coming from? Whose is it? Is it the author's? If not, is the narrator anonymous and impersonal, without a life to go with the voice? Is the narrator that entity with no more than a voice in things? Or, as in, say, Gabriel García Márquez's *The Autumn of the Patriarch* or Samuel Beckett's *Texts for Nothing*, does the narration amount more to something like polyphonic recitative, staged by a presence "off" who chooses the words only, but has no more overt presence than that of an impresario? Often, too, as in Woolf, a first-person text has given way to a third-person one, but eccentric verbal shadings have remained, to give the oddest double flavor of unabashed intimacy and savvy remoteness. For example, you first write: "I think, daily, of my silky little bladder," then switch it to "She thought, daily, of her silky little bladder," which puts your third-person narrator in a curious bladder-fancying stance. There are some words that a character will use about him- or herself which a narrator cannot use without seeming tendentious. "*Thought felt,*" the Germans still call it, which sounds awfully vague, but it amounts to delineative precision of a subjective kind. You might make a whole novel of it, in this day and age anyway, and thus dispense with watching. Just listen. Make the voice the personage, in both its utterances and its thoughts. That, in a sense, is what the late Arno Schmidt created in his *Evening Edged with Gold*, a massive split-screen tome with big pages like sails on which you see-hear all the different tellers of the same "Fairytale," having your ear rove with your eye as the page breaks up vertically or horizontally. The complementary opposite of this, I suppose, is what Woolf does here and there in *To the Lighthouse*, scooping up a long conversational exchange, in all its twists and turns, its runs and stutters, and then with an almost censorious ear compressing it into an oral contingency sample of only one-third of a page's length, setting it off to show that she has done her duty (*they were talking, thus*) without being slavish about it.

You might go further, taking Nabokov's dictum that character is merely a compositional resource and extending it to dialogue as well. No people, as such, and no talk; but lots of minds at work in the silence. It may be said that characters are the meat the burglar feeds the housedog while he gets to work on the house's mind, while dialogue in fiction is for the eye only—it need not replicate actual talk, as, I think, among others, Woolf and Ivy Compton-Burnett proved. If you're willing to give up some things you're used to, you'll get other things you've rarely had. That goes for the old-fashioned omniscient narrator, too, a term too Platonic to be useful inasmuch as there is no all, no total, so no narrator can know it. The thing's a hedge, a front, fostering, as Sarraute has said, a false attitude to the knowability of both people and characters. There is no narrator in everyday life, so why rehearse for it in novels that take you inside strangers' heads? I can see her point, but all the same would point out that readers don't always read to fit themselves for everyday living: they read to escape, to break free, to take the impossible on trust and imagine what it would really be like to take the lid off someone's head and know everything that is going on in there, for the sheer bugging of it. By the same token, they might go to the antinovels of Robbe-Grillet, Sarraute, and the recent Nobel laureate Claude Simon, for the sheer novelty—after so much quasiomniscience—of seeing people from the outside only, none of whom they get to know half as well as they know their daily friends. In old Spanish novels a little lame devil called Asmodeus used to lift off the roofs of people's houses, in an extremer version of the mood that sent Virginia Woolf around London at night, peering in at windows. People are curious about people, but not always; and, sometimes, we are curious about their very incuriosity about us. The novel has made this its stock in trade for years, but novelists are entitled to work the market both ways, revealing *and* denying, opening *and* closing up shop. And to ring the changes is not to aim at a sharper realism, but to make the various movements in the prose symphony contrast with one another. The gesture is aesthetic, not informative.

Other issues that need to be thought about include the selection of narrative tense: the past looks firmer and more final, the present more immediate and less congealed, the future altogether the most open of all, whereas in fact it is the most fate-ridden (they *will* go here, they *will* go there, and their napkin rings *will* gather a faint patina of mold). In fact, the whole thing is illusion: the past seems to confer on what's in it a certain security, but the words holding that illusion in place are just as arbitrary as those supporting an illusion in the present. At best, the past is a tone-retainer, like the present. All time in fiction is made of words, and the true, ecumenical time of fiction is the order in which the words reach the reader's eye, whether or not that is the order in which the novelist thought of them.

Speaking of illusion, there is such a novel as *Gulliver's Travels* which, especially at the outset, wants you to believe it isn't fiction, and then there is Howard Nemerov's *Journal of the Fictive Life*, which flaunts its very fictionality. Surely both ways are artful. It isn't an either/or problem. In a sense, a novel corresponds exactly to nothing but itself, and yet it cannot be made out of nothing, so the novel is derivatively nonmimetic and, like any other text, a verbal area to focus on, so as to have it in common with others, more or less. But it is almost inappropriate to refer to a certain novel by Flaubert as *Madame Bovary*; the only accurate, unskimping mode of allusion to it is to read aloud the whole novel each time you want to refer to it. To do so would surely end all generalization and install in its place something good: a devout, patient, endless act of reading. That, maybe, is the only way of making permanent contact with the mind, Flaubert's, which his novel evinces: the fable's manger, so to speak. And that, of course, you could not do with prose that has no personality; prose — of a kind only too common — whose most blatant virtue is that, in aiming low, it makes no grammatical errors, and is intended to be read only once, certainly not to be pored over, and then junked. The exceptions, Bunyan and Swift, but surely not Orwell or Dreiser, have an interesting mind behind them, and the plain prose gets you to it sooner, whereas with most all you get to sooner is the vacancy.

Well, it might be said at this point, as things fall away, if you have no personages, no talk, and possibly no plot, all you have left are the vicissitudes of a voiceless nobody, whereas all these things rather than ruling the roost have come to rest as components of style — as color, noise, vigor, as faces, gabble, shove, accommodated into a sentence or two, serving the novel instead of the other way around. Everything, even a news item, is a story these days, so the novelist may be forgiven for not always telling one, as perhaps for no longer feeling obligated to a certain national or local tradition when all the planet heaves into view. Call it the holistic novel; it comes into being on the heels of the Museum Without Walls of André Malraux, with all the world's art becoming available through postcards and reproductions. And now the planet as a whole has swum across our screens with entire oceans affixed to its hide, held down by the spin: an epiphany, I suggest, not just for Sf writers, to whom it was far from new, but for all novelists, all poets, even if all it does to Our Town is install it in a wider and more baffling context.

Daily the presses churn out routine novels, noticed with routine politeness by reviewers who will never know better. Such is the last behavioral waltz of the nineteenth century. Fiction and the novel have moved on, never mind in how awkward and befuddled a disarray, reductive or bloated. Literary art may never offer a beginning, a middle, and an end, in that order again, except out of nostalgia, and maybe not even those three in any causal relationship whatever. The plural novel will have middles, ends, beginnings, held together in the auteur's mind, and the novel will have finally begun to catch up, technically speaking, with Pollock and Rothko, Debussy and Messiaen. Sheer consumerism has always kept the novel back, making it into a commodity rather than an art form whose calling is to say what it is like to be alive in a certain time, to remind us of our intimate selves by being there, on the paper, in the ink, as brand-new, warm, and tweakable as we are. And just as apt to be forgotten, overlooked, or left for dead.

CONTRIBUTORS

MAX APPLE is the author of *The Oranging of America*, a collection of short stories; the novels *Zip* and *The Propheteers*; and *Free Agents*, a collection of prose pieces.

ANDREA BARRETT has published short stories in *The Northwest Review, Spectrum,* and *Prairie Schooner,* as well as two novels, *Lucid Stars* and *Secret Harmonies*.

NICHOLAS DELBANCO has published ten novels, including the trilogy of *Sherbrookes, Possession,* and *Stillness*. He has also published two books of short stories, a book of literary history, *Group Portrait: Conrad, Crane, Ford, Wells, and James,* and a different kind of group biography, *The Beaux Arts Trio,* as well as a travel book about Provence, *Running in Place: Scenes from the South of France*. He directs the Master of Fine Arts Program at the University of Michigan.

STEPHEN DIXON has published four novels, *Fall & Rise, Too Late, Work,* and *Garbage,* as well as some 225 short stories. He is Associate Professor in the Writing Seminars at Johns Hopkins University.

STEPHEN DUNNING is the winner of the James B. Hall Short Fiction Award and of a PEN Award in 1986. He has published fiction in

New Letters and *Indiana Review*, and poems in over a hundred literary journals. A collection of short stories, *To the Beautiful Women*, appeared from Samuel Russell (Croton-on-Hudson, N.Y.), in 1990.

RICHARD ELMAN is the author of twenty published books of fiction, poetry, and journalism, including *An Education in Blood*, a trilogy comprised of *The 28th Day of Ellul, Lilo's Diary*, and *The Reckoning*. *Cocktails at Somoza's*, a reporter's notebook of the Nicaraguan revolution, and *Disco Frito*, a book of fiction, reflect his continuing interest in Latin America.

WANDA HAYNES FRIES is a short story writer living in Somerset, Kentucky. "Mel's Back" is her first published story.

GEORGE GARRETT, Henry Hoyns Professor of English at the University of Virginia, has published in the 1980s a *Collected Poems*; a collected short stories, *An Evening Performance*; a novel about Renaissance England, *The Succession*; a literary satire, *Poison Pen*; and a critical study, *Understanding Mary Lee Settle*.

LAURENCE GOLDSTEIN, editor of *Michigan Quarterly Review* and Professor of English at the University of Michigan, has published two volumes of literary criticism and two books of poetry, and is coeditor (with David L. Lewis) of *The Automobile and American Culture*.

IHAB HASSAN is Vilas Professor of English and Comparative Literature at the University of Wisconsin-Milwaukee. He is the author of *Radical Innocence, Paracriticisms, The Dismemberment of Orpheus*, and *The Postmodern Turn* among other books.

MAXINE HONG KINGSTON is the author of two critically acclaimed memoirs, *The Woman Warrior: Memoirs of a Girlhood among Ghosts* and *China Men. Hawai'i One Summer*, a collection of twelve prose sketches, was published in 1987; her first novel, *Tripmaster Monkey: His Fake Book*, appeared in 1989.

M. G. LORD is editorial cartoonist for *Newsday*. A volume of her political cartoons, *Mean Sheets*, appeared in 1982.

BERNARD MALAMUD's great career as a fiction writer began with the publication of *The Natural* in 1952 and culminated in his last published novel, *God's Grace*, in 1982, *The Stories of Bernard Malamud* in 1983, and a posthumously published collection, *The People: And Other Uncollected Fiction*, in 1989.

CONTRIBUTORS

EUGENE MIRABELLI is the author of three novels, *The Burning Air*, *The Way In*, and *No Resting Place* as well as a variety of shorter works in fiction and nonfiction.

GREGORY L. MORRIS is the author of *A World of Order and Light: The Fiction of John Gardner* and is a regular reviewer of contemporary fiction for literary journals. He teaches at Pennsylvania State University, Behrend College, in Erie.

JOYCE CAROL OATES's recent novels are *You Must Remember This*, *American Appetites*, and *Because It Is Bitter, and Because It Is My Heart*. She is the author of many volumes of short stories, poems, and essays, including *(Woman) Writer*. She is the Roger S. Berlind Distinguished Lecturer in Creative Writing at Princeton University.

CONSTANCE PIERCE has published a collection of short stories, *When Things Get Back to Normal*. She teaches at Miami University in Ohio.

PAULA RABINOWITZ is Assistant Professor of English at the University of Minnesota and coeditor (with Charlotte L. Nekola) of *Writing Red: An Anthology of American Women Writers, 1930–1940*.

SCOTT RUSSELL SANDERS teaches literature at Indiana University. He has published a novel, *Bad Man Ballad*; a book of stories, *Fetching the Dead*; and a collection of personal essays, *The Paradise of Bombs*.

LYNNE SHARON SCHWARTZ has written six books, including the novels *Disturbances in the Field* and *Rough Strife*, and the short story collections *Acquainted with the Night* and *The Melting Pot*.

DAVID R. SLAVITT has published many volumes of poetry as well as many novels, including *Alice at 80* and *The Hussar*. He does not teach anywhere.

KYNA TAYLOR, born in Washington, D.C., and educated at the University of Maryland, is currently enrolled in Cornell University's Master of Fine Arts Program where she is completing a collection of short stories.

ALLAN VORDA has conducted numerous interviews with 1960s rock groups as well as with minimalist composer Steve Reich and novelist Ron Hansen.

PAUL WEST received an Award in Literature from the American Academy and Institute of Arts and Letters in 1985. He has published many books of fiction, including *Gala, The Very Rich Hours of Count von Stauffenberg, Rat Man of Paris, The Universe and Other Fictions*, and *Lord Byron's Doctor*.

GLORIA WHELAN's first collection of stories, *Playing with Shadows*, appeared in 1988.

Note: Rather than include ninety entries to the Contributors pages of this volume, the editors have elected to omit biographical notes for the authors represented in the Symposium.